TREES ON THE MOUNTAIN
An Anthology of New Chinese Writing

RENDITIONS **BOOKS**

are issued by the Research Centre for Translation
The Chinese University of Hong Kong
publisher of *Renditions*, a Chinese-English Translation Magazine

General Editors

Stephen C. Soong
George Kao

This book is published
with the aid of the
WING LUNG BANK FUND
for Promotion of Chinese Culture

TREES ON THE MOUNTAIN
An Anthology of New Chinese Writing

Edited by
Stephen C. Soong and John Minford

A *RENDITIONS* Book

The Chinese University Press
Hong Kong

Distributed by
The University of Washington Press
Seattle and London

Typesetting by Goldwind Photo Typesetting Co.
Printing by Ngai Kwong Printing Co., Ltd.

CONTENTS

In Lieu of a Preface

At the creation, when Pan Gu chiselled the universe out of Primordial Chaos, the purer elements ascended to form the heavens, the baser descended to form the earth. So legend has it. Our story tells of the continent of Sinim, easternmost of the Four Great Portions created round the world's axis; it tells of Sinim's sacred peaks, and the greater and lesser trees that adorn them and protect them from the ravages of wind, rain and snow, providing an enduring reminder of the original unity of earth, heaven and man.

But let us proceed with our story: one fine spring day, on one of the highest peaks of the centrally situated Arsyversian Mountains in the aforementioned land of Sinim, a white-whiskered old gentleman dressed in the loose-flowing robes of a Daoist hermit was seated beneath the branches of Lithodendron, the fabled Stone Tree, mumbling to himself (as was his wont), when suddenly he sensed an alien presence, and rising to his feet beheld a youth standing close by, peering through a glass at the patterns traced by nature on the Tree's leaves. The youth's features (when finally he turned his head and answered the old man's gaze) at once proclaimed him to be a citizen of the westernmost of the Four Great Portions, the distant realm of Bullbary, and from his short and much-patched robe and the hempen sandals on his feet, he was clearly a like-minded, if somewhat bedraggled, Seeker of the Way.

Deasil (for so the old hermit was named) and young Widdershins exchanged credentials, and upon discovering that they were both members of the Hermetic Fraternity of Lithodendric Masons (the existence of which, Gentle Reader, I must beg you not to divulge to another living soul), were instantly swept away in a flood of koans and enthusiasms, that soon progressed from the riddle of the Stone Tree itself to other plants and herbs and botanical arcana of Sinim.

> *In Sinim's Land stand two beneath the Tree of Stone;*
> *Eastern and Western rapt in hybrid polyphone.*

As the two conversed, imperceptibly the Golden Crow of the Sun commenced his descent, and the shades of evening drew in around them. Reluctantly, and only after agreeing to renew their acquaintance at a later date, our two pilgrims went their separate ways.

In a twinkling spring turned to summer, and at the time appointed the two met once again beneath the Stone Tree. Widdershins seemed a little agitated.

'Friend Deasil,' he began without further ado, 'let us leave this Stone conundrum till another day. For the present, I beg you to accompany me to a locality not far from here, in which there is something that concerns us both.'

Deasil agreed, and the two set off at a brisk pace in an easterly direction. They skirted a small wood and clambered down a neatly terraced mountainside, after

1

which the terrain became more wild and unmanageable. They were obliged to force their way through a dense thicket of brambles, tearing their robes and cutting their arms and legs on the coarse thorns. Finally the very thorns seemed to lose heart, and gave way to a bleak prospect of barren hillside, denuded and scarred by flood and fire. In the distance, on a ledge set into this undulating wasteland, the two pilgrims beheld a pile of uprooted trees, arranged in the manner of a giant funeral pyre.

Sadly they turned their backs on the desecrated highlands and wended their way down the lower slopes to a valley fresh with green and bathed in a luminous mist. Behind the mist, however, they perceived an arc of impending storm cloud, and even as they stood contemplating this scene of light within darkness, there was a rumbling of thunder, which hurried them onwards and down to the end of the valley. Here they crossed a little stream and came to the ocean. They sat on the sand and looked out across the water. Their journey across the mountains had left them weary. Night fell, and it seemed they were spirited over the ocean and into the dark vault of the heavens. Pinpoints of light could be seen below, stretching out in patterns of great beauty over the no longer visible waters of the ocean, drawing the Four Great Portions together in a single net. At the same time they heard the sound of an antique music, a mellow peal as of stone chimes echoing through the firmament. Gradually light and music faded, and a voice could be heard in the darkness, solemn, but gentle, and a little humorous:

'Welcome aboard Axis Mundi, my friends. Allow me to introduce myself: Athanasius K., Keeper of the Centre. I had the honour of accompanying the Son of Heaven on his last ritual peregrination through the Five Sacred Peaks of Sinim, and was able to make some trifling adjustments to the Great Calendar, in token of which he appointed me Keeper in Perpetuity of the Five Talismans. These talismans I have guarded through the troubled centuries. Seeing you wandering on the Central Peak and stumbling down to the ocean, I felt it my bounden duty to take you on board for a little trip. Those plants and trees you have seen growing between the wasteland and the sea are all recent avatars of the old line. They (and others of their kind which I will leave with you) possess healing properties and are destined to play a part in the gradual atonement of man and nature. On your return journey the two of you must carefully collect and preserve specimens of these, and later transplant them to the Realm of Bullbary. You will thus be carrying on the work begun with *Amoenitates Exoticae* and *Hortus Kewensis*, continuing the search that will end only with the rediscovery and worldwide diffusion of the Magic Fungus. Gather the specimens together and place them in a casket made of tablets of jade. And before you deposit this casket in Bullbary, take a stone leaf from Lithodendron and carve upon it an inscription relating the circumstances of your expedition and the nature of the collection.'

When he had spoken these words, Athanasius turned and drifted away through a glowing archway, on which could be discerned the words (or were they stars?) *Litterarum Virtus*.

Deasil and Widdershins awoke to see the first rays of the sun rising above the sea. Beside them on the sand lay scattered a handful of blooms of a rare and novel beauty, such as they had seldom seen before. They gathered them together and hurriedly retraced their steps up the valley, here picking a blossom or a shoot, there uprooting (with tender care) a sapling, and only when they had gained the foothills of the Arsyversian Mountains did they stop to look back. In the valley shadowy figures were already at work, relentlessly weeding.

'Ah!' sighed Deasil, when finally they reached the Tree and both sank exhausted to the ground, 'what a day and night we have spent!'

Widdershins said nothing, but as soon as he had recuperated his energies, he set the specimens out in some sort of order, and choosing a leaf from the Tree, began at once to carve an inscription in miniscule characters. What follows is a much enlarged rendering of that inscription, together with the marginalia of Deasil, added over a period of days.

Signs of Nature

THIS IS a testimony to survival. Throughout Chinese history, art and literature have been inseparable from a central tradition of spirituality. The impact of the West, the fragmentation of the Chinese universe since 1949, the intense ideological pressure brought to bear on creative artists have in their different ways posed threats to both the art and the tradition. But both have survived far worse threats in the past.

By bringing together literature from China, Taiwan, Hong Kong and the Chinese 'diaspora', we are not inventing a cultural entity; we are reflecting the profoundly cohesive force of the Chinese written word, *wen*, and the continuing power of the traditional conception of literature, *wenxue*.

> *Originally* wen *designated the footprints of animals, or the veins of wood and stone, the set of harmonious or rhythmic 'strokes' by which nature signifies. It is in the image of these natural signs that the linguistic signs were created, and these are similarly called* wen. *The double nature of* wen *constitutes an authority through which man may come to understand the mystery of nature, and thereby his own nature. A masterpiece is that which restores the secret relation between things, and the breath that animates them as well.*
>
> —*François Cheng:* Chinese Poetic Writing

The Way

François Cheng's words echo those of Liu Xie 劉勰, written fifteen hundred years earlier:

> Wen *has a great virtue indeed. It is born together with heaven and earth.*
> 文之德也大矣，與天地並生者何哉!

And the Virtue stems from the Way, the unnameable source, the Void. As Cheng wrote of his fellow Parisian exile, the painter Zao Wou-ki:

> *His quest could not but lead him towards the Open. Beyond existential experience and technical experiment the ultimate aim is nothing less than to attain a genuinely spiritual vision. The more he masters the primeval void and frees the vital inspiration emanating from it, the more he approaches the Source, that point where the human gaze, painter's and spectator's alike, becomes lost in the very origin of all forms. Thus the living space that Zao Wou-ki's brush opens up for us transports us into a region of metamorphoses that we ourselves have always confusedly desired. And it is thus that the singular fire that burns in the artist's starlit night becomes, at each encounter with his paintings, the pure expression of our personal mystery.*

Zao's quest for the Open, the Source, is less a deliberate choice, more a spontaneous expression of his individual genius. Things just happened that way, it was an almost haphazard chain of discoveries and self-discoveries. As the poet Zhao Yi 趙翼 *wrote, these things are 'three parts human endeavour, seven parts fate'* 三分人事七分天. *What a shame this old man* 老朽 *never learned fortune-telling in his youth, or mastered the hexagrams of the* Book of Changes!

In a remorseful mood—Deasil

Or, in the words of another modern artist, Liu Kuo-sung, one of the founders of the Fifth Moon school in Taiwan:

> *Zen is absolute stillness in motion and absolute motion in stillness; though dark it shines forever; though shining, it is forever dark; motion and stillness are the two things that can explore into the original source of life itself. The highest expression in art is to 'go beyond the shapes'* . . . .

Both Zao and Liu are 'intuitively journeying towards the mysterious centre of Chinese philosophy.'

Liu Kuo-sung and the poet Yu Kwang-chung ventured into the modernist camp at the same time, and both eventually found their way back into the tradition. In retrospect Yu wrote: 'There are three types—the Filial Son 孝子, the Prodigal Son 浪子, and the Prodigal Son Returned 回頭的浪子. I was like a nice, quiet girl who starts to elope with a wolf . . . . Half way down the road, I ran back home.'

Remembering the past—Red Codicil

 ## The Void

Fiction seeks its vision in the interplay of society and individual, in the shadow-play of Void and Form, illusion and reality. *The Story of the Stone* is the classic Chinese example. All three pairs of stories in this anthology are concerned with outcasts, 'persons in exile', outsiders, and with what Lucien Miller calls " 'thingness' . . . the pattern of character which unfolds in a particular society". Their common theme is alienation, the penumbra which the individual must pierce to 'understand the mystery of nature', of his own self and of the society he or she lives in.

 ## The Quest

Are the younger artists and writers, and especially the younger generation inside China, whose recent works occupy well over half the pages in this anthology, also 'journeying towards the mysterious centre of Chinese philosophy'? Their journey has to be seen in its political context. Since the brief but intense 'Peking Spring', democracy has been suppressed and experimental art has been all but forced underground. In 1980 the veteran actor Zhao Dan pleaded from his deathbed:

> *Artistic creation is highly individual. It cannot be approved by a show of hands. You can comment, criticize, encourage or applaud. From a historical point of view, art and literature must be free from any restriction.*

But during the recent 'spiritual pollution' campaign, the latest in a series of inward contractions that began in 1980, experimental writers

were branded, either by name or by innuendo, 'polluted' and 'pollu-
ters'. These writers (practitioners of *wen*) are inheritors of the old line,
in Athanasius' sense. They are following, in their various ways, a
common calling to restore through literature the 'secret relation between things'. They are exercising their freedom to search, and for this
they are suspect. Their quest continues, but within stricter confines.
Literature is a dangerous art to practise in China.

Their spirit is well expressed by Xiao Ling, in Zhao Zhenkai's
story 'Waves':

> *Perhaps the search itself is what already epitomizes our genera-*
> *tion: we will not easily accept death, or silence, or obedience to*
> *any fixed judgement.*

Zhao (writing this time as poet—Bei Dao) issues a challenge on behalf
of a whole generation:

> *Let me tell you, world,*
> *I—do—not—believe!*
> *If a thousand challengers lie beneath your feet,*
> *Count me as number one thousand and one.*

Yang Lian in his poetry traces the often bewildering spiritual transition
from a loss of certainty to a newfound and still unfamiliar faith:

> *A secret horizon*
> *Ripples, trawls distant dreams to the surface*
> *Distant, almost boundless.*
> *Only the wind rousing a song*
> *In place of the broken sundial buried in the earth*
> *Points to my dawn.*

This same paradoxical spirit of disenchantment and determination is
found in the work of the young Taiwan poet, Xiang Yang:

> *The one thing China has not known is light : . . .*
> *Soon the bright day will dawn,*
> *But till then, in the thick rain, the ink-splash rain,*
> *In the bold raising of hands,*
> *And the determined eyes,*
> *Let me take you sailing.*

In Hong Kong, Huang Guobin returns again and again to his theme of
the inner quest which is at the same time a cosmic journey:

We believe too much in ourselves.
We never let our roots reach into the soil
To listen to the song deep in the ground
And the ore racing in the veins of igneous rocks.
We never stretch ourselves like seedlings
To put forth soft green tender leaf-tips . . . .
And finally, amidst the silence of lakes and mountains,
Hurl headlong into the boundless space beyond the heavens.

Living Tradition

These young writers and artists, like their predecessors in the 'old' *avant-garde* of the 50s and 60s, are confronting the challenge of being both modern and Chinese. An essential part of their artistic growth, and a key to the harmonious reconciliation of these at first sight disparate elements, is the freedom to choose and experiment. Modernism is not a *cul-de-sac*, but a sometimes necessary phase of openness to change. In the same way, tradition is not an immutable canon, but rather a constant source of renewal. The ultimate goal is, just as it was with Zao Wou-ki, 'nothing less than to attain a genuinely spiritual vision'. The young writers have followed many paths toward this goal, drawing on tradition and modernism in different measures. The young playwright, novelist and critic, Gao Xingjian, talks of bringing the old lyrical and symbolic spirit of Mei Lanfang and infusing it into a reborn modern Chinese theatre—already revived in his own plays with transfusions of Theatre of the Absurd and Theatre of Cruelty. Hong Huang in his 'Misty Manifesto' draws on traditional Chinese poetics to bolster the case for modernism in poetry. Yang Lian looks anew at many neglected areas within the tradition, areas he considers fertile for the contemporary artist; while Yang Mu argues that the 'new poetry' in Taiwan has at last come of age, after a hard-earned apprenticeship in the 60s and the violent 'indigenous' reaction in the 70s.

In his Sui Garden Poetics, *Yuan Mei analyses the word* chuan 傳 *(tradition) into Man + Special* 人加專: *in other words, it is men of special talent who perpetuate, transmit, create tradition. Tradition is not an orthodoxy, an accepted canon; it is a continuous process of growth, in which new cells replace old and diseased ones. So tradition does not really stand in rigid opposition to the modern. The great artists of the modern age see tradition in a new light, interpret it afresh, and thereby give it vitality.*

In a serious moment—Deasil

During a recent lecture-recital in Hong Kong, the great master of *Kunqu* opera, Yu Zhenfei, now in his eighties, demonstrated, with an extraordinary blend of charisma and childlike humour, how the centre of the practice of *Kunqu* lies in Daoism, how the best entry to stage-craft is *Taijiquan*, and how the only convincing stage laugh comes from the alchemical furnace, the *dantian*.

Yu also stressed roundness in movement and gesture, the Ultimate (taiji) *circle, essence of this martial and meditative art.*

After my morning practice—Deasil

To a casual observer this venerable old actor and the young experimental writers may seem to belong to two different worlds; but at a deeper level they are part of a continuum. The authors of *The Impostor* and *The Bus-stop* are also searching, through humour, satire, and the theatrical expression of human absurdity, for a truer and more 'genuinely spiritual vision' of man and society.

Antiquity Before Us, Face to Face

There are signs that the tradition is making itself felt again, like an inexhaustible subterranean spring. Few books can claim a greater antiquity, and simultaneously a greater modernity, than the *Book of Changes*. In its Wilhelm/Baynes version, it has come to permeate the modern consciousness of the West. The Chinese have largely forgotten it, especially the young, always eager to read the latest in American fiction, but incredulous if told that this very fiction contains their own distant past. Yang Lian is an interesting exception to this rule. In a short essay published in September 1983, he points to the *Changes* as an unexplored repository of indigenous Chinese symbolism. He is merely bringing home to China what the West has briefly borrowed. In the words of Liu Xie again:

Antiquity, however remote,　　　　　　　終古雖遠，
Appears before us, face to face.　　　　　　偄焉如面。

Trees on the Mountain

Bei Dao, in one of his most recent poems, 'On Tradition', muses:

the mountain goat stands on the precipice
the arched bridge decrepit
the day it was built
who can make out the horizon
through years as dense as porcupines
day and night, as sombre
as tattooed tribesmen
are the wind-chimes; none hear the ancestral voices
the long night silently enters the stone
the wish to move the stone
is a mountain range, rising and falling
in history textbooks

tr. Bonnie S. McDougall

The *Book of Changes*, when consulted concerning our enterprise, was more cautious and reassuring:

Development—Gradual Progress

A tree on the mountain develops slowly according to the law of its being and consequently stands firmly rooted . . . . Within is tranquility, which guards against precipitate actions, and without is penetration, which makes development and progress possible.

Hexagram 53 (Wilhelm/Baynes version)

Gradual—what a deceptive and terrifying world! Where water flows, there a channel forms: 水到渠成 . *Think how many great monuments have eventually succumbed to this gradual and silent process: the slow erosion of a mansion by termites, the relentless decline of the Jia family in* The Story of the Stone. *The achievements of many a great artist or poet are indeed built on the dead bones of innumerable lesser forerunners:* 一將功成萬骨枯. *Such is the gradual progress of history. Alas! A sobering thought!*

During a sleepless night—Deasil

Old Deasil nodded thoughtfully as he read the inscription once more through to the end. The two men began their journeys home, and while they walked, and before they parted ways, Deasil addressed these words to his young friend, speaking inwardly, almost as if to himself:

'The mountain is young. It will always remain so, and the grass and trees will continue to take root on it. The soil nourishes, and the trees in their turn when once they grow to maturity, protect the mountain, cleanse the air, and enrich the very soil that gave them birth.

'Come, you had better do as Athanasius instructed, take this batch of absurd specimens with you to Bullbary, and see how they fare there.'

This record written during a typhoon, with heavy rain beating on the windowpanes.

Postscript

The fabled Stone Tree is of course *The Story of the Stone*, original title of the novel popularly known as *The Dream of the Red Chamber* (whence 'Redology', and its acute form, 'Reddiction'). This novel was indeed our original point of intersection, and became a point of departure for this adventure into the modern world. The large characters in the margins are taken from early rubbings, some from steles or rock-inscriptions on the sacred peaks themselves. The seal-carving, and the calligraphy on pages 181, 271 and 305, are by Wu Zijian 吳子建. The calligraphy on page 9 is by Professor Jao Tsung-i 饒宗頤. The Magic Fungus 靈芝 scroll-pattern on pages 11, 81 etc. is taken from a Yuan dynasty blue and white bowl in the collection of the Art Gallery, The Chinese University of Hong Kong. François Cheng's 程抱一 thoughts on Zao Wou-ki (pp. 4 and 13) can be found in the catalogue prepared by the Hong Kong Arts Centre for Zao's retrospective there in 1981, and his thoughts on the nature of *wen,* in *Chinese Poetic Writing* (Indiana University Press, 1982), p. 213. Liu Kuo-sung 劉國松 on Zen is from *Liu Kuo-sung: The Growth of A Modern Chinese Artist* by Chu-tsing Li, Taipei 1969. The remark about the 'mysterious centre of Chinese philosophy' is from Chang Chung-yuan's *Tao: A New Way of Thinking*, Perennial Library 1977.

We wish to take this opportunity of thanking our friends Geremie Barmé, Bonnie McDougall, William Tay, Brian Blomfield and Rachel May, who gave most generously of their time and advice (even if it was not always heeded). Xi Xi, Yang Mu, Yu Kwang-chung and Zao Wou-ki were extremely prompt in replying to our many queries and requests.

S.C.S.
J.M.

Prose

PIAZZA September, 1951
Courtesy of the artist

許芥昱：趙無極畫布上的顏色與光亮

Colour and Light in the Canvases of Zao Wou-ki

By Hsu Kai-yu

Translated by Diana Yu

THE GRAND PALAIS, that famous nineteenth century building standing south of the Champs Élysées and north of the Seine, between the Arc de Triomphe and the Place de la Concorde, is so named not only for its architectural grandeur and dignity, but because its immediate neighbour to the right is the Petit Palais. Despite its royal title the building never served as the abode of any kingly personage, and with the coming of the Republic its spacious rooms with their lofty ceilings were re-furnished and converted into exhibition halls. This was no place for ordinary artists to display their talents. For a century only artists of the first order in the western world have enjoyed the honour of being sponsored by the French Ministry of Culture to hold exhibitions there. On 12 June 1981, Zao Wou-ki's (Zhao Wuji 趙無極) one-man retrospective of works covering a period of thirty years opened on the first floor, while the works of his friend, Nicolas de Staël (1914-1955), a painter who enjoyed wide popularity in France, were displayed on the ground floor of the same building.

Most of the thirty-six paintings on show in that exhibition—oils and water-and-ink—were large-scale works. The largest of them, a triptych, occupied the spacious wall facing the entrance staircase, an irresistible expanse of bright yellow accented by fat virile lines of dark brown and black. The earliest of the paintings, *Arezzo 1950*, is a canvas of soft yellows and light leaf-green tones. Yellow, a neutral colour, is like the earth, while the green, peering behind the yellow, tells of budding life. On such a background fine black lines form shapes resembling symbols (both orthographic and non-orthographic). But where have we encountered these symbols before? On some ancient stele? Or are they the traces of pictograms executed on walls by cave-men in an even more remote age? What forms are these mingled among them, tree-bark corrugations, rock fissures, a legacy of Nature's master-strokes! Yellow and green are congenial colours, not in the least menacing or strange, and standing in front of this painting I recalled the words of the French poet Henri Michaux, when as early as 1952 he wrote of Zao Wou-ki's art:

> To display while concealing, to break the direct line and make it tremble, to trace in idleness the twists and turns of a walk and the doodlings of a dreaming spirit, that is what Zao Wou-ki loves; and

This essay originally appeared in Ming Pao Monthly, *November 1981.*

then, suddenly, with the same air of festivity that enlivens the Chinese countryside, the picture appears, quivering with joy and delight in an orchard of signs.

Montrer en dissimulant, briser et faire trembler la ligne directe, tracer, en musant, les détours de la promenade et les pattes de mouche de l'esprit rêveur, voila ce qu'aime Zao Wou-ki, et, tout à coup avec le même air de fête qui anime campagnes et villages chinois, le tableau apparaît, frémissant joyeusement et un peu drôle dans un verger de signes.

But how has this come about?

Learning from postcards

1950 was the third year of Zao Wou-ki's stay in France. A mere three years and he had achieved so much. This was because when he arrived in France he was far from empty-handed.

Zao had left China armed with fourteen years of professional training at the Hangchow School of Fine Arts, the encouragement and mentorship of many a Chinese pioneer of the western painting tradition, the success of two exhibitions, and a huge pile of postcard reproductions of famous works of western painting. These postcards were important; without them Zao would perhaps never have become the internationally acclaimed artist that he now is.

Years earlier a younger brother of Zao's father, who used to travel frequently to Europe, had brought back large numbers of these postcards after every trip, to please the young Zao. Zao's own father, a banker and a gentleman of sophisticated tastes, quite renowned in Shanghai and Hangchow, was also fond of painting and had once himself won an international award for painting. He was very much in favour of his son's studying fine arts, and though the boy's mother entertained hopes that he might one day distinguish himself in the conventional manner and become a banker like his father, it was Father's and Grandfather's wishes that prevailed. Zao was born in 1921 in Peking. When his family moved to Shanghai he was just a few months old. At home, Grandfather taught him calligraphy. He learnt to recite some traditional axioms by heart and can still vaguely recollect the gist of one: "Written characters should be animated, and the ink should be infused with life." But what does "life" mean? Later Zao reached this conclusion: a work of art must touch the viewer's heart; the first impression it makes must be an indelible one. His family owned a collection of valuable paintings, and often the elders would lay out these family treasures and point out to sons and grandchildren the merits of an ink-dot landscape by Mi Fei or a work by Zhao Mengfu. As time went by such familiarity bred a tender liking. The young Zao was unable to point out what exactly distinguished Mi Fei's art. He only realized much later that a Mi Fei landscape had a cheerful vivacity like that of the autumn sun. It sparkled through the paper. In 1979 the French writer Jean Leymarie, commenting on Zao's art, said he had combined the cheerful and vivacious qualities of Mi Fei and Ni Zan, stating at the same time that the same qualities were to be found in Cézanne. These remarks are not unfounded. The Mi Fei's were a family heirloom, while the

Cézannes had been available in the form of postcard reproductions brought home by the uncle—Cézanne, Picasso, Matisse, and outstanding works by the Impressionists, the Fauvists and the Expressionists, as well as more classical masterpieces by sixteenth and seventeenth century Italian, Dutch and French painters. Zao's admiration for western painting dated from that period.

In 1935 Zao entered the Hangchow School of Fine Arts. In the traditional Chinese painting classes, students were ordered to copy works of Ming and Qing painters as a kind of discipline, a practice in which Zao participated very unenthusiastically because he believed that imitation and art were completely different things. This irritated the class master Pan Tianshou 潘天壽 so much that he nearly expelled the rebellious student. As for western painting, students had to practise drawing plaster models for three years and drawing the human body for two years before they were permitted to start on oils. Zao had no patience for such rules and before a year had gone by at the school he launched into oil painting secretly at home. When in lack of a model he would beseech his little sister to sit down and let him paint her face. In the school, most of the teachers of western painting had been trained in Belgium or France in the academic tradition, and demanded that students delineate every grin or frown on the model's face with realistic precision. Zao believed that precise representation of separate parts could not reflect the entirety of the model's presence, such an entirety being the organic unity of all the parts. Already he had been convinced by Picasso and Matisse, and felt that his own disposition was quite akin to theirs. He himself admitted that all the works displayed in his very first exhibition, which he held upon graduation in 1941 in Chungking, were modelled on this handful of European masters who had exerted such an influence on him. In spite of this, his performance attracted considerable attention in the Chinese painting scene of that time. Chinese artists were unsure of their direction within the confines of tradition, and it was not until the War of Resistance came to an end that they committed their first open act of defiance against traditional painting. On the eve of the Hangchow School of Fine Arts' return to Hangchow, the principal of the school, Lin Fengmian 林風眠, together with Ding Yanyong 丁衍庸, Zao and others, held a joint exhibition in Chungking.

Even before he went abroad, Zao had decided to pursue the essentials of the visual experience by departing from visual resemblance, to try to make his canvas a medium for intellectual and emotional communication between viewer and work. To paint an apple that looked like an apple, or a landscape that looked like a landscape, was not enough. Already he had begun to try to make line and colour express certain things that ordinary language could not (or very often could not) easily express—a certain feeling, certain imaginations, a question—things that lie sometimes within the realm, if only relatively so, of pure beauty, or sometimes are simply the substance of life's dilemmas.

Le Moulin-Vert: taking flight

His paintings of 1950, though a first attempt made on arriving in France, were ample evidence that he had already taken flight.

Certainly it was his talent that propelled him upwards: his painting talent was his chief asset, and on top of that a talent in living and getting along with people.

These were qualities it was impossible to counterfeit. His lively spirit (which his white hairs in no way diminish), that mellow air with which he still talks, all suggest the charm he must have exerted three decades or more ago. In Chungking he had become acquainted with Vadime Elisseeff, French cultural attaché in China at that time. When Elisseeff returned to Paris in 1945 to take up the post of curator of oriental art at the Musée Cernuschi, he took with him twenty paintings by Zao and displayed them in the museum as Zao's début in France. Zao arrived in Paris on 1 April 1948, just in time for the postwar period when painters of distinction from all over western Europe were flocking to Paris. Twenty or thirty of these artists— Nicolas de Staël, Pierre Soulages, Roberto Sebastian Matta, Georges Mathieu, Hans Hartung, Alberto Giacometti, Jean-Paul Riopelle, Sam Francis, and others, met regularly, mostly at the Galerie Nina Dausset on the Rue du Dragon. Zao soon made friends with them, and was taken seriously. He went to the Grande Chaumière (the oldest atelier in Paris) to practise drawing the human body, and very soon felt himself quite at home in the art atmosphere of Paris. In less than a year, and though he was still hardly able to speak French, he won the class prize for drawing. In May 1949, having settled in Paris for barely a year, Zao held his first show. The preface of the catalogue was contributed by Bernard Dorival, curator of the Musée National Moderne, who evoked the special quality of Zao Wou-ki's art:

> Chinese in their essence, modern and French in some of their aspects, the pictures of Zao Wou-ki succeed in creating a most enjoyable synthesis.

This statement is still relevant today.

It all began in the Rue du Moulin-Vert in Montparnasse, favourite haunt of Parisian writers and artists, where Zao had his first studio and home. A famous neighbour was Giacometti, from whose philosophical vision emerged elongated, emaciated figures capturing the essence of humanity. On the second anniversary of Zao's arrival in Paris, fortune knocked on the door—the famous poet Henri Michaux brought an influential gallery owner, Pierre Loeb, to see him and at one stroke Loeb bought twelve of Zao's paintings. The connection continued for eight years, through which Zao's works found a steady market in western Europe. Michaux also collaborated with Zao, publishing his own poetry and Zao's prints together in book form, each to the other's benefit. In the following two decades Zao continued to work with poets and writers, making prints to accompany Harry Roskolenko's texts, Arthur Rimbaud's poetry, André Malraux's writings and the works of many others. Malraux, who was France's Minister of Culture for many years in the 1960s, made truly outstanding contributions to the arts and letters of Europe, and also did much to boost the livelihood of writers and painters in Paris. Artists were granted low rents for residences and studios and free use of government cultural facilities. The book which Malraux and Zao co-authored, *La Tentation de l'Occident*, discussed the influences, especially the harmful influences, exerted by modern western culture on traditional Chinese and French culture. It showed Malraux's great penetration and admiration for the cultural tradition of China, and was also a factor, by no means insignificant, in Zao's swift rise to success.

For Zao, whose initiation into western painting had begun with closely observed reproductions, the works of Paul Klee became a great attraction as early as 1950, although to be exact his private devotion to Klee dated from 1951, when he had the opportunity to view Klee's paintings closely for the first time in the museums in Switzerland. Klee's use of linear symbols (which so enriched and condensed the meaning of painting) stimulated Zao to try the use of traditional Chinese symbols (written characters) in his own art. It was a new departure that coincided with some of Zao's own chief preoccupations; on the one hand, having been for so many years steeped in Chinese calligraphy, he could now re-examine the Han steles, the oracle-bone script, ancient bronze and stone inscriptions with renewed interest; and on the other hand, Klee's merging of eastern and western elements pointed Zao to an *avant-garde* direction for art in the West.

Even today Zao Wou-ki says, "My art developed very naturally and very logically. From Klee to my present style—don't you see how easy it is to comprehend?"

Yes, the earliest painting included in the Grand Palais retrospective already shows traces of Klee's influence. The teenager's ostentation has been abandoned, and unpretentious brushwork and unadorned clarity prevail. This was in line with the good old tradition of Chinese landscape painting which Zao could not erase from his memory entirely. He felt that working on his paintings (though not every one of them) was an enjoyment, and this, at least, was very much a Chinese *literatus* painter's attitude.

In the early 1950s, Zao became keenly interested in the calligraphy found on prehistoric Chinese oracle-bones, and in the bronze and stone inscriptions. It was no coincidence that his painting style should change so dramatically. The canvas *Wind* (painted in 1954, now in the artist's own collection), a work of historical significance, is a vertical rectangle that suggests the big centre-piece hung on a Chinese wall, while the two rows of oracle-bone writing (are they bird script or tiger script?) and the dark sombre purple remind the viewer that he could well be looking at an ancient stele or reading the fragments of a message excavated from the Yin Ruins. But this is no ordinary, cold lifeless stone, for in its purplish-red hue a spiritual light flickers, bespeaking the scriptless (or scripted?) mystery of a stone plaque's Heaven-ordained message. Zao's use of symbols resembling ancient writing was complementary to his print-maker's style, producing an art which western viewers found especially interesting. As Alain Jouffroy wrote for the 1955 exhibition of Zao's lithographs and engravings in Cincinnati's Museum of Fine Arts, "The work of Zao Wou-ki shows us clearly how the Chinese vision of the universe, in which the blurred and far-off reflects the spirit of contemplation rather than the thing contemplated, has become a modern, universal vision. And men as different as Paul Klee, Mark Tobey or Henri Michaux have likewise had recourse to it." Indeed, calligraphic symbols were as much of a revelation to Zao as ancient Spanish grotto symbols were to Juan Miró.

Probing these depths tended to lead towards greater and greater mysticism. For two years (1953-1954) Zao's paintings found no buyers, because nobody understood them.

A *cul-de-sac* necessitates change—though the path Zao had taken was not purely a *cul-de-sac*.

Jonquoy: soaring

From Edgar Varèse, composer and Zao's great friend, Zao acquired a taste for traditional music as well as electronic music. A new penetration into the mysterious beauty of Nature was on its way—the analysis of sound into its basic elements by science and not via the usual musical instruments, and then the synchronization of these elements into musical pieces. Zao first met Varèse in 1955 and the two men developed a deep friendship which ended only with Varèse's death in 1964. In that decade each exerted great influence on the work of the other. The script-like symbols in Zao's paintings became larger and larger and wilder and wilder (as can be seen in a work done in October 1955, now in the Sherwin collection in New York), and then grew faint, misty 朦朧, even invisible (as in *My Country* and several other works from 1957). In *My Country*, a warm lyrical piece that expresses an exile's nostalgia for home, a shape roughly resembling the map of China occupies the entire canvas. In the upper area (which corresponds to the Shaanxi/Gansu region?) loom several heavy black forms which vaguely (but not necessarily) resemble Chinese written characters. Dense clouds hang over the north-western corner, and similar clouds, only lighter, cover eastern China and the lower Yangtze. In China sufferings were plenty. Accompanying his parents or his school, Zao had moved from place to place, and in his mind's eye his country was always engulfed in the flames of battle. Throughout that wide land gunsmoke and turmoil always prevailed, yet there were quiet places nonetheless, the patches of bright yellow and orange red shown on the painting.

Open-hearted blissful lyricism was still relatively rare in his works, and was more often outweighed by powerful pangs of emotion. Even when he painted lovely floral visions of his homeland Zao often let loose nightmarish forms on his canvases. In *Night is Stirring* (1956, title given by Michaux) the images are extremely powerful: dark shadows hang from the upper part of the painting like giant trees, their branches suddenly ablaze when they reach the area in the centre, while dark blues and blacks press hard towards the centre, the patches of light always accompanied by looming shadows. The heavy, rough-hewn symbols are back again, most prominently in the 1957 painting titled *The Two of Us*, now in Harvard's Fogg Museum. On this painting, which is of great historical significance, two half-faded Chinese characters "*wu ji*" 無極 (infinite)* are discernible on the right, while the shape of what appear to be two other characters looms on the left, perhaps indicating the name of the artist's wife. Zao and his wife went through an emotional crisis that year, and their works produced during that period, which was also one of great creativity, bore the obvious mark of such a crisis. In *Tempest* (painted 1957, now in the Guggenheim Museum, New York), a black beast charges madly into the canvas from upper left and is stopped dead by torrid flames, while dark clouds, pregnant with faint dark shadows (are these symbols?), close in on all four sides. In another work, completed in 1956 and now in the Walker Art Centre, Minneapolis, Mont Riven is a pure mountain of fire in whose blazing flames innumerable tiny forms (symbols again?) dance and leap. When the fire in the artist's heart was too strong for him to bear he had to desert his home, leave Paris, and re-

---

Wou-ki in the French EFEO romanization —*tr.*

visit America. In that country he met many painters and made friends with Franz Kline, Mark Rothko, Guston Philip, Adolph Gottlieb and Hans Hoffman. The uninhibited daring of these artists, verging on self-indulgence, gave him a new stimulus. In 1957 he produced a large work (97 by 221 cm.) in his younger brother's residence (the painting is now in the Detroit Institute of Art's collection), in which the tension, so obvious in *Tempest*, has become greatly toned down, although the confrontation of red and black pulling across a barrier of rough-hewn symbols is still quite visible.

The profusion of works produced in these last years of the 1950s is remarkable in various ways. The works have one thing in common—each canvas, no matter how dim and depressing its colour scheme, invariably contains a patch of pearly-white light. This is something more than a mere light-and-dark contrast, it is the re-emergence of "the void", that crucial element in Chinese painting. "The void" is far from being total emptiness, for it embraces all essence and all origins not plainly perceivable by man—it is the void, the state of nothingness, of Daoist philosophy. To critics in the European tradition this was highly enlightening. In F. Elgar's words, that light was the light of the east, or the light of the west shining in an eastern sky.

After having spent over a year travelling, first visiting the United States, moving from the east coast to the west coast, then going on to Hawaii, to Hong Kong where he met and married his second wife, then returning to Paris via the Middle East, Zao settled down again and moved his home to the Rue Jonquoy. This was a beautiful place which his architect and designer friends helped to create, with garden and fish pond, where the artist could work to his heart's content. His paintings became ever larger and larger. He says he never does rough sketches, never makes small paintings to magnify upon. One painting is one painting. A large painting sometimes requires to be laid on the floor as he works on it, and then he can really "walk into it", as it were. A small painting has to stay on an easle and the painter faces it, stands opposite it, never enters it; the same applies to the viewer of small paintings. Zao wants his viewers to "walk into" his paintings, and on this point he is close to Jackson Pollock and Mark Rothko.

A mounting sensitivity as well as a gradual suppression of the narrative element in his art showed that Zao was moving in the direction of pure painting. Except for a few pieces that were given names primarily to commemorate some worthy event, most of his works done after 1957 are untitled—the art is there for the viewer to appreciate. Sometimes even a poet's lines seemed redundant. Some works were executed very slowly, retouched again and again, the final version appearing only after ten years had passed (the *Mont Riven* mentioned above was an example). But there were others that he completed at one sweep overnight, like *6-1-60*, now in a private collection in Paris, painted on 6 January 1960. The heart of this picture is a spread of gleaming white, and darkness surrounds it on all four sides; shadows, like those of winging vultures, appear in and out between the light and the dark, while a touch of blue makes itself visible behind the white light and conjures up dawn on the sea. It is perhaps inappropriate to describe these works of the artist in terms of natural and concrete images. Perhaps we should only say that each work of this period has a central element acting as the focus of the painting, and that there is always the presence of a void, pregnant with spiritual meaning, which palpitates incessantly as if performing the function of the pulsating heart.

But why is it wrong to speak of Zao's art in terms of natural images? In 1961 he himself confessed that in Paris he had rediscovered China. "Certainly Paris exerted a decisive influence on me in my artistic formation, but as I developed into maturity in Paris I also gradually rediscovered China." His paintings make the principle of his pictorial construction quite clear—the artist's view of the universe is elucidated by a centrifugal movement that extends from centre to the four sides in varying modes and patterns while the principle remains unchanged. The attraction and significance of a painting is not confined by its frame, but extends into the remote and unseeable distance—or, to put it in an old Chinese way, into the realm of the imagination, inaccessible even to the brush. In fact, these canvases bear obvious landscape traces. *18-1-63*, a work painted in 1963 for Michaux, is nothing other than gleaming white waves on a beach, waves whose presence echoes a trail of white clouds in the sky, only that sky looks like a summer night sky laden with rain clouds. Both *7-6-63* and *31-1-63* are seascapes, while *18-2-63* is a picture of meadows in early spring.... The year 1963 marked the artist's return to Nature. In his own words: "Of course our paintings manifest Nature's phenomena, for life is encaged in concrete forms. Strictly speaking, no form is ever abstract, and any painting that depends on forms to convey thoughts and feelings is no abstract painting."

Storm, Calm, Nature

The happy peaceful days of the early 1960s brought many paintings characterized by a serene beauty. But the storm was destined to return. *29-9-64* shows clouds scurrying across the blue sky, signalling the onset of the storm. *29-1-64* shows a giant tree making its protest to an evening sky baked red by the setting sun. In the two years that followed the paintings were quieter. In *13-2-67* the sea is boiling again, and the leaping form (a dragon?) on the right hurls itself towards the blinding white light; the light surges forward, and as it does so, so does the darkening storm on the left; thunder and lightning illuminate a crag in the very moment of disintegration. Those were days in which the artist's emotions were on trial, for beginning from 1964 his wife had been ailing, her health sometimes seeming to improve but gradually worsening, until in March 1972 she died. During the periods when she was seriously ill Zao could not bring himself to plan any large-scale oil painting, and only dabbled with Chinese water-and-ink, which resulted in a number of charming works in the Chinese ink-splash landscape tradition, somewhat resembling the impromptu pieces of Ba Da Shanren 八大山人 and Shi Tao 石濤. These he continued to execute very occasionally up to 1979. Half a year after his wife's death, in a big painting painted in memory of her (200 by 525 cm., now in the Musée National d'Art Moderne), he returned to the basic tones of yellow and brown which he was so fond of in his early period. The red in the upper-left corner and the black in the upper-right are life and death at loggerheads with one another; a few dark patches in the centre and below are also thrown in, in antagonistic positions. All in all it suggests a union and a confrontation, and finally, a burial in the earth of all the joys and woes of this encounter. From that point on Zao's paintings became

OIL, July 9, 1964
From the collection of Mrs. Ruth P. Smith, N.Y.
Courtesy of Kootz Gallery, N.Y.

ZAO WOU-KI

The artistic destiny of Zao Wou-ki is not merely individual; it is intimately linked to the development of a pictorial tradition several thousand years old, a tradition that bears the mark of the written sign. Has there ever been a country where the written sign was held in such honour as in China? "In the beginning was the sign" is the primary affirmation that defines this most singular culture. In the archaic Chinese myths the Creator does not reveal himself in the "word" or in Holy Writ; he leaves traces which inspire humans to create their own divinatory or linguistic signs. These, through their architectural and figurative qualities, have given rise to a double art (calligraphy/painting) in which the man drawing and the sign drawn are one. From then on the brush becomes the passion of a whole people. Through its mediation, through the primordial rhythm of its gestures, the Chinese immerse themselves in signs which express both the vital breath animating the created universe (qi) *and the internal lines inherent in all things* (li).

— François Cheng

HSU KAI-YU

Professor Kai-yu Hsu, who died tragically in the fierce storms that struck Northern California in January 1982, is remembered by his colleagues, students, and friends as a man of many talents and interests. While art, classical scholarship, and pedagogy occupied much of his thoughts and time during his two and a half decades at San Francisco State University, his most tangible and lasting professional contributions may well have been in the area of modern Chinese literature.

Kai-yu began his work in modern literature with his Ph.D. dissertation at Stanford University (1959) on the poet Wen Yiduo, who was Hsu's mentor at the National Southwest Associate University in Kunming. In 1980, Wen I-to, *a revised and expanded version of this work, was published in the Twayne World Authors Series (G. K. Hall), the last book to bear Kai-yu's name as author. In the intervening two decades, Kai-yu's contributions to modern and contemporary Chinese literature—including research, translation, personal contacts and sponsorship—reflected his interests, talents, and energy level. In addition to publishing many essays and articles in English and Chinese, attending conferences all over the world, and entertaining writers from the PRC, Taiwan, and Hong Kong, Kai-yu authored three important books in the field of modern Chinese literature:* Twentieth Century Chinese Poetry: An Anthology *(Doubleday, 1963; Cornell, 1970),* The Chinese Literary Scene *(Vintage, 1975), and* Literature of the People's Republic of China *(Indiana, 1980). These works, which continue to be read, used, and enjoyed today, serve to remind us of Kai-yu Hsu's dedication to Chinese belles lettres and to the men and women whose writing, research, and translating he so admired.*

Howard Goldblatt
San Francisco State University

even more liberated in spirit. Strong, rich colours intruded boldly into the quiet calm of his canvases—for calm these paintings still are, their pictorial design bearing still the ideas of landscape, with black occupying crucial points and upholding designs as daring as his ink-splash impromptu pieces (such as *13-9-73* etc.). The intrusion of rich colours brings along a strong breath of life, and yet so artfully are these colours thrown in that the overall effect is by no means jarring or disruptive.

Occasionally there re-appeared strong pangs of emotion and more agitated convulsions. More than a year after the death of his second wife, Zao painted *1-10-73* which has a pitch black upper rim suggestive of a bank of dark clouds, below which peers a little dark blue—it is a picture of a storm-ridden sky. The heavy black symbols, together with the semi-spherical dark reddish-brown shape haunting the lower region, make it quite impossible for the gleaming white patch in the centre to strike any balance between light and shade, no matter how desperately it tries. And even the intrusion of an almost colourless area, indicating the void with its spiritual significance, cannot temper the uneasiness which the entire pictorial design conjures up. *The Two of Us Again* (*10-3-74*, 280 by 400 cm., a large painting in the artist's own collection), has a very delicate pictorial design, the soaring black form in the upper-right corner balanced by the crouching black form in the lower-left, mesh-like black threads between them seeming to explain their close and yet remote relationship. The heat of the red and the quiet of the dark subdued red reflect certain conditions of the heart. The pictorial design is rendered complete by white areas in the background (the void in which the spirit flows) linking the various elements together, while pale greens, pale reds and light yellows sprinkled here and there lighten up the whole tone. But all in all it is a violent sight.

During these last two or three years Zao has been painting mainly quiet pictures, a representative work being *21-4-80*. The mossy stones that lie under the crag by the waterside, the exuberant life on the crag, the faint hills and remote streams in the upper-right, and, what is more, that thin thread of orange-red and dark purple on the extreme left edge, which adds so much to the painting's charm —all that charm only comes through fully in the original. Another 1980 work, the large triptych hanging on the main wall of the first floor of the Grand Palais, has patches of yellowish-green that warm up the entire canvas (200 by 525 cm.), and only one relatively heavy black form looms in the lower-left corner, the rest of the black having all thinned out, as if it were the substance of smoke, or mist, or dream.

Colour and light

The opening ceremony on 12 June was divided into two sessions. The morning was reserved for guests invited in a more or less official capacity—V.I.P.'s from the Ministry of Culture, and Parisian celebrities, while artists and professionals came mainly in the afternoon. At the opening ceremony I met Zhu Dequn 朱德羣, Chen Jianzhong 陳建中, Peng Wanchi 彭萬墀 and other painters, and of course Xiong Bing-ming 熊秉明 was there. In a suit of light blue, with a dark blue tie, Zao moved handsomely among his guests, and we exchanged greetings. For a really good talk with him I had to wait until the morning of 25 June, when I paid him a visit at his residence on the Rue Jonquoy. The small courtyard on to which the main entrance opens justly deserves the reputation it has gained for its décor—it contains a stone sculpture by Zao's late wife, and under a tree a small work by Henry Moore beckons to the guests. The shelves in the sitting-room were all lined with books, and vases of flowers, altogether eight of them, decorated the tables, window-ledges and staircase entrance. Zao's studio is located upstairs in the house we first entered. It has only a skylight and a window opening on to the courtyard. When Zao paints he needs to be alone. When Paris seems too noisy for him he drives for an hour and a half to another studio which he owns in the country. When he is not happy with a work in progress he turns it over and lets it stand with its face to the wall, leaving it there until his interest in it revives. Because of this some old works have had to wait several years before they are completed. He does not have the habit of inviting friends to comment on his paintings, nor does he ask them for suggestions if he gets stuck. He would rather confront the canvas alone and conceive his own solution. It is not a question of pride. He does so simply because to him artistic creation is a lonely struggle, and no one else can contribute to it. Sometimes art critics deliberately contradict him, because they want to avoid his influence; at other times they claim to find ideas in his paintings that have never entered the artist's mind. The only comment he will make on the Daoist idea of void and spirit is: "I take up my brush and paint. I paint and paint, and a painting is born. Prior to that I have no concrete or predetermined plan."

"And so your art is a natural flow, as in the natural flow of the Dao, is it not?" asked Xiong Bingming. "What do my thoughts have to do with Daoism or Confucianism? My thoughts are only engaged with the principle of void and substance on the surface of my canvas. It was you who helped me by giving it its Daoist interpretation after that long talk we had so many years ago."

Zao seems a sincerely modest man, although his is not the kind of false modesty that prevents him from expressing confidence in his own achievement. He is not concerned whether his paintings are called eastern or western, just as he knows full well that although he holds a French passport he is ultimately Chinese. All this is true and not to be debated. But he admits that what the French poet Henri Michaux, the writer Jean Leymarie and the Chinese scholar Cheng Baoyi say about his art makes a lot of sense. Cheng Baoyi has said that for Zao the artist, apart from technical experimentation and experiential exploration, the ultimate goal, so persistently pursued, has always been the authentic vision of the Spirit, for which his brush has opened up new vistas. To look at his paintings is for us to experience again the pure expression of our own personal mystery.

For Henri Michaux, Zao's art, while it is already divorced from form, is still organically linked to the flesh and bones of Nature. It is an art neither weird nor strange. The warm, flowing colours are no longer colours; they have been transformed into light, radiating, torrential light. R. Caillois said that Zao has transformed light into fire, fire into reflections of light, reflections of light into transparency, and finally, transparency into the crystallization of shimmering light. As for the artist himself, he has said he has no preference for any colour in particular. Each colour is a radiation of energy. Colours fill life in space, and at the same time colours describe light in its distribution.

And so it is perhaps in Zao's understanding and treatment of colour that we are given to see a corner of that secret mystery that is the artist's.

余光中：中國山水遊記的感性

The Sensuous Art of the Chinese Landscape Journal

By Yu Kwang-chung

Translated by Yang Qinghua

Yu Kwang-chung claims to be ambidextrous: a poet with his right hand and a writer of prose with his left. But he must surely be a reincarnation of the legendary Buddha of a thousand hands, so continuous and varied has been his output: translations, of modern English and American poetry, of a life of Van Gogh and recently of Turkish poetry and Oscar Wilde's The Importance of Being Earnest; *familiar essays and critical essays; and all this in addition to his own poetry, and his teaching and participation in a wide variety of cultural activities during all the years since his undergraduate days. After teaching in Taiwan and U.S.A., he has been a Reader in the Chinese Department of The Chinese University of Hong Kong for the past nine years. He is considered by many the doyen of modern Chinese poets, and was voted by Taiwan's young poets the 'uncrowned Poet Laureate' in 1983.*

His thirteenth volume of verse was published in 1983. But the work of his left hand is not to be treated lightly. In prose he is a master stylist, blending classical allusion with a modern sensibility, and at the same time creating a fluent and idiomatic Chinese style free from the prevalent Anglo-Americanisms. His latest series of three articles on the Chinese landscape journal demonstrates the wide range of his scholarship and his penetrating critical insight. It is a modernist's sympathetic treatment of a neglected traditional genre.

THE VARIETIES of prose are so numerous and diversified as to defy any attempt at classification. But if one were to endeavour to bring about an assortment in terms of psychological effect, then they would fall under two categories: the sensuous and the intellectual. The landscape journal, consisting as it does of narrative and scenic description, belongs, by its nature, to the sensuous category. Its author's sensory perceptions are extremely fine; they are data recorded by highly acute sense organs. We can talk of a writer as "highly sensuous" if in his writing, in his narrative and description, his use of sensory data enables the reader to visualize, to be there, and share the experience. And visualization on its own is really in-

This essay originally appeared in Ming Pao Monthly, *November 1982.*

sufficient; the other senses must also be exploited, hearing, smell, touch, taste, etc. Sensory experience is a natural part of human experience, but when it comes to expressing it in words, ordinary people, even the common run of writers, resort to clichés, and produce puerile, vague generalizations. Only prose-writers of real distinction can transcend limitations of language and get directly at the essence of things. Archibald MacLeish, the American poet, says in his "Ars Poetica":

> A poem should not mean
> But be.

This profound aphorism can equally be applied to prose.

Let us see how Wang Zhi 王質 of the Song dynasty describes the moon:

> Boundless mountains and hills, shadowy trees. An eyebrow of new moon hung above the towering cliffs, modulating its pace to the movement of man.
>
> —*from his "Donglin Journal"*

We often compare the new moon to an eyebrow or talk of an eyebrowlike new moon, but it is certainly novel to employ "eyebrow" as a measure word. The expression "modulating its pace to the movement of man" 遲速若與客俱 is reminiscent of Li Bai's lines:

> *Descending the verdant hills at nightfall,*   暮從碧山下，
> *We were followed home by the mountain moon.*   山月隨人歸。

But Wang's expression is more sensuous, more dynamic, more cinematic. What a vivid conception of the moon, to say that it will follow us slowly if we move at a leisurely pace, and will increase its speed as we accelerate. Let us see again how the same author describes a boating experience:

> Nothing but lotuses were to be seen. The wind came from ashore, bowing the plants before it. They were a-rocking and stirring, a confusion of sprawling red and prostrate green, and wafts of heady fragrance filled the air, clinging obstinately to our breasts and sleeves. We moored our boat by the roots of an ancient willow tree, and purchased a couple of jarfuls of wine and some water caltrops. Back in the lotuses again, we broke into riotous singing and laughter, which was echoed back to us by the surrounding valleys. A light breeze arose on the water, and ripples were born like fine scales. Fireflies flitted to and fro, as if in alarm or fright. The night was now far advanced. The peaks towered higher than ever, yet seemed near, looming over our heads as if they were about to reach down and snatch us. Not a trace of cloud could be seen in the sky. The stars were all out and shining brightly, tumbling in the water, like pearls rolling on a mirror, irretrievable.
>
> —*from "Donglin Journal"*

As scenic depiction this is really superb. Visual, auditory, and olfactory experiences are all woven together and brought to life. When fragrance "clings obstinately to our breasts and sleeves" 冲懷冒袖, 掩苒不脫, the olfactory experience is fused with the visual and the tactile. And the visual experience is so dynamically expressed: when the lotuses respond to the motion of the wind, they begin "a-rocking and stirring, a confusion of sprawling red and prostrate green"; a light breeze brushes the water, and ripples "are born like fine scales"; the ghostly flame of the fireflies flits "to and fro, as if in alarm or fright"; and the peaks "loom over our heads as if they are about to reach down and snatch us".[1] But most vivid of all is the description of the stars reflected in the water, likened to "pearls rolling on a mirror, irretrievable". Pearls as an image of stars and mirror as an image of water: these are static comparisons, and commonplace enough. But to speak of "pearls rolling on a mirror" is to bring motion into the matter. The fluctuation of the ripples on the surface of the water is thus brought out in a highly sensuous manner. From this we may draw the general conclusion that the best way to describe a scene is in fact to narrate it. Even the most static of scenes should be made to appear somehow in motion. In this way the landscape comes alive. To put it another way, run-of-the-mill scenic descriptions use a lot of epithets, but a truly striking description uses more verbs. In this respect it is cinematic.

Now let us look at a passage by Ma Ge 麻革 of the late Yuan dynasty. This is from his "Trip to Dragon Mountain":

> (We) went to sit again under Manjusri Crag and began to treat ourselves to some drinks. The sun had set, and a light mist and vaporous clouds mingled with the approaching dusk. Presently, a cool moon rose, casting a pale gleam over the rocks. The doleful murmuring of the pines was carried to us from the nearby ravines. We all looked around us in awe and hearkened in silence. The more rarified the atmosphere grew, the more remote were our thoughts from the world. Then said we to each other: "Could anyone in this world know joy greater than this?"

Both visual and auditory senses are involved here. The author has succeeded not only in conjuring up the moonlit night and the murmuring of the pines, but also in summarizing in a few pithy words the human response to both: "We all looked around us in awe and hearkened in silence." In scenic description and narrative, it is indeed sometimes more effective to state the results of perceptions, rather than their causes. For instance, if one wishes to evoke the beauty of a girl, it is

---

[1] A pity that parts of this description plagiarize the Tang dynasty poet Liu Zongyuan's 柳宗元 "Yuanjiake Journal", which I quote here for comparison:

> The wind would often descend from the mountains all around, shaking the tall trees, bending the multitudinous blades of grass, leaving a confusion of jumbled red and frightened green. Heady wafts of fragrance filled the air. The brook dashed on, with swift eddies, and formed pools in the depth of the valley.

The lush vegetation was rocking and stirring all the time.

The author also plagiarized Su Shi's "Trip to the Hill of the Stone Bells" which contains the following sentence:

> A gigantic rock towered by the side a thousand feet high, resembling some ferocious animal or hideous ghost about to reach down and snatch us.

MT. HUA, SACRED PEAK OF THE WEST. Ming dynasty woodcut, from *Ming kan mingshan tuban huaji* 明刊名山圖版畫集, Shanghai People's Art Publishing House.

sometimes a better strategy to show the admiration and wonder her beauty inspires in the beholder, rather than to give a direct account of her charms. Similarly, a direct description of a ghost or hideous monster is less effective than an account of the horror it instils in the hearts of those who encounter it. The human response ("we all looked around us in awe and hearkened in silence") throws the objective reality into relief most effectively, and keeps the reader in suspense (a trick all movie directors are familiar with).

Narrative can be every bit as sensuous as description. Take the following example from the "Mt. Hua Journal" of the great traveller Xu Xiake 徐霞客 of the late Ming dynasty:

> Descended to Shaluo Flat. Night pressing in; hurried out of the
> valley. Dark-walked for 3 *li* and stayed the night at Shifang Convent.

Night falls more slowly on the plain. "Night pressing in" is a mountain phenomenon, and dusk fell even more speedily for the author, as he was walking down the mountain. The words "pressing in" lead naturally on to the word "hurried". But all the hurry was to no avail, for man cannot outstrip the heavens, which were already dark by the time the traveller was out of the valley. In other words, night had overtaken him. The three expressions "pressing in", "hurried", and "dark" bring out the mobile relationship between night and man in a manner that is both urgent and dramatic. The highly dense expression "dark-walked" is sensuous to the point of saturation.

Xu Xiake, in his narrative, often employs singular expressions. This singularity is sometimes caused by his highly individual way of seeing things. The following passage, also from his "Huangshan Journal", is a good example of this:

> A small band of monks slowly alighted from the sky, where the pines and the rocks were lost in a tangle. Clasping their hands in salutation, they told us that they had been snowbound for three months and had fought their way through in search of food. They inquired how we had managed to climb this far up.

Xu Xiake and his party had braved the snow in order to attempt the hazardous ascent. Looking up, they saw this small group of monks descending from the very summit. Hence the singular expression, "slowly alighted from the sky". Even King Hu 胡金銓 would find it hard to outdo this, in one of his "kung-fu" adventure films.

Another shift in the camera-angle, and we find ourselves looking downwards from above, as in the following scene from Xu Xiake's "Yunnan Journal":

> (I) then clambered to the summit of the peak again. Walking all the way round, I had a view of the southern face, which was dotted with little shrines from top to bottom, like cells of a honeycomb or swallows' nests, ready to tumble down at any moment. They were all outbuildings of the Lohan Temple to the north and south of it.

In the postscript to his "Huangshan Journal" Xu has the following sentence describing a similar view:

> Leaning on my staff, I ascended in the direction of Cinnabar Convent. A climb of 10 *li* brought me to Huangni Ridge. The peaks which had loomed so high in the clouds emerged one after another and then dropped below my staff.

That the misty peaks dropped one by one below his staff demonstrates clearly the height he had scaled. It is surely an expression at once delightfully attractive and full of a sense of motion.

Chinese mountains and Chinese men of letters seem to exist in a symbiotic relationship. They need each other in order to be fully accepted into the halls of fame. Nature needs the *imprimatur* of the Muse, the Muse requires the *nihil obstat* of Nature. Thus every one of China's Great Peaks has at one time or another been immortalized by one of her Ancient Bards or Old Masters. Huangshan is known for its beauty all over China, and Huangshan Journals of one sort or another are too numerous to mention. The most renowned in ancient times are those from the hands of Xu Xiake, Qian Qianyi 錢謙益 and Yuan Mei 袁枚, while among contemporary writers, there is Ji Xianlin 季羨林. The journals written by these four writers differ in length, but even the shortest runs to approximately one thousand characters, and is therefore too long to be reproduced in full. In order to achieve a comparison, I shall cite passages describing pine trees:

HUANGSHAN. Ming dynasty woodcut, same source.

Every sheer precipice and overhanging crag is, without exception,
encrusted with knotty and fantastic pines, the taller measuring less
than ten feet and the smallest only a few inches. They are flat-headed,
with short bristling branches, convoluted roots and knotted trunks.
The shorter the older; the smaller the more extraordinary. Who would
have thought to find such a singular phenomenon as this, in a mountain
landscape that is already singular enough in itself? . . . On the way
down from Guide Cliff, halfway over a snowy slope, a crag rose
abruptly before us. From a crevice on its summit sprouted a pine tree
less than two feet high, its branches extending obliquely, twisting
round and round, coiling into a verdant canopy that stretched over
thirty feet. Its roots threaded their way up and down through the rock,
almost spanning its entire height. This is known as the Disturbed
Dragon Pine.

—from "Huangshan Journal" by Xu Xiake

The top of Old Man Peak was gained. Many strange-shaped pine
trees could be seen growing over the precipices, jutting dangerously out
from the rock-face. Thenceforward, every tree, without exception, was
a pine. And every pine, without exception, was in some way grotesque.
There were some with a trunk no thicker than a man's calf, but with
roots coiling over almost one sixth of an acre. There were some whose
roots did not cover more than ten feet, but whose branches extended
a long way, providing a dense shade over the path by their side. Others

followed the contour of the hillside and their extended boughs formed an arch over a gully. Yet others burst from a crevice and seemed to be growing almost horizontally. Some were light as feathered canopies, some writhed like dragons. Some ran close to the ground, then rose into the air, then returned to the ground again. Others projected sideways, came to a sudden halt, and then continued to project sideways again . . . . Standing on the north slope of Shixin Peak, one could see a pine growing out of the southern rock-face opposite, its boughs extending right across the gorge in between. That was what is generally known as the Guide Pine. To its west, a gigantic crag projected vertically upwards, surmounted by a pine which was only a little over three feet high, and yet covered almost one sixth of an acre. Its crooked trunk emerged from the rock and worked its way down and through it, splitting it in two near the middle. Its twisted and interwined branches snatched at one another. This was the Disturbed Dragon Pine. On the peaks of Stone Bamboo Shoot Cliff and Elixir Refining Bluff, every rock was a carefully placed part of the whole. There was no part that was superfluous or out of place. And every isolated piece of rock was topped by a solitary pine and looked like a head with a hairpin, or a carriage with a canopy. Viewed from afar, silhouetted against the sky, they resembled so many blades of grass. It was indeed a fascinating sight, beyond imagination and quite indescribable. These pines did not grow in the soil, but on the bare rock. Their trunk and bark were stone. Nurtured by the rain and clouds, enduring snow and frost, they were

HUANGSHAN, THE CRANE-CRESTED PINE, by Huang Binhong 黃濱虹.

HUANGSHAN SCENE, painted by Huang Binhong in 1954.

conceived from the very life-essence of Nature and engendered from the depths of antiquity. They belong with the elixirs and magic mushrooms of legend and are certainly not ordinary plants. And yet there are vulgar people who think of digging them up and keeping them in pots for their entertainment.

Ascending a snowy steep and turning east, we encountered a giant prostrate pine, wriggling its way across our path. Reduced to its present state by a thunderbolt, it stretched along the ground, spanning a distance of hundreds of yards, twisting and turning, with ruffled scales and angry bristling whiskers. Passers-by all thought it a sad sight. But I gave a chuckle, and said: "Isn't this a master stroke of Providence, to have thwarted it thus? Think what a still more imposing sight it will be in centuries to come when it becomes even more entangled and knotty."

—from "Huangshan Journal" by Qian Qianyi

Climbing Lixue Terrace, we came across an ancient pine. Its roots were in the east, while its trunk stretched along the ground westward, and its treetop extended southward. The whole tree had grown into the rock and then broken through and burst out of it. The rock seemed alive and hollow, sheltering the pine within itself. Rock and pine were totally assimilated with each other. It also seemed as if the pine stood in fear of heaven and did not dare to grow upwards. Its height was less than two feet, but it took quite ten people to link their arms around it. Other pines, there were, as bizarre as this, and too numerous to be mentioned.

—from "Huangshan Journal" by Yuan Mei

The pine trees found on Huangshan are even rarer than those in other places. They are the rarest of the rare. You only have to look at the names of the more noted ones, to have some idea of this: "Hassock Pine", "Interlocked Pines", "Fan-shaped Pine", "Black Tiger Pine" . . . "Guide Pine", and innumerable others, besides all the nameless tall pines, dwarf pines, ancient pines, young pines, pines growing on overhanging cliffs and sheer precipices, in the most unimaginable places. Endowed with myriad graceful forms, bizarre beyond all measure, they grow in violation of all the rules by which trees normally grow. In any other place, pines a thousand years old would look quite doddery and senile; but here, they are still young maidens in their prime, and their branches and trunks are not that thick either. In any other place, pines grow only in the soil. Here, they grow on the bare rock-face. In any other place, pines bury their roots in the earth. Here, the trees expose their roots quite unashamedly, all of them, bigger ones, smaller ones, thick ones, fine ones, on the surface of rocks, to the anxiety of the onlooker.

—from "Climbing Huangshan" by Ji Xianlin

Huangshan is famous for four things. First and foremost among these are its pine trees. No account of Huangshan would be complete without a mention of them. If we compare the four passages quoted above, we are obliged to rank Qian's first, Xu's second, Yuan's third, and Ji's last. It seems that when it comes to writing "Huangshan Journals" we Chinese are going gradually downhill. Huangshan is indeed the most extraordinary of all mountains; and the pine trees on Huangshan are the most extraordinary of all pine trees. It is only fitting therefore that there should be

HUANGSHAN,
by Liu Kuo-sung (1966)

something extraordinary in the way of prose to celebrate them. The grotesque beauty of Disturbed Dragon Pine won the acclamation of three distinguished travellers successively from the Ming and Qing dynasties. It should truly be named a wizard among pines. Yuan Mei made his trip to Huangshan one hundred and sixty-seven years after Xu Xiake,[2] and the tree was then still in full vigour. It must have been in existence for hundreds of years. But Ji Xianlin, enumerating as he did twelve celebrated pines of Huangshan in one breath, did not even mention it. Can it have freed itself from the rock and flown away? Qian Qianyi, in his descriptions of the pines of Huangshan, employs both panoramic long-shots, and close-ups. His close-ups of the two grotesque pines are highly sensuous. The images he creates are condensed and charged with tension. In his long-shots the other queer pines are also presented in a lifelike and animated way. Ji Xianlin, on the other hand, does a very perfunctory job, resorting to such abstract and unimaginative clichés as "endowed with myriad graceful forms".

A writer's ability can often be gauged by an examination of the way he uses figures—whether he uses them appropriately, vividly, uniquely. Qian's comparison of the solitary pine on the isolated rock to a hairpin on the head or a canopy on a carriage is highly graphic; the hairpin is an especially ingenious conceit. In his description of a prostrate pine, he uses first the expression "twisting and turning" and then "with ruffled scales and angry bristling whiskers". The apt reference to a dragon thus recurs like a motif. Neither Xu nor Yuan take any particular pains to give an elaborate description of the pines, yet the images they create are unforgettable. Ji Xianlin, by comparison, is very disappointing. Though he gives a whole string of names for these extraordinary trees, he fails to be at all specific and only succeeds in leaving a vague and generalized notion in the reader's mind. Time and again he resorts to enumerations: the pines are "tall, dwarf, ancient and young"; their roots are "bigger, smaller, thick and fine"; and all this with the avowed intention of demonstrating their "myriad graceful forms". Such rollcall-like enumeration, however, is sadly one-dimensional; it lacks perspective or texture. It is, in sensuous terms, impoverished. The sensuous quality of a piece of writing can roughly be assessed by an examination of the way the writer uses verbs. Ji's pine trees "grow", "bury" and "expose"; whereas Qian's pines "coil", "snatch", "twist and turn", "wriggle", "ruffle and bristle"—all, again, hinting at dragon motion. It is plain at a glance which set of verbs is the more expressive, which is the more sensuous.

Mount Tai is universally renowned, and has even found its way into many old Chinese sayings. Many accounts have been written of it, among which the most celebrated is probably the "Ascent of Mount Tai," by Yao Nai 姚鼐 of the Qing dynasty. The most acclaimed section of this journal is the passage describing the sunrise. The high point of the "The Southern Sacred Mountain", by another Qing dynasty traveller Qian Bangqi 錢邦芑, is similarly a sunrise description. We may compare the two by juxtaposition:

---

[2]Xu Xiake made two visits to Huangshan. The first was in the 44th year of the reign of Wanli (1616 A.D.). Yuan Mei's visit was in the 48th year of the reign of Qianlong (1783 A.D.).

MT. TAI, SACRED PEAK OF THE EAST. Ming dynasty woodcut.

Far, far away, along the horizon, stretched a thin streak of cloud of a rare hue. In another instant it was dappled pink. The sun was rising, vermilion like cinnabar, borne on a bed of stirring red light. Some said this was the Eastern Sea. I turned to look at the peaks to the west of the Sun Observing Peak; part of them had caught the sun, part had not, so that they were streaked red and white. But all of them appeared to bow before Mount Tai.

—from "Ascent of Mount Tai" by Yao Nai

The deep gloom gradually receded, but the air was still frosty against one's brow. To the east in the whitish mist a thread of rosy cloud soon broke into bright gold. It stretched the length of the eastern sky, from south to north, thousands and thousands of miles. Soon it grew brighter still, and multi-coloured, while the red glow in the due east became more luminous than ever. Another instant, and a disc of blood scarlet struggled up from beneath layers of cloud, radiating a myriad shafts of dazzling light. The earth was restored to brightness again. Heart and eye felt free.

—from "The Southern Sacred Mountain" by Qian Bangqi

In the last sentence of the first passage cited above, Yao has endeavoured to describe the effect of the first rays of the risen sun on the various peaks. Some had caught the sun and turned rosy in colour; others were untouched by the sun and retained the pristine white of their snow drifts. But all were lower than Mount Tai and seemed to be bowing to it. By comparison the last part of Qian's description, consisting of sixteen Chinese characters, is flat and insipid and far inferior. But in describing the sunrise itself, Qian seems somewhat more successful; his prose is more colourful and abounding in the sense of motion. Yao has a magnificent phrase "borne on a bed of stirring red light" 下有紅光, 動搖承之, which expresses the sense of motion most vividly. But Qian's range of colour is much wider, and shows more gradation, from "deep gloom" to "frosty nip", from "whitish mist" to "a thread of rosy cloud", from "bright golden" to "shining red" and "blood scarlet". The verbs Qian employs are also more diversified ("recede", "break", "stretch", "dazzle" and "struggle"), and more intense in feeling. The Tongcheng School of the Qing dynasty, to which Yao Nai belonged, prided itself on a prose style that was "light in flavour, scanty in words, orderly in appearance and leisurely in pace" 味淡聲希, 整潔從容. We would expect the works of that school to be characterized by a flatness of expression and a slackness of tempo. Yao's passage quoted above is mainly composed of short sentences, many of them conventional four-character locutions, and they inevitably fall short of the thrilling climax of Qian's "a disc of blood scarlet struggled up from beneath layers of cloud". In a word, Qian's prose is more sensuous.

*   *   *   *   *   *   *

In ascending Mount Kuocang by the water route, beyond Exi, the boat must inch its way forward, the boatman's sweat mingling with the water of the stream. The sky is brow-beaten by the mountains, the water begs the rocks for release. Only on arrival at Xiaoyang does the vista open out.

Wu Hongzhong brought Ruiru to see me off, and they sat with me on the bow. We had a few drinks, and the boatman entertained us with boating songs. We were at the game of finger-guessing, when suddenly we looked up and gave a loud cry of astonishment, for the colours we saw were not those of this world. But as I am ignorant as to how colours are named in heaven, I shall have to content myself here with their worldly approximations.

The setting sun was half a disc on the horizon, a ball of rouge fresh from the furnace. West of the river the peaks were verdant as the feathers of a parrot or blue-black as the rear-plumes of a crow. Overhead a vast expanse of scarlet cloud stretched for five thousand feet across the sky, a huge rift revealing a patch of azure firmament, all this reflected in the water, like red agate against an embroidered cloth.

The sun went further down. The sand-dunes were soft blue and tender white, and across the river, reeds and moon-reflections were scarcely distinguishable from one another. The mountains were now the hue of old watermelon-rind, and seven or eight flakes of downy cloud, a mellow lychee gold, converged into two banks, which began to glow a translucent grape-purple. Waves of night vapour rose up in the air, silvery white like the belly of a fish. They penetrated the furnace-fresh vermilion above, and all merged in a haze of glittering gold. At that moment, the whole universe, sky, earth, mountains, waters, the glorious sunset, the rosy clouds, all was in concert to present a most magnificent spectacle. One cannot help wondering why Nature should have troubled to produce such a masterpiece of painting and dyeing. Could it be that she wished to arouse the jealousy of the Fata Morgana, to outshine the Buddha Aksobhya, by giving us this glimpse of her own insurpassable beauty?

—*from "Xiaoyang" by Wang Siren* 王思任 *(Ming dynasty)*

This sunset description is even more sensuous than the two sunrise descriptions quoted above. Sunrise and sunset are breathtaking visual experiences, and descriptions of them are frequently to be encountered in Chinese literature. But the painter is better equipped to capture the richness of such fleeting and variegated colours. Words can seldom do justice to such a subject, and the writer will more often than not heave a sigh of helpless wonder when confronted with such grandeur. If he tries to push his medium to its limits, he may possibly rival Xie Lingyun's 謝靈運:

Clouds and sun help each other's brilliance,
Air and water are equally crystaline and fresh.

It was still early when we left the valley,
But the sun was already fading when we boarded the boat.
Trees and dales garnered the dusk,
Clouds and mists closed the evening.

Famous lines; but not what one would call richly sensuous. And it would take a prose genius to equal Su Shi's 蘇軾 line:

Scales of sunset-cloud stretching down the sky, fish-tail red.

Such a grandly conceived, masterfully executed and totally graphic representation of the roseate splendours of the sunset as Wang Siren's is really quite unprecedented in Chinese prose. As a matter of fact, in the whole realm of Chinese literature, including poetry, such sensuous depictions of visual beauty are extremely rare. The great novelist Cao Xueqin, in describing female costume and ornaments, paid a lot of attention to the discrimination of colours. He was never so crude as to represent things in sheer red or green. There is a passage in the forty-ninth chapter of his *Story of the Stone* which goes:

[Dai-yu] put on a pair of little red-leather boots which had a gilded cloud-pattern cut into their surface, a pelisse of heavy, dark-red bombasine lined with white fox-fur, a complicated woven belt made out of silvery-green shot silk, and a snow-hat.[3]

[3]Tr. Hawkes, Penguin Classics, pp. 478-9.

MT. EMEI. Ming dynasty woodcut.

But Cao's marvellously delicate sense of colour is mainly devoted to the description of costume and objects of beauty. It is seldom applied to matters such as the clouds and the sky.

Chinese painting has traditionally been divided into two schools: the Northern and the Southern. The Northern School was founded by Li Sixun 李思訓 of the Tang dynasty, famous for his "blue-and-green" landscapes, with their gold and red highlights. The Southern School is descended from the poet-painter Wang Wei 王維 of the Tang dynasty, whose paintings were characterized by large areas of tonal wash and relatively little linear detail. Later on, the monochrome ink-and-wash paintings of the Southern School, with their "mild" brushwork and "remote" inspiration 筆淡意遠, occupied a dominant position with critics of traditional Chinese painting, and the use of colour was very much relegated to second place. As to the problem of light and shade, this was of even less concern to the Chinese painter. No wonder Constable complained that the Chinese "have painted for 2000 years and have not discovered that there is such a thing as chiaroscuro". Wen Zhengming 文徵明 of the Ming dynasty wrote of landscape painting:

> I hear that in ancient times most painting was done in colour, and the use of ink was considered a secondary technique. Therefore most paintings were executed in blue and green. Later, in the middle ages, people began to paint in umber and varieties of ink and wash also made their appearance.

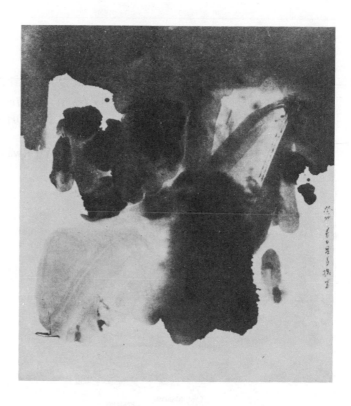

LANDSCAPE,
by Lui Shou-kwan
(Lü Shoukun 呂壽琨), 1963.

In the umber landscapes of Huang Gongwang 黃公望 of the Yuan dynasty light strokes in umber and indigo are added to a groundwork in ink and wash. After the Yuan dynasty, literati paintings became progressively more "mild" and "remote", using more ink and less colour.

Laozi's saying, "The five colours make men blind", is somewhat hard to accept in the 1980s, when people spend so much of their time watching colour movies and colour television. But it is very much in accordance with the Daoist predilections of ancient Chinese painters. In all the world the Chinese must surely be the race most capable of appreciating the charm of black and gray. Qian Zhongshu 錢鍾書 points out, however, in his essay "On Chinese painting and poetry", that whereas "in the field of Chinese painting, the beauty characteristic of the Southern school —dilute, mild, limpid and remote 冲淡清遠—has gained wide acceptance, the similar views of the 'spiritual harmony 神韻' school of poets has never been accepted into the mainstream of Chinese poetics." Such a statement is correct in a certain sense; but as Qian himself has also observed, to a non-Chinese eye, such differences of emphasis in Chinese poetry and painting are relative, more quantitative than qualitative. A typical Chinese classical poem, in terms of its colouration, is still ink and wash, or, at most, umber from the brush of Huang Gongwang. We may explore this idea further by looking at the poems on painting by some of the great poets. Du Fu 杜甫 had one of the keenest eyes for graphic art, and wrote many poems about paintings. These poems, though highly vivid, are strangely "mild" in terms of colour. This is true not only of his poems about pictures of horses, but also of those on

THE FIVE PEAKS

至少五嶽還頂住中國的天
At least the Five Peaks
Are still supporting the Chinese sky.

Yu Kwang-chung: "Music Percussive"

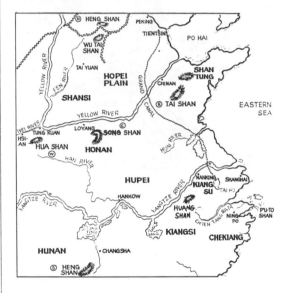

EAST CHINA AND
THE FIVE SACRED PEAKS,
with Huangshan added;
from *Hua Shan*
(Hong Kong, Vetch &
Lee, 1973).

THE FIVE SACRED PEAKS, from an ink-squeeze of an inscription incised on a stone stele at Songshan. The five curious Daoist ideographs represent the 5 Peaks, East, South, West and North (clockwise) with Songshan in the Centre.

The connection between religion and the surface of the ground originates in the conception of Chinese sacred mountains. The whole country is divided according to the points of the compass by the five Sacred Mountains, one in the north, south, east, west and centre . . . . The conception of these mountains characterizes to a high degree the need of the Chinese to find a perfect equality between their innermost convictions and nature herself . . . . The whole country should be regarded as a single temple.

Ernest Boerschmann,
Picturesque China *(London,*
Fisher Unwin, circ. 1910).

landscape paintings, such as "Song on a painted landscape screen newly drawn by the Vice-prefect Liu of Fengxian County", and "Lines written in jest on a landscape by Wang Zai". Su Shi also loved to write poems about paintings, and his use of colour is equally muted. See for example his "Lines on Wang Jinqing's Misty Rivers and Peaks, in the collection of Wang Dingguo" and "On Li Sixun's Yangtse River and Precipitous Isles". In the former poem, we can still find some sense of colour, as in the lines:

> *Crows brushing scarlet maple leaves settle by the waterside for the*
> * night;*
> *Snow falling from tall pines startles a daytime nap.*

But the latter poem is entirely monochrome. This is worth noting, since Li Sixun, the painter in question, is precisely the founder of the gold-and-blue school of landscape painting of the Northern Song dynasty. And Wang Jinqing is another important painter of the same school. If poems about paintings of the Northern school are so lacking in colour, how much more so poems on works of the Southern school?

The "mild limpidity" of the ink-wash paintings of the Southern school was further promoted in the literati-paintings of the Yuan and Ming dynasties and later. No wonder the literati writers were influenced by it in their landscape journals. I have already quoted passages from ancient Chinese landscape journals characterized by a particularly strong sensuous appeal, but such prose is by no means common. The authors ordinarily exhibit an understated charm, a "mild limpidity", rather than a vigorous sense of grandeur and colour. The landscape sketches of writers such as Yuan Hongdao 袁宏道, Zhong Xing 鍾惺, Tan Yuanchun 譚元春, Li Liufang 李流芳, and Zhang Dai 張岱, are all executed in simple strokes and "mild" washes, creating an impression of viewing the landscape at a distance. The prose of the Tongcheng School of the Qing dynasty is never sensuous, and this deficiency is most apparent in the landscape journal. The literary heyday of the Tongcheng school was rather short-lived. Yao Nai, a third generation Tongcheng writer, still produced several readable pieces in this genre. With Guan Tong 管同, however, of the fourth generation, the movement was more or less on its last legs:

> Lying alone in the dead of night, I felt so inexpressibly happy, listening to the sound of the soughing wind and the roaring billows on my pillow, dreaming often of dragons and fish dancing in the waves. In the fourth month, in early summer, Zhou Baoxu of Jingxi came from Soochow. A good friend of mine, he had always been fond of unusual sights, and on the sixteenth night of the lunar month we went together to watch the sea from the bund. The waves came in like crumbling mountains, the moon shone on the sea like fragments of silver. It was all so vast and cool. We looked at each other as if we were in another world. I was immensely delighted.
>
> —*from "Baoshan Journal" by Guan Tong*

Journals such as this are lacking in sensuous appeal, are written in a language that is positively banal, and contain many expressions derived from earlier writers. In the same journal from which this excerpt is taken, we find a passage describing the sunrise:

> Several days later we went together again to watch the sunrise. It was still dark when we arrived. We could make out nothing even at close quarters, and only heard the roaring of the waves, which was like the sudden breaking of a storm. In a little while, the dawn came. And the sun rose. But it did not rise at once. First a thin thread of light was seen, and the sun loomed behind it, sometimes higher, sometimes lower. It struggled like this for quite a moment, and then rose.

By writing of the sunrise in such a dull and indifferent manner, without animation, totally devoid of artistry, Guan proves himself inferior to his master whose description of the sunrise on Mount Tai we have reproduced above. Therefore, we can see that in the entire literature of both the Ming and Qing dynasties there was no one to equal Wang Siren's masterly and uninhibitedly sensuous description of the glorious afterglow. To rival such dazzling light and brilliant colour, we would have to go to the paintings of the French Impressionists. And for the depiction of colour in words, we can perhaps only find another example of similar brilliance in John Ruskin's famous description of J. M. W. Turner's painting "The Slave Ship".[4]

HUANGSHAN, 1982, by Liu Haisu 劉海粟 (born 1896)

[4] See *Modern Painters*, Vol. I, Part II, Section V, Chapter 3. I am of the opinion that Wang Siren's description is even more commendable, for he had to describe Nature directly, while Ruskin had the painting of the same title to use as the basis of his description.

Modernism and Tradition:
A Symposium

Editors' Note

During the past seven or eight years, Western modernist literature in translation has once again become available to Chinese readers, and has provided the material for a prolonged debate, the pros and cons of which fluctuate according to the prevailing political wind. Yuan Kejia's *Selected Works of Foreign Modernism* began to appear in 1981, and is an ambitious project, as can be seen from a glance at the table of contents of the first two volumes, reprinted overleaf. Apart from this valuable compendium, countless journals publish foreign literature in translation, together with critical essays and 'potted introductions'.

Yuan, who is the senior scholar of contemporary foreign literature at the Academy of Social Sciences in Peking, suggested to the editors of *Renditions* that the most suitable introduction to the complex debate surrounding Modernism would be the lengthy article that appeared in the *People's Daily* on the 13th September 1983. We followed his advice, and invited Geremie Barmé to translate the article and add to it a commentary making the debate a little more intelligible to the uninitiated observer. To this we have appended three prose extracts by young modernist writers in China: the first is taken from Gao Xingjian's short book on contemporary fictional technique; the second is from Xu Jingya's controversial essay on Modernism in Misty Poetry; the third is what might be termed a modernist view of the Chinese tradition by Yang Lian. Gao, Xu and Yang Lian were all attacked during the Spiritual Pollution campaign of late 1983. Xu became one of its chief targets, and the extraordinarily abject self-criticism he was obliged to make (see pp. 65-8) is a reminder that however open China's economic door may be, artists and writers are as vulnerable, as easily humiliated, as expendable as ever. Finally we have translated the full text of a speech delivered by the distinguished poet and critic Yang Mu in Taiwan, which, while removed from the heat of the Mainland debate, deals with essentially the same theme. The search for a mode of expression that is both modern and authentically Chinese concerns every contemporary Chinese artist, and transcends the tendency towards a xenophobic obsession with ethnic and ideological purity ('Will the Stream-of-Consciousness flow into China'—a true title, the implication being that if it does, it may bring with it a tide of filth!).

Selected Works of Foreign Modernism, Vols. I and II (Shanghai, 1981)

Table of Contents

未來主義	**Futurism**		
馬利涅蒂	Marinetti *tr Lü Tongliu*		呂同六譯
阿波里奈	Apollinaire *tr Wen Jiasi*		聞家駟譯
馬雅可夫斯基	Mayakovsky *tr Zhai Houlong*		翟厚隆譯

意識流	**Stream of Consciousness**		
普魯斯特	Proust *tr Gui Yufang*		桂裕芳譯
沃爾夫	Woolf *tr Wen Meihui & Gou Xu*	文美惠	郭　旭譯
喬伊斯	Joyce *tr Jin Di*		金　隄譯
福克納	Faulkner *tr Li Wenjun*		李文俊譯
橫光利一	Yokomitsu Riichi *tr Ding Min & Dan Dong*	丁　民	丹　東譯

超現實主義	**Surrealism**		
布勒東	Breton *tr Jin Zhiping & Zhang Guanyao*	金志平	張冠堯譯
艾呂雅	Eluard *tr Luo Dagang & Zhang Guanyao*	羅大岡	張冠堯譯
阿拉貢	Aragon *tr Ye Rulian*		葉汝璉譯
查拉	Tzara *tr Fan Yuanhong*		樊元洪譯
托馬斯	Dylan Thomas *tr Wu Ningkun*		巫寧坤譯
埃利蒂斯	Elytis *tr Li Yeguang & Yuan Kejia*	李野光	袁可嘉譯
安德拉德	Mário de Andrade *tr Zhu Jingdong*		朱景冬譯

存在主義	**Existentialism**		
加繆	Camus *tr Meng An & Zheng Kelu*	孟　安	鄭克魯譯
薩特	Sartre *tr Zheng Kelu & Jin Zhiping*	鄭克魯	金志平譯
椎名麟三	Shiina Rinzō *tr Dan Dong*		丹　東譯
安部公房	Abe Kōbō *tr Sun Lüheng & Sun Changling*	孫履恒譯	孫昌齡校
沃爾馬	Varma *tr Ni Peigeng*		倪培耕譯
拉蓋什	Lakash *tr Ni Peigeng*		倪培耕譯

Modernism and China:
A Summary from the *People's Daily*

By He Li

Translated by Geremie Barmé

TRANSLATOR'S INTRODUCTION
Do You Have to be a Modernist to be Modern?

GAO XINGJIAN has commented that the discussion concerning Modernism is a 'non-debate', such is the ignorance about modern Western literature among both specialists and laymen in China. A legitimate dialogue on Modernism and its relevance to Chinese culture would be a sisyphean undertaking. A survey of the discussion as it has developed in China since 1979 certainly does reveal a woolliness about the history and literature of Western Modernism that is only paralleled by the enthusiasm with which writers and critics alike have joined the fray, disputing issues involving everything from Italian Futurism to the black humour of Kurt Vonnegut and William Burroughs.[1] There is no denying it, the 'cult of the Modern' has taken root in Chinese soil once more, and it is a cult that craves to have a '*modeng*' 摩登

---

[1] Futurism, with its obsession with machinery, has understandably attracted the attention of some Chinese critics. The Italian school of Futurism led by Filippo Marinetti into the welcoming arms of Mussolini is cited as an example of the *avant-garde* doing the goose step, while Russian Futurism is seen as being more progressive in that it was 'absorbed' into Bolshevism after the October Revolution. See "Three Topics in Western Modernist Literature" 西方現代派文學三題, Yuan Kejia 袁可嘉, *Wenyibao*, January 1983. Yuan is one of the most informed writers involved in the debate, though he falls down in his analysis of class struggle and Modernism. Vonnegut has fared surprisingly well in China, and is widely translated. Even the voluble Zhang Jie 張潔 has nothing but praise for his eccentric behaviour, professing herself to be his Chinese 'soul mate' in an article in which she also roundly condemns American culture as bankrupt and wizened (see *Dushu* 讀書, 1983.5; "Kurt Vonnegut Says: No!"). Joseph Heller of *Catch-22* fame is lauded as the 'creator of black humour', and his novel is available in Chinese; while his long-deceased British cousin in the grotesque, Saki (H.H. Munro) is only known to students of English. Burroughs, the contemporary master of literary cut-up technique, has been mentioned in passing in a number of articles on black humour, but one can hardly imagine his works will ever appear in Chinese. Yet, for all the material now available in Chinese on Modernism, Yuan Kejia's lengthy introduction to the massive compendium of *Selected Works of Foreign Modernism* (*Waiguo xiandaipai zuopinxuan* 外國現代派作品選), Shanghai 1981, Volume I, is one of the only well-researched studies on the subject.

culture all of its own.[2]

In many ways the situation in post-Cultural Revolution China mirrors Europe after World War I. A sense of spiritual dissolution and crisis has become a salient element of the society, while the decay of political orthodoxy and the increased pressure to industrialize and make projections about the future have caught millions of Chinese, especially the so-called 'lost generation', in a dilemma between Self and Society. The attraction certain 'classics' of Modernism hold for such people — Kafka's *The Metamorphosis* and *The Trial* being among the most popular[3] — is hardly surprising. Yet among the *sino-cénacles* of the new literature there are many trendy supporters of the faith who are willing to apply modernist literary devices to the tenets of socialism, and are basically more in sympathy with the positivistic views of Germany's late-nineteenth century *avant-garde*.[4]

In considering the complex, confused and at times simply muddle-headed arguments surrounding Modernism in China today the Western observer may well feel a sense of *déjà vu*. Living in a world based on economic prosperity and avaricious consumerism, in a contemporary culture that is fragmented and elitist, it seems to the onlooker that Modernism is hardly something that can easily be limited to a specialist debate on historical detail or literary techniques. In fact, the discussion concerning Modernism and China has broken free from such academic confines to become a crucial issue in the cultural and political arena.

[2] In recent months the veteran writers Ba Jin and Xia Yan have both commented on the positive influence of Western literature in China up to 1949, and much 'foreign-inspired' literature of the 20s and 30s has been reprinted. Some of the more thoughtful proponents of an absolutely contemporary literature along the lines of one or another Westernism are coming to the belated realization that what appears to them to be so new, is in actual fact a continuation of a major trend in post-May 4th literature. In this context, mention should be made of Leo Lee's 李歐梵 fascinating article "Modernism and Modern Chinese Literature: Studies and Comparisons in Literary History" (in Chinese, printed in a collection of essays entitled *Langman zhi yu* 浪漫之餘, Taipei, 1981). Although basically a study of the continuation of the modernist tradition of 30s Chinese literature by Taiwanese writers in the 60s, many of the points that Lee makes, especially those concerning Taiwanese modernists' excessive concern with technique even to the extent of excluding humanity (here he quotes Chen Yingzhen), are of relevance to the study of modernist writers in the mainland.

[3] 'Kafkaesquerie' (to indulge in a neologism) in China promises to be an intriguing field for research. Even Gao Xingjian has managed to read a tale of proletarian woe into *The Metamorphosis* (see his *Techniques* page 38, and Zi Wei's *A Portentous Parable Concealed in Absurdity*, in *Waiguo wenxue yanjiu* 1980.1 — an interesting cross-cultural and political

comparison can be made between Zi Wei's rather holier-than-thou comments on this story and Vladimir Nabokov's analysis of it in his *Lectures on Literature*, Picador, 1983). Kafka, along with Camus, is one of the most widely read 'modernist' writers in China. The attraction of his scarifying records of desperate isolation and mordant gloom perhaps hold a special fascination for many Chinese. Not all readers are similarly impressed, however; and one critic declares that "for a mentally healthy person to read him . . . requires a great effort of will so as to overcome one's psychological and even physical revulsion . . . (his) world is too distant from our own." ("An Unfamiliar and Confused World", a review of *Selected Works of Foreign Modernism*, by Mu Mu, *Waiguo wenxue yanjiu*, 1983.1).

[4] Their approach may best be summed up in the following quotation: "Suffusing the entire 1880s' sense of the modern was a confident faith in social advance, a readiness to believe that to expose abuses was to invite their annihilation, that to repudiate the conventional past was to clear the way for a healthy moral growth, for welcome ideals. Hard work, clear vision, courage, purposefulness — these were the keys to the future, to the evolution of new types of men, of society, of art" (*Modernism 1890-1930*, edited by Malcolm Bradbury and James McFarlane, Penguin Books 1976, p. 41). All you have to do is change '1880s' to '1980s'!

'Que sommes nous, d'où venons nous, où allons nous?'
'What are we, where do we come from, where are we going?'

—*Paul Gauguin*

WOODCUT by the English artist Leon Underwood for *The Dragon Beards versus The Blueprints* by Hsiao Ch'ien (Xiao Qian 蕭乾), London, The Pilot Press, 1944.

The following article appeared in China's leading daily newspaper, the *People's Daily*, on the 13 September, 1983. He Li, the author of this resumé (in all probability a pen-name, as it just happens to be a homophone of the word 'reasonable'), takes the articles that have appeared on Modernism in the Writer's Association *Literary Gazette (Wenyibao)* as his major frame of reference and covers the debate by summarizing a few key articles which have expressed conflicting views on the analysis of Modernism, its place in China, and Modernist writing techniques. The format used in the article is typical of other 'hundred flowers' debates that have been so obligingly summarized for the average reader in the pages of the *People's Daily*. The present digestible compendium of abstracts makes a pretence of objectivity (a striking departure from traditional Chinese mud-slinging journalese), outlining the controversy and the conflicting opinions with seeming impartiality. Upon slightly closer scrutiny, however, the bias of the *People's Daily* reveals itself. Even the writer's introductory remarks betray his heart-felt concern that "certain disturbing tendencies have become evident" in the discussion, and indicate that he is anxious to counteract the influence of writers who have "expressed an unprincipled and open admiration for" Modernism. He Li is perturbed by "the clamour for a 'Chinese literature of Modernism'", and unabashedly regrets that the majority of the hundreds of articles on Modernism are in favour of it. Perhaps then it is in a spirit of fair-play that he attempts to redress this overwhelming one-sidedness by using this article as a forum in favour of the critics of Modernism. The casual reader may verify this statement by measuring the amount of type-space given to either side; I think you will find that the 'majority opinion' in favour of Modernism gets not quite half the space of their right-thinking opponents. Yet we should console ourselves with the knowledge that although the dice are loaded, it is pretty grand of the *People's Daily* to let the other side play at all.

The first protracted debate on Modernism in China was carried in the pages of *Researches in Foreign Literature* (*Waiguo wenxue yanjiu* 外國文學研究) from December, 1980 up to March, 1982 when Xu Chi 徐遲, who apart from being the originator of a bizarre form of prose he calls 'scientific reportage' is also the Editor-in-Chief of this journal, concluded the discussion with his article "Modernization and Modernism" 現代化與現代派. This is without doubt one of the most amazing and confounding arguments in favour of Chinese Modernism that has appeared to date, and it is little wonder that *Wenyibao* chose it as a fulcrum in its own discussion of the topic. Xu states that he was reluctant to write anything on the subject, but distressed that most critiques of Modernism had failed to note the primacy of economics in the evolution of 20th-century Western literature, he felt obliged to make a few comments. He makes the interesting point that at the moment when China took its first decisive steps in the direction of modernization, abstract paintings, vague (or misty, *menglong* 朦朧) poetry and stream-of-consciousness novels made a fleeting appearance. He regrets that the sprouts of a Chinese Modernism were trammelled by adverse criticism and a change in economic policies, yet although Chinese culture is now based on revolutionary realism once more, he is convinced that in the not too distant future, when a modernized socialist China begins to take shape, "we will finally produce *a modernist culture based on a combination of revolutionary realism and revolutionary romanticism*".[5] (My italics.) Xu sees such a 'neo-modernism' as a natural by-product of government economic policy. And until the day when it is possible he enjoins everyone to use Marxism to study Modernism, concluding his article with quotes from *Das Kapital* to demonstrate that Karl Marx had actually foreseen the development of Marxist Modernism![6]

It is only by reading articles such as the above or even the opposing opinions of writers such as Li Zhun 李准 in "Is there necessarily a link between Modernization and Modernism?" 現代化與現代派有着必然聯繫嗎?[7] that one realizes that the whole question of Modernism is even more confused and confusing in China than it is in the West (impossible though that may seem). Therefore, I caution the reader not to expect too much from Chinese theoretical discussions of Western Modernism, for the burden of literary orthodoxy and intellectual isolation still weighs heavily on even the most well-informed Chinese critics and writers. Works by Kafka and Pinter,

[5]This topsy-turvy piece of reasoning was first printed in *Waiguo wenxue yanjiu*, 1982.1 (see page 116 of that issue for this quotation), and later reprinted in *Wenyibao*, 1982.11.

[6]*Op. cit.*, p. 117.

[7]See *Wenyibao*, 1983.2.

after all, were only tentatively introduced to Chinese readers in 1979, and it was not until 1981 that the first selection of modernist literature became available in translation.[8] The important thing in all of this is that the Pandora's Box of twentieth century 'isms' (including many that are already 'wasms') has been opened in China, giving all who wish it the knowledge that socialist realism and a fickle Party line are not the be-all and end-all of literary and artistic creation. Some writers, like the dexterous Wang Meng 王蒙, have already managed to find a common ground between a dogged faith in Party politics and technical innovation; others like Dai Houying 戴厚英 and more recently Liu Xinwu 劉心武 prefer to use their new skills to build a bridge to their own humanity.[9] If the debate about Modernism can validate and encourage individual diversity and a touch more creative license, then the conflicting and ill-argued opinions summarized in the following pages will not have been in vain.

WE ARE fortunate indeed to be able to avail ourselves of a concise survey of the debate on Modernism, and thus avoid the arduous and unrewarding task of sifting through those four hundred-odd articles on the subject ourselves, searching for the essential elements of disagreement in a skein of contention. The polemical style of this type of writing retains none of the terse cut-and-thrust of argument characteristic of the classical language; while the rhetorical devices and obfuscation of the most unlettered style of Chinese prose have found a haven here. In translating this article I have taken some time to read a number of the original works quoted herein. The majority of them are, to take a line from Clive James, of such length and tediousness that the mere reading aloud of them would put a whirling dervish to sleep in midspin. Unfortunately, even in this summary we are not spared all of the turgid turns of phrase and overstated platitudes of the originals. Not of a mind to make Chinese jargon more acceptable to an English-reading audience through translation than it is to Chinese readers, I have been at pains to keep as close to both the letter and the spirit of the original as possible. After all, this is the record of a complex politico-literary debate, not a tea-party.

---

[8]See Note 1.

[9]For further comments on Dai Houying, see Note 12. Liu Xinwu's literary pedagogy tended to alienate many of his readers, but with the publication of his novella *As You Wish* (*Ruyi* 如意) a few years ago, his writing has taken a new, more independent direction. His recent short story "The Black Wall" ("Heiqiang" 黑墙, *Beijing wenxue*, 1982.10) is a quantum leap towards an honest and individual style. *Wenyibao*, again in the role of judge and jury, printed a scathing criticism of this story (see "Green Leaves — Black Wall — Gold", by Li Bingyin, *Wenyibao*, 1983.4) in which Liu's present writing is described as being "self-indulgent" and "twisted". Liu, with characteristic humour, has commented that he feels honoured that this criticism is actually longer than his original story.

何理：＂文藝報＂等報刊關於西方現代派文學與我國文學發展方向問題的討論
He Li: The Discussion Concerning the Question of Western Modernism and
the Direction of the Development of Chinese Literature, Being Held in
Literary Gazette (Wenyibao) and Other Journals and Papers

OVER THE LAST few years, newspapers and periodicals throughout the country have acted as a forum for a discussion concerning Western Modernism and the future of Chinese literature. In the twelve months since *Wenyibao* reprinted Xu Chi's essay "Modernization and Modernism", along with a rejoinder by Li Di 理迪,[10] that magazine has published over twenty articles on the question of Modernism, while other journals and newspapers have printed numerous studies and introductory articles on the subject. From its very inception, this discussion has revealed clear-cut differences of opinion among writers and literary critics.

Many comrades have pointed out in their articles that in developing our own socialist literature in the past, we learned from and assimilated all of the outstanding elements of foreign writing, and that to do so has been both correct and necessary. With literature coming to reflect modern life with greater force and depth in recent years, some writers have begun to experiment with the use of certain artistic techniques that originated with Western Modernism, thereby hoping to enrich the means of artistic expression at their disposal. An exploratory use of such artistic forms and techniques should be encouraged as long as it roots itself firmly in our own national life, and does not lose sight of our aim to develop a socialist literature with a Chinese na-

tional character. It must be noted, however, that in the discussion concerning such experimentation and the evaluations of Modernism, certain disturbing tendencies have become evident, such as:

1. Despite the fact that a few of the numerous articles and books—over 400 articles and more than ten books—that have appeared give an appropriate evaluation of Western modernist literature, the majority have expressed an unprincipled and open admiration for it; and,

2. Some of the literature produced recently, in both describing and commenting on Chinese society, reflects a social outlook and philosophical approach typical of Western Modernism.

Of even greater concern than the above is the fact that a number of highly questionable proposals concerning the future direction of Chinese literature and the evaluation we should make of Modernism have come to the surface. Some comrades have even declared that Chinese literature should aim at developing along the lines of Western Modernism. According to this view our revolutionary socialist literature is "the product of the steam age", and as such is now hopelessly antiquated; while Western modernist literature is the creation of "the electronic and atomic age", and "represents a definite advance in human thought". They even go so far as to clamour for a "Chinese literature of Modernism", and claim that "Marxism needs Modernism".[11]

Below follows a summary of the three major points of controversy that have emerged from this discussion as it has developed in *Wenyibao* and the press.

1) Are we going to make a critical evaluation of Western Modernism and take from it what we need, or are we to accept it as the future direction of Chinese literature?

---

[10]These articles were printed in the November issue of *Wenyibao*. Li Di, who is most probably a staff writer for the magazine, does little more in his reply "Questioning 'Modernization and Modernism' " than list his queries. It is reasonable to assume that while Li Di's article is not aimed at orchestrating the discussion, it definitely did try to set the tone for the controversy as presented by *Wenyibao*. For a reply to Li Di, see Jie Fei and Mei Ni's "Some Questions for the 'Inquisitor' " (*Waiguo wenxue*, 1983.2).

[11]These last two quotations are from Xu Chi's article.

Those comrades who are enamoured of Western modernist literature are of the opinion that Chinese Modernism is a necessary corollary to modernization. To them, the advent of modernist art is "an inevitability which is both a negation of realism by modernist writers and a negation of realism by itself".[12] Some comrades have said that "the present reform is in effect a revolution in literature", and that "it is an 'historical necessity'". "If the society is to modernize, why shouldn't we have 'Modernism' in literature?" In his article "Modernization and Modernism", Xu Chi writes, "With the realization of the Four Modernizations of socialism, a 'culture corresponding to modern thought and feeling' will appear", which will "mean Modernism in art and literature", and thus he concludes that "there should be a Marxist Modernism". Other comrades have stated that "the appearance of a modern Chinese poetry has undermined the principle of realism in poetic creation" and that, "in the final analysis, Modernism will become the mainstream of Chinese poetry".

In pointed contradiction to the above opinions, some comrades have stated that the appearance of Modernism is by no means the inevitable result of material development, but rather it is the product of definite historical circumstances peculiar to Western societies this century. The nature of our socialist system is fundamentally different from that of societies under monopoly capitalism, and because of this basic difference we are not influenced by the historical conditions that gave birth to Modernism in the West. The dramatic changes that Chinese society has undergone in recent years have merely highlighted the need for us to develop and enrich the scope of artistic expression available to our socialist literature. To

do so we must make an exhaustive critical appraisal of all artistic forms, including those of Western modernist literature, and assimilate whatever will be useful in the description of the changes occurring in our society, and which will both satisfy the demands of the masses and further the development of our socialist literature.

In an article entitled "Is there necessarily a link between Modernization and Modernism?", Li Zhun states that, "Every literary and artistic genre as well as every intellectual trend has specific social origins, including economic, political and sociological and ideological factors, while the material forces of production can only be said to play an indirect role. Take for example the advent of Romanticism at the beginning of the nineteenth century: it was the direct result of the French Revolution, the climax of the movement for democracy and the struggle for national independence at that time. Critical Realism which made spectacular developments in the mid- and late-nineteenth century, had its origins in the continued dissolution of the feudal social structure and the increased manifestation of the inherent contradictions within capitalism ... yet it is extremely difficult to pinpoint the exact origins of either of these developments in the changes taking place within the material means of production at the time."

In "Three Topics in Western Modernist Literature", Yuan Kejia states that the origins of Western modernist literature are complex, yet can be seen as the reaction of bourgeois and petit-bourgeois Western intellectuals to the changes and pressures that had developed within the material and spiritual civilization of the West since the advent of monopoly capitalism. The objective causes of Modernism may be considered to be the concrete historical and social changes in the period of monopoly capitalism, including changes in the relations of production, social relations, the standard of living, science and culture, and so on. On the subjective side there are changes in the class status of modernist writers, their world view and artistic perception. The clash of these various subjective and objective elements has resulted in the bizarre and seductive phenomenon known as modernist literature. Thus, although these conditions resulted in Modernism, they do not equal modernization.

[12] See the Postscript of Dai Houying's novel *Oh, Humanity!* (*Ren a, ren!* 人啊！人 Guangzhou, 1981). Dai was the first writer not only to attempt to use a dramatic new technique of narration in a novel-length work of fiction, but also to deal with the dangerous theme of the humanity of man. Her Postscript contains an illuminating autobiographical sketch along with an argument in favour of 'literary renewal'. Dai's more recently published works, a novel called *Death of a Poet* (*Shiren zhi si* 詩人之死, Fuzhou, 1982) and *The Chains Are Soft* (*Suolian, shi rouruande* 鎖鏈，是柔軟的, Guangzhou, 1982), do little to fulfil the promise shown in her first book.

Li Di says, "Modernist art and literature, or simply Modernism, is a concept with a definite historical connotation covering the various 'isms' of Western bourgeois art and literature in the 20th century. The content and nature of Modernism is quite clear, and it constitutes an ideological system and world view which is in direct opposition to Marxism. Just as it is impossible to talk of 'Marxist idealism' or 'Marxist Dadaism', it is equally erroneous to advocate 'Marxist Modernism', and to do so is tantamount to adopting modernist Western art and literature."

2) Are we to carry on and develop the outstanding traditions of progressive and revolutionary literature that date from the May 4 period, or negate and abandon these traditions?

Those comrades who propose to negate and abandon our revolutionary literary tradition are of the opinion that authority and tradition are obstacles to the liberation of thought and the reform of literature. They claim that our literary tradition is the result of past historical conditions, and its conservative and narrow aspects are thrown into relief now that those conditions no longer exist.

Sun Shaozhen 孫紹振 writes that, "All traditions, including artistic ones, have a conservative side, and if artistic reform is to be successful, then we must be extreme when we first challenge those traditions" ("Give artistic reformers an atmosphere of greater freedom" 給藝術的革新者更自由的空氣). While Xie Mian 謝冕 declares that, "Because of the antiquity of the Chinese race and the fullness of our traditions, the burden we bear from the past is heavier than that of other peoples" ("After Losing Equanimity" 失去了平靜以後). Xu Jingya 徐敬亞 in his "Volant Tribe of Bards—a critique of the modernist tendencies of

Chinese poetry"[13] says that one of the objects of "the inevitable literary negation that follows on a [major] social negation" is to condemn "the increasingly narrow path along which Chinese poetry has been moving for the last thirty years. A path that was initially characterized by a basic rehash of the Romanticism of the nineteenth century; then progressing from the joyous pastoral ballads of the 50s and the orgiastic lyricism of [the poetry of] the 60s . . . to the quasi-religious Hosannahs of the ten year Cultural Revolution. . . . [The new poetry moves to negate this trend that] all but submerged Chinese poetry in a vast sea of small production poetasters locked into their formula of 'Classics + folk songs = poetry'." He goes even further to state that the contemporary trend of poetry is "to break free of the traditional realist principles [of writing] and express anti-realism and anti-rationalism . . . so that poetry can finally rid itself of the shackles of millenia of tradition and work in favour of expressing the 'feeling of the here and now' of a modern society."[14]

The comrades who oppose the above opinions regard culture as an historical accretion and consider that when dealing with the relationship between tradition and the development of culture in a period of transition [such as the present one], it is necessary to make a detailed and historical analysis of the traditions in question and not simply to condemn them out of hand. In "On Reading *A Preliminary Discussion of Contemporary Narrative Techniques*", '現代小説技巧初

---

[13]*Cf.* pp. 59-68 below. See *Contemporary Literary Trends* (*Dangdai wenyi sichao* 當代文藝思潮, Lanzhou, 1983.1) for the full text of this sensational and highly controversial view of Chinese poetry. Xu, a young poet in Jilin, argues convincingly, albeit with uncommon acerbity, in favour of the modernist tradition of post-May 4th literature and the more recent vague (or misty) poetry. See Bonnie McDougall's introduction to her selection of Bei Dao's poetry in *Notes from the City of the Sun* (Cornell, 1983) for an excellent summary of the debate surrounding the new poetry.

[14]Again this is a sentiment that recalls the *Zeitgeist* in Germany at the end of the nineteenth century. A poem by Arno Holz, a leading theorist at the time, insists: 'Modern sei der Poet/modern vom Scheitel bis zur Sohle (Let the poet be modern/Modern from head to toe)' (*Modernism, op. cit.*, p. 38). For the reader whose palate has been jaded by all of this heady fare, I recommend a dose of Tom Wolfe. Wolfe in *The Painted Word* (Bantam Books, 1975) and *From Bauhaus to Our House* (Abacus, 1983) offers a refreshing antidote to the tedious dead-pan of discussions on Modernism and the *avant-garde*, be they from the East or the West. Fewer Chinese writers and critics would view Modernism with such an almost religious sense of awe if they could read what one of the most voluble critics of the modern world has to say on the subject.

探' 讀後,[15] Wang Xianpei 王先霈 states that China has its own solid tradition of fiction writing, and a number of narrative styles beyond those of the 'chapter novel' (*zhanghui xiaoshuo* 章回小說) and the 'sketch novel' (*biji xiaoshuo* 筆記小說). This tradition, he continues, has produced a wealth of outstanding works as well as bequeathing to us a unique national form and artistic technique. There is a great amount of material on narrative technique contained in traditional theoretical works on the novel which reflect the aesthetic concerns of Chinese writers of the past. And Wang points out that it is clear from the developments of recent years that writers have been hindered in realizing their full artistic potential for the very reason that they have failed to make a serious study of our own outstanding national traditions, and have neglected to develop a [contemporary] fiction with definite national characteristics.

Miao Junjie 繆俊傑 in his "Thoughts on the Question of Literary Innovation" 關於文學創新問題的思考 says that Marxism has always put an onus on developing outstanding national cultural traditions and on "indigenization" 民族化 in art and literature. "The question of whether China's socialist art and literature is to 'indigenize' and develop her own national style is not merely a question of literary form, but also of crucial importance if we are to start a new phase in the development of our art and literature, effectively respond to the needs of the masses in this new period and advance along the correct path. It is for this reason that we must lay particular emphasis on the issues of inheriting our national tradition and making 'indigenization' a matter of artistic innovation . . . . The art and literature of every national group has its own unique national character."

In "A Critique of One View of Contemporary Poetry" 評一種現代詩論,[16] Yang Kuanghan 楊匡漢 says, "An artistic tradition is full of vitality, it is like a mighty river, continually surging anew with the confluence of other streams; it should not be, indeed it cannot be, dammed up. [As] Lenin says, we are not trying to create a new proletarian culture from nothing, but rather to build on the excellent models, traditions and achievements of the existing culture in accordance with a Marxist world view, and an attitude based on the realities of life and struggle under the dictatorship of the proletariat. Be that as it may, the author of the tract 'Volant Tribe of Bards' is calling for nothing less than the wholesale rejection of our poetic tradition. He ridicules all classical poetry as an abomination spawned in 'a union of feudal politics and morals with an economic base of small production'; he indiscriminately reviles all folk songs as 'feudal pastoral ditties'; and, furthermore, he regards the new age of poetry that was ushered in by Comrade Mao Zedong's *Talks at the Yenan Forum on Art and Literature* in 1942 as nothing more than a 'vast sea of small production poetasters'. He even goes so far as to declare that the venerable tradition of realism in Chinese poetry is no more than a 'creative label with the adaptability of a chameleon' which he claims should be 'given well-considered rejection'. In the final analysis, however, it is the spiritual doubt evinced by a certain group of people, doubt in the basic need to fight for socialism, that is the root-cause of their deviation from the tenets of socialist literature in their creative work. Thus, it is inevitable that the 'three negations' [social negation, political negation and artistic negation] will cut artists off from the source of their artistic life and end in their abandoning realism and divorcing themselves from the people and the present age."

3) Are we to adhere to and continually pursue the rules that govern art, or are we going to negate them?

Some comrades say that any artistic innovation necessitates a clash with and in some cases the

[15] See *Wenyibao*, 1983.6. Wang's criticisms of Gao Xingjian are not unreasonable. Unlike Gao, he is aware that modernist writing techniques are not universally popular in the West today (France being an exception to a certain extent), and that Gao has been too hasty in attempting a post-mortem on realism, since it is still alive and well in Western literature. Unfortunately, Wang's tenuous claims that "we had it first", citing examples of classical Chinese literature, tend to detract from an otherwise clear-headed argument.

[16] See *Wenyibao*, 1983.3. Clearly affronted by Xu Jingya's extremism, Yang attempts to refute the "biased, confused and incorrect" views expressed in "Volant Tribe of Bards". In fact, he succeeds in being little more than condescending and dogmatic.

destruction of pre-existing aesthetic tastes and artistic habits. They say that traditional and popular artistic tastes are the very object of [the present literary] renovation. Gao Xingjian in his book *A Preliminary Discussion of Contemporary Narrative Techniques* 現代小說技巧初探 claims that the Balzacian novel should be regarded as classical form and that modern writers do not aim at creating individuals, or indeed at depicting an environment as Zola does of Notre Dame. In modern novels, he says, plot has given way to a variety of new structural styles. The examples that Gao gives of traditional methods of writing prose fiction are, the refining of plot, the description of scene, creation of characters, types, . . . etc; while those of modern fiction are the use of stream-of-consciousness, the bizarre and non-logic, artistic abstraction, and so on.

Xu Jingya asks: "Is human art to be forever limited to realism and romanticism? Do we want to, or more importantly, *can* we free ourselves from 'concrete art' and move towards 'abstract art'? . . . The answer to this question will not only determine the way in which we evaluate world art, but is also of pressing relevance to the future of art and literature in China, and to the way in which we approach certain phenomena already evident in some contemporary Chinese works."

Sun Shaozhen declares that "the present clash with artistic traditions is in reality a clash of artistic habits", and, "for artistic innovation to be made possible, we must first carry out a struggle against traditional artistic habits."

Other critics are of the opinion that Western modernist literature has only been concerned with "imagism and poetic techniques", and lacks substance, as a result of which characters in modernist works are quite colourless; while even if a certain personality is created, it is inevitably abstracted to become a universal character type. A lack of characterization, especially the lack of character-types with a high degree of individuality and generality, is a major indisputable failing in modernist literature. Not to see this defect for what it is—an example of failure—but rather to advocate it as a success is, to say the least, quite inappropriate.[17] The creation of artistic types is a universal rule in the arts, and at the core of this rule is the need to create definite character types. This is so because literature is the reflection of the true nature of life. To exhort writers to describe psychological states, feelings, ideas, thoughts and settings, and not to aim at typicalization—to emphasize the description of feelings, psychological states, fantasies and the expression of the individual in opposition to the need for the creation of artistic types, thereby negating the basic rules of art—can only be of the greatest detriment to our literature.

In "The Upgrading of Literature and the Clamour for Modernism" 文學的提高和現代主義的呼聲, Guan Lin 關林 declares that the anti-traditionalism professed by the modernists is not only a denial of traditional literary views but also of traditional philosophical views. Ideologically, modernist arts and modernist philosophy are inseparable. They have both abandoned the Rationalism that has come into being since the Age of Enlightenment, and lean heavily in the direction of anti-rationalism and irrationalism, emphasizing intuition and the role of the subconscious to the exclusion of all else. Artistically, the basic premise of Modernism is the negation of realism. It opposes writers dealing with objective existence and encourages them rather to concentrate on the Self and the internal world of the individual. Certainly, it cannot be denied that Modernism has given rise to a number of unique artistic techniques; nevertheless, its deep-rooted anti-traditionalism inevitably leads to a wide-sweeping rejection of accepted artistic maxims. For

[17]This is a very valid point, and one that Chinese modernist enthusiasts would be wise to take heed of. In praising the use of interior-monologue (or stream of consciousness), Chinese writers have been known to quote Virginia Woolf's famous dictum that the task of the novelist was to record life itself—"not as a series of gig lamps, symmetrically arranged; but a luminous halo, a semi-transparent envelope surrounding us from the beginning of consciousness to the end . . . ." As J.B. Priestley in *Literature and Western Man* so wisely remarks, "If his [the novelist's] fiction is concerned with men in a particular society, and with the character of that society, then this highly subjective, interior-monologue, halo-and-envelope method will not serve his purpose . . . . It is one thing to feel free of that series of gig lamps; it is quite another thing to atomize narrative, construction, scene, character, so that nine-tenths of what is valuable in fiction vanishes . . . . " (p. 435). Chinese writers such as Zong Pu 宗璞 and Wang Meng have made attempts to construct a "luminous halo" around that very "series of gig lamps" with some interesting results.

SKETCH OF THE FIRST ANNUAL CONVENTION of the Chinese Society for
Foreign Literature, held in Chengdu, November/December 1980 (from *Foreign
Literature Studies*, 1981.1).

example, it denies the importance of plot, characters and scene-setting—all crucial elements of
narrative art. Its further rejection of typical types
leaves the reader with nothing more than an 'anti-
novel'. It is clear that the Modernist world view
is one that is diametrically opposed to that of
Marxism.

In "The Road of Life and the Road of Realism" 生活之路和現實主義之路, Wu Yuanmai
吳元邁 states that following the raising of the
standard of living individuals are finding increased
opportunities for self-fulfilment, and the descriptions of characters in realist literature should
reflect these changes as a matter of course. Styles,
forms and techniques can ossify and need to be
supplemented or even replaced by new ones. This
on-going dialectical process in realist literature in
which the new replaces the old will continue as
long as life does itself. For this reason, realism
remains eternally young and will never be super-
seded. Yet it is crucial that we do not rest in our
efforts to explore and innovate in literature along
the guide-lines indicated by life itself. We must,
above all, avoid stagnation. Realism rejects none
of the things of value and meaning in the progressive art of the past or the present, nor does

it reject those things of value and meaning in
Modernism. However, the elements of Modernism
that disrupt and confound the rules of art cannot
be assimilated into realism.

Wang Xianpei says that for the short story/
novel to flourish and develop it is essential that it
retains the unique elements that go to make it up;
it must continue and develop the artistic tradition
that has accrued over its long history, and it will
be disastrous if this is abandoned. To disperse with
artistic rules, and replace an artistic style and a
form of literature that has its own special techniques with some pie-in-the-sky "modern techniques", far from being the "salvation" of the
novel, will only result in disaffecting large seg-
ments of the reading public.

The discussion outlined above continues un-
abated in the pages of *Wenyibao*, and other
journals and newspapers throughout the country.
No doubt our literature will be able to make large
strides along the road of socialism if we cling fast
to the principle of "letting one hundred schools of
thought contend and one hundred flowers
blossom" and continue the present discussion in
an energetic, thorough and healthy way.

高行健：現代技巧與民族精神

Contemporary Technique and National Character in Fiction

By Gao Xingjian

Translated by Ng Mau-sang

I

WHAT IS usually meant by national form in Chinese literature? As far as poetry is concerned, it is more or less clear: it means primarily the tonal patterns and rhyme schemes of classical poetry, and the form of the folk ballad. National form in poetry refers to these two different poetic traditions. In Chinese fiction, we have, strictly speaking, only the traditional "linked-chapter" (*zhanghui* 章回) style, which very few novelists of today still employ. The fictional form which most Chinese writers have used since the May Fourth (1919) Movement is largely derived from the Western fictional tradition of the 18th and 19th centuries.

What traditional Chinese techniques has modern Chinese fiction continued to use after it relinquished its traditional "linked-chapter" style? The most talked about technique in classical Chinese fiction is the method of "direct-portrayal" (*baimiao* 白描)—a term borrowed from painting: sketching the outline with clearcut and simple strokes, and then adding the finishing touches to bring the work to life. As a way of writing fiction, this method is certainly unique. The writer interrupts his narration at a high point, having aroused the interest of the reader, who then has to wait for the outcome of the action in the next chapter.

Some novelists successfully employ this traditional fictional technique. Some use it, but simultaneously adopt other techniques learnt from the Western realistic tradition. The adoption of Western technique does not necessarily deprive a work of national character. The question is this: have those writers since the May Fourth Movement who have *not* used the traditional direct-portrayal method as their chief means of expression (and they are by no means a minority), by abandoning tradition in this way, thereby lessened or even obliterated the national character of their work? The answer is clearly "no".

This extract is taken from Gao's book A Preliminary Discussion of Contemporary Narrative Techniques 現代小説技巧初探, *Huacheng Press, Guangzhou, 1981,* pp. 111-17. For more on Gao, see Geremie Barmé's *introduction to the play* The Bus-stop.

II

WHAT THEN is national character in literature? Turgenev spoke well when he said that his "nation" was the Russian language. A writer creates through language; the national character of his work derives first and foremost from his ability to exploit the artistic potential of that language.

China is a country of many nationalities, where *Hanyu* (the language of the Han people) is most commonly used. We may say that any literary work written in *Hanyu*, or in the languages of the other ethnic groups, reflects in varying degrees the character of the nation.

Language is a medium through which we think and convey our thoughts. A piece of work written in the native language of a nation will naturally reflect that nation's cultural tradition, way of life and mode of thought. Irrespective of how a Chinese writer may borrow from foreign techniques, inasmuch as he writes in good, typical Chinese, his work will definitely have a national flavour. The more he grasps the essence of his national culture, the more distinctive will be the national character of his work. The Italy depicted by Gorky will remain Italy-in-Russian-literature. The same is true of the United States as seen by *émigré* Chinese writers. Their delineation differs fundamentally from that of their American counterparts.

III

AS LONG AS a writer depicts national life in his native language, the more vivid his portrayal, the richer the national character of his work. The kind of technique employed is beside the point.

The Goddess, an anthology of Guo Moruo's early poems, was obviously composed under the inspiration of Walt Whitman. Nobody however thinks these are foreign poems. The simple, free verse style of Ai Qing has not only taken nourishment from the impressionist and symbolist school, it also reflects the poet's conscious effort to break away from the Chinese poetic and folk ballad form. Lu Xun was even more extreme in advocating the "principle of taking whatever is useful" (*nalai zhuyi* 拿來主義). In his fictional and poetical writings are blended the techniques of western critical realism, romanticism, impressionism, symbolism and even surrealism.

In his "Kuangren riji" (The diary of a madman), Lu Xun anticipated Kafka; he borrowed from Gogol the technique of the grotesque. His prose-poem "The Passer-By" differs little in form from the plays of Pirandello, and was written several years before the plays of Ionesco and Beckett. He used the technique of symbolism in his "Medicine" and "Revenge"; of impressionism in his "The story of the good", "Snow", "The beggar" and "Autumn night"; and of surrealism (which had only then begun to emerge in the West) in "Dead fire", "The epitaph" and "Vibration". Even the way in which "The true story of Ah Q" was written has no precedent in classical Chinese fiction. Because Lu Xun focussed on the suffering and spirit of resistance of the Chinese people, their vacillation and cries of woe, and because of his superb mastery of the language, his work radiates a modern spirit—the revolutionary spirit of a people awakened from sleep, intent on liberating itself from the fetters of imperialism and feudalism.

IV

THE MOST distinguished modern Chinese novelists, Mao Dun, Ba Jin, Lao She and Ding Ling, have all blended western fictional techniques to form their own individual styles. The depth and breadth of reality reflected in their work, and the vivid depiction of characters from different strata of society far surpassed the achievement of those writers who closely adhered to the traditional way of writing. In the process of artistic creation, as long as the writer depicts social reality and characters vividly and realistically, he will automatically represent the social customs, the spiritual world and mode of thought of his nation. His work will have a distinctive national, or indigenous, character. The kind of technique used is beside the point.

Indigenization should not merely follow one singular pattern, just as a national language is not confined to a single style. National language is derived from the literary language of writers with the most character and stature. Once a writer has formed a style of his own, he will contribute to the national literature.

V

WHEN LU XUN wrote his "The story of Ah Q", he might not have been consciously seeking a national fictional form. However, his uniquely sober tone, which blended sympathy with satire, enabled him not only to recount the life and soul of a destitute peasant, but also to reflect the life and spirit which pervaded the semi-feudalist and semi-colonial society of the time. When Romain Rolland, steeped in Latin culture and brought up in an entirely different society from that of Lu Xun, read this story, he was moved to tears. Ba Jin's *Family*, which dwells on the destiny and aspirations of Chinese youth before and after the May Fourth Movement, also aroused the sensibility of many Western readers. This shows that if a writer succeeds in truthfully describing the life of the people, readers from other nations can equally be affected, can equally comprehend.

The appeal of a national literature lies in its ability to depict the life of the people as it truly is. Let us hope that the quest for a national form will not surplant this quest for truth.

(Sections VI, VII and the first paragraph of section VIII have been left out in this translation.)

VIII

ARTISTIC TECHNIQUE transcends national frontiers. It is not the monopoly of one particular nation. The spirit of a nation has its own long and distinctive history, much stronger and more lasting than the relatively short lifespan of a technique. It is the sum total of the nation's cultural tradition, social customs, psychological modes, aesthetic tastes and ways of thinking (as formed by the national language). The pursuit and absorption of new techniques is never an obstacle to the healthy development of a nation's literature.

The search for artistic devices and methods does not always bear fruit. If we are thwarted in our search, let us admit our failure. Almost all great artists and writers have experienced the bitterness of defeat. They do not consider that all their works will become classics and be handed down to posterity. There are indeed great works which, when first published, were not given recognition by society. History however holds the balance. Even if a work becomes a classic, it will be better if it serves as a stepping-stone for posterity, rather than a weight on their shoulders. This is the attitude one ought to take on the matter of tradition and innovation.

THE GREAT WALL,
by Yin Guangzhong 尹光中.

徐敬亞：崛起的詩羣──評中國新詩的現代傾向

A Volant Tribe of Bards
— A Critique of the Modernist Tendencies of Chinese Poetry

By Xu Jingya

Translated and adapted by Ng Mau-sang

I SOLEMNLY BESEECH poets and critics to remember the year 1980 in the same way that sociologists remember the ideological thaw of 1979. 1980 was a time of important innovation for our New Poetry, an artistic watershed. It witnessed the disintegration of the old monolithic and monotonous way of writing poetry, a way that had prevailed since 1949, and saw the emergence of a new richness and variety, of a poetry with strong modernist overtones.

The first officially published poem to proclaim the new movement was Bei Dao's 'The Answer', printed in *Poetry* (Shikan), March 1979, at a time when the praises of the heroes of the April 5 Incident of 1976 were still ringing in the air:

The Answer	回答
Baseness is the password of the base,	卑鄙是卑鄙者的通行證，
Honour is the epitaph of the honourable.	高尚是高尚者的墓誌銘。
Look how the gilded sky is covered	看吧，在鍍金的天空中，
With the drifting, crooked shadows of the dead.	飄滿了死者彎曲的倒影。

Xu Jingya is a young poet and critic who was born in 1951 and graduated in 1982 from the Chinese Department of Jilin University in N.E. China. In 1979 he became a member of the Jilin branch of the Writers' Association. After graduation he was assigned to the editorial staff of Shenhua 參花, *a magazine devoted to popular or folk performing literature. He is married to the poet Wang Xiaoni, and they have a young daughter.*

His controversial essay 'A Volant Tribe of Bards' was first published in Xinye 新葉, *a Liaoning student magazine, early in 1982, and was reprinted in* Dangdai wenyi sichao *(Contemporary Literary Trends)* 當代文藝思潮, *1983:1. This translation represents only a fraction (approximately one tenth) of the lengthy original. Nearly all of the detailed discussion of individual poems and of poetic technique has been omitted. Some twenty extracts are here linked together, to give the reader a general idea of Xu's argument.*

The English title is taken from one of Wordsworth's sonnets:

A Volant Tribe of Bards on earth are found . . .

A more literal translation—'A body of emergent poetry'—is given by Bonnie McDougall in the introduction to Notes from the City of the Sun.

For an anthology of Misty poetry, see below, pp. 181-270.

The Ice Age is over now,	冰川紀已過去了，
Why is there still ice everywhere?	爲什麼到處都是冰凌？
The Cape of Good Hope has been discovered,	好望角發現了，
Why do a thousand sails contest the Dead Sea?	爲什麼死海裏千帆相競？
I come into this world	我來到這個世界上，
Bringing only paper, rope, a shadow,	祇帶着紙、繩索和身影。
To proclaim before the judgement	爲了在宣判之前，
The voices of the judged:	宣讀那些被判決的聲音：
Let me tell you, world,	告訴你吧，世界，
I—do—not—believe!	我——不——相信！
If a thousand challengers lie beneath your feet,	如果你腳下有一千名挑戰者，
Count me as number one thousand and one.	那就把我算作第一千零一名。
I don't believe the sky is blue;	我不相信天是藍的；
I don't believe in the sound of thunder;	我不相信雷的回聲；
I don't believe that dreams are false;	我不相信夢是假的；
I don't believe that death has no revenge.	我不相信死無報應。
If the sea is destined to breach the dikes,	如果海洋註定要決堤，
Let the brackish water pour into my heart;	就讓所有苦水都注入我心中；
If the land is destined to rise,	如果陸地註定要上昇，
Let humanity choose anew a peak for our existence.	就讓人類重新選擇生存的峯頂。
A new juncture and glimmering stars,	新的轉機和閃閃的星斗，
Adorn the unobstructed sky.	正在綴滿沒有遮攔的天空。
They are five thousand year old pictographs	那是五千年的象形文字，
The staring eyes of future generations. [1]	那是未來人們凝神的眼睛。

By 1980, this kind of modernist poetry was being widely published and attracting a lot of attention both among poets and with the public at large. It already had a strong following among the young in China.

What was the nature of the impact which these poems had?

Feeling is the soul of poetry. The single most important characteristic of these poems is that they vibrate with the spirit of their times. Stoical calm in the midst of intense suffering, equanimity in the face of cold hostility, the tragedies and joys of an epoch are here transformed into a threnody, a lament in monologue form. Here are ordinary members of modern Chinese society, feeling and experiencing life from a perspective that differs utterly from that of their predecessors.

Since 1949, Chinese poets have adhered to the principle of realism, of 'art as representation of life'; their dogmatism has turned their poetry into mere description. The new poets stress the subjectivity and individuality of poetry, they stress the dynamic role of the aesthetic subject, they call on poetry to witness an experience of the kaleidoscopic emotions of life . . . . [The old poetry was] a mirror held up to the external world. For the young poets of the 80s 'poetry is a mirror

---

[1] Bonnie McDougall's translation, from *Notes from the City of the Sun* (Cornell, 1983), p. 38. Xu himself does not quote the poem, as he would assume that his readers knew it anyway.

with which to see oneself', 'it is the history of the human soul'; 'the poet creates his own world.' This is the new manifesto. 'Poetry is a special means of communication between the human heart and the external world.' Poetry that merely reflects the external world is not art. This conception has distanced the new poets from the simple and mimetic poetic practices of their predecessors . . . .

For example, when a new poet writes of the landscape, he dwells entirely on his own personal feeling. He has immersed himself totally in the scenery he describes. One 'reads' therefore not only rivers and mountains, but also the unsettled emotional world of the poet. Landscape has thus been 'humanized', and 'poetry is a mirror with which to see oneself.' Some of Gu Cheng's poems[2] (many of which focus entirely on the poet's personal feelings) have been labelled 'misty'; this is because of their psychological nature. The majority of Bei Dao's poems use external imagery to symbolize the poet's own psyche, and the images are organized in stark fashion. The poetic 'leaps' of Jiang He and Yang Lian are even more a direct expression of the heart's rhythm . . . . For these young poets poetry is a medium for the unfolding of the soul. They merge the subjective with the objective, and fuse a fresh and vibrant emotion with the world around them. In so doing, they have discovered a poetic perspective quite different from that of their immediate predecessors. By stressing the aesthetic quality of poetry, they have dissociated themselves from the mimetic description of classical poetry, or the intuitive lyricism of romantic poetry. They strive to transcend the confines of realism, and are intent on forming a new entity between the self and the external world. The poet turns from external reality and looks inwards, forming his images in accordance with his own feeling and sensibility. Such are the principles according to which Bei Dao, Shu Ting and Jiang He create their poems . . . . The result is not mere poetic imagining, but the poet's instantaneous response to reality. Once the door of the soul and the door of nature have been opened, the world is no longer monotonous and drab; the richness of the soul imbues it with a renewed splendour. One and the same stream acquires a hundred colours, a hundred different shapes of motion. This departure from the old pictorial aesthetic, this new merging of the temporal and spatial in art, has taken poetry into a new and wider domain, has rekindled the very life of poetry.

Many, finding the broken images, the apparently disjointed structure, and the seemingly end-less ending of these poems unpalatable, have cried 'I can't understand this!' Bereft of those elements they are used to seeing in poetry — a distinct story line, a logical sequence, whole incidents, complete images, the poet exerting himself at the end of the poem to achieve a heightening effect — bereft of all this, the reader is at a loss and cries out in protest, 'This is plain bad!' This demonstrates a divergence in the whole conception of poetry. To the young poets themselves, poetry is a radiation of the life-force, an unbosoming of emotion. The importance of a poem rests not with its plot or its concrete content, but with the poet's feeling. When a poet succeeds in communicating his feeling to the reader, he can be said to have achieved his purpose.

---

[2]For a selection of poems by Bei Dao, Gu Cheng, Jiang He, Shu Ting and Yang Lian, see 'Mists', below pp. 195-248.

Footprints of the Younger Generation

It is precisely because Chinese society has undergone such an extraordinary experience that its poets have produced such 'extraordinary' poems, poems which have transcended the boundaries of our tradition. Looking at their poems, one can see truthfully and distinctly the mental contours of a generation . . . . As Comrade Xie Mian aptly pointed out in his essay 'After Losing Equanimity', the young poets' response to the life they have experienced can be summed up in four words: 'I do not believe.' Their attitude towards the future is one of yearning and aspiration, the keynote of their poetry is one of hope and determination. What I want to say here is that these poems are the footprints of a whole generation of young people, of a decade, footprints of restless wandering, of depression, of defiance and passionate indignation, of contemplation and aspiration . . . . In these poems we see the image of youth that has been injured and insulted, but that no amount of oppression can crush or deceive.

Bei Dao: All

All is fate
All is cloud
All is a beginning without an end
All is a search that dies at birth
All joy lacks smiles
All sorrow lacks tears
All language is repetition
All contact a first encounter
All love is in the heart
All past is in a dream
All hope carries annotations
All faith carries groans
All explosions have a moment of quiet
All deaths have a lingering echo

一切

一切都是命運
一切都是煙雲
一切都是沒有結局的開始
一切都是稍縱即逝的追尋
一切歡樂都沒有微笑
一切苦難都沒有淚痕
一切語言都是重復
一切交往都是初逢
一切愛情都在心裏
一切往事都在夢中
一切希望都帶着注釋
一切信仰都帶着呻吟
一切爆發都有片刻的寧靜
一切死亡都有冗長的回聲

Shu Ting: This, Too, Is All
A reply to a young friend

Not all trees
 are broken by the storm;
Not all seeds
 are left rootless in the soil;
Not all feelings
 dry in the deserts of the heart;
Not all dreams
 let their wings be clipped.

No, not all
Is as you say!

這也是一切

不是一切大樹
 都被暴風折斷;
不是一切種子,
 都找不到生根的土壤;
不是一切真情
 都流失在人心的沙漠裏;
不是一切夢想
 都甘願被折掉翅膀。

不, 不是一切
都像你説的那樣!

> *Not all flames*
>   *consume themselves alone*
>   *do not shed light on others;*
> *Not all stars*
>   *point only to the dark*
>   *do not announce the dawn;*
> *Not all singing*
>   *brushes past the ears*
>   *does not stay in the heart.*
>
> *No, not all*
> *Is as you say!*
>
> *Not all appeals*
>   *lack reverberation;*
> *Not all losses*
>   *are beyond repair;*
> *Not all abysses*
>   *spell destruction;*
> *Not all destruction*
>   *falls upon the weak;*
> *Not all souls*
>   *can be trampled underfoot*
>   *to rot in the mud;*
> *Not all endings*
>   *are stained with blood and tears*
>   *and joyless faces.*
>
> *All present is pregnant with the future,*
> *All in the future grows from its yesterdays,*
> *Hope, and the struggle for it—*
> *Bear this all on your shoulders.*
>
>   *tr. Bonnie S. McDougall*

不是一切火焰，
　　都只燃燒自己
　　而不把別人照亮，
不是一切星星，
　　都僅指示黑夜
　　而不報告曙光；
不是一切歌聲，
　　都掠過耳旁
　　而不留在心上。

不，不是一切，
都像你說的那樣！

不是一切呼籲都沒有回響；
不是一切損失都無法補償；
不是一切深淵都是滅亡；
不是一切滅亡都覆蓋在弱者頭上；
不是一切心靈
　　都可以踩在腳下，爛在泥裏；
不是一切後果
　　都是眼淚血印，而不展歡容。

一切的現在都孕育着未來，
未來的一切都生長於它的昨天。
希望，而且爲它鬬爭，
請把這一切放在你的肩上。

Two poems, 'All' by Bei Dao, and 'This, Too, Is All' by Shu Ting, epitomize this image of youth. Many see these two poems as representing two types of young people. This is a misreading of the poems and a misunderstanding of the poets themselves. These two poems are typical of all the works of the young poets; they are two refractions of a unifying belief of our young people: their outright rebellion against falsehood and ugliness, and their single-minded aspiration towards beauty, truth and perfection. Together these two refractions form the thematic foundation of the new poets.... Bei Dao negates the old world, while Shu Ting affirms her belief in humanity. Theirs is clearly a different expression of a single feeling.... In the hearts of the younger generation and in the works of the young poets, the feelings of negation and aspiration are closely aligned, inseparably mingled like milk and water. Bei Dao affirms his belief with brows tightly locked, while Shu Ting continues her quest with a smile....

The Expression of the Self

In their poems the young poets advocate 'a self with a modern character', believing this to be the 'content of a modern poetry'. They consider that the self proclaimed by the poetry and art of the past (i.e. since 1949) was a sort of non-self, 'a grain of sand', 'a pebble for paving the road', 'a gear wheel', or 'a screw'—not a human being with human feelings, thoughts and doubts. The young poets voice their opposition to this 'religious self-abnegation'; they firmly believe in human rights, human free will and all the just demands of a human being; they believe that man should be his own master, so much so that the lyrical persona in their poems is often an individual being pure and simple . . . . Through the first person narrator, who is a real existing entity, they recite to the world, to the reader, or to nobody in particular, their muted interior monologues—strong yet calm, melancholy and steadily paced . . . . The poems of Bei Dao, Jiang He and Yang Lian all deal with a common theme from the perspective of the 'self' . . . . Because they stress the relationship between the poet and the outside world, between the 'person' and the 'thing in objective reality', because they expose the internal contradictions in life, their work constitutes a striking contrast to the poems of the past, which either simple-mindedly illustrate life, or glorify its positive elements, or condemn its negative aspect. The new poems reflect to a greater extent the complexity of life, its many facets.

Complexity of Theme

The complex experiences and feelings of a generation have determined the complexity of their poetic themes. In this they have broken away from the poetic formula of the 50s and 60s (still widely prevalent)—namely, description at the beginning, followed by elaboration in the middle, and elevation at the end . . . . As far as poetry is concerned, this change is sure progress.

Thus there emerges in poetry multiple meaning and indirect treatment of theme . . . . Because such modernistic poems stress expression through implication, the theme is frequently a synthesis of several trains of thought, and creates at times a feeling of apparent contradiction . . . . To deal adequately with such themes, the poets have found an appropriate technique, a mode of expression based on symbolism. These poems thus tend in general to show a certain abstraction, a certain surrealism, a random association of ideas.

Bei Dao: Life   生活

Net   網

This is the most succinct of symbolist poems. It uses the image contained in the monosyllabic Chinese character *wang* (網, net) to symbolize the disyllabic title, *shenghuo* (生活, life). Without going into detail as to whether this is a poem of the first order, one can safely say that from an aesthetic point of view the associations triggered by it exceed those of a thousand mediocre poems put together . . . .

The Path of Poetry

A nation, in order to achieve greatness, must develop from its own foundations. This is also true of a literary form. What then is the most immediate foundation for modern Chinese poetry? It is not classical poetry, nor is it folk ballads; it is the fine tradition established since the May Fourth Movement (1919), under the influence of western poetry. This is the new poetry's 'own foundation'.... The poetic mainstream of the future flows from the May Fourth tradition (especially as seen in the poetry written before and during the 40s); to this can be added a modernist technique, with an emphasis placed on critical learning from foreign modernist poetry. On this foundation, we can build a truly diversified and pluralistic poetic structure.

Conclusion

The young poets of today have a glorious but difficult task. The future and its new art are largely dependent on their present efforts. Our admiration (and our compassion) go out to them. They must continue to carve out a new path through innumerable difficulties.... There is nothing ahead of them, not a single footprint. They must continue on their journey, must turn back from time to time to explain themselves to those behind them, must slow down because of the 'drag' from behind. But nothing can stop them. Their quest is predestined. The beginning has already been made. They will move forward to success, carrying their mission with them.... The earth will receive their fruits, the earth will record their names—this Volant Tribe of Bards!

徐敬亞：時刻牢記社會主義的文藝方向

Postscript: Xu Jingya's Self-criticism in the *People's Daily*
"Keeping the Socialist Orientation of Literature and Art Constantly in Mind"

Original editor's note:

Comrade Xu Jingya is the author of one of the so-called Three Volant Essays, which have attracted much attention in poetic circles. His long essay, 'A Volant Tribe of Bards', published in Contemporary Literary Trends (1983.1), advocated a series of erroneous ideas departing from the socialist orientation in literature and art. These ideas cover the relationship between art and politics, between poetry and life, and between poetry and the people; and some problems of fundamental principle, such as how to treat our country's classical and ballad poetry, and how to treat the revolutionary tradition of New Poetry since the May Fourth Movement. The essay provoked incisive criticism from the general reading public and in literary and art circles. The Jilin Provincial Party Committee and Jilin literary and art circles also repeatedly gave the author serious criticism and patient assistance. Recently, Comrade Xu has to some extent realized the error of the views he advocated and has written this self-criticism.

MY 'VOLANT TRIBE OF BARDS' has since its publication been severely criticized by theorists, critics and poets. During this time, I have read many critical essays and taken part in a series of conferences and forums. Being a young student fresh from college, I am lucky to have obtained instruction and help of this kind from theorists and leaders of the older generation as well as from my teachers, lucky to have received their earnest criticism both in written and spoken form. I have benefited a great deal from this. In receiving their criticism I have often re-examined, dissected and analysed my former viewpoints. I have had a deepening recognition of my errors in departing from the socialist orientation and have acquired a greater understanding of the socialist orientation of the new poetry and in literature and art in general. During this time, I have also had the opportunity to recall the course of my growth. I have summed up my experience, and clarified my orientation. In my short literary experience, this discussion will live forever in my memory.

'Volant Tribe of Bards' is an essay I wrote at university in 1980 and early 1981. At that time, my discontent at the monotony and the formulaic nature of poetic creation during the devastating rule of the Gang of Four, and my excitement at the experiments that were taking place, led me to make these observations on the orientation of the new poetry appearing in 1980. However, the rampant trend of capitalist liberalism influenced me so deeply, that my own explorations and observations took a wrong direction, and I made great errors on a whole series of matters of principle. In my essay, I cursorily negated the cultural tradition of our classical poetry; I played down and even negated the development of the revolutionary poetry of the past decades; I negated the realistic principle of poetic creation; I blindly recommended Western Modernism in the arts, praised some younger poets as a Volant Tribe of Bards, and made an inappropriate evaluation of their work; I propagated idealistic literary viewpoints such as 'anti-rationalism' and 'self-expression' etc. It is especially serious that in my analysis of the conditions for the development of artistic schools, I advocated the need of a 'unique social outlook which can even be discordant with the concerted main voice of society'; and that I erroneously used the words 'I do not believe' to sum up the poets' attitude toward the past. This is not merely a literary mistake, it is a political one. After its publication, my essay had a very bad effect in literary circles. Today, when I read it from a new point of view, I am shocked. I have often asked myself, 'Why did it happen?'

I AM A YOUNG writer who embarked on a literary career after the smashing of the Gang of Four. In my university years, along with the movement for ideological liberation, came some erroneous trends of thought. I was greatly influenced by the trend towards capitalist liberalism for a period of time, and became confused and both ideologically and artistically lost. I slackened my efforts to remould my world view, and was quite uninterested in the study of Marxist literary theory. I regarded as rare treasures Western modernist capitalist theories in philosophy, aesthetics and psychology, theories such as existentialism, intuitivism and psychoanalysis, which were pouring in at that time. And I indiscreetly passed judgement on some important issues in China's new poetry, using the limited knowledge of Chinese literary history (of the recent past and of the contemporary period) which I had just acquired. Thus, as a result of my ideological confusion and the heterogeneous nature of my artistic training, I dashed off the essay with only a smattering of knowledge of some important theoretical issues, and an incorrect ideological inclination crept in. This distorted my discussion of a serious artistic question and was responsible for the deviation from the correct socialist orientation in my discussion of the relation between art and politics, poetry and life, poetry and the people. I made many irresponsible observations which contain serious mistakes in political standpoint. Reading some of the critical articles and my own essay together, I now feel that there are many good lessons I should draw. Just as many comrades have pointed out in their critiques, my 'Volant Bards', seen as an overall view of the orientation of our new poetry and of its artistic development, fails to be guided by Marxist theory and is permeated with the idealistic view of art and the metaphysical way of thinking. The absence of correct ideological guidelines led to its deviation in the analysis of life and art, and hence to the inevitable failure to explicate literary phenomena in a scientific way. Recalling the writing of the essay, I feel that I wrote such an erroneous piece because during the period when liberalism was rampant I neglected the study of Marxist theory. And later I did not promptly grasp the essence of a whole series of Party instructions on literature and art. For a long time after the writing of the essay, I was not aware of the errone-ous viewpoints contained in it. In the struggle against capitalist liberalism in the fields of litera-ture and art, a struggle led by the Party, I did not promptly examine myself in a critical light, and as a result many ideological and artistic errors remain in 'Volant Bards'. After the 12th Party Congress, the Party Central Committee resolved to build a socialist spiritual civilization with communist ideology as its centre; but I still failed to examine my essay in the light of the Party's resolution, and still less did I correct my viewpoint by approach-ing the problem from the higher level of a socialist orientation in literature and art. I was still too engrossed in the minute artistic analysis of detail, and consequently made the mistake of allowing the essay to be published in January 1983. As a result, some of my uncorrected errors spread again in theoretical and poetic circles, doing harm to the cause of literature and art.

Whether as a writer or as a young person, I should not for a moment depart from the socialist direction. Exploration without a correct direction is dangerous.[1] In the early stages of the discussion of my essay, I came to realize some of its artistic and academic faults—but that was all. It was only after the subsequent help I received from or-ganizations and comrades at various levels, es-pecially after several large-scale forums and serious, conscientious, practical, realistic, word-by-word, paragraph-by-paragraph, point-by-point analysis and criticism, that I began to realize the seriousness of the matter. During this time, many of my colleagues, friends and teachers talked with me in a spirit of friendship and reason, with patience and restraint. Some older literary comrades compared the errors in my essay with their own in the 50s, and praised with deep feeling the Party's policy on literature and art, and the lively cultural situation since the Third Plenum of

the Eleventh Central Committee. All this filled me with a variety of emotions. While receiving this severe, but calm and comradely criticism, I went through my essay and dissected it thoroughly, and came to realize that it does indeed deviate from the cardinal principle, in literature and art, of serving socialism and serving the people. This whole discussion woke me up with a jolt. Climbing the ladder of knowledge is not an easy matter. Criticism is a kind of remoulding, a process of learning which causes pain and shame, and self-criticism is a similar process of self-correction and self-moulding. Our artistic growth took place during the devastating rule of the Gang of Four, and the younger generation of writers like myself have never experienced the normal life of artistic criticism. During this discussion, I realized, from the transformation of my own perception, that artistic criticism is as necessary to the cause of literature and art as washing is to the human face. Constant criticism and self-criticism are the ef-fective guarantee of a correct orientation in litera-ture and art.

Here I would like to mention in passing that while 'Volant Bards' was being criticized in literary and artistic circles within China after its publica-tion, some foreign scholars took pleasure in it and commented on it with ulterior motives. I think that they know nothing about the concrete situation of Chinese poetry today. Their motives are completely different from ours. They do not share our desire to debate the rights and wrongs of an issue so that artistic creation may prosper. Our discussion is entirely part of the normal order of things in the literary and artistic life of our society. To adhere to the truth and to correct mistakes, these are also scientific principles that everyone engaged in artistic creation and research should follow. As for those foreigners who take pleasure in sowing discord and stirring up trouble, the less said about their deeds and motives the better. Perhaps they will never be able to under-stand the weapon of criticism and self-criticism as it functions in our revolutionary literature and art.

Since I graduated from university, I have been involved in a considerable amount of popular cultural work. And during two years of work as an editor, I have also had the opportunity to read quite a few poetic works written in the vein of

[1] Editor's note: Exploration *with* a 'correct direction' is surely a contradiction in terms!—J.M.

classical poetry and folk ballad—which I attacked in my essay as 'that same old stuff, awkward and difficult to read', and as 'feudal pastoral'. In my leisure time, I too came to feel the bias of my former viewpoint. My contact with many amateur writers made me feel all the more the serious harm done to poetry by the erroneous views of 'Volant Bards'. The whole debate has clarified many of my confusions and rectified my ideological direction. Our country, our people, the rapid economic development of our society, our unique national spiritual life, all require our literature and art to take the socialist road, the Chinese socialist road. It is imperative that we take this road; it is unimaginable to be without the guidance of Marxism, the leadership of the Party and without the thousands of years of our cultural heritage, the decades of the more recent revolutionary tradition in literature and art. The tendency in artistic creation to break away from life and the people, and the theoretical ideas that support this tendency, jeopardize the normal development of literature and art. Life is already teaching and warning us all.

Recently, after studying the *communiqué* of the Second Plenum of the Twelfth Central Committee, and Comrade Deng Xiaoping's talk on eliminating spiritual pollution, I felt clearer about the duty of every literary worker; and at the same time, I felt sorry for the harmful effects of my past mistakes. What is done cannot be undone. The road ahead is still a long one, and I will take this opportunity to examine myself carefully, to eradicate the influence of capitalist liberalism, and to keep forever in the forefront of my mind the socialist orientation in literature and art. I have recently reflected that although 'Volant Bards' was written only three years ago, and although my own experience as a writer, and my exposure to erroneous thought, were not of any great duration, the incorrect viewpoints expressed in the essay, and other confusions not verbalized, but implicit in it, have intrinsic causes and social roots that must not be overlooked. Therefore my own ideological and artistic study and remoulding will be a long-term task. Today's self-criticism still needs to be continuously deepened, the freshly established and correct viewpoint needs to be gradually consolidated. From now on, I will consciously expend more effort in the study of Marxist theory of literature and art, will firmly take the literary road to serve socialism and the people, will go deep into life, close to the people—this is the resolution that has formed itself in my mind. And also, I believe, through this discussion, our new poetry, and the cause of literature and art, will surely develop more healthily along the socialist road.

March 5, 1984

tr. ZHU ZHIYU

楊煉：傳統與我們

Tradition and Us

By Yang Lian

Translated by Ginger Li

IT EXISTED LONG ago, it exists now, it will continue to exist into the future. It is more than a word, more than that river, that never-ending mountain range some people claim it to be. It is a solution within our very blood, a component of our every cell, a part of every tremor of our spiritual being. It is formless, but potent! It is a constant reminder to us that nothing we do today can be a negation of yesterday. Yesterday was, and will not perish. In the gradually receding eye of the future, yesterday and today are a sequence, each a sign of its time.

This is tradition, the tradition that none of us can cast off. We are rooted in a common culture, in the unique linguistic form of a psychological structure. It is a form, in that it never determines the modernity of the subject-matter, but instead dictates certain peculiar modes of feeling, thinking and expression. It commands our obedience in each act of artistic creation. I believe that no individual artist in his creative work can betray his tradition. Either consciously or unconsciously, every artist's work, his "individual entity", is to a greater or lesser degree permeated with the "intrinsic elements" of his tradition. This is the premise of his very existence. Tradition should be seen as a series of such "individual entities", independent of each other and yet at the same time linked by the continuity of these "intrinsic elements". It is like a train held together by invisible couplings. It lives in the way we individually forge our links with it. Through the specific essence of individuals it reveals the national quintessence.

"Intrinsic element" and "individual entity" are terms I have proposed in the course of my inquiry into tradition. The former denotes those qualities by virtue of which tradition continues to be tradition after all its incidental characteristics have been stripped away. The latter denotes the individual artistic styles that different writers of different times have created for themselves out of a variety of elements. For instance, when we study the "individual entity" of the great Chinese poet Qu Yuan, we observe the various unique artistic characteristics that distinguish

Yang Lian was born in Berne, Switzerland, in 1955, and returned with his family to China in the same year. He began writing poetry in 1976 while working on the land near Peking, and now works for the Central Broadcasting Commission in Peking. In 1981 he became a member of the Peking branch of the Writers' Association. This short essay appeared in the Guizhou journal Shanhua 山花, *September 1983. For a selection of Yang's poems, see below, pp. 249-255.*

WOODEN FIGURE, Early Western Han dynasty;
excavated in 1982 at Liuyuangang, Guangzhou;
in the collection of the Guangzhou Municipal
Museum.

him from contemporary and subsequent poets, but we also observe the common
ground. To be specific: Qu Yuan, in his poems "Tian Wen" 天問 and "Li Sao" 離騷,
expresses with vigour and passion man's aspiration towards a direct mastery of
nature, society and self; he succeeds moreover in furnishing this aspiration with a
complete symbolic system embodying the Chinese national quintessence; he also
succeeds in creating a feeling of overwhelming aesthetic delight; in all this he has
essentially fulfilled his mission of rediscovering tradition. It is precisely his most
original (individual) and transforming quality that brings him closest to the tradition: his (radical) use of that most compelling myth of Chu culture, the "intrinsic
element" of Shamanism.

Similarly, in our own time, several thousand years after Qu Yuan, it is still the
task of every artist to form the "individual entities" that link the "intrinsic
elements" of tradition. To emphasize the significance of tradition is not to propose
it as a sole artistic criterion. Actually, no single standard of the "past" can ever be
used to measure the things of "today". To emphasize tradition is to emphasize
"historicity"—a familiar term, but one that has not attained a full creative mani-
festation. It is to emphasize the need for a clear resolution of the creative dilemma:
which parts (of the tradition) should be discarded, and which retained? This in fact
is to emphasize the "present". It is only through a comparison with the "past" that
the "present" can attain a precise meaning. But this fundamental issue is so often
avoided by the blind and the timid. Some issue indiscriminate condemnations of
the "abandonment of tradition", while others make pretentious claims for their own
"anti-traditionalism". Both attitudes betray the same ignorance and lead to the same

end-result. He who inherits only the outer garment of our great ancestors is a clown, not a true successor; while the endless imitation of external influence only makes a writer the stupid slave of that *other* tradition. Both camps are engaged, simultaneously but from different directions, in the process of self-annihilation.

What is it that we want to build for ourselves today? We must ponder this question, *now*.

We must create a new synthesis. The power and inner life of poetry derive from the accumulation of a diversity of human experiences. The poetic tradition can grow at an orderly pace only if radically new creative work can be inserted organically into it. It is the easiest thing in the world to affirm or negate indiscriminately. But the great masters of past and present, of China and the world, have bequeathed us a more formidable task, of a quite different nature.

We must try every possible means to acquire the knowledge, to equip ourselves with the basic resources for analysis and comparison; we must confront and master our ever-changing and developing national spirit, and the thread that runs through all of its changes; we must rediscover, explore and secure once again those things in our history that answer our own aspirations; we must pick out from the numerous and diverse sources the "inner core" that is still strong and vital; this is the vitality and strength that Yeats called mature wisdom. Wisdom is not intelligence, the essential difference between them being that intelligence moves from the simple to the shallow, while wisdom moves from the complex to the profound. Intelligence may dazzle for a while with innate flair and novelty; but the origins of wisdom lie in breadth of experience, and its fruit grows through painstaking pursuit to firmly structured conception. Without this inner substance, so-called feeling seems to me to be an illusion. It is only in the works of those comparatively few artists who have matured in this way and who possess this firm consciousness, that bright imagery is endowed with a precise and emotionally convincing meaning. This is the only real kind of "creation".

When we talk of analysis and comparison, what we are proposing is a "critical spirit". A poet should possess a sensitivity towards his own needs, but he must also be able to select, if he is to draw the knowledge that will satisfy those needs. An artist is a true artist only when he can discern the "inner gravity" of the work through the superficial effects of language. That is why Repin[1] endlessly praised Mayakovsky, why Rodin was so fond of Phidias[2], while Eliot evolved a whole artistic philosophy out of Dante's poems—these masters of entirely different styles were connected by their profound sensitivity to the essence of art. Then we often see how some poets, having produced spectacular works in their early career, "dilute" themselves through endless duplication. This is another manifestation of the lack of critical spirit. This spirit is essential to the poet's own growth. The life of a poet should be a life of self-rejuvenation; he should be unafraid of destroying the existing equilibrium, should forever seek a new equilibrium at a higher level. The "critical spirit" is the premise that validates the "nourishment" (guarantees its authenticity), while "self-rejuvenation" is the prerequisite of creativity. Substance and void are

---

[1] Ilya Yefimovich Repin, 1844-1930, Russian painter of historical subjects.

[2] The Chinese text must surely refer to the famous 5th century B.C. Athenian sculptor.

OIL, 110 x 90cm, 1981, Qu Leilei (born 1951).

each irreplaceable, and together contain the whole mystery of the poet's growth.

Looking at the current poetic scene, I must say that some of those who flaunt their fidelity to "tradition" do not seem to understand what that "tradition" is. They seem happy to voice a dying echo of yesterday's thunder. Those, on the other hand, who rely solely on individual intuition, and mistake that for "anti-traditionalism", will soon wither on the very soil they despise, because they lack roots firm enough to sustain healthy growth. These two groups forget that the "self" is not confined to the individual instinctive impetus, nor to the collective general principle, but is a blend of the two. The artist's calling demands the simultaneous embodiment of individuality and of the entire tradition.

So, what steps should we take if we want to sustain our tradition? In my view, the poet must first conceive his position clearly, know where he stands. Let us imagine a co-ordinate series, with the poet's own cultural tradition as the vertical axis and the human civilization of the poet's time—philosophy, literature, art, religion, etc.—as the horizontal axis; the poet (having located himself) can look back continuously on his own tradition from the vantage-point of the latest achievements of the global civilization of his time. In this way, his vision embraces much that he was previously unaware of, because the level of his understanding was lower. This is "rediscovery". For example, when we seek to create a "poetic world" that resonates with and yet defies the real world, we can see our endeavour "validated" by the great example of Qu Yuan. That lode of genius lying deep within the literary works of our ancestors reveals its lustre, its true value, afresh. Our poems, situated at our "point of intersection", will then possess a certain awareness, a sense of breadth and profundity. The interpenetration of the two areas (of each axis) bestows a quality that is at the same time Chinese and contemporary.

This essay is too short to discuss in any detail the specific nature of the "intrinsic elements" of our tradition. However, as relevant constituents of the Chinese cultural tradition, I would propose several items:

(1) China's own unique symbolic system—as far as I know, nobody has ever investigated the *Book of Changes* 易經 closely in this respect;

(2) certain repeatedly emphasized themes in traditional Chinese philosophy, art and religious belief—the objectivity, the tendency to synthesize, the transcendental tradition (transcending utilitarianism);

(3) the poetic conception of nature, nature imagery—the unique visual language of Chinese poetry, that is, a consciousness of multi-gradational concrete imagery;

(4) the "unconscious impetus" which appeals to the reader not through words but through mental conception;

(5) the organic compound structure of the poetry of Qu Yuan;

(6) typical oriental modes of thinking such as "enlightenment" 悟 and "tranquility" 靜, which in the past were hastily dismissed as mystical and metaphysical (玄學).

Tradition is an eternal present; to neglect it is to neglect ourselves. We should, in the course of creation and criticism, begin from an exploration of the "intrinsic elements" of tradition, absorb them into our poems, and then enrich that tradition with our creations. In this way the poetry itself will contain a truly *poetic* feeling and strength. The more of tradition we can lay claim to in this way, the more distinct will be our realization of our own creative and innovative mission, the greater will be our place in history.

PEKING TOTEM,
Wang Keping (born 1949).

楊牧：新詩的傳統取向
The Traditional Orientation of China's New Poetry

By Yang Mu

Translated by Xiang Liping and John Minford

STRICTLY SPEAKING, New Poetry in Chinese literature has a history of no more than seventy years. But in a broad sense it is a part of a timeless pattern. Every generation has its share of poetic genius; and every talented writer, however lofty his ideals and aspirations, however infinite his resource and skill, realizes that ultimately what he endeavours to do is more than just an incomplete and imperfect part of that timeless pattern. His transmission of the past is meaningful only by virtue of his determination to explore new frontiers. Mere compilation and collation are hardly the chosen mode of expression for the transcendent wisdom or profound passion of a genuis. So, at the threshold of each major era, we may say that literature depends for its continuing forward impetus on the pioneering efforts of its New Poets, the literary reformers of their time.

Wen Yiduo 聞一多 believed that the historical significance of the Four Masters of Early Tang (Wang Bo 王勃, Yang Jiong 楊炯, Lu Zhaolin 盧照鄰 and Luo Binwang 駱賓王) lay in their redemption of the prevalent 'court style' 宮體. They opened up a new realm, created a new path for the poets of the new empire to explore. They were the New Poets of their time, forerunners of the subsequent Golden Age of Li Bai 李白 and Du Fu 杜甫, Wang Wei 王維 and Meng Haoran 孟浩然. After the Mid-Tang, when the poetry of Yuan Zhen 元稹 and Bai Juyi 白居易 was so popular, its influence spreading even beyond the confines of China, it was the young Du Mu 杜牧 who took a lone stand against this poetic fashion, and resolved to rescue poetry from what he saw as a decline. He was the New Poet of *his* age. The limitations of his time and of his own ability prevented him from setting a new poetic fashion and from extending the boundaries of the art. But his aspirations and his dedication were lofty, deriving as they did from a firm resolve to establish something markedly new. We do not judge a hero by the extent of his success: it is this creative dedication that we respect and emulate as the true mark of the New Poet.

From this pattern of continuity and growth in Tang literature we can observe that New Poetry is indeed a broad term, and one which we would like to see recurring frequently in the annals of any literature. The very frequency of its recurrence is testimony to the splendour of a tradition. It recurs time and again in the history

Yang Mu 楊牧 *is the pseudonym used by C.H. Wang* 王靖獻 *when writing as a poet and essayist. Though now a professor of Chinese and Comparative Literature at the University of Washington, Seattle, he was and is first and foremost a creative writer. In 1983, he was voted one of the top poets in Taiwan by his fellow poets of a younger generation, and continues to be prolific as scholar and critic. Perhaps the following selection of titles from his many publications illustrates best his awareness of the heavy responsibility of his generation in carrying forward the tradition into the future* 繼往開來.

> The Traditional and the Modern 傳統的與現代的 *(essays in Chinese, 1974)*
>
> The Bell and the Drum: "Shih Ching" as Formulaic Poetry *(University of California, 1974)*
>
> *"Chou Tso-jen's* 周作人 *Hellenism" (*Renditions *No. 7, Spring, 1977)*
>
> *"Ch'en Yin-k'o's* 陳寅恪 *Approaches to Poetry: A Historian's Progress" (*CLEAR, *Vol. 3, No. 1, Jan. 1981)*

of Chinese literature. English literature, with its relatively shorter but equally rich history of one thousand years, consists in effect of a series of such New Poetry movements, each with its rise and its fall, one leading into another in a continuous succession to the present. In German literature the long, dark and dismal centuries between the Middle Ages and the end of the eighteenth century produced hardly anything worthy of special mention. It was not until the stormy entrance of figures like Goethe and Schiller upon the scene that the true soul of Germanic Europe was manifested. Herein lies Goethe's significance as a New Poet.

When we talk of New Poetry in China today, we refer specifically to the kind of poetry which originated on the eve of the May Fourth Movement (1919). This poetry underwent the various experiments of the twenties and thirties, it tested out new grammar and rhyme, it grappled with new themes, it earnestly explored the very essence and scope of art in all its aspects; and after the gradual process of condensation and introspection of the 40s, it was on the verge of attaining a distinctive identity of its own. At precisely that juncture (1950) it disintegrated—for political reasons—to resurface later in Taiwan and the Chinese 'diaspora'. Subsequently, ideological interference reduced poetry in Mainland China to a convenient propaganda tool, in the process making it perhaps more popular, but depriving it of its depth and artistic quality. At the same time in Taiwan, there was an obvious literary discontinuity—similarly for political reasons. It was impossible for many of the fine Chinese works of the 40s, or even the more successful earlier experiments, to gain acceptance. The existing 'tradition' in Taiwan was one of a rather exquisite, sentimental style of verse, an immature exoticism and a kind of vernacular poetry 白話詩 written by native poets in coarse Chinese during the days of the Japanese occupation.

HAN DYNASTY POTTERY FIGURE
of a folk performer.

Recent observation indicates that now, after more than thirty years of turbulence, New Poetry on the Mainland is re-emerging, rediscovering its sense of
artistic value. But things are only just beginning to change, and since the lack of information makes accurate assessment difficult for the moment, I have chosen to
leave this new development undiscussed here. It is in Taiwan, and in the Chinese
'diaspora' which looks to the Taiwan literary scene as its centre of gravity, that the
bold development of the New Poetry is a palpable and incontrovertible fact. Its
progress has been sometimes slow and circuitous, sometimes sudden and dramatic.
This New Poetry is rooted in the specific geoculture of Taiwan. It recognizes
Taiwan's past and simultaneously looks to her future. It has inherited the positive
spirit, alive from the May Fourth years until the 40s, has held fast to it, and finally
surpassed it, to establish a complete literary system of its own. We shall discuss the
traditional orientation of the New Poetry with reference to this particular branch
of the great tree of Chinese literature.

Central to the traditional orientation of China's New Poetry is its creative
spirit. This seeming paradox is essential both to a meaningful understanding of the
New Poetry and to a positive affirmation of tradition. Tradition is the accumulated
achievement of history. In the realm of literature, it is a composite of the finest
writings through the ages. It is what we often call 'The Classics'. The total corpus
of tradition is at once pluralistic and unified, background and prospect. It is a daily
increasing stock of inspiration derived from the classics—sublime, weighty, vast in
extent. But how is it that such a literary tradition can perpetuate itself for three
thousand years without degenerating or losing its vitality, can indeed continue to
build, wave upon wave, into a magnificent, surging torrent? I have already suggested
that this very longevity of tradition is the fruit of the constant creative experimenta-

tion of dedicated men of letters, of their vision, their spirit of exploration, their persistent craftmanship.

Take the currently denigrated Rhymeprose of the Han dynasty. Mei Sheng 枚乘, Yang Xiong 揚雄 and Sima Xiangru 司馬相如, in a spirit of the utmost enlightenment and objectivity, chose the basic mode of *The Songs of the South* for their poetry; and then, in a spirit of bold inventiveness, proceeded to integrate into this mode the rhetorical style of the political strategists of the Warring States period. It was only by dint of endless technical experimentation, through infinite exploitation of verbal resources, out of an astonishing breadth of knowledge in the natural sciences, that these poets could forge a style that was free and dynamic, variegated and supple, and could finally create an imposing body of literature and establish for the mighty Han Empire its most appropriate literary genre, in whose all-embracing and expansive features can surely be seen a reflection of China's very unity. However, from the Six Dynasties onwards, the Rhymeprose degenerated, and its place in the literary vanguard was taken by other genres. And this chain of literary transmutation has continued through the past thousand years.

China's achievement in literature is due to the creative innovations of generations of New Poets. They select the finest part of the classical tradition and discard its dross, guided by a total sense of literary historicity and exercising at the same time their individual judgement and invention to the fullest. They are witnesses of their time. The pioneers of modern poetry in this century are the poets who have mastered this creative spirit inherent in our cultural tradition.

Innovations and breakthroughs in poetry derive from the lessons of tradition. In the empirical craft of writing, the New Poets may have broken with the techniques and modes of their immediate literary tradition; but spiritually they have proved that creation is the only way to keep a great tradition from falling apart.

'Poetry voices intent.' This is the basic definition of poetry in the Chinese tradition. 'The intent arises within the mind, and issues forth in verbal form as poetry.' It is a definition that cannot be questioned. The alternative formulation of poetry, 'growing along with emotion', amounts to much the same thing. Or, if we wish to draw a fine line between 'emotion' and 'intent', we may say that the traditional concept of poetry is that it is an artistic product growing along with emotion in the voicing of intent. It may take on numerous forms—delicate and graceful, bold and rousing, simple and solemn. In short, the intent is the fruit of emotional impact, the crystallization of thought: when actualized in a literary process, it is what we call theme, the long gestated burden of the poet, the deep conception crying out for birth.

Our study of Chinese and Western literature tells us that such literary themes are actually limited in number. Despite the tomes and tomes of literature that have been written, there is very little 'new matter' to be expressed. The variety of themes is rather small. Strictly speaking, all literature and art revolves around two subjects —love and death. Such large-scale matters as the confrontation between man and heaven (or nature), and the relationship between an individual and his state, as well as such smaller-scale attachments as exist between men and women, between parents and children, between friends, and even such poetic topics as plants and animals— all these have to do with feeling; whereas matters such as spiritual and bodily destruction, the despair that numbs the soul, the degeneration that arises from ignorance, these can all be subsumed under death. Writers may handle these themes of love and death with supreme insight, they may go on to explore lack of love, transcendence of death, their techniques may be new, but their basic themes remain unchanged.

Since the New Poetry movement began, poets have certainly been producing works which differ from the classics in appearance; but these very poets have been working within the Chinese intellectual tradition, in their themes, in their search for the salvation of man and society, in their doubts and affirmations. We are all familiar with the works of the period up to the 40s; but even the modern poets of the past thirty years in Taiwan have generally been working with traditional themes. Understandably, most modern poets are no longer content with such traditional topics as 'Grief for the Past' or 'Sorrow at Parting'. Instead they have turned inward to describe the inner world of the human psyche and its undulations. They are more interested in the portrayal of the fears and doubts, the various states of helplessness created in the twentieth-century industrial and commercial world. We may say that the modern poets have not only recognized the positive meaning of traditional literary themes, but have also tried to unfold its 'negatives'. They wish to reveal more fully the causes, the images and the nature of love and death. They are not only continuing the traditional themes, enlarging and extending previous discoveries, they are also hoping to surpass their predecessors through the insights gained from their own altered perspective. It would be rash of us to pass judgement on their attempts. If ultimately they are deemed to have succeeded, they will be considered 'classics'. They will then have become part of the tradition.

The radically new perspective, the rejection of traditional modes and the opening up of new paths are all methods employed by the modern poet to create a new literature, the 'avid pursuit' of modern form. Old forms and ways of thinking, imperfect inferential principles and stereotyped imaginative patterns (imagery, metaphor etc.) all need to be seriously examined, and the dead wood discarded. Otherwise the New Poetry will be too weighed down to grow effectively. After the May Fourth Movement, we adopted the vernacular as the major poetic medium, broke the myth of language and rejected the authority of the classical mode of expression, *wenyan* 文言, and the rhetorical parallelism that went with it. We believe the vernacular language has the potential to express modern man's consciousness. Despite this, the New Poetry still has very much a traditional orientation in matters of language. Many leading New Poets introduce classical grammar and a classical flavour into their vernacular. They can even transform classical rhetorical patterns with ease. Among the New Poets in Taiwan today, the leading masters of language are generally those who adopt the vernacular as their basic style, at the same time embellishing it with a refinement taken from the classical language and borrowing extensively from the best of foreign languages. They borrow, they synthesize, so as to meet the demands of modern expression.

This change in language has determined the form of the New Poetry. When 'vernacular poetry' was first introduced into Taiwan, it was for a time referred to as 'free verse'. This did not mean that it was undisciplined or wild. The term was used specifically to indicate a new variety in form, a freedom in relation to the

A REPRESENTATIVE WORK
by the Taiwan sculptor Lin Yuan 林淵.

long-established prosodic rules of the 'old-style' and 'regulated' verse, even to the relatively loosely-organized metres of the 'lyric' verse (*ci* 詞 and *qu* 曲). It is the New Poet's belief that in order to portray effectively the complexity of the modern world, Chinese poetry must be freed from its traditional forms. To avoid the habitual ways of thinking and imagining, it is permissible for Chinese poetry to abandon its own traditional forms and to borrow from the West. For even if a Chinese modern poet writes in the sonnet form, he is unlikely to feel restricted and confined by this ultimately *alien* European tradition. On the contrary, he can through such limited imitations transfuse new artistic qualities into the bloodstream of Chinese literature. Time has proved the significance of the poetic experiments of the 30s. Over the past three thousand years, the New Poets, the poets with radical ideals and creativity, have frequently turned to other countries in the process of reform, drawing on foreign artistic methods and philosophical concepts. So when the New Poet of the twentieth century occasionally follows in the footsteps of Western masters, he is not really straying away from tradition, he is simply following a natural spiritual tendency. Since the 50s, the New Poets in Taiwan have occupied themselves more vigorously than ever with experimentation, imitating and transmuting the various modern poetic forms which emerged in Western literature after the First World War. They have successfully proved that foreign literature, like foreign science and technology, can be applied in China to serve China's own ends.

Over the last decade, however, the demand has been for New Poetry to return to the Chinese tradition once again. This reflects a concern for matters of style and form. New Poetry has gone through the stage of being free and Western, and has largely attained its maturity. The cry is not so much for a wholesale return to the ancients, but for a new mastery of the classical literary spirit, a new transformation of the classical poetic models. In my view, the modern poet should concentrate on learning from the poetry written in the classical period before Shen Yue 沈約 (441-513). For structural principles, he should even study the organic prosody of the *Book of Songs*. This new emphasis on classical quality, this attempt to transmute classical prosody, are not to be confused with the restoration of classical poetry. They merely constitute one of the most immediately effective manifestations of the New Poetry in its traditional orientation.

In brief, during the past seventy years, China's New Poetry has outgrown its exploratory stage, a stage of many innovative achievements in both form and content. The courage and self-confidence of the New Poets derive from their extensive reading in both Chinese and Western literature, from their understanding of literary history and its inevitability. The extent of their success actually depends on their traditional orientation, an orientation which varies only in degree, which may be either deliberate or unconscious. The New Poetry as it has developed in Taiwan over the past thirty years or so has beyond doubt established its own artistic identity which distinguishes it not only from the literatures of other countries, but also, fundamentally, from the New Poetry written in Mainland China during the same period. Creative writers must appreciate the lessons of history, evaluate the heritage of their own tradition and draw on foreign resources. They must also be concerned for the society in which they live. Above all, they need a reasonably free environment. It is in Taiwan that China's New Poetry has been able over the past thirty years to develop a unique style and philosophical content; this is because the majority of poets have felt a sense of cultural mission. With a strong will, in the face of many attacks and much mockery, they have been able to sustain their artistic beliefs, experimenting and exploring, destroying and rebuilding. The modern poetry of Taiwan is quite distinct from its Mainland counterpart in this same period, because the most dedicated poets in Taiwan are willing to recognize the reality of Taiwan's geoculture, are able to understand the destiny of the island. Taiwan's past, present and future have to find their appropriate expression in poetry.

Twenty years ago, some people had the mistaken notion that the New Poetry had to be a product of an anti-traditionalist spirit. There have also been those who have advocated 'horizontal transplantation' 橫的移植 as a means of accelerating the modernization of the New Poetry. Events have shown that throughout its process of modernization, the New Poetry has always had a correct traditional orientation. Dante cast aside the elegance and archaism of the Latin language; using the vernacular Italian as his medium, with his emotional roots firmly planted in the soil of Florence, he evolved from folk poetry a completely new form and rhyme. In his *Divine Comedy* he transmitted the Christian teaching on the relationship between God and man. He was the great New Poet of his time, the most effective harbinger of the Renaissance. And yet Dante too was, in absolute terms, oriented towards his tradition. He said that all of his creative achievements, in literary consciousness, in artistic skill, could be traced to a writer who used Latin, a writer who considered his model to be the Homeric epics, a Roman writer totally ignorant of Christian culture, the 'man of Mantua', the great Virgil.

We wait for a Dante to appear among the ranks of our New Poets.

November, 1983

Fiction

Two Stories by Chen Yingzhen

Translated by Lucien Miller

TRANSLATOR'S INTRODUCTION

TO NUMBERS OF Chinese living in or outside Taiwan today, Chen Yingzhen is a legend in his own time. He is not simply one of the more important contemporary Chinese writers, but *the* intellectual godfather to many artists and critics. For some of these he epitomizes the socially concerned writer—one who has suffered imprisonment for his convictions and who continues to address social ills in writing published after his release. Both sympathetic critics and detractors note the presence of an ideologue within the godfather as well—a person whose passionate commitment to ideas sometimes appears to be more important than their artistic expression. But many readers find that it is the very intensity of Chen Yingzhen's vision which establishes a unique empathy with character and event and gives his writing its aesthetic strength. For the Western reader unfamiliar with the author, a few salient facts about his life and the development of his fiction are necessary to understand his importance as writer and social critic in contemporary Taiwan. Such information will also enhance reflection on the relation between artist and ideologue in the two stories which appear here for the first time in English translation.[1]

For the record I should state that the exact accusations which led to Chen's arrest were never made public, although rumours abound.[2] The author was charged with "subversive" activities by the Taiwan Garrison Command in a secret military

[1] My book of translations of Chen's short stories is awaiting publication.

[2] While they lack evidence, some fantasize that Chen may have belonged to a study group interested in social problems and critical of the government, and that there was some informer within the group. Knowing that Chen reads Japanese, others conjecture that the authorities found Japanese translations of materials which looked vaguely "Communist" in his house. One rumour has it that the author was jailed for writing about disillusioned lower-middle-class intellectuals. Perhaps the wildest but most entertaining opinion is that the word "red" (*hong* 紅) was caught by the censors—in "A Race of Generals" pigeons are taught to fly by the waving of a "red flag" (*hong qi* 紅旗).

trial. His original ten year sentence which began in June of 1968 was commuted through an amnesty honouring the death of General Chiang Kai-shek, and Chen was released in September of 1975 after serving seven years. My own impression is that there is a kind of "Dance of Intellectuals" always going on in Taiwan which at least partially explains the author's plight, a dance which one may find in any country in the world where martial law is the norm. Persons of differing political persuasions are ever dancing in some great ballroom to the same well known patriotic song. The rhythm may shift suddenly or the lyrics blare, depending on the whim of the maestro and the boys in the band. The dancers are mostly dressed alike and imitate one another making identical movements, but just on the outskirts of the circle some couples wear bizarre clothes and try to see just how far they can go creating new dance steps of their own while still keeping the basic beat. A few get so carried away that they forget where they are and dance themselves out of sight on an adjoining verandah. Such is the game played by socially concerned intellectuals in Taiwan. They try to press as far as they are able, given the specificity of political regulations and the obscurity of their enforcement. Magazines and newspapers are periodically closed by the government and re-emerge later under some new rubric. Voices are silenced and perhaps disappear altogether, never to be heard again, but others may take their place. Somehow or other, Chen danced too fast or too slow and was noticed too much. Whether he actually did something "wrong" we will probably never know. The important thing is that he is writing again.

Chen's social concern and his passion for ideas may be at least partially attributed to his experience of material poverty and human degradation as a child. A native Taiwanese, he was born November 19, 1937, in Zhunan, Taiwan, and his early childhood years were spent in Yingge or Banqiao, both small villages in the district of Taibei. His family of six brothers and two sisters was so poor that at an early age he was sent to live with a childless uncle. During his youth two shattering events occurred which were to have a bearing on his later years; aspects of both events are explored in his fiction.[3] One was the death of his twin brother at age nine which brought about an identity crisis that lasted for several years. The other was Chen's witnessing of the sale of a twenty-year-old neighbour by her destitute parents. She had been like a beloved big sister to him. As we see in the two stories which follow, female enslavement and child prostitution are recurring motifs in Chen's writing.

Still another subject from Chen's past which occasionally appears in his writing —one that seems oddly unfamiliar in the context of modern Chinese fiction—is religion. In "Poor Poor Dumb Mouths" the hypocrisy and superstition of a Christian minister are parodied, while in "A Race of Generals" folk beliefs in an afterlife receive reverential treatment. The author describes his father as being a deeply religious Christian whose faith made a lasting impression, and he speaks gratefully of the influence of persons such as Albert Schweitzer on his youth (an influence which may also be traced in his own writing).[4] But while noting the religious ele-

---

[3]See Chen's brief autobiographical essay, "Whip and Lantern", *"Pianzi he tideng"* 鞭子和提燈, in *The Biases of Intellectuals, Zhishiren di pianzhi* 知識人的偏執, by "Xu Nancun" 許南村 (pseudonym of Chen),

Taibei: Yuanjing, 1976, pp. 19-28.

[4]*"Pianzi he tideng"*, p. 27.

ment in a few of Chen's stories, I believe it is important to dismiss the speculations of persons such as Yu Tianzong, an editor, writer, and friend, who allege that the author's incarceration was the result of the Taiwan government's failure to understand his Schweitzerian idealism.[5] Such an assertion is more likely a fantasy intended to defend Chen against charges of being "socialistic", a taboo ideology in Taiwan.

Lastly, a central formative experience of Chen's youth was his discovery, around the time he was in the sixth grade of elementary school, of a collection of writings by the irascible twentieth-century Chinese short story writer and satirist, Lu Xun. Chen does not mention Lu Xun by name, since the latter's works have long since been banned in Taiwan along with many other modern mainland Chinese writers, but there is no question whom he is referring to. As a matter of fact, students in Taiwan commonly read such proscribed mainland authors, although surreptitiously. While Chen says that he did not understand every story, his repeated reading of the collection had a dramatic impact:

> . . . this tattered volume of short stories ended up becoming my most intimate and profound instructor. It was then that I knew the poverty, ignorance and backwardness of China, and that that China was me.[6]

He was especially touched by an unnamed character whom we easily recognize to be Lu Xun's "Ah Q," a peasant buffoon and misfit whose fantasies of power and self-deception symbolize diseased Chinese society. In all probability this early reading of Lu Xun fostered in Chen the hope that literature might be light against darkness—a hope that proved to be somewhat premature if not naïve. Lu Xun himself bitterly admitted being frustrated in his aspirations for social change through literature. And in contemporary Taiwan, as is generally true elsewhere, media such as radio and television are more influential than writing, and students and intellectuals are typically more interested in material well-being than in social reform.

Chen's personal experiences of poverty and loss, his youthful exposure to the power of satire in Lu Xun, and the influence of Western literature and social and religious thought, gradually sensitized him to issues in Chinese society. And of course the seven years of forced "exile", as his imprisonment is euphemistically termed, represent a period of sobering silence and reflection. The evolution of his consciousness and of his own self-awareness is reflected in his essays or implicitly embodied in the twenty-two stories he wrote between 1959, when his first work appeared in print, and 1967, the year he published his last story before being imprisoned in 1968. In the half-dozen or so stories written after the author's release in 1975, the relation between the individual and oppressive social conditions is made more explicit. The narrative voice sometimes reminds us of the didacticism of a Theodore Dreiser or a Lao She rather than of the distant aesthetic stance of an Eileen Chang or Flannery O'Connor. Occasionally, there is a certain ideological tendentiousness which overshadows the prose as in the post-imprisonment piece

[5]Yu Tianzong 尉天驄, "*Muzha shujian*" 木柵書簡, in *Chen Yingzhen xuanji* 陳映眞選集, ed. Joseph S.M. Lau, Hong Kong: Xiaocao, 1972, p. 429.

[6]"*Pianzi he tideng*", p. 26.

ILLUSTRATIONS by children of Lo-tsu village arts and crafts programme, Taiwan, led by Father Ron Boccieri, Maryknoll priest.

entitled "White-Collar Worker". On the other hand, the consciousness which directly informs "Big Brother", another story published recently which is set in the Vietnam war era, is precisely what makes its social message enormously appealing.

In the earliest of the pre-imprisonment stories we generally encounter idealistic individuals whose aroused social consciences swiftly turn nihilistic once they find they are no match for the status quo. Towards the end of the pre-imprisonment period, the point of view is more that of the pained onlooker who has a cool view of society and whose attitude is one of sad mockery or even sarcasm. The two stories translated here, both published in 1964, fall between the poles of romantic nihilism and parody of the pre-imprisonment era. "Poor Poor Dumb Mouths" moves more clearly in the direction of skepticism and social criticism, while the tone of "A Race of Generals" is both humorous and tender.

Soon after his release from prison in 1975, Chen collected many of his short stories in two separate volumes, *My First Case* and *A Race of Generals*. Incidentally, the latter volume from which I have selected two stories for translation was proscribed in Taiwan immediately after its publication for reasons which remain obscure, but probably as a form of harrassment. At any rate, Chen wrote an introduction to both volumes under the pseudonym of "Xu Nancun", entitled "On Chen Yingzhen".[7] As a kind of apologia in disguise, the essay provides a critical account

[7]See "On Chen Yingzhen" (*Shilun Chen Ying-zhen* 試論陳映眞) by Xu Nancun, in *Jiangjun zu* 將軍族 *(A Race of Generals)*, Taibei: Yuanjing, 1975, pp. 17-30. Also in *Diyijian chashi* 第一件差事 *(My First Case)*, Taibei: Yuanjing, 1975, pp. 17-30.

of the writer by a supposedly disinterested commentator. Under the guise of a pseudonym, Chen assumes what is to my mind a somewhat affected remorseful persona and dismisses his earlier writing as being naïve. What is implied is that there will be no more depressed intellectuals, guilt-ridden romantic nihilists, and idealistic reformers who are prisoners of a short-sighted individualism. This introduction is in effect a declaration which gives Chen a fresh start as a writer after a seven-year silence, and it may also be meant to be a kind of response to those who would accuse him of writing "socialistic" fiction—the reader is informed that these earlier stories reveal the author's ingenuous belief that failure and disillusionment were simply the plight of the poor lone individual.

The protagonist in "Poor Poor Dumb Mouths" accords with a typical pre-imprisonment story pattern—he is a young lower-middle-class ("petty bourgeois") intellectual who suffers from a sentimental emotionalism and an ignorance of the connection between his sick self and a sick society. His world is a nightmare in which repressive human relations and the violence of murder and slavery are but aches and obscure memories. His release from the hospital is a rather routine and mechanical form of escape. In reality there appears to be no cure for personal and social ills. What distinguishes "Poor Poor Dumb Mouths" from earlier pieces is its belated expression of hope—the hero echoes Goethe's deathbed wish when he pleads in a dream: "Open up the window, let the sunlight come in!" The world briefly appears to brighten, but as a whole the light is faint and its presence feels somewhat forced. The individual is undone by the weight of self and a morbid fatalism, and is helplessly unable to bring about a new world or effect any change.

As a matter of fact, even prior to his incarceration in 1968, Chen's awareness of a growth in his own social consciousness led him to criticize much of what he and other writers in Taiwan had published during the 1960s.[8] To brand the writing of this period "socialistic" would probably seem critically naïve to the author, if not politically malicious, since the relation between the individual and society is left undeveloped. The change in consciousness that we do see in the pre-imprisonment short stories and essays is a gradually deepening social concern and an awareness of personal responsibility which are later most clearly articulated in Chen's post-imprisonment stories. What is more significant for our understanding of the context of the stories translated here is that in the pre-imprisonment essays there is a more direct exposition of the position of the writer in Taiwan society. Chen speaks of an orphan mentality, a feeling of exile, and an escapist attitude which must be overcome.[9] Many Taiwanese educated in Japan during the era of Japanese colonialism (1895-1945) were cut off from modern China and their own native Taiwanese roots, and this privation has left its legacy, claims the author. The separation from mainland Chinese literature of the 1930s coupled with the inundation of Western

---

[8]See Chen Yingzhen, "Modernism Rediscovered: Random Thoughts After a Performance of *Waiting for Godot*" (*Xiandai zhuyi di zai kaifa* 現代主義的再開發), in *Chen Yingzhen xuanji*, p. 20, "Preface".

[9]See "The Song of the Exile" (*Liufangzhe zhi ge*

流放者之歌), in *Chen Yingzhen xuanji*, pp. 381-390. Essay first published in *Wenxue jikan*, 1967. For the orphan theme, see Chen Yingzhen, "*Shiping Yaxiya di guer*" 試評亞細亞的孤兒, in *Taiwan wenyi* 台灣文藝, No. 58, March, 1978, pp. 245-256.

values and culture have fostered the sense that the Taiwanese writer is living in exile. In a story such as "A Race of Generals" we detect the felt need for the appreciation of native roots, both Taiwanese and mainland, a need which must be expressed in the face of an escapist mentality which the author finds prevalent among modern young Chinese intellectuals. And in both "A Race of Generals" and "Poor Poor Dumb Mouths" we find suggested something which is made more explicit in the essays—a criticism of those who have buried their capacity to care about their own people, who are embarrassed by poverty and lowliness, and whose one desire is to "go abroad". As the mental patient's student friend says in "Poor Poor Dumb Mouths", "we are all rootless people." There is a kind of "patriotism" embodied in this criticism which readily reminds us of Lu Xun—a desire to grow new shoots as well as to uproot a false consciousness.[10]

Central to the appreciation of "A Race of Generals" is our understanding that it is written in a reflective mode which provides the possibility of transcending its dominating existential ambiance. It is possible to view "A Race of Generals" as a triumph of transcendence and thus ultimately a work of comic vision, once we are sensitive to what montage and point of view call forth from us. In the story, Chen Yingzhen juxtaposes conversations with reflections, and thereby sets forth a whole series of acts of recognition between the characters so that the ending of their lives strikes us as a conversion rather than a tragedy.[11] The characters discover they are misfits—she is a teenage Taiwanese who is forced into prostitution while he is a middle-aged mainland Chinese who was formerly married. Despite age and ethnic differences, they come to share nicknames and to recognize personal idiosyncrasies —a particularly duck-like raspy voice, a way of sucking on a cigarette. In the end their bodily postures in death suggest they have become familiar with one another as persons set off from the rest of the world.

On the other hand, for the college student in "Poor Poor Dumb Mouths" who has been a mental patient for a year and a half, isolation and the concomitant inability to communicate have become conditions of human existence. He seems to find it necessary to be private, to lie back from the world, simply in order to survive mutilated inter-personal relations. For him, the distance between language and feeling is nearly absolute. He admires the bodies of Taiwanese railroad workers glistening with sweat—unconsciously translating them into art objects—but their toil is unintelligible to him. For a brief moment his isolation seems ended when in describing the disfigured body of a young prostitute he suddenly recalls Mark Antony's depiction of "sweet Caesar's wounds, poor poor dumb mouths". But he does not guess that the girl's wounds, like Caesar's, might speak of a general social malaise of which his mental disease is but a part. The fundamental disquiet he experiences leaves him feeling uneasy but unchanged. His consciousness has expanded, but his conscience is yet unformed.

Once we become aware of our own affirmation of a growth in both consciousness and conscience in "A Race of Generals", we begin to understand why we accept

[10]See "Whip and Lantern," p. 26, for Chen's allusion to Lu Xun's patriotism.

[11]The existentialist approach here follows Gabriel Marcel's terminology and philosophical reflections in *The Mystery of Being*, 2 vols., Chicago: Henry Regnery Company, 1950.

so readily the peaceful sleep of Three Corners and Little Skinny Maid. Their deaths are testimony to a mutual faith, a native belief and openness which involves a pledge to follow with all of one's being.[12] There is a dominant mode of inter-subjectivity which is altogether absent from "Poor Poor Dumb Mouths". Lastly, as we consider the element of light which illuminates "A Race of Generals" we find still another contrast. The light-against-darkness motif found throughout "Poor Poor Dumb Mouths" denotes a blindness to social ills and a fear of personal death. In the ending of "A Race of Generals", the coruscating trumpet and flashing baton symbolize an opening to joyous life. Through their mutual recognition Three Corners and Little Skinny Maid share a form of purification which leads to their final radiance in death.

If these deaths are a testimony of faith and affirmation of a certain sort, what does such witness say about the world? In the last analysis, Three Corners and Little Skinny Maid are "Generals" who share a victory. They are what Gabriel Marcel calls "persons in exile" who have lost their way and are strangers to themselves until they discover one another.[13] But what they both come to recognize is the impossibility of their relation in this life. Thus their triumphant end and peaceful sleep have an otherworldly quality. Their option for "the next life" where they agree they both will be "pure as babes" may be read as social criticism. As outsiders, we are left with the sense that there is no place in the Taiwanese world for this odd couple and that theirs is a fitting death. We are witnesses to a simple radiant faith which causes us to join in their triumph even as it separates us from their milieu. They are indeed a ludicrous pair.

Clearly, there is an intimate relation between Chen's personal experiences of hardship, his reading, and the growth of a social consciousness. The fact that he is a native Taiwanese who sees his writing as part of the Chinese literary tradition is central. He does not view himself as a regional writer and laments a separatist mentality. But he does steep himself in his Taiwanese roots and is concerned with what the English poet Gerard Manley Hopkins terms "inscape", the particular interior pattern or design of an individual thing which makes it what it is. For Chen Yingzhen as a fiction writer, the "thingness" with which he is concerned is the pattern of character which unfolds in a particular society—the atmosphere of time, place and event in Taiwan which transforms consciousness. In "Poor Poor Dumb Mouths" and "A Race of Generals", the conscience of protagonist, writer and reader begins to bud if not to flower.

---

[12]*Mystery of Being*, Vol. 2, p. 84.

[13]Richard Hayes, introduction to *Gabriel Marcel: Three Plays*, New York: Hill & Wang, 1965, p. 16.

陳映眞：將軍族

A Race of Generals

By Chen Yingzhen

SUCH GOOD WEATHER for December. To have the sun so sparkling bright and shining down on everything, especially on Burial Procession Day,[1] gave the mourners a secret delight. An alto saxophone could be faintly heard blowing the tune, "Moon Over the Barren City"—a very Japanese air. It sounded so mournful, but like the weather, there was a pleasant feeling of romance to it. Three Corners had just fixed the slide of Bean Pole's trombone, and now, pursing up his lips, he tried blowing a few notes on it towards the ground. Then he pointed it towards the street and warmly harmonized with "Moon Over the Barren City".

Suddenly he stopped. He had only played three notes. Ordinarily, his little eyes were narrow and squinting, but now they were staring wide open. He kept gazing like this along the direction of the sliding trombone at a woman.

Bean Pole stretched out his hand and took the instrument.

"OK, OK," he said. "Thanks."

There seemed to be something on Bean Pole's mind. He fixed the trombone under his arm with one hand, and with the other pulled out a crumpled cigarette which he stuck before Three Corner's eyes, nearly hitting him on the nose. The cigarette was so wrinkled it looked like a crushed earthworm. Retreating a step, Three Corners shook his head resolutely and screwed up his lips to force a smile. There wasn't much difference between this look and the puckery face he wore when he was about to blow his horn. Bean Pole lipped the cigarette and straightened it with his fingers. There was a flash of light from a struck match, then a sucking sound as he began smoking.

As Three Corners sat on a long wooden bench, his heart was palpitating strangely. Probably it

was five years since he had seen her, but he recognized her in a single glance. The woman stood in the sunlight, the weight of her body resting on her left leg, causing her rump to curve seductively leftward like the arc of a mandolin.

"So she still stands in that way," he mused to himself. "But now it's more fetching than ever."

She had stood that way before him several years ago. Then they had been in the Health and Pleasure Musical Troupe,[2] and almost every day they went all about for performances bumping along together in a huge truck.

"HEY, THREE CORNERS , how about singing a tune?" she had called, her hoarse voice rasping like a duck. He had quickly turned his head around to see her standing in that old familiar way, hugging a guitar. She was more scrawny and slight then, and in the moonlight she looked especially funny.

"It's too late! Can't be singing now."

But she kept standing there deliberately, standing in that way. He patted the sand beside him and she sat down amiably. The moonlight in the water was breaking into myriads of flashing fish scales.

"Then just tell a story!"

"Chatterbox."

"Just one story, that's all." She took off her go-aheads, then bored her bare feet into the sand like a pair of crickets.

"At sixteen or seventeen, you shouldn't be listening to stories!"

"Tell one about your home. A story about when you were in China, on the mainland." The girl lifted up her head. The moonlight spread gently over her withered little face, and made her slight undeveloped body appear all the more gawky and clumsy.

[1] The day chosen for mourners to accompany the casket of the deceased to the cemetery for burial.

[2] A popular military band of semi-professional musicians which plays at public functions and gatherings.

90

Three Corners gave his slightly thinning scalp a bit of a rub. In the past he had made up a lot of stories—stories about horse thieves, civil wars, and lynchings—ah, but none of these would do for charming a homely girl like her. What a delight it was to look at these girls of the Musical Troupe with their long hair beautifully set and their little mouths gaping as they listened trans-fixed! But aside from hearing his stories, they were always fooling around with the young male musicians. It made him so forlorn. The musicians were ever poking fun, saying,

"Hey, our Three Corners, he's nothing but a celibate saint!"[3] And he would always grin and smirk, blushing at each corner of what was most assuredly a triangular shaped face.

He took the guitar and strummed a chord. The sound clanged in the empty darkness. Far away fishermen's lights were now brightening, now fading. He felt so homesick—how could he tell a story about it?

"I'll tell a story," he sighed. "One about a monkey." It was a story which had appeared in a little Japanese children's pictorial. His older sister had told it to him while he sat just looking at the inserted colour plates. Then they were living in the northeast part of China that had been occupied by the Japanese.

"Once upon a time there was a monkey who was sold to a circus. His life was very hard and difficult. One night there was a full moon, and the monkey began longing for his dear home in the forest. He longed for his father, mother, elder brother, and elder sister . . . . "

She sat there, hugging her bent legs, weeping quietly.

"It's all in fun!" he exclaimed in a panic, his lips trembling. "What's this?"

The girl stood up, so pathetically scrawny, a bony skeleton with a dress on. After a while, her body weight gradually shifted to her left leg—in just that way.

IN JUST that way. Today, however, the woman had on a uniform—one that was just a trifle too small for her. Its deep blue colour was embroider-ed throughout with a gold pattern. She was bathed in the light of the December sun, and it softened the startling blue of the uniform. She was wearing sunglasses, and her face looked more plump and fair than in the past. Her attention was completely focused on pigeons that were flying in elliptical circles across the sky. A red flag was being waved to them.

He could have walked into the sunlight and shouted:

"Little Skinny Maid!"

And she could have used that raspy voice box of hers and called out to him. But he just sat there, watching her. In fact, she was no longer a "Little Skinny Maid". And as for himself, he sensed that he was indeed aging like an old patched drum or one of those mended brass horns that is misshapen and dolorous sounding. During those years with the Health and Pleasure Musical Troupe, he had gradually reached forty. Yet, while one year followed another, he never had had that feeling of growing old. He hadn't realized it, but long ago the men and women musicians already considered him as an "Uncle". He kept on smiling, not because he refused to concede his age. It was just that in both body and mind he had always been a Bohemian. The first time he had really begun to feel old had been that evening.

HE REMEMBERED it very clearly: at first he was alarmed by this girl who was standing there in that way and shedding tears ever so lightly. Then he felt sorry for her. But all this ended when there welled up in him a sense of his age. He realized that he had never experienced this emotion before. In that instant, his heart was transformed into the heart of an older man. Such a stirring immediately made him dignified and self-possessed. He kept assuring her,

"It's all in fun, Little Skinny Maid! What's this all about?"

There was no response. The girl made an effort to control herself, and after a while there was no more sound of sobbing. The moonlight was ex-quisite. Glowing so tranquilly over the long sandy beach, the fort, and the beamed roofs of the barracks, it caused one to wonder: what use was it for Heaven to take this beautiful moment and secretly unfold it in the depth of a night devoid

[3] The original text makes an allusion to a scholar of the Spring and Autumn period (the Confucian era), Liu-xia Hui, who was famous for his ability to withstand female temptations.

of human presence?

Three Corners looked over the guitar, then randomly plucked a few chords. Making an effort to please, he sang in a light bantering voice,

"There once was a man named Gaffer Qi,
His job was to feed young chicks with tea,
'Cluck-cluck!' went the sound,
'Pluck-pluck!' all around."

The girl couldn't help bursting out laughing. She turned her body about and, using one of her scrawny legs, lightly kicked some sand at him. Immediately she turned around again and blew her nose profusely. Before her childlike vivacity his heart was like a flower bud that bursts into full bloom with the passing of noon. He kept singing,

"There once was a man named Gaffer Qi
. . . ."

She wiped her nose, then folded her legs and sat down cross-legged before him.

"Any smokes?" she asked.

He quickly fished around in his pocket and brought out a single snow-white cigarette and lit it for her. The bright red flame from the lighter illuminated the tip of her nose. For the first time he discovered the girl had a very good one, fine and strong. He noticed it was running slightly, which made him feel cold. She inhaled deeply, lowered her head, then rested her cheek in the same hand that was grasping the cigarette. With her left hand she drew several small crooked circles in the sand.

"Three Corners. I have something to talk about," she said. "You listen." As she spoke, the smoke came curling about her lowered head and wafted upwards.

"Sure," he answered. "Sure."

"I had a good cry. I feel much better now."

"I was talking about a monkey, not about you."

"Almost."

"Eh? Are you a monkey, Little Skinny Maid?"

"Almost. The moonlight is almost the same too."

"Umm."

"Ay, ay! This moonlight. As soon as I ate dinner, I knew something was wrong," she said. "When the moon grows really big I always get homesick."

"Like me, no? And now I don't even have a home."

"I have one, so what? What good is it?"

Using her buttocks as an axis, she pivoted about in a half circle away from him. Slowly she smoked her cigarette as she faced the full golden moonlight now becoming tinged with red. A faint "sss" could be heard from the burning tobacco. She was tugging at her hair with long strokes. All at once she spoke again:

"Three Corners."

"Hey," he said. "It's very late. Don't you be dreaming and worrying about home. Of course I'm homesick too, big deal." With that he stood up. He used his sleeve to rub the evening dew off the guitar, then released the pegs one by one. The girl continued to sit. She was carefully dragging on the cigarette butt. With a shot, a fine red arc of light broke into a myriad of fiery red stars on the sand.

"I'm homesick, but at the same time I hate home!" she exclaimed. "Do you feel the same way? No, not you."

"Little Skinny Maid," he replied, lifting the body of the guitar and shouldering it like a gun. "Little Skinny Maid, what good is it to think about what's gone? If I were to be like you, always moping, moping, I wouldn't want to go on living a single day!"

The girl jumped up, knocking the sand from her clothes. She stretched and yawned broadly. Her eyes were blinking as she looked at him.

"Three Corners, you have seen a lot," she stated in a quiet voice. She paused a moment, then went on. "But what it feels like to be sold, that's something you know absolutely nothing about."

"I know," he responded fervently, his eyes opening widely. The girl gazed at his balding head, his face which truly was shaped like a triangle. She couldn't resist a smile.

"Sold just like one of our country pigs or a cow," she observed. "For six hundred dollars. I was to be his for two years." She stuck her hands in her pockets, shrugged her stiff little wooden shoulders, and turned her back to Three Corners. As ever, her body weight shifted to the left leg. She kicked at the sand lightly with her right leg, like a pony.

"When that day arrived to take me away, I didn't shed a tear. My mother was hiding in her room crying. She cried real loud, just so I could hear. But I didn't shed a tear. Nothing! Hang it!"

"Little Skinny Maid!" he said soothingly. She turned to look at him and saw how upset he was. His face was twisted all askew.

"Three Corners!" she laughed. "You think you know: you know as much as a fart!" As she spoke, she bent her head again and wiped her nose. "It's getting late. Time for bed."

They walked towards the Guest House. The moonlight cast two ludicrous silhouettes and illuminated two lone lines of footprints, trailing behind. The girl put her hand through Three Corner's elbow. She was very drowsy, and her mouth broke into an enormous yawn. He could feel her skinny little chest against his elbow, but his own breast was filled with a warmth of a different kind. As they parted, he remarked:

"If my old lady had had a baby girl after I left home, she'd probably be about your age."

The girl made a face and went trudging off towards the women's quarters. The moon was slanting downward in the eastern sky, an inordinately round sphere.

IT WAS the moment for the Drum and Gong cortege to go to work.[4] Tightly drawn brittle skin drums accompanied jolting brass gongs. The afternoon tranquility began to be disrupted. Three Corners pulled his hat lower and stood up. He saw something glittering brightly in the woman's left hand—she was clasping a flashing silver baton which she held under her right arm. The tiny brass tip of the baton gleamed as it began to move, and it made a faint sound like the whinnying of a horse. "So she is a conductor!" he thought.

A number of young female musicians also dressed in blue uniforms were assembled. They began to play the American folk song "Massa's in the Cold Cold Ground" at half tempo.[5] In the spaces between the ear-splitting sound and deafening roar of the gong and drums, the melody floated up unhurriedly. It blended with the moaning cries of filial sons and grandsons which alternately rose and fell. The mournful dirge was interwoven with sparkling sunshine, thus giving form to the human

[4] At a funeral procession there are commonly two musical groups, one Chinese and the other Western. The Drum and Gong cortege is Chinese.

[5] At Taiwanese funerals both Chinese and foreign songs are commonly played.

comedy of life and death. The men's band also assembled and, as though they were joining in the merrymaking, they began to improvise and participate. With a very imposing air, Bean Pole was slipping up and down the trombone slide and mouthing "The Chant of the Wanderer" fervently. He too retarded the tempo by half—as if any tune could serve as a requiem. As long as the tempo was slowed, any tune would be all right.

Three Corners placed his trumpet to his lips, but didn't really blow. He merely pretended that he was playing. He was watching the woman who was such a dignified conductor. The golden yellow tinsel at the tip of the baton flew and danced about following the sweep of her arm. After a while he realized there was a half beat difference between the baton and the music. It was then that he remembered Little Skinny Maid was slightly tone deaf.

YES, SHE was tone deaf. So she couldn't be a vocalist in the Health and Pleasure Musical Troupe. But she could dance very well, and was an excellent female clown. She would take a broken red-lacquered ping-pong ball and stick it on her one beauty spot—her nose, then stand on the stage platform, a skinny wooden figure. A wave of giggling would roll up from the audience. Then she would give one more deadpan wink and a greater guffaw would well up. She really couldn't sing on stage, and even off stage she seldom tried. Unfortunately, if once she started to feel good, she would sing, and for hours on end she would croak in her rasping voice. She would take a good tune and sing it in such a disjointed incoherent way that there was no melody left.

One morning Little Skinny Maid began softly singing. She sang the same song again and again with intense feeling. Three Corners was in the room next door repairing an instrument. He could not help listening to her plaintive song about their homeland.

> *"Green Island*
> *so like a boat*
> *tossed about*
> *on a moonlit night . . . . "*

She would sing it through once and stop a while, then sing it again from the beginning. The tenderness with which she sang deepened with each rendition.

"Three Corners," she called out, abruptly.

He made no answer.

She knocked lightly on the plywood wall. "Hey, Three Corners!"

"Eh?"

"My house is close to Green Island."[6]

"You're sick."

"My home is in Taidong."

He made no response.

"Mother Fuck! Not been back for so long!"

"*What* did you say?"

"I haven't gone home for many years!"

"What *else* did you say?"

Little Skinny Maid stopped for a while, then began giggling and snickering. There was a sigh, and she called again:

"Three Corners."

"Chatterbox!"

"Got any smokes?" He stood up, felt in his jacket for a cigarette, and threw one over the plywood wall to the girl. He heard the sound of a match striking. A streak of blue-black smoke wafted over from her room and disappeared out his small window.

"The man who bought me took me to Hualian,"[7] she went on, spitting a thread of smoke through her lips. "I told him, 'Smiles for sale, but not my body.' When he said that wasn't good enough, I split."

Three Corners stopped his handiwork on the horn and lay down on his bed. The ceiling leaked, and looked mildewed in places.

"So!" he exclaimed, "you're a fugitive!"

"So what!" she shouted. "You aren't going to report me to the cops, are you?"

He burst out laughing.

"I received a letter from home this morning," she went on. "It says that because I ran away, my family has to sell several plots of land in compensation."

"Oh, oh."

"It serves them right! *It serves them right!*"

---

[6] Green Island is located off the coast from Taidong, a small town on the east side of Taiwan. Little Skinny Maid's song, "Green Island Serenade", was a popular melody in Taiwan, and signifies the island of Taiwan.

[7] Hualian is another small town on the eastern seacoast of Taiwan. Little Skinny Maid is alluding to being forced into prostitution.

They both fell silent. He sat up and rubbed some rust off his hands. The trumpet that he had been repairing lay on the table. In the sunbeams from the window it glittered quietly with a silver white glow. He didn't know why, but he felt depressed. After a while, the girl spoke in a hushed voice.

"Three Corners."

He swallowed, then said quickly:

"Ay."

"Three Corners, in two days I'm going back home."

He half-closed his eyes and looked out the window. All of a sudden he opened them wide, stood up, and spoke haltingly.

"Little Skinny Maid!" He could hear her yawning resignedly. It seemed she was stretching her limbs.

"With the land," she stated, "life is already no good, but without it, it will be even worse. If they don't sell me then that will be the end of my younger sister."

He walked over to the table and picked up the trumpet. Using a corner of his shirt, he polished it until the brass became bright, gradually producing circles of red and purple light. He thought for a while, then said numbly:

"Little Skinny Maid."

"Um."

"Little Skinny Maid. Listen to me. If there was someone who loaned you money to repay the debt, wouldn't that be OK?"

She fell silent, then suddenly burst out laughing.

"Who's going to loan me the money? It's six hundred and fifty dollars! You!"

He waited for her to stop laughing.

"OK?" he asked.

"OK, OK," she said, rapping on the plywood wall. "OK! You loan me the money, and then I'll be your old lady."

He blushed a deep crimson, as though she were facing him. The girl laughed until she was gasping for breath. She pressed her hands against her stomach and leaned against the bed frame for support.

"Don't be embarrassed, Three Corners," she said. "But I know you scratched a little hole in the wooden wall so you could watch me go to bed." She exploded with laughter.

In the neighbouring room Three Corners hung his head. His ears flooded ochre-red like the colour of pig's liver.

"Little Skinny Maid," he said to himself. "You do not know me."

He could not sleep that evening. The next night, very late, he sneaked into Little Skinny Maid's room and left his bank book of seven hundred and fifty dollars beside her pillow. Then he calmly walked out of the quarters of the Health and Pleasure Musical Troupe. Once on the road he knew for certainty he had no regrets about that military retirement money, but he wasn't sure why his tears would not stop.

SEVERAL DIRGES had been played. And now the woman was again standing there in the sunlight. She gracefully removed her uniform hat, pulled a handkerchief from her rolled up sleeve, and wiped her face. She propped up her sunglasses, and with something of a disdainful air gazed about at the onlookers who were standing in a circle.

Bean Pole sidled up to Three Corners and said, teasingly:

"Hey, get a look at that conductor! What an elegant woman, eh!" Whereupon he pursed up his lips and picked his nose.

Three Corners said nothing, but did chuckle softly. Even when he smiled like this his whole face was covered with wrinkles. The woman's black hair flowed down in an ebony sheen, and at the very top of her head it was brushed into a small bun. Her face looked longer, and it brought into relief especially well her naturally fine nose.

"One grows and develops," he thought. "The other withers. And all within a mere five years!"

The air was warming up gradually. Pigeons lighted on house gables which were opposite one another. No matter how hard their owner waved his red flag, they would not fly again. They merely cocked their heads, flapped their wings, and as usual cuddled close together to roost, dumbly watching the flag. Ashes from paper funeral money curled up in burnt rolls and floated about not far above the ground.

Three Corners stood there and suddenly perceived the woman facing towards him. It was hard to tell whether she was really looking at him because of the sunglasses she was wearing. His face went pale, and his hands trembled a bit. He noticed the woman was also standing there woodenly, her lips parted. Then he saw her walking in his direction. Three Corners lowered his head and tightly gripped his trumpet.

He sensed a blue figure approaching him, pausing a moment, then standing and leaning against the wall as he was. His eyes were burning, but he kept his head bent down.

"Excuse me," the woman said, addressing him.

He would not answer.

"Is it you?" she asked. "Is it you? Three Corners, is . . . ." Her voice was choking. "It's you. It is *you*."

When he heard her sobbing he immediately felt a deep calm, just like that night on the beach.

"Little Skinny Maid," he said in a low voice. "You dumb Little Skinny Maid!"

He looked up and saw her covering her nose and mouth with a handkerchief. Seeing her hold herself back in this way, he knew that she had really grown up. She looked at him and glowed. He probably hadn't seen a smile like that for decades. The war had ended and he had returned home. His mother had smiled ecstatically then, in that way.

Suddenly there came the sound of wings beating, and the pigeons again flew up, cutting slanting elliptical circles. They both watched the birds and then fell into a silence. He paused before speaking again.

"I've been watching you wave the baton. You certainly look imposing!" She giggled. He studied her face. Beneath the sunglasses there was a small pearl-shaped tear, sparkling finely. He grinned and asked:

"So you still like to cry that way?"

"I am much better than I used to be," she replied, lowering her head.

Again they were quiet for a while, both watching the pigeons slicing elliptical circles farther and farther away.

He clasped the trumpet under his arm and said:

"Let's go. We can have a chat." They walked shoulder to shoulder past the dumbfounded Bean Pole.

"I'll be right back," said Three Corners.

"Oh," stammered Bean Pole. "Yes. Oh, yes!"

The woman walked gracefully, but Three Corners' back was hunched. They strolled out the end of a verandah, past a small stage and a row of dormitories, and then over a little stone bridge. A strip of cultivated fields greeted them. Flocks of sparrows were perched together on the power lines above. Away from the fragrance of incense and burnt paper money, they felt the air to be exceptionally fresh and brisk. A variety of crops painted the farmland fields into squares of dark and light green. They stood for a long while, neither of them saying anything. A feeling of happiness such as he had never known before flooded Three Corners' chest. Unexpectedly, the woman thrust her hand through his arm as they ambled along a path on an embankment through the fields.

"Three Corners," she said in a quiet voice.

"Hmm?"

"You've aged." He felt his half-bald bony head, then clutched it with a laugh.

"I've aged!" he agreed. "I've aged!"

"But it's only been four or five years."

"Only four or five years, yes. You're the sunrises, and I'm the sunsets!"

"Three Corners . . . ."

"Those days in the Health and Pleasure Musical Troupe, they were good times," he said. He squeezed her hand tightly underneath his arm, and with his free hand he brandished the gleaming trumpet. "After I left," he went on, "I was a vagabond. Then I understood what it feels like to be sold to another."

Suddenly they fell silent. He was vexed with himself for his impertinent remark, and his normally relaxed face grimaced. But she kept on clutching his hand. She lowered her head and watched her two feet strolling along. Some time passed before she spoke again.

"Three Corners . . . ." He hung his head dejectedly and fell silent. "Three Corners, give me a smoke," she requested. He lit a cigarette for her, and then the two of them sat down together. She took a puff and said, "I've really found you at long last." Three Corners sat there rubbing his hands, thinking about something. He lifted his head, looked at her, and then said in a hushed voice:

"Found me. Found me for what?" He was agitated. "To give me back my money, right? . . . Did I say something wrong?"

The woman stared at his anxious face through her sunglasses. All at once she impulsively removed her uniform hat and stuck it on his bald head. She scrutinized him closely and then laughed with delight.

"Don't make such a face, please!" she explained, adjusting her glasses. "It makes you look exactly like a General!"

"I shouldn't have said that. I've aged. I'm to blame."

"Don't be silly," she said. "I've found you to ask for forgiveness." Then she added, "When I saw your bank book I cried all day long. People said I had been wronged by you, so you ran away." She started to laugh. He began laughing too.

"I honestly never thought that you were a good man," she said. "At that time, you were getting older. You couldn't find anyone else. I was an ugly little thing, so easily pushed about. Three Corners, don't be angry at me for always being on the defensive then."

He blushed awkwardly. It wasn't that he had never had any desire for her. He was the same as any other man in the Health and Pleasure Musical Troupe: an independent bachelor ever fond of whores and gambling. For such a one, lust is not dependent on a pretty face.

"When I took your money and went home," the woman continued, "I expected to end this business. But they took me again to Hualian to see some big fatso of a man who drilled me with his sharp tongue. Still, his accent reminded me of you and that made me happy. 'Smiles for sale, but not my body!' I insisted. Jelly-belly giggled like crazy. They blinded me in my left eye shortly after."

Three Corners grabbed her sunglasses and saw that her left eye was shrivelled up and closed. The woman put out her hand and took back the glasses. She put them on again very calmly.

"But I don't have any resentment," she said. "A long time ago I decided that somehow I was going to go on living just to see you one more time. Returning the money wasn't the main thing —I wanted to tell you that I finally understood. I made enough money to pay them back, and, more than that," she added, "I even saved up seven hundred and fifty dollars. Finally, two months ago I joined a music group, and unexpectedly found you here."

"Little Skinny Maid!" he said.

"I said before I'd be your old lady," she said, smiling somewhat. "Too bad, I'm unclean now, so it's no good."

"How about the next life?" he suggested. "My body stinks more than yours."[8] From afar the shaking clamour of funeral music began to rise up and reverberate. He glanced at his watch—it was the moment for the mourners to accompany the Burial Procession.

"Perfect!" she exclaimed. "Let it be the next life. Then we'll both be pure as babes!"

With that they both stood up and wended their way more deeply along the embankment. Before long, he began to play the tune, "The March of the Prince", and as he did so, he goose-stepped on the path, waving from side to side. Peals of laughter came from the woman. She retrieved her uniform hat and put it on, and wielding her silver baton, she went before him, likewise goose-stepping. Young farmers and village youth waved to them in the fields and cheered. Dogs began to bark from every direction. In the slanting light of the afternoon sun, their ecstatic silhouettes disappeared down the long embankment.

THE NEXT MORNING a pair of bodies was discovered in the sugar-cane. The man and woman both wore the uniforms of band musicians. Their hands were crossed over their chests. A trumpet and a baton were laid neatly at their feet, giving off sparkling flashes of light. They looked both composed and ludicrous, but there was a kind of dignity in their absurd appearance.

After stopping to look at the corpses where they lay within a circle of onlookers, a big lanky farmer rode his bicycle on down the road. He met a squat little peasant who was shouldering buckets of liquid excrement on a pole.

"They were both laid out at attention!" he exclaimed. "So dignified and straight. Just like a pair of Generals!" With that, the two of them, the big farmer and the little peasant, laughed uproariously.

---

[8]An earlier version of the story has Three Corners say at this point: "In this life and generation, there is some force pushing us towards tragedy, shame and ruin."

陳映眞：淒慘的無言的嘴

Poor Poor Dumb Mouths

By Chen Yingzhen

AFTER CHANGING into a clean bed shirt, I forced myself to lie down flat on the bed again. Nonetheless, my heart was pounding stubbornly, the same as ever. It made me feel uneasy—after all, my sickness was not completely cured. But then I thought to myself:

"You aren't all well yet, that's all. But you'll get better, no question of that."

ONE DAY half a month ago, that young doctor—but he is balding—sought me out for a chat. It's part of regular hospital procedure. As we spoke, he was dashing everything down in sweeping strokes on a set of note cards. At the end of the session, he said:

"OK, that's it."

I stood up. He groped for a cigarette in his slightly soiled white lab-coat, thrust it in the corner of his mouth, and at the same time, put in order the card stack and locked it away. I stared at his long white filter-tipped cigarette, and began to feel disgruntled. As soon as you are admitted into the hospital, you're told: "Quit smoking." Right away I concluded this: any doctor who smokes in front of a patient who has been forbidden to smoke plainly has no integrity at all. Yet all he did was say:

"OK, that's it. That's it."

His face had a kind of pleased expression. It was a look that is seldom seen on the cold disinterested faces of the professionals around here. Just then Mr. Guo, a seminary student, entered the office. He looked as if he were already dead beat, but the moment he saw me, he broke into a smile—I won't say there was any malicious intent, but it was manifestly hypocritical. He patted my shoulder as though he were coaxing a child. In times like that all I can manage is a benign smile. The doctor stood watching us with his hands stuck in his lab-coat pockets. With that I walked out.

He'd consistently been one to think he was right, just like most young doctors.

I hadn't gone but a few steps out of the office when I heard the doctor saying to Mr. Guo, in Japanese:[1]

"That guy—it's obvious *he's* getting better."

I stood there dumbly for a few seconds. After a while I realized I simply wasn't up to attending my afternoon piano lesson, so I returned to my room to lie down for a rest. For the first time I figured out that I had already been in this mental hospital for a year and a half.

Not long after this conversation with the doctor, I was actually granted permission to take afternoon walks outside the hospital.

I SAT UP in bed and smoothed out the wrinkles in my clothes, then stuck my hair into place with my fingers and walked to the duty desk. I didn't expect Miss Gao to be there. She was sitting reading a very fat Japanese magazine. I stood in the doorway looking from a distance at magazine's illustrations. She raised her head. Our glances met one another in our images reflected in the glass window. I flashed a smile. She, however, clearly did not. It was a bit awkward having to wipe off my grin. She is a stout person, no beauty it's true, but she is not an ugly woman either. She tore out a pass and filled it in.

"For how long?" she asked.

"The usual, eh? Same as always."

[1] A few select Taiwanese were trained in Japanese medical schools when Taiwan was under Japanese control (1895-1945), and many Taiwanese studied in Japan after World War II. Japanese language ability is a vestige of Japanese domination (when all public school instruction was in Japanese), and is sometimes a mark of superior education.

"Be back at 5:00."

"Uh-huh."

As she was fixing the seal to the pass, I spotted a car coming through the big gate of the hospital. Miss Gao laid the pass on the corner of her desk.

"Miss Gao," I addressed her. She turned her head and gazed at me. I gave her another smile. "Here's a patient."

She opened the window. A man was being carried in who was shaking all over. His family trailed behind bringing bedding, a wash basin, and a hot water bottle.[2] The scene made me sick, but Miss Gao just put on her uniform cloak indolently, affixed a marker at the page she was reading, and shut her magazine. She leaned back against the wall and turned to me:

"What are you doing still hanging around?"

As she was putting her magazine in a drawer I walked out. The sun was shining on the hospital's little stretch of lawn. A hired car blocked the main gate and two children were sitting in the shade of the car. They looked like they belonged to the new patient's family. Seeing those guileless unhappy faces, I hastily elected to leave by the back gate.

A south wind was blowing over the rich glossy green of the rice paddies. I followed along the high wall of the hospital thinking of Nurse Gao's taciturn facial expression.

"What are you doing still hanging around?" she had said, wrinkling her brow.

I know just how she was thinking: "How come you're still here? I've got a new patient, right? I must get busy!" I wouldn't say she was acting phoney, but I'll not forget an incident that happened over seven months ago, that would be sometime in March probably. It was one of those evenings when I'd be alternately lucid and incoherent. I don't know why, but I was all alone in my room and I started crying. Nurse Gao happened to pass by—a coincidence, I guess. She opened the door and came in, but as soon as she did I stopped crying. It seems to me a man suffers a great loss of face if he weeps in front of a woman. She asked all sorts of questions, but I wouldn't pay any heed to her. I think she wanted to leave yet she stood there a while. Suddenly she

was drying my tears with her handkerchief. She kept drying my cheeks, and I heard her say:

"You're a big boy in college now—what are you doing crying?"

Her voice sounded weak, nervous, and somewhat hoarse. I lay there very quietly, not making a sound. I don't know when it was exactly, but I became aware that in place of the handkerchief there were the steady movements of a hand as soft as cotton lightly massaging my cheeks.

For a long time after this I have had a complex about Miss Gao. It is a mixed bag of nervous fear and familiarity. In the daytime, for instance, she is really good at looking as though nothing has happened, just like that moment at the duty desk. I would insist that this is a kind of shameful hypocrisy. But it is just as the doctor says: whether people are normal or abnormal, everybody has two or even several faces. Sometimes perhaps it would be better stated: the person who is able to balance his life wearing a variety of different faces may be called "normal".

But I'll never forget that soft hand continuously stroking my face, and all the more so since I have been studying piano with Nurse Gao in the hospital, and it is one and the same hand that practises the piano so well.

"You dummy!" she often explodes, while I gaze silently at her flashing eyes. It is only then that there is something about her that would be called beautiful. She will play three or four measures for me enthusiastically. Yet admittedly I really am a "dummy" at playing the piano, though I have a good ear. Once I heard her play a bit of the first part of Tchaikovsky's "Meditation". Encore! Encore! It was simply magnificent. Yet that Mr. Guo in his ignorance disdains her potential talent. One time I almost had a fight with him about it. He also plays, but without the finished style that comes from training and discipline.

AS I LEFT the hospital grounds I decided to visit Mr. Guo at the little Christian Mission Centre where he was living during his internship as a theology student. I remember one occasion when I asked him the following question:

"From the viewpoint of theology, what is mental sickness?"

"Ah, ah," he said.

---

[2]Such items are considered personal and are brought to the hospital by relatives.

With that his whole being sank into a profound meditation. He worked hard explicating the difference between mental illness and spirit possession.

"If I didn't have personal experience of this myself," he said, "it would be difficult for an intellectual like me to mention it." Thereupon he began to narrate his "personal experience".

He said once he went with his teacher to see a country doctor who was possessed. As soon as they entered the latter's door, the evil spirit spoke using the doctor as a mouthpiece.

"Reverend, this is a personal grudge. There is no use in your concerning yourself. If you insist, I'll lay bare your deepest secrets, as well as those of others of your type, before a host of people."

The doctor underwent this ordeal until the day he died. According to Mr. Guo, the whole affair was a matter of sin. The evil spirit was reputed to have been a man the doctor had killed in order to run off with his wife. This adulterous woman who became the doctor's wife ended up a suicide.

And so on and so forth.

Surprisingly, I was spellbound by this story. I've always been one with a yen for mysticism, so that's how Mr. Guo and I became intimate.

MR. GUO came out to open his door scantily clad in rather grubby underwear. This was the first time I had seen his physique. He was quite well built. We are about the same age, but in comparison to me he is very hairy.

As I entered his room, I noticed a record revolving on the turntable with some chorus singing an American folksong. I thumbed through his bookshelf and took down a volume, flipping through it casually, and waited for him to speak. He has always been the first to open his mouth. Though I kept turning pages for a long while, he did not say anything.

I looked him over. He seemed to be just sitting there, wrapped up in the music.

"There's another patient in the hospital," I said. He looked at me, as though in a daze.

"What?" he mumbled.

I spoke louder:

"Another patient has been admitted to our hospital."

He nodded, then abruptly shut off the phonograph. In an instant, the room fell silent. I could hear water dripping faintly.

"You didn't turn off the faucet?" I asked.

"It's broken!" he said, smiling.

Our conversation ground to a halt. After a while I laid the book down on the desk and said:

"That person was trembling and jerking all over. I didn't know there were so many kinds of mental illness."

Mr. Guo said nothing, but poured me some tea.

"Thanks," I said.

"How the way of the world is changing!" he exclaimed.

"It seems God has abandoned the world," I commented. "It is so chaotic and disordered."

He puzzled over this a while. Again there was silence between us. Whenever in an argument, he always ends up retreating to the defense and valiantly adopting the position of a student of theology.

"That's not accurate either," he offered hesitantly. "It's what it says in the Bible: at the end of the world there will be revolutions, endless natural calamities, wars, massacres, and strange diseases . . . . And mental illness is one of the 'strange diseases.' "

I thought of those patients with minor conditions who sit out on the lawn in the afternoon sun. Every face pale and wan, every pair of eyes a passive expression of helplessness, all of them smothering a chill bitterness. Often these sad faces will smile mischievously, causing you to start. It is as though someone were penetrating into your deepest recesses.

"Sin," I remarked casually, "the offspring of the poisonous snake!"

He paid no regard to my ridicule. He was being quite deliberate about turning on the phonograph and setting the volume low.

"I've thought it through," he went on. "It's like you said. The majority of the mentally ill are victims who are crushed and ground up by society. But Christianity cannot help but perceive human sin in the very midst of social oppression."

I noticed he lowered those honest eyes of his. It seemed he was really making an effort to protect the principles he relied on for his words and actions, but he himself had long since lost hope for the New Jerusalem. And where is my Jerusalem? All that remains is that fated grand calamity, the End of the World.

The conversation made us pensive. Though the source of depression in each was not identical, it had the same character.

At that moment my glance happened to light upon a white card beside my tea cup. I picked it up and realized it was a photograph. It was an old picture of a female student. I felt anxious lest he be angry, and I immediately put it back where it was. But he thrust out his hand and took it. He looked at the photograph and all of a sudden an awkward shyness caused him to blush around the eyes.

"Your sweetheart?" I asked.

"Probably it was stuck in that book you had and fell out."

"Probably so," I said. He merely smiled and put the photo in an English-language dictionary which was close at hand.

"Boy, that was a long time ago," he said finally.

Apparently, there was some scar in this. Suddenly I felt remorseful, so I made an offhand remark:

"Romantic attachments have never gone very smoothly for me."

He looked at me directly and turned off the phonograph. His neat tidy face was gradually suffused with empathy.

I began to panic and throw together a very unsatisfactory story about some love affair.

"And later on?" he asked solemnly.

"Later on?" I repeated, feigning a long face. "Later on the girl became sick and died. Before she died she said she still hated me."

"But I believe she actually loved you," he said ardently.

Mr. Guo began to talk about women himself. He considered himself quite a big man, one who had gotten all sorts of women to fall for him. I was really surprised. This proved he was even worse than those single men who brag about their exploits.

He proceeded to talk about Miss Gao. "I just thought we shared an interest in music. I certainly did not expect that one day I would receive a passionate note from her."

"Eh!" I exclaimed.

"You'd never think she was that kind of a woman," he said with a self-complacent air. "And she's older than us."

I loathed his mention of "us". Of course I didn't believe anything he said from the start, but I began to feel bored and vexed by him. Maybe from jealousy.

All of a sudden, he asked:

"Have you ever touched a woman?"

It took me a little while to get what he meant.

"Umm," I said.

"Eh?" he inquired.

"Once a woman felt my face."

He was perplexed for a moment, then burst out laughing. I stood up and said I had to go.

"I won't see you off," he said.[3]

I left his room, again hearing the dripping of the leaky faucet. I felt somewhat disconsolate.

Just opposite the Christian Mission Centre lay this wearisome little town's street, the same as always. As I walked along I kept telling myself:

"Eighty percent of what Mr. Guo said is bunk. Men of his ilk are always like that."

Then I remembered a fellow student at the university who was nick-named "Baby Ox". He was one of those students who got into college through the "Minority Peoples" quota system. He was a little like Mr. Guo. Much to people's disgust, Baby Ox was always venting his shallow male chauvinism. So the Miss Gao affair had to be just as phony. Of course I thought about it this way: "Whether real or not, it's of no consequence to me, especially since I'll soon be completely well and able to get out of here."

I was really hopeful I could make it to Taibei[4] and see off a good classmate of mine, Yu Jizhong, who was going abroad. Yu had come to see me four times, and he was very diligent about writing. He had a head full of nothing but "the American way of life". What he often said was:

"It's always good to leave. A new sky, a new earth. Nothing can be the same."

I never commented one way or the other, but I remember asking him casually:

"Isn't that just floating? Or even plain exile?"

Suddenly he looked me straight in the eye. His handsome countenance was that of a man set on going abroad.

"You're not just floating too?" he asked,

[3] A common polite expression when friends part.

[4] The capital of Taiwan and site of several universities and colleges.

incredulously. He laughed. "We are all rootless people."

I can recall how low I felt at that time. Still, I did not oppose his way of thinking. Partly because we were good friends, but also it seemed there was nothing untrue about what he said. Wasn't my very dejection witness to its accuracy? I didn't know then that Yu's statement, "It's always good to leave", would be such a source of refreshing joy to me now.

And I am going to leave here too. The doctor said so himself. Too bad for him and the rest of them that they always assume I don't know Japanese. It was an elective at college. People like them are so fond of speaking a foreign language—it's enough to show they don't have roots either. But the fact that I do not harbour any resentment towards them for liking foreign languages proves I'm really a rootless person myself. What Yu Jizhong said was not all wrong.

SINCE IT was not to be long before my release, I wanted to have a look at some sugar-cane fields nearby. In the past, I'd always gone to the right at the railway crossing and followed along the sugar factory's narrow gauge railway so as to watch the workmen at the warehouse there.

Always there are just about ten men. On their feet they wear things that are made out of rubber tires. What I love most are those sandal-like shoes. Each pair is matched by well-built muscular legs. They really make me think of Roman soldiers. I was once nearly an art student and accordingly have a great predilection for the workers' beautiful legs and bodies. They are so rich in form, and they look as though they are carved by their sweat. To see these ten or so men in the brilliant full sunlight put their shoulders to a fully loaded boxcar and push it slowly forward—this really is a moving sight.

Often in my letters to Yu Jizhong I write an uninhibited description of this scene, and tell him that this is excellent material from everyday life for a sculpture relief. But he is ever cold and insensitive. What a pity it is he does not understand art.

Besides watching the labourers at work, I would also see them gnawing on sugar-cane in a boxcar, or two or three of them squatting playing chess. Such a pleasant sight. Regrettably, I don't understand their dialect. Besides I would have on the kind of distinctive hospital garb that people here could recognize easily, so ordinarily I just watched them from afar.

But today I decided not to go over to the warehouse area. When I reached the railway crossing, I walked to the left. As I looked up along the narrow-gauge rails of the little railway, I became aware of the openness of a strip of sugar-cane field far in the distance which lay between the rails and was set in relief by them. The scene was so enchanting that I stepped out along the railway ties. There was a bit of the child in me yet.

I hadn't gone very far when I discovered that today there appeared to be a lot of people walking along the railway, and moreover they were all passing me as they walked towards the warehouse. I asked what was going on and was told that someone had been murdered.

I turned around and went back stepping along the railway ties. And of course I walked very quickly, really it was almost a run. But the ties weren't evenly distributed, so it was awkward going. In fact, it turned out that there really was a large number of people gathered at the side of the warehouse. There was noise and bustling all about. A murder is something you often hear about, but I had never seen one with my own eyes.

The emaciated yet well developed corpse of a young girl lay stiffly on the ground, her face in the mud. Her skirt and top had been cut open by the police investigators, and her back looked the waxen colour of dead flesh. To the right of her spine and separated quite distinctly from each other were three gashes, black with congealed blood. The blood from one of these had stained the strap of her brassiere a tangerine red.

An inspector, wearing a sportshirt, inserted a delicate dissecting knife into the mouth of the stab wounds.

"Tsk-tsk, look at that!" an old woman exclaimed among the onlookers.

"Used a chisel," said a man. "Attacked her from the back. Hack, hack, hack. Three of them." The late arrivals listened attentively.

A police sergeant waved his hand, stopping several children in the circle of onlookers from flocking about the dead body. The sun was already slanting to the west, illuminating the warehouse well with a faint blush of red.

People crowded together, their stares cold and indifferent, as though they were gazing at the dis-

memberment of livestock. The Inspector thrust in the dissecting knife as deeply as possible, turned it to the left and right, and then withdrew it. He used a ruler to gauge the depth. To the side an assistant marked down numbers and notations on the profile of a body outlined on a sheet.

"The killer?" somebody asked.

"Ran off. Over towards the sugar-cane fields."

I overheard someone say the girl was a fledgling prostitute who had been attempting to run away. She'd been killed by the person who sold her.

The inspector stood up and began to turn over the body to check the front. The crowd could see now many more little spots of congealed blood. At first glance, it looked as if some flies had settled lightly on her body. But actually every black spot was a chisel hole.

When the bra was scissored open, a pair of stiff little breasts were exposed. In one breast there was a small chisel hole that was very clean. There wasn't even any fluid or blood in it. Her face looked thin, and from the corner of her mouth saliva hung mixed with blood. One could not tell whether her face was attractive or ugly. It was covered with the pallor of death. Her hair was soaked in mud and of course excessively filthy.

At first all the men were busily engaged in speculating and talking. But with the exposure of a naked body like hers, they fell into a wondrous silence and the women who normally love to ask questions also shut their mouths.

I squeezed my way through the crowd. Maybe it was because I felt it was time to get back to the hospital, not to mention the fact that I had not brought a watch. For a while I was in a stupor, wandering aimlessly along toward the hospital. This was the very first time in my life I had seen the naked body of a woman. I thought of that pair of little breasts. My impression was that they were a little like yesterday's steamed dumplings, dried by the wind. But what gave me the most anxiety was that head of filthy hair.

Back at the hospital I saw the doctor at the entrance gate chatting with the family of the new patient who had been admitted that afternoon. Because they and their car were blocking the main gate, I just stood to one side looking at the children who were now sitting in the car. The youngest little boy was asleep with his head aslant.

Immediately, I began to feel upset.

The doctor saw me standing there and stood well aside for me to get by. As I squeezed through their midst I overheard the doctor saying to the family:

"Let's give it a try, OK? We'll keep in contact."

I walked slowly across the grass; the weather felt a little cooler. All of a sudden I recalled Mark Antony's speech in *Julius Caesar*:

"I . . . .

Show you sweet Caesar's wounds, poor poor dumb mouths,

And bid them speak for me."

Act three, scene two, I think. I had it in an exam once. I remember our Shakespeare professor, Father Huang, reciting the original scene aloud in his exquisite English. The iambic cadence was melodic, like the harmonious song of a pipe organ. I really delighted in that experience. But it is not until now that I realize how cruel and gloomy the literary work of a great talent is which makes an analogy between human mouths and mortal stab wounds on a body, wounds of congealed blood.

THE NEXT DAY happened to be again the time for my routine check-up and diagnosis.

"I think you can probably be released now," said the doctor.

"Oh," I replied.

He looked at me. After a while, he asked: "Don't you feel happy?"

"Uh. Uh-huh. Of course I'm happy," I said. The doctor began to smile slightly. I don't know why, but I blurted out impulsively:

"Yesterday I had a dream, a very entertaining dream."

"Eh?"

"I suppose it was kind of boring really, not worth mentioning."

"Go ahead and describe it, let's see."

"I dreamt I was in a dark room. There wasn't a ray of light. Mildew had been growing there for a long time and was covering everything."

The doctor tore off a sheet of wrapping paper, and began writing in sweeping strokes. I felt some anxiety creeping up. Actually, I couldn't remember for sure whether I really had had a dream. But I kept speaking.

"A girl was lying down in front of me. There were mouths all over her body. Many of them."

"Many what?"

"Many *mouths*." I pointed to my mouth. "Lips," I said.

The doctor stared at me, wrinkled his brow, and said:

"And then?"

"The mouths talked. And what did they say? 'Open up the window, let the sunlight come in!' "

The doctor was listening very conscientiously. Seldom was he that way. Generally I'm of the opinion that egocentric people hardly ever listen to what others are saying. His way of inclining his head to listen carefully made his face look rather intelligent. Because he was paying attention I went on.

"Have you heard of 'Ge-de'?"

"What?"

I stuck out my hand and he handed me another sheet of paper. I used the quill pen on the table and wrote out the name of 'Ge-de' in full. He read the name in German:

"Johann Wolfgang von Goethe."

"It's what he said when he was dying: 'Open up the window, let the sunlight in!' "

"Oh, oh!" said the doctor.

"After that there was a Roman soldier. He took a sword and split open the darkness, and the sunlight shot in like the shaft of a golden arrow. All the mildew faded away; the toads, the leeches, the bats dried and shrivelled up. And I too dried up and withered away."

I was grinning, but the doctor was not. He pondered for a while, then carefully took the piece of paper and stuck it in the stack of file cards. He glanced up and looked at me. His eyes had a look of hidden pity. I stood up.

"In fact it is a very entertaining dream," he commented.

NONETHELESS, after a week I was released from the hospital in the best of health. As I left, I asked again about the meaning of my dream, and the doctor answered:

"You are no longer a sick person now, so as far as I'm concerned, your dreams have no meaning."

We looked at one another and laughed. But I have never been able to remember clearly whether I really had a nightmare or not.

Two Stories by Xi Xi

Introducing Xi Xi

ZHANG YAN 張彥 herself denies any deliberate reference to direction in her pen-name Xi Xi 西西 (literally West West). At the same time she insists that it is formed along quite different lines from proper names like Mississippi 密西西比, Sicily 西西里 or St. Francis of Assisi 聖法蘭西斯‧阿西西. It is a graphic representation of a young girl in a skirt, her legs spread within a chalked frame, playing a game called 造房子, Building a House, popular among young Chinese girls to this day.

She was born in Shanghai into a family originally from Guangdong province, and came with her family to Hong Kong in 1950 to complete her secondary school education. She then received her training as a school teacher at Grantham College of Education. After graduation, she was a primary school teacher for 20 years, then, after a four year gap, returned to teaching. There is a streak of childish delight observable in some of her stories and a spontaneous, childlike enjoyment of life in some of her characters. In *My City* 我城, 1979, the hero of the novel is a young apprentice in a telephone company; he looks at everything with wonder and awe, and his subjection to a physical examination, of which he completely fails to understand the significance, is quite hilarious.

But Xi Xi has never deliberately written for children, and her expressions of childish delight are often restrained. Her style can best be described as sophisticated, a sophistication masked by a deliberate and deceptive simplicity. Her first attempt at serious writing was "Maria", a short story published in 1965 in the *Student Weekly* 學生週報. It describes the harrowing experience, during the Congo war of "liberation", of a Belgian nun, who tries to give water to a captured French mercenary on the point of death. She leads him to a stream and he almost reaches it, only to be shot seven times from behind by the African "leopards". It is extraordinary that a young Chinese school teacher should have begun her writing career with such an outlandish subject, one which was quite beyond the confines of her own personal experience. The story won acclaim from the critics, and her writings from then on have showed a versatility in dealing with a variety of themes from different points of view, and a determination to avoid repeating herself. She writes creditable *baihua*, and has succeeded in overcoming the influence of the local Cantonese dialect, which has hampered most young writers educated and brought up in Hong Kong. But she differs from Eileen Chang and Bai Xianyong, in that she does not set out to be a deliberate stylist. Stylistic perfection, of course, attracts imitation. But the stylist either tends to become stereotyped, or disappoints his loyal following by adopting a new approach. Xi Xi has no such qualms. The form and language of her stories are tailored to fit the subject matter.

The unique quality of her writing may in part be explained by the unique nature of the Hong Kong environment. A free port and international commercial centre, it paid no attention to "culture" until the late sixties. A few early and valiant attempts to publish literary journals failed. Eventually small groups of writers got together and managed to put out publications, financed, written, edited and even distributed by themselves. Such groups have been steadily growing in numbers over the years. Xi Xi once edited a magazine called *The Thumb* 大姆指, and now belongs to the Su Ye 素葉 group, which has a bi-monthly magazine and publishes its own series of books. This sort of thing is quite common in cosmopolitan cities. But Hong Kong possesses two distinct advantages. Hong Kong is relatively free from the obsessive influence of the May 4th Movement, and because of its two-stream educational system and the preference given to the English language it is not unduly preoccupied with the Chinese "identity crisis" and the search for "roots". It is entirely up to the individual writer what attitude he wishes to adopt towards the main stream of the Chinese tradition. And Hong Kong is in a better position to assimilate international cultural trends. Interestingly, the younger writers and artists are much more sympathetic to writers outside the English language. According to Xi Xi, the works that have had the greatest impact on her are fairy tales, European and Japanese films and Latin American and European writers. It does not follow that she rejects the Chinese tradition. On the contrary, she is essentially a Chinese writer. But she is more cosmopolitan than insular in her outlook. Her second novel *Deer Hunt* 哨鹿 is an historical account of Emperor Qianlong's 乾隆 deer hunt in Inner Mongolia, a juxtaposition of historical fact and fictional fantasy, demonstrating her ability to combine past and present through creative imagination. She has also published a volume of verse, while her latest publication *Cross Currents* 交河 is a collection of essays and short stories.

S.C.S.

西西：像我這樣的一個女子

A Girl Like Me

By Xi Xi

Translated by Rachel May and Zhu Zhiyu

IT REALLY ISN'T right for a girl like me to have any love affairs. Which only makes it all the more surprising that such a strong attachment should have developed between Xia and me. I think it must be entirely the cruel hand of Fate that has landed me in this situation from which I cannot extricate myself. And I am powerless to fight against Fate. They say that when you really like a man, you can sit in a quiet corner just looking at him, and one little smile from him, even a very casual sort of smile, can make your spirit soar. That is exactly how I feel about Xia. So when he asks me—Do you like me?—I can tell him what I feel without holding back. You see, I am not a girl who knows how to protect herself, and the things I do and say are forever making me the laughing-stock of other people. You might think I look very happy when I am sitting with Xia in a café; but inside, my heart is heavy with silent grief. Inside I am really extremely unhappy, because of my premonition of where Fate is leading me. And I only have myself to blame. Right at the beginning, I never should have agreed to go with Xia to visit that school friend I hadn't seen for a long time; and then afterwards, I never should have accepted that first of many invitations to go to the cinema with him. Well, it's too late for regrets now. But the fact of the matter is that whether I do have regrets or not, I am no longer as worried as I was by the thought of our coming separation. Soon, everything will be over—for I have agreed to take Xia to the place where I work, and right now I am sitting in a corner of the café waiting for him.

I'd already left school long before the time when Xia and I started getting involved with each other; so when he asked me whether I had a job, I told him that I'd already been working for several years.

—So, what do you do?
He asked.
—Make-up. I make people up.
I answered.
—Oh, you do make-up.
He said.
—But your own face looks so beautifully natural.
He said.

He said he didn't like it when women wore make-up, he much preferred them to look natural. I don't think it was this conversation which drew his attention to the fact that I don't use make-up, but rather the uncommon paleness of my face. And of my hands. It was because of my work that my hands and face looked paler than those of other people.

I knew that Xia had got totally the wrong end of the stick about what sort of work I did, just like every friend I'd ever had always did. He must have imagined me at work, beautifying the faces of ordinary ladies, or embellishing brides in readiness for their wedding day; and he can only have felt even more certain that he was right when I told him that I had no regular holidays in my work, and that I was often busy on Sundays. After all, there are always so many brides on Sundays, or on holidays.

But making up brides is not what I do. What I do is to give a final embellishment to those who no longer have life; I make them up so that they will look peaceful and soft when they depart this world. In the old days I used to tell my friends exactly what I *did* do for a living; as soon as I thought they had jumped to the wrong conclusion, I would put them straight because I wanted to let them know what kind of person I was. But this honesty had cost me most of my friendships. It was me they were afraid of—as if I, sitting with them over a cup of coffee, was the embodiment of every dreadful spectre in their minds. I don't blame them for reacting like this—because after all, we are each of us born with a primitive fear of the mysterious and of the unknown. And so I had answered Xia without offering any explanation. There were two reasons for this: firstly, I didn't want him to be frightened—I felt that I would never be able to forgive myself if I ever again upset one of my friends by disclosing the macabre details of my employment; and secondly, I'd always been bad at putting things into words, and little by little I was getting used to keeping things to myself.

   —But your own face looks so beautifully natural.
   He said.

When Xia said this, I was acutely aware that it boded ill for our future together. And Xia?—he was perfectly happy, happy to be with a woman who didn't make herself up. His heart was light, but mine was heavy with sadness. I'm always wondering who in this world will do my make-up for me, at my end. Aunt Yifen? But Aunt Yifen and I are the same, and we both feel very strongly that we never want to do make-up for our nearest and dearest as long as we live.

I can't think why I carried on going around with Xia so much of the time, even after that bad omen cast its shadow. Perhaps I am only human after all, unable to control myself, marching left right, left right, in the footsteps of Fate. I really cannot come up with a rational explanation for anything I've done, and then I think to myself . . . well, isn't that only human nature, to be irrational? Much of human behaviour *is* inexplicable, even to the person who is acting in that way.

   —Can I see where you work?
   Xia asked.
   —I can't see why not.
   I said.
   —Will anyone mind?
   He asked.
   —No, I don't suppose anyone will.
   I said.

The reason why Xia wanted to come with me to work was because I had to go there every Sunday morning, when *he* had nothing in particular to do. First he said he'd just like to accompany me there; but then he thought that since he

would have gone all the way there anyway, why not go in and have a look around. He said he wanted to feel the excitement of the brides and bridesmaids, and he wanted to see how I made them as beautiful as roses, or how their natural beauty was spoilt by the make-up . . . whichever! I agreed without a moment's thought. I knew that Fate had brought me this far, to the starting-line, and that it was something I had to go through with. So, right now I am sitting in a small café, waiting for Xia to come; and then we shall go to the place where I work.

And when we get there, everything will become clear to him. Xia will realize that the fragrance he has taken all along to be a perfume that I wear especially for him, is actually nothing more than the smell of antiseptic which clings to my skin; he will also realize that the reason I always wear white clothes is not because I am deliberately trying to cultivate an air of innocence, but because these clothes afford me a measure of convenience in entering and leaving my place of work. The smell of that strange lotion not only clings to my skin, but must also have worked its way through to my bones by now—I tried everything I could think of to wash away that smell, but I never managed to get rid of it, and finally I gave up trying. I don't even notice it any more. Of course, Xia doesn't know anything about all this. He once said to me: What an unusual perfume you are wearing! Soon everything will be out in the open.

You know, I'm something of a hairdresser and I can do a stylish cut; and I am also an expert hand at doing up a tie. But where does it get me? Look at my hands. Just think of all the times they have trimmed the hair and beards of silent customers, and tied up ties around stiff and solemn necks. Could Xia stand it if this same pair of hands were to cut his hair, or knot his tie for him? These hands are really warm, but they seem icy cold to others. These hands should be quite at home cradling a new-born baby; but other people look at them as though they had turned into white bones, to hold and soothe skeletons.

THERE ARE PERHAPS many reasons why Aunt Yifen decided to pass on her skill to me. And from the kind of things she says, people would see it all very clearly: of course, with a skill such as this, a person really wouldn't *ever* have to worry about being out of a job, and the pay is pretty good too! How could a girl like me, with little formal schooling and a limited intellect, possibly hope to compete with others in this human jungle where the weak are the prey of the strong.

I think the reason why Aunt Yifen imparted the valuable secrets of her unique skill to *me* was purely and simply because I am her niece. She never allowed any visitors when she was working, and it was only after she took me on as her apprentice that she let me follow her around, learning from her little by little; and I didn't feel afraid, even when I was standing in front of those naked and cold corpses. And I even learned how to take the crushed or shattered bits and pieces of a human body, or the fragments of a fractured skull, and fit them together and sew them up, as though I were only a wardrobe mistress making up a costume.

I lost both my parents when I was a child, so I was brought up by Aunt Yifen. What has happened is that gradually, over the years, I have grown strangely like my aunt, and have even assimilated her reticence, her pale face and hands, and her slow way of walking. In every way I have grown more and more like her. Sometimes I can't help wondering who I really am—maybe I am a carbon copy; maybe the two of us are really one and the same person; maybe I am only an extension of my aunt.

—From now on, you won't need to worry about food or clothing.
      Said Aunt Yifen.
—You also won't have to be dependent on someone else for your keep, like other women are.
      She said.

Actually, I didn't know what she meant by this. I didn't see what was so special about learning her particular skill—surely there were plenty of other occupations that could provide for me just as well, where I wouldn't have to worry about food and clothes, and where I wouldn't have to depend upon someone else to support me, the way other women had to. But I was so very ignorant of the world, and definitely not equipped to compete with other women—and that's why Aunt Yifen thought to help me by passing on to me her special skill; she had only my best interests at heart. And if you think about it, what single person in this

whole city can do without our help?—it doesn't make any difference whether he is rich or poor, a beggar or a king; when Fate delivers him into our hands, we shall be his last source of comfort, and we shall make him look peaceful and calm, and soft beyond compare. Aunt Yifen and I both have wishes of our own; but quite apart from these, there is one wish that we have in common, which is that never, as long as we live, do we want to do make-up for our nearest and dearest.

That's why I felt so sad last week. I'd already heard a little about this tragic thing that had happened, and then I discovered that it was my younger brother who was involved. As far as I understood the situation, my little brother had been in love with a girl who was not only attractive and nice-natured, but also very talented—they were so happy together that I thought they must be meant for each other. Despite all of this, however, their happiness proved to be very short-lived, and it was not long before I heard that she had got married to a man she didn't love, goodness only knows why. What sense does it make when two people who love each other cannot get married, but must instead spend the rest of their lives suffering, pining for each other. My little brother is a changed person, and not so long ago I heard him say: I might as well be dead!

I don't know what to think. Surely it's not possible that I shall have to make up my little brother?

—I might as well be dead!
      My little brother said.

I simply don't understand why things have turned out like this, and neither does my little brother. Supposing she had said: I don't love you any more. Well, there wouldn't have been much my little brother could have done about it. But they do love each other, and it was not because anyone owed anyone a favour or needed the money that she married this other man. Surely in this day and age, there are not still young ladies who are being forced by their parents to marry against their will? Why should she have surrendered her whole life to Fate in this way? Ah, let us hope that we never have to do make-up for our nearest and dearest, as long as we live.

But who can look into the future? When Aunt Yifen informed me of her decision to teach me her highly unusual skill, she said to me: You must promise me one thing before I take you on as my apprentice. I couldn't think why Aunt Yifen was being so serious, but she carried on in a solemn voice: When my time comes, you must make me up all by yourself; don't let anyone else touch me. I didn't think it would be a difficult promise to keep, I only wondered why Aunt Yifen was being so insistent. I myself feel quite differently about it —for I can't see what difference it makes *what* happens to my body after I am gone. Still, it was the one hope that Aunt Yifen cherished above all others, and I felt that provided I was still alive when that day came, I must do whatever I could to ensure that her hope was realized. Aunt Yifen and I are the same as we make our long journey through life in that we don't have 'great expectations'—Aunt Yifen's hope is that I shall be the person who does her make-up for her at her end; and mine is that I shall be able to put my skill towards creating a 'sleeping beauty', a corpse more peaceful and calm and soft than all the others, just to make it seem as though death is really no more than the deepest and best of sleeps after all. Whether I ever actually manage to do this or not, it is only a game I play when I am feeling bored with life and I'm trying to kill time. And anyway, any effort I make is bound to be in vain . . . for isn't everything in the world devoid of meaning?

Supposing I ever *do* create my 'sleeping beauty', can I hope to be rewarded?—the dead themselves know nothing, and none of their relatives ever realize just how much mental and physical energy I expend on my work; and I shall never be able to hold an exhibition and let the general public appreciate the quality and the innovative skill of my work as a make-up artist; and it is even less likely that anyone will ever write a review or a comparative study, or do research, or hold a seminar, in order to discuss the making up of the dead; and even if there *were* people who did this sort of thing, so what? Theirs would only be the buzzing of bees and the busy-ness of ants.

My work is nothing more than a game of solitaire I play in a small room.

Why then do I have my ambition if not to provide the incentive for carrying on with my work—because my work is, after all, solitary, and I am alone; and in the game I play there is no opponent and no audience, let alone the sound of applause. While I am working, I can hear only the sound of my own soft breathing; and even though the room is full of men and women, I am the only one breathing, softly. I can even hear my heart sighing and lamenting; and the sound of my own heart seems all the louder because the hearts of the dead are no longer uttering their sad cries.

Yesterday, I thought that I would make up a young couple who had committed suicide, who had died for love in fact. I stared at the face of the sleeping boy, and suddenly I felt that *here* was the raw material out of which I would fashion my 'sleeping beauty'. His eyes were shut, his lips were lightly closed; there was the trace of a scar on his left temple; he looked as though he was asleep, sleeping peacefully. Over the years I had made up faces by the thousands—many of these faces looked anxious, though by far the majority looked fierce. They were my standard repertoire, and I did the appropriate mending, sewing and patching, so that they would come to look infinitely soft. But the boy I saw yesterday, his face had an indescribable air of calm—had it been a real source of pleasure to him, killing himself? Anyhow, I knew that I for one wasn't taken in by his outward appearance, and I regarded what he had done as an act of extreme cowardice; and as far as I was concerned, a man who lacked the courage to fight against Fate was not even worth a second glance. Not only did I abandon the idea of turning this young man into my 'sleeping beauty', but I refused to do any make-up on him altogether; I thought him and the girl so stupid for just dumbly accepting whatever it was Fate had in store for them, and so I passed the two of them on to Aunt Yifen, leaving her with the job of beautification, of carefully covering over the burns on their cheeks that had been caused by drinking a particularly lethal poison.

EVERYONE KNOWS ABOUT what happened to Aunt Yifen, for there were people around at the time who saw for themselves. Aunt Yifen was still young in those days, and she liked to sing as she worked, and would talk to the dead lying before her as if they were her friends. Her reticence, you see, came later. Aunt Yifen used to pour out her heart to her sleeping friends—she never wrote a diary but she 'talked' it instead; and those who were sleeping in front of her were the most wonderful listeners in the world because they could listen endlessly to every detail of her tireless talk. They were first-rate at keeping secrets too. Aunt Yifen would talk to them about the man she had got to know, and she would say how they were as happy together as lovers could be, but how from time to time they also had their cloudy days, which now seemed so far away. In those days, Aunt Yifen went to a school for beauticians once a week to learn the art of make-up. She went there regularly over the years, rain or shine, and mastered virtually every technique that the teachers there had to offer—even when the school told her that she had nothing more to learn, she still insisted that they try to think if there was not *some* new technique they could teach her. Her passion for make-up was so intense it was almost as if she had been born with it, and her friends thought that she was bound to open up some large beauty parlour. But she did not, and instead she dedicated the fruit of her studies to the sleeping bodies in front of her. Her young lover was ignorant of all this—he had always assumed it was part of their nature for girls to be preoccupied with their appearance, and he thought it was just that she liked make-up . . . that was all.

Until one day, when she took him to the place where she worked. And pointing to the dead bodies around them, she told him that hers was very lonely and dreary work, but that here there were at least no worldly cares, all conflicts over jealousy, hatred, fame or money ceasing to exist; and she told him that when people sank into the darkness, they would become peaceful and calm, and soft. He was so shocked, never having thought that a girl like her could be doing work like hers —he had loved her, he would have done anything for her, he had solemnly sworn that he would never leave her no matter what happened, and that they would remain devoted to each other for the rest of their lives, and that their love would always be true. Yet, before a silent gathering of dead bodies which could neither speak nor breathe, he completely lost the courage of his former convictions, and letting out a loud cry he turned round and dashed out, pushing all the doors open as he went. All along the way, people saw him running in blind panic.

Aunt Yifen didn't see him any more after that, but she was heard talking alone in the small room to her silent friends: Didn't he say he loved me?

Didn't he say he would never leave me? Why was he suddenly so frightened? Gradually, Aunt Yifen became more and more reticent. Perhaps she had said all she had to say, or perhaps her silent friends had heard it all before and there was no need for her to say anything more—you know, there are some things which don't really need any elaborating. Aunt Yifen told me a lot about herself when she first started teaching me her remarkable skill. Of course, it was not the only reason why she chose me instead of my little brother, but it was the main reason . . . because I was not a coward.

—Are you afraid?

She asked.

—No, I'm not afraid.

I answered.

—Have you got a strong stomach?

She asked.

—Yes, I've got a strong stomach.

I answered.

It was because I was not afraid that Aunt Yifen chose me to follow in her footsteps. She had a premonition that my fate might mirror hers, though exactly why we have been becoming more and more like each other is something that neither of us could explain—perhaps to start with it was because we were neither of us afraid. We were completely fearless! When she told me her story, Aunt Yifen said: But I always maintain that in this world there must be people like us, who fear nothing. Aunt Yifen had not yet become totally withdrawn in those days, and she would let me stand beside her so that I could see how she put red on an unbending mouth and how she gently stroked an eye that had been wide open for so long, inviting it to rest. In those days, she still talked incessantly to her gathering of sleeping friends: And you, why are you frightened? How is it that a person who is in love can have no trust in that love but is a coward in love? Among her sleeping friends there were more than a few who were fearful and cowardly, and they were more reserved than the others. Aunt Yifen knew quite a bit about her friends and would sometimes tell me about them, like once when she was putting powder on a girl with a fringe she said: Gracious, how pathetic this girl is!—to have abandoned her sweetheart simply in order to play the fine-sounding role of the 'dutiful daughter'. Aunt Yifen knew that the girl over here had died in settlement of some obligation or other, and that the girl over there had died in mute acceptance of her fate— they had both surrendered themselves helplessly into the hands of Fate, as though they were not human beings made of flesh and blood, with human thoughts and feelings, but only pieces of merchandise.

—What an awful job.

One of my friends said.

—To put make-up on dead people! Ugh!

One of my friends said.

I was not afraid, but my friends were. They didn't like my eyes because my eyes were often fixed on the eyes of the dead; they didn't like my hands because my hands often touched the hands of the dead. At first it was just that they didn't *like* my eyes and hands, but gradually they came to fear them; and at first it was only my eyes and hands that they feared, but later it was my whole body. I have watched them leaving me one after another, like animals in the face of a raging fire, or farmers in the path of a plague of locusts. I asked them: Why are you so scared? *Someone's* got to do this kind of work—I'm good at my work, aren't I? And I'm qualified to do it, aren't I?

But gradually I became content with things the way they were; and I got used to my loneliness. There are always so many people looking for nice cushy jobs, and wanting everything to be all roses and stardust. But how can anyone test his strength and show his confidence when cushioned by star clouds and rose petals. I have few friends now, for they felt in my hands the coldness of that other fathomless world, and they saw in my eyes a myriad of drifting and silent spirits, and they were afraid; and even though my hands had warmth and my heart had fire, and my eyes could shed tears, my friends were blind to this. I began to resemble my aunt, having only the sleeping dead before me as my friends.

I wonder what made me tell them, when all around was a deathly hush: You know, tomorrow morning I'll be bringing a man called Xia to see you. Xia asked me whether you'd mind. I told him that you don't mind. Now, are you sure you don't mind? Xia will be coming here tomorrow, and I think I know how things will turn out in the end because my fate and Aunt Yifen's fate have already merged into one. I expect I shall see Xia

struck with panic when he sets foot inside this place—gracious, we'll both scare each other out of our wits in our different ways! But I won't really be frightened by what happens—you see, there have been so many signs, I already know how it will all end. Xia once said: Your own face looks so beautifully natural. Yes, it is; beautiful to Xia. But even its natural beauty is powerless to dispel a man's fear.

I HAVE THOUGHT of changing jobs; surely I am capable of doing the kind of work that other girls do? There's no way that I could be something like a teacher now, or a nurse, or a secretary, or an office-clerk; but couldn't I work in a shop, maybe sell bread in a bakery . . . or what about some kind of domestic work? A girl like me only needs three meals a day and a roof over her head—isn't there some way that I can fit in? Looking at it realistically, what I ought to be doing, with my particular skill, is making up brides—but I can't bear to even think about it. Imagine how I'd feel if I was putting lipstick onto a customer's lips, and suddenly they parted in a smile!—no, too many memories stand in the way of my ever doing the very work which suits me best. Suppose I *did* change jobs: would my hands and face ever lose their pallor? and that antiseptic which must have worked its way through to my bones by now, would its tell-tale smell ever completely disappear? and would I still keep it secret from Xia, my previous job, the kind of work I am doing now? It is disloyal to conceal the past from the one we love; and even though there are countless girls in the world all desperately trying to gloss over their lost virginity and their slipped-away years, I despise them for it.

I'm sure I *would* tell Xia that all this time I've been doing make-up for the sleeping dead. And he must know and come to accept that I *am* this kind of girl. So, it is not the smell of an unusual perfume that clings to me, but the odour of antiseptic lotion; and it is not because I am striving to cultivate an air of innocence that I am often dressed in white, but because I have to think of my own convenience, in entering and leaving my place of work.

But these are only insignificant details, like drops of water in the ocean.

When he knows that my hands often touch

those sleeping dead bodies, will he still take hold of them—say, if we were jumping over a rushing stream? Will he still let me cut his hair, or do up his tie? Will he be able to tolerate my eyes gazing on his face? Will he lie down before me without any fear? I think he will be scared, very scared; and then after the initial shock, like those other friends of mine he will start to dislike me; and finally he will turn his face away altogether—all because of his fear. Aunt Yifen said: If it is love, what is there to be afraid of? But this thing, this so-called 'love'—though it may seem on the surface to be both strong and indestructible, I know that it is actually very frail and easily broken. A mask of courage is only a sugarcoating. Aunt Yifen said: Maybe Xia *isn't* a coward. It is the feeling that she could be right which partly accounts for why I haven't told him anything more about my job, the other reason being of course that I'm not one of those people who is good at putting things into words. Maybe it wouldn't come out right, maybe I would choose the wrong time and place altogether, or maybe the weather would be unfavourable—any of these factors might distort my meaning. To fail to enlighten Xia that my work did *not* consist of beautifying brides was in fact a test for him because I wanted the chance to observe his reaction when he finally sees the objects of my work —if he is scared, he is scared. If he immediately takes to his heels, then let me say to those sleeping friends of mine: It's as though nothing had happened.

—Can I see where you work?

He asked.

—I can't see why not.

I said.

So now I am sitting in a corner of the café, waiting for Xia. I've just caught myself wondering whether it isn't perhaps unfair of me to inflict this on Xia—after all, what's so wrong with it if he *is* frightened by the kind of work I do? Why should he be superhumanly brave? Why should there be any connection between a man's fear of the dead and his fear when it comes to love?—they might be two totally separate things.

My parents died when I was very small and I was brought up by my aunt—my little brother and I are orphans, we have no mother and father. I knew very little about my parents or what sort of

lives they had led, and everything I *do* know was told me by Aunt Yifen later on. I remember her telling me about my father, how he too did make-up for the dead in the days before he got married. And that after he had decided he wanted to marry my mother, he once asked her: Are you afraid? And my mother answered: No, I am not afraid. I think it's because I take after my mother, and because her blood is flowing through my body, that I too am not afraid. Aunt Yifen said that my mother would live forever in her memory because of something she once said: It is love that makes me completely fearless. Perhaps this is why my mother will also live forever in the inmost recesses of *my* memory, even though I cannot remember the sound of her voice, or even what she looked like. But if my mother said that love made her fearless, I think that was only the way my mother felt, and it doesn't give me the right to expect everybody in the world to feel the same as her. I probably have only myself to blame, for having submitted to this fate, for having committed myself to such an unacceptable occupation. Who in this world *doesn't* go for girls who are soft and warm, and sweet as sugar? . . . and girls like that ought to be doing some pleasing form of work that is both graceful and ladylike. Not like *my* work, which is sombre and bleak, and cold as ice; and I think it has overshadowed my whole being with its dark cloud for such a long time.

So what makes a man as radiant as the sun strike up an acquaintance with such a gloomy sort of woman? If he were to lie beside her, wouldn't he find himself thinking of how her everyday companions were corpses?—and if her hands were to touch his skin, wouldn't the thought cross his mind, how often these same hands had caressed the flesh of the dead? Oh, it really isn't right for a girl like me to have love affairs with anyone at all. It all seems like a huge mistake, and I'm responsible—so why not leave this place and go back to work? I've never in my life known a man by the name of Xia; and, by and by, he will forget that he once knew a girl who did make-up for brides. But it's too late for all this, for through the window I can see Xia coming along the other side of the street. What is it that he's carrying in his hands? Why, what an enormous bunch of flowers! What big day is it today?—somebody's birthday? I watch Xia as he catches sight of me sitting in this dark, quiet corner, and walks over from the door of the café. There is bright sunshine outside; he has brought the sunlight in with him, for his white shirt is reflecting that brightness. He lives up to the meaning of his name—Xia, never-ending 'summer'.

—Hello. Happy Sunday!

He said.

—These flowers are for you.

He said.

He is obviously feeling happy, and he sits down to have a cup of coffee. We have had such happy times. But what is happiness after all—happiness is always quickly over. My heart is weighed down by so much sorrow. Only a short walk, no more than three hundred yards from here, and we'll be at my work-place. And then, just like what happened many years ago, a panic-stricken man will go dashing out through those large doors, and curious eyes will follow him until he completely disappears from sight. Aunt Yifen said that maybe there are still some courageous people left in this world who fear nothing. But I knew at the time that what she said was only conjecture, and I thought exactly the same thing again when I saw Xia walking along the other side of the street with an enormous bunch of flowers in his hands... because this was a bad omen. Oh, it really isn't right for a girl like me to have love affairs with anyone at all. Perhaps I should say to those sleeping friends of mine: Don't you think we're the same, you and I? Decades can flash past with the blink of an eye. It is totally unnecessary for anybody to be scared to death by anybody else, for no matter *what* reason. The enormous bunch of flowers Xia has brought into the café, they are so very beautiful; he is happy, whereas I am full of grief. He doesn't realize that in our line of business, flowers are a last goodbye.

ILLUSTRATION by Choi Ho-chuen (Cai Haoquan 蔡浩泉).

西西：十字勳章

Cross of Gallantry

By Xi Xi

Translated by Cecilia Tsim

BHUNAH TOOK OUT a handful of peanuts from his pocket and put them on my lap. Taking one for himself, he started shelling it and the skin fell in flakes all over me. Whenever Bhunah sees me sitting at my own door, he always comes over for a talk. He is like a younger brother to me, because, like my brother, he is also nine years old. I have no relatives in this city, and Bhunah always reminds me of my father, my mother, my young brother and sister. Ah, my father, what will he be doing now? Sitting on the rush mat in our house, forever making those leather drums. As for mother, she will probably have a big blanket wrapped round her, and she and my younger sister will be huddling beside the iron pan over the charcoal fire to keep themselves warm; for in my homeland, the weather usually gets cold around this time of the year. My younger brother is probably in the town square, sitting on the steps of the Stone Lion, trying to sell firewood, stacks of it all lined up beside him. I wonder if trade will be good today?

'Uncle Deehan, father says that you are going to slaughter the bull this year.'

'I will do it if everybody says so.'

'Not everyone can kill a bull.'

'Many people do.'

'My father can't!'

'He can.'

'No, he can't! He said so himself. This was what he said. He said, "I can't do it, I am too old." '

'He was being modest.'

'How did you learn to do it?'

'Learn to do what?'

'Cut off the bull's head with one swing of the chopper.' As he spoke, Bhunah raised his hand and cut through the air in one swift motion. He then took out some more peanuts from his trouser pocket, and put them on my lap again.

Bhunah likes to shell a peanut, throw it up in the air, and catch it in his open mouth. Sometimes he catches it, but sometimes he misses. And when he misses, he picks up the peanut (however covered it is with soil or dust), gives it a rub with his hands or brushes it across his trousers, and pops it into his mouth.

'Father said it will be a grand occasion.'

'What will be a grand occasion?'

'When the bull's head falls at the first swing?'

'Oh, you're still on about killing the bull.'

'It has to be absolutely spot on, doesn't it?'

'Yes.'

'How did you learn to do it?'

'Practice.'

'But how can you cut off a great big bull's head with just one swing?'

'It's a matter of practice.'

'Uncle Deehan?'

'Yes?'

'Can you teach me how to cut off a bull's head?'

'You want to learn how to cut off a bull's head?'

'When I grow up I want to be like you.'

'Good at cutting off a bull's head?'

'Yes, with just one swing of the sword.'

'You wouldn't think like this if you were a bull.'

'Why did you want to bring the bull into this?'

'If you were a bull, would you want to be slaughtered?'

'Uncle Deehan . . . . '

'You still want to learn how to cut off a bull's head?'

'Will you teach me how?'

'Ask your father to teach you.'

'No, I want to learn it from you.'

'You will have to finish your homework first.'

'That's a deal!'

'But you must do your homework first!'

'All right, I'm going back to do my homework right this minute!'

He ran off, leaving behind him a pile of peanut shells on the floor, and peanut skins littered all over me. On my lap were some peanuts still in their shells; beside the peanuts was my kukri. In my spare moments, sitting beneath the shade of the tree in front of my house, I like to take my kukri out and carefully inspect it, inch by inch. In fact there are not many inches to this kukri, but every inch of it is precious to me. This dagger is my only prized possession in this city; it is my only friend. It has been with me for many years; it has travelled with me from home to several countries. And now, in this city, it is all I have left. In my homeland, floods or droughts have caused havoc over the years. Food is short and life is very hard. That was why I joined the army so young.

In the old days, my father was a soldier too. But now he has grown old, and an old soldier cannot earn enough to support his family. So he gave me his kukri and got me into the army. The kukri which my father left me is very old. The patterns on the sheath—the rings of circles on the mouth of the sheath, the symmetrical hexagonal shapes around the middle portion, the grid of criss-crosses at the bottom—are all so faded as to be almost unrecognizable. The brass nail on the sheath has also long disappeared. But this is still a good dagger. Even in my homeland now, it is not easy to find another as good as this one. You can feel its weight when you hold it in your hands. And when you take it out of its sheath, its edge still radiates sharpness. Who would have expected such a good knife from its dark and tattered sheath? Towards the upper end of the dagger, near where the handle is, are etched the uneven marks of ringed corrosion. That strange dent looks like a bat in flight. The upper end of the dagger is tapered; the middle is shaped like the neck of a vase; the lower end spreads out and bends sideways, curving outward, so that if I raise the dagger in my hand, it looks like a blazing torch, its flame blown sideways by the force of the wind. Sitting in the shade outside my house, I like to polish my dagger with care. I will never let it rust. I know this dagger so well. I can count the number of plum blossom nails on it, and the number of flowers the nails have formed themselves into. I can also remember the exquisite patterns carved on the face of the dagger, the dotted lines forming into leaves and the entwining creepers which give this tough blade an enduring charm. The two small knives that come with the sheath were already a little rusty when the dagger was given to me. But I have always kept them well oiled. And now, they are as bright and smooth as razors. This dagger will stay with me always. If I should return home in future, all I will take with me will be this one dagger which has followed me everywhere like a shadow.

BHUNAH IS ONLY nine years old, but he is a strong and robust boy. He has thick black hair and a sun-tanned complexion typical of his Mongol blood. When he goes jogging with me, he can go half way up a mountain before pausing for breath. He could run further, but I won't let him, because jogging, like all other sports, has to be taken slowly and needs to be reinforced with regular, daily practice. No one should overdo it. When we jog, I deliberately slow down to keep him company. It makes him very happy, for he thinks he is running almost as fast as I am, although in fact he is still quite a lot slower. These days, he works really hard, and I can see that he is constantly improving. One day, he will be a very fast runner, better even than I am.

If my brother were with me now, he would be like Bhunah. He would jog up the mountains with me. In my spare time, I would take him on hikes; we would climb mountains and he would learn to tell the trees by their names, he would know how to star gaze and predict the weather just by looking at the clouds. My brother would also grow up to be a strong young man. Bhunah is luckier than my brother; he can live with his parents here. And life here is definitely better than life at home. The question is whether, having grown up in this city, one should go back home? And if not, what could a Nepalese youth do in this alien, foreign city? I don't know the answer. As far as I know, everyone who has come here from my native land is a soldier. We first enlisted with the army and then we got posted with the garrison to different places. If I had not been a soldier, would I have come to this city? And if so, how? As a tourist? A student? On business? In this city I have not met anyone from my country who is an engineer, teacher, doctor or even a common clerk. Those who have come from the few big cities near my homeland are all standing guard in front of the shops. Only the very rich among my countrymen have been exceptions to this rule. What will Bhunah do, if he grows up here?

Maybe my brother is better off staying at home. During the Yerma Festival, he will sit against the wall with the sacrificial fruits and flowers all arranged in front of him in circles, and he will let his sisters make a red mark in the middle of his forehead. And they will say, 'We plant thorns on the door of the God of Death, may our brother live to be a hundred years old.' Many years ago, my elder sister planted such a red mark on my forehead and I became a strong and healthy lad. But my poor sister, she married a man in the country while she was very young. They now live in a thatched hut of clay and she toils in the fields with my brother-in-law. They do not even own an ox. I have seen my brother-in-law tilling the soil, using the plough that he made, while my sister, all in black and with a big plaid behind her, was holding a bamboo sieve with both her hands, scattering the seeds against the wind. She is only two years older than I am, but I feel she looks like a middle-aged woman.

A letter from father tells me there's been a flood in the country. The fields have been destroyed. They will have another poor harvest, and it will be difficult to make ends meet. People who live off the land live at the mercy of fate, they depend on the whims of the heavens above; they have no choice. They cannot move into their parents' place in the city. Everyone has his share of trouble to bear. If we were not poor, I would not have become a soldier.

Now my livelihood is not a problem any more. I do not need to worry about my meals and accommodation here. In fact my life in this city has actually turned out better than I expected. I send all my salary home, in the hope that my family will live a better life. Some day . . . but I don't want to think about the future. What sort of future does a soldier have? It is not like being in business; it is unlikely that I will earn enough money to buy a small house for my parents, younger brother and sister. The future? I'd rather leave the future to tomorrow.

'Uncle Deehan?'

'Yes.'

'I didn't do badly today, did I?'

'You did better than last week.'

'I practise every day.'

'It's good if you can keep up your practice every day.'

'I will try very hard.'

'Good boy!'

'I want to run as fast as you.'

'You will with more practice.'

'Really?'

'Yes, really.'

'I don't believe you. You are the fastest. You have to tell me why you are the only one who can run so fast.'

'There are other fast runners too.'

'Don't try to fool me, you are the fastest.'

'Your father also runs very fast.'

'Father said he really looks up to you, because you always come first at running uphill.'

'That's because I always start ahead of the others.'

'That's not true! I have seen you run before! Everybody starts together but in no time at all you've reached the top of the mountain. You move like lightning. Doesn't it exhaust you?'

'You get used to it after running for a while.'

'Why am I out of breath after running less than half way up the mountain?'

'If you practise every day, you won't get out of breath.'

'Is it all a matter of being able to make your breath last the distance?'

'With controlled breathing and more practice, you can run faster.'

'Did you say my father can run very fast too?'

'He can run very fast and he can really run uphill.'

'He said he is no match for you, do you know why?'

'Why?'

'He said it's because he likes to drink beer and drinking too much beer has slowed him down.'

'It doesn't matter if you drink once in a while.'

'Uncle Deehan, you stay away from beer and cigarettes because you want to keep fit and run fast, right?'

'No, I stay away from beer and cigarettes because I don't particularly like them. Also, I want to save up more money to send home.'

'If I drink beer, will it slow me down too?'

'Kids should not be drinking beer.'

'Uncle Deehan?'

'Yes.'

'I've had enough rest now. Let's run again, all the way to the peak.'

'All right, let's go.'

The breeze is cool and refreshing. I know the hills and tracks around here well. Every day I make several trips up and down the mountain. I can almost recognize every single tree and the position of every stone. If I were not with Bhunah, I would have reached the peak a long time ago and would have made it back to the foot of the hill again by now. If I were not with Bhunah, I would have left this well-trodden path and would have headed up into the more difficult terrain. I would find my way through the thick scrub and the wild rocks. I really surprise myself sometimes. I am becoming more and more like a hunter. Only a hunter leaves the beaten track for the wilds, because he knows the most precious species are always hiding there, where few men venture.

'UNCLE DEEHAN! Uncle Deehan!'

'Is that you, Bhunah?'

'Can I come in?'

'The door is not locked. Just give it a push and come in.'

Bhunah pushed open the door and like a whirlwind he jumped in. I had on a long-sleeved shirt and was buttoning up one of the sleeves.

'Uncle Deehan, you've arrested a lot of people today.'

'Yes, some.'

'Father said he caught five altogether.'

'He told you already?'

'He said you caught more, is that right?'

'I don't remember.'

'Father said you caught seven all by yourself.'

'It was a joint effort. Everybody had a hand in it.'

'Are there many people trying to sneak in?'

'There are more these days.'

'And they are difficult to catch?'

'It depends.'

'They were saying that you did a great job this time. You arrested seven all by yourself. They said you're a brave soldier.'

'Has your father come back?'

'Yes, he has. That's why I know you caught so many people today.'

'This happens every day.'

'Uncle Deehan, are your hurt?'

'It's nothing, it will be all right.'

'There's blood on your hands.'

'Oh, it's only red spirit.'

'Why are you wearing a long-sleeved shirt? Quickly, let me have a look! Are you hurt like my father? Why don't you go to hospital? Father went. He was bandaged there and came back. He said those people were really fierce; some of them with knives even. Are you hurt? Show me.'

'It's nothing. My skin was slightly scratched. I've already put some red spirit on it. If I were really hurt, I would have gone to hospital, wouldn't I?'

'Did they really have knives?'

'Some of them did.'

'Did they use their knives on you?'

'Yes.'

'Did you fight them with your dagger?'

'No.'

'Why didn't you? You had a good dagger with you, didn't you?'

'There was no ill feeling between us.'

'But they stabbed you with their knives!'

'They did that because it was a matter of life and death for them.'

'But it was dangerous not to fight back with your knife!'

'I didn't want to hurt anyone.'

'But they could have hurt you, even killed you!'

'Danger is part of a soldier's life. You can get killed any minute.'

'But we are not at war.'

'It's exactly because we are not at war that I could not use my dagger.'

'They were difficult to catch?'

'Some more difficult than others.'

'Father said they were like foxes, very hard to catch.'

'But they're also like lambs, unable to really run away.'

'But unlike lambs, they had knives.'

'Many didn't have knives, many were still children; and there were some women too.'

'Father said the women didn't have knives, but

they scratched with their nails and bit with their teeth. There are teeth marks on your hands. Were you bitten by them?'

'That's their only defence. They had no other way.'

'Uncle Deehan, see, your arms have been scratched all over!'

'It's nothing. They will be all right in a few days.'

My arms were not too seriously hurt. There were just scratch marks left by a woman's nails. After I had applied red spirit, they were all right. That woman was so skinny, but she had great strength. I found her hiding behind the rocks, curled up in the undergrowth. First she retreated backwards, until there was no more space for her to retreat into, and then she lay there like a wounded lamb. She knew that once we found her, there would be no hope of escape. She would be taken away and, after a while, she would be repatriated to wherever she had come from. I could see despair in her eyes. She was so disappointed and frightened. And then all of a sudden, she shot out from the undergrowth and got down on both her knees at a short distance from me. She bowed and kowtowed, started kowtowing to me non-stop. I did not understand her language, and I could not tell what she was actually saying. But what she wanted was quite clear. Similar incidents had happened to me many times before. They would kneel before me, amongst them young children, young women, old women, and even young men, and they would entreat with the plaintive look of despair and with tears all over their faces. All of a sudden, she reminded me of my poor sister back home. But I cannot be soft-hearted. I am a serviceman. I am a soldier. My duty is to catch illegal immigrants on these woods and hillsides. I am an enforcer of the law. I must carry out my responsibilities as a soldier, obey the orders of my superiors, arrest all who break the law, and help maintain law and order in this city.

If they run into me, they don't stand a chance. I know the terrain here. They are only intruders in a foreign land. None of them is my match when it comes to running, how can they get away? Even if they are not arrested by me, there is really no escape. There are troops everywhere, and like me, all the soldiers have undergone intensive training. They are good at combing the mountains and the rough country and they know the geography around here like their own back gardens. Ah, what good will it do them to kowtow to me?

Having decided what to do, I shot forward like an arrow, and in one movement I reached out and locked both her hands behind her back. There and then, she became like a beast in an arena; she scratched at me and bit my hands. But I know how to ward off such attacks and, one by one, I arrested them all.

The ones with knives are more difficult to handle. Of course, if I drew my dagger, they would not stand a chance against me. I can cut off a bull's head with one swing of the chopper. It would be child's play to cut off their heads. But I am always in control. I never allow myself to use the dagger. If I had used it, my kukri would be all covered with blood. I really have no grudge against these poor people. I assume that they too must have parents, brothers and sisters at home, that they are just a bunch of poor oppressed creatures driven to desperation by fate? And I am only a man who arrests, I am not a killer. But if they have knives with them, I have to handle them more carefully. That's why some troops arm themselves with assault rifles when they go on patrol. With rifles, of course, you've only got to aim at their faces, and these people have to give up.

Even without a rifle and without using my dagger, I still managed to arrest them one by one. I was not hurt. One girl made several scratches on my arms, and left a long mark with her nails, but these scars will heal. Today, I arrested seven illegal immigrants altogether. I suppose it was seven, because they said it was. Bhunah's father got five. He was slightly hurt. He must have returned home from hospital by now. In the barracks we were hailed as two brave soldiers.

I READ MY father's letter under the light. He said he had received the money I sent him, that they were all well at home and that I needn't worry about them. But the letter also said my brother-in-law had an accident while working in the fields. His hoe scraped one of his toes and he lost a lot of blood. When my sister saw what happened, she passed out. My brother-in-law became very weak and had a high temperature; it was not known whether the rust on the hoe would give him tetanus. They would write again if there was further news.

A lot of people came into my house just now. When they left, I did not close the door, and Bhunah popped his head in. I folded the letter properly and put it inside my pocket. Bhunah walked carefully into the house. He came in very slowly because he was holding a paper cup in his hand, and in the cup was a piping hot drink. Beside the cup he was holding, he also had a paper bag between his fingers.

'I'll treat you to a hot dog, Uncle Deehan.'

'You bought these at this late hour?'

'There's hot chocolate in the cup, your favourite drink.'

'Your pocket money will not go very far if you spend it like this.'

'I can go without breakfast for a week, but I must come here to offer my congratulations.'

'Where is your father?'

'He's at home, they are very noisy, drinking. I was here just now but there were so many people, so I did not come in. Luckily I had not bought the drinks and food first, or else they would have gone cold by now.'

'Thanks for the chocolate and the hot dog.'

'I salute you, Uncle Deehan. Congratulations on getting the Cross of Gallantry.'

'Thank you, Bhunah.'

'Oh, where's your Cross? Where have you put it?'

'In the drawer.'

'Why don't you put it on display? Father certainly won't put his medal away in the drawer. He'll show it to everyone who comes inside the house. They are all very envious. This is a great honour. Everybody says so.'

'Bhunah, have you finished today's homework?'

'All done, Uncle Deehan! Why don't you show me—your Cross of Gallantry? Is it the same as my father's?'

'The same.'

'Father said the ceremony was very grand, was it?'

'Yes, very grand.'

'Father said London is a big place, there are lots of pigeons in one of the squares, some Houses of Parliament by a river, and there's a big clock somewhere that strikes, and when it does the sound it makes is exactly like the sound of ferry bells here. Is it true?'

'Yes.'

'Father said the parks over there are very big. Inside one of the parks, you can row boats, and there is a big church with stained glass, right?'

'Yes.'

'Father said there were others who were awarded medals, and that there were different kinds of medals; the highest kind of medal is called the Victoria Cross. Is it true?'

'Yes.'

'It is such an honour to be awarded a medal!'

'Bhunah, do you have to go to school tomorrow?'

'Yes I have to, but the house is packed full of people. I can go back a bit late. I cannot go to bed even if I go home now.'

'This hot dog is very big. Shall we share it between us?'

'I bought it specially for you. We're celebrating!'

'We'll each have half, like brothers.'

'Good, half each.'

'Do you want some hot chocolate too?'

'We'll both have half?'

'Yes, each of us will have half.'

'Uncle Deehan, it would be so nice if you were my real brother.'

'Aren't you like my own brother now?'

'Uncle Deehan, I don't know why, I really admire you very much.'

'Don't say such silly things.'

'It's true, I really admire you, you are the fastest at running uphill, you can cut off the bull's head with one sweep of the chopper and now you have been awarded this medal.'

'Your father is the one you should really admire.'

'Uncle Deehan? When I grow up, will I be able to get a medal too?'

'All soldiers have the same chance of getting medals.'

'When I grow up I want to be a brave soldier, and I want a medal too.'

'Bhunah, it's getting late now. You should be going to bed.'

'I am so envious of people who have the Cross of Gallantry. Uncle Deehan, tell me, what are the people who have been awarded the Victoria Cross like? They must be great men, right? When I grow up, I shall be a good soldier, a brave soldier, and I want a medal.'

'Bhunah, it is getting very late now, go home and sleep.'

Finally, Bhunah went home. I locked the door, took out my father's letter and re-read it once more. My poor sister, her problems have got worse. I hope my brother-in-law will be all right. I opened the drawer and put the letter inside. On opening the drawer, I saw my Cross of Gallantry. It is a medal for bravery. I am a hero because in one day I arrested seven illegal immigrants. Bhunah said when he grew up he wanted to be a heroic soldier and he wanted the medal for bravery. Why does anyone want to be a soldier? If I had the choice, I would rather be a doctor or a teacher. Why can't I sell stamps over the counter in the Post Office, or be a driver in a public vehicle, or a carpenter making tables and chairs?

Today, I did not polish my kukri. I unfastened it from my waist and put it on the table. For how many more years will this dagger be with me? I don't know. Will I some day give this dagger to my child, just as my father handed it to me? I hope there will never be blood on this dagger. I even hope that this dagger will disintegrate with my body when I die. Or be used for nothing but chopping wood. My brother sells fire wood in the town square, sitting on the steps of the Stone Lion. Can the dagger be used to chop wood? I don't know. I have not tried. When it is Festival time, sister will put a red mark on my younger brother's forehead, saying as she does, 'We plant all thorns on the doorsteps of the God of Death, may our brother live to be a hundred years old.' Now, at Festival time, there is no one to put a red mark on my forehead. My sister is so skinny, standing there, thrashing husks against the wind in the open fields, dressed in black. How strange that the girl hidden behind the rocks was so like my sister! She made two blood-stained marks on my arms, one longer than the other, a vertical and a horizontal. They formed the sign of the cross.

ILLUSTRATION by Choi Ho-chuen,
courtesy Suye Magazine.

Two Stories by Zhao Zhenkai

The Poetry and Fiction of Bei Dao/Zhao Zhenkai

IN DECEMBER 1978, the pages of an unofficial magazine, *Jintian* 今天, were pasted up in three places in Peking: on a wall at Xidan soon to be known as Democracy Wall; on the wall of the Ministry of Culture; and on the gate of the offices of *Shikan* 詩刊 (Poetry), an official national magazine. In January the following year, these big-character posters appeared in magazine form, typewritten and mimeographed, and subtitled in English *The Moment* (later issues renamed *Today*). Unlike most of the other unofficial journals connected with the Democracy Movement, which focused on political analysis and issues, *Today* was essentially a literary journal, featuring poetry, prose, literary criticism and translations from foreign literature.

The writers who contributed to *Today* expressed a strong awareness of the independence of literature from politics; their literary goals were broader and deeper than those of both the politically-oriented writers of the Democracy move-ment and the "new literary tide" which had been officially recognized in December 1978 at the Third Plenum of the Eleventh Party Congress. Unwilling to allow that literature is basically just a tool for class struggle or that the uniqueness of the in-dividual is subordinate to social or class character, the *Today* writers sought to explore hitherto restricted areas in art and politics in China: the relationship between the individual and society, the fundamentals of human nature, the full expression of the self. Such explorations could not but imply an inherent question-ing of the present system as a whole. The *Today* group, in its particular concern with the state of literature, extended its questioning to a re-evaluation of the Chinese cultural tradition, urging a "broader perspective" in cultural matters as a necessary means of revitalizing Chinese literature. Although closed by the authorities in September 1980, the *Today* publications and their writers have left a permanent mark in the Chinese literary world.

Zhao Zhenkai 趙振開 was one of the chief editors of *Today*. Under various pseudonyms he also published a rather large body of his own work in *Today*, in-cluding the two stories and most of the poems by him in this special issue of *Rendi-tions*. He was born in Peking in 1949, but his family was originally from the south. His father was then, and still is, a professional administrator; his mother was a nurse, later a doctor. His education, at one of the top high schools in Peking, was inter-rupted by the Cultural Revolution, and for a brief period he was a Red Guard activist. In 1969 he was assigned work in a construction company in Peking, where he remained until 1980. Since 1979, when one of his poems was published in *Poetry*, many of his poems and stories have appeared in the official press, and he has enjoyed a strong following throughout China, especially among the young. He is currently an editor at *El Popola Cinio*, China's Esperanto magazine.[1]

At first glance the poet and the fiction writer appear to be two different persons inhabited by two widely different sensibilities. In fact, they represent two aspects of a profoundly complex personality: a traveller in search of spiritual solace, and an observer of spiritual sterility. The two sides overlap: in the bitter edge of despair which surfaces in the poems like a reef at low tide, and in the tenderness which informs the rare moments of shared love in a lifetime of rejection and betrayal. Nevertheless the contrast is sufficient to justify the choice of different pen-names by the author for his work. Bei Dao 北島 is the name he has been using almost invariably for his poems; for his fiction, first published under the pen-names Ai Shan 艾珊 and Shi Mo 石默, he has now reverted to his real name, Zhao Zhenkai.

The poet Bei Dao[2] is a traveller on a quest which leads him in many directions. Most often it leads him to the sea, to a lonely island or shore pounded by waves; but without a boat ticket, he is reduced to dreaming of the ocean and what lies beyond. Sometimes his quest takes him to a river bank, a sheltering haven to the poor and needy; sometimes it takes him to a valley, protected from the winds and time; sometimes it takes him to a deserted temple, where perhaps an omen of regeneration lingers about the ruins; sometimes a park with trees and a pond in the middle of the city offers temporary refuge. At the end of the quest lies the ideal, the union of loving hearts dwelling together in a centre of peace like the eye of a cyclone. The mood is subdued, but not hopeless, and companionship alleviates the trials of the journey through hostile territory. The consolations of nature and love are real, and dreams are true. Nevertheless even in the more tranquil poems the unasked questions intrude: what forces the traveller forward and at the same time impedes his journey? From what does he seek refuge? Some of the poems contain a note of despair, some an overwhelming cry. The ordinary acts of daily life are fraught with an unknown but menacing danger; all that is precious in life becomes meaningless and fades away; for years beauty has been a lie, and deception a kind of devotion; night stretches on interminably, without promise of dawn.

In fiction the author is not pursuing his private quest but becomes an observer of the present moment in the lives of others. Selecting passages in a man or woman's life when inner torment threatens or destroys the mask of cynical indifference, he frequently portrays a kind of spiritual brutality or corruption. But despite the ugliness that emerges under the author's pen, there is no sense whatsoever of any hidden perversity of taste. The acuteness of the author's perception and his honesty as a writer force him to confront the viler aspects of existence, a confrontation that leaves him exhausted and depressed. There is no sentimentality or tacked-on ending to strike a false note of sensationalism. Instead the brutality is relieved by moments of great delicacy when love or memory reveals the potentiality of human worth amid sterility and betrayal. With great subtlety, the author suggests in these moment the self-awareness and self-disgust that co-habit with corruption. The objectivity of the author's voice prevents the self-disgust from spilling over

---

[1] For further biographical detail, see "A Poetry of Shadows: An Introduction to Bei Dao's Poems", in *Notes from the City of the Sun: Poems by Bei Dao*, edited and translated by Bonnie S. McDougall, Cornell University China-Japan Program, 1983.

[2] For a selection of Bei Dao's poems, see below pp. 195-208.

in a melodramatic bid for the reader's sympathy. Instead the bleak but under-dramatized narrative permits the reader to imagine that betrayal and sterility are not the necessary and inevitable condition of the human race, but a failure of courage under unusually adverse circumstances.

"Waves" is the author's longest, most complex and most experimental work. The original draft was completed in November 1974, revised in June 1976 and revised again in April 1979. As his first major effort in fiction, Zhao Zhenkai has an affectionate regard for it though admitting its relative naivety. For him its value lies in its authenticity and spirit of rebellion. This modest appraisal does not do justice to a work that testifies so positively to the creativity latent in young Chinese writers despite the rigours of the past thirty years. "Waves" is a patchwork of reflections in the minds of several characters. There is no detached author, and the reader is present as the action unfolds, piecing together the story from the characters' individual perceptions. The unifying element in "Waves", linking the fragmented composition verbally, structurally and thematically, is suggested by the title itself, literally "wave motion" or "undulation".[3] Past and present alternate in the minds of the characters, scenes change fluidly, relationships intertwine. Reality is seen as a composite of multiple reflections and permutations, a pattern which undulates through time and the simultaneous perceptions of individuals. Life is a wave-like experience of fluctuations between illusion and reality, between a person and society, within relationships and even within a single personality. While the vision, structure and title of Zhao Zhenkai's "Waves" all suggest Virginia Woolf's most experimental novel, *The Waves*, the former was written before the author came in contact with Western modernist writing. Even since the efflorescence of the late seventies, Zhao Zhenkai's remarkable achievement in "Waves" has rarely been challenged.

"Moon on the Manuscript" is a very different kind of writing: controlled, detached, ironic. The reader is not obliged to sympathize with the first person narrator, simply to observe the way his mind works under the pressures of a highly competitive and demanding society. The brutality of this story is not physical but mental: violence is done to conscience, not to body. One of Zhao Zhenkai's most brilliant achievements to date, "Moon" is a masterpiece of the short story form.

One of the most striking characteristics of Bei Dao as a poet is his great courage —in a daring break with the practice of the past thirty years in China—in speaking with his own voice about his own hopes and fears. In his fiction, he avoids auto-biography (also a rare phenomenon in contemporary Chinese fiction), but neverthe-less expresses the fears and confusion of his own generation in a particularly compelling way. Whether as a poet or a writer of fiction, Zhao Zhenkai is concerned with what is universal and basic in human nature and human relationships. While critics carp at the difficulties of his "eccentric" and "disjointed" style, readers who share his concerns about the life and death of the human spirit have little trouble following his train of thought. The style is indivisible from the content: a continuing exploration into the human condition.

—SUSETTE COOKE and BONNIE S. McDOUGALL

[3]Compare the passage in Yang Mu's essay, p. 78 above: 'Most modern poets ... turn inward to describe the inner world of the human psyche, and its "undulations" 內心靈魂的波動.' (ed.)

趙振開：波動

Waves

By Zhao Zhenkai

Translated by Susette Cooke

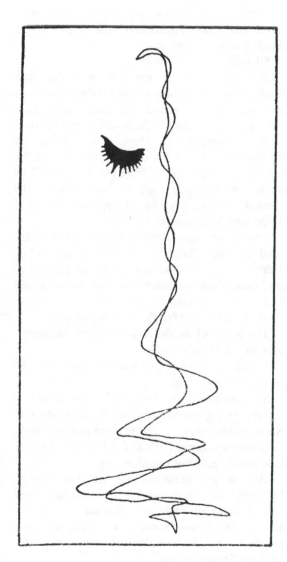

This translation ('work-in-progress') represents a little over two-thirds of the original story. Condensations of the omitted passages are printed in italics. The complete story will appear in a forthcoming anthology of Zhao Zhenkai's fiction.

I

1A *Yang Xun*

PULLING INTO THE station, the buffers screeching. Outside the window the flash of streetlights, shadows of trees, a line of pulsating railings. The train attendant opens the door, lets down the step-ladder, mutters something indistinct. A stream of fresh air hits my face. I breathe in a deep draught of it, and step down from the carriage.

The platform is deserted. In the distance the locomotive spouts jets of steam, a sickly-pale spotlight wavers in the rising fog. From the long shadow of the train comes the clanging ring of small hammers.

Night, flowing gently along the breeze.

The old ticket-collector leans against the railing, napping. On his chest a loose brass button quivers a little. He stretches, pulls a fob-watch from his pocket. "Huh, late again, the loafers." He turns the ticket over and over, then gives a long yawn and hands it back. "I've been to Peking ... Tian Qiao, Dazhala'r, the flower market ... it's nothing, nothing."

I give him a cigarette. "When were you there?"

"In '34." He strikes a match, sheltering it from the wind with his hand, the flare jumping from between his fingers to his forehead. He inhales greedily. "That year I'd just got myself a wife. Went shopping for a bit of printed cotton and stuff."

A sweet, greasy smell of mildew and decay wafts about the little station square. There's a big cart stopped in the light from the waiting-room doorway. The shaft-horse snorts from time to time, sniffing about on the ground. The driver lies sideways across the top of the cart, one foot dangling down. I put down my bag, light a cigarette and throw the match into a pitch-black puddle

125

nearby.

There are no streetlights, no moon, along the road, only a faint gleam from somewhere reflected on the narrow blades of grass in the ditches by the road side. Suddenly, from behind some rustling sunflowers, a lighted mud-brick house flashes into view. It stands all alone in a vegetable patch. A bunch of red peppers hangs on the door, very distinct in the light.

I change my bag from one hand to the other and walk up.

"Excuse me." I knock on the door. "Could you give me a drink of water?"

Not a sound.

I knock hard. "Excuse me——"

A scratching noise. I sense someone standing behind the door, trying not to breathe. At length the door opens. The outline of a young woman's face is caught in a faint ray of light, surrounded by translucent strands of hair . . . how weird!

"I'm sorry, I've just got off the train, it's a long way to the factory and I'm terribly thirsty . . . . " I explain awkwardly. The shadows gradually fade; I see a pair of large, watchful eyes.

She gestures with her hand. "Come in."

The room is furnished very simply, the wall-paper peeling in places. On the table stands a photograph of a little girl mounted in a glass holder, a pen and blue notebook lying carelessly beside it.

"Sit down." She points to a stool beside the door. With one hand held behind her back she retreats a few steps and sits down on the bed opposite. The light falls across her face. I am struck dumb: what a beautiful girl.

"Pour it yourself, the thermos flask and the cup are on the box beside you." She opens the blue notebook, her other hand still held behind her back.

The water is scalding hot. I blow on the steam and ask: "Do you live here by yourself?"

She raises her eyes, stares at me, after a time nods abstractedly.

"Just been sent back from the countryside?"

"What?"

I repeat my question.

"A year ago."

"Which production team were you in before?"

She raises her eyebrows in surprise. "Anything else you'd like to know?"

I am taken aback for a moment, then smile. "Yes. For instance, what's that in your hand?"

"You must have been brought up on the *One Hundred Thousand Whys*." She produces a glinting dagger from behind her back and lays it on the table.

"On the contrary, I wasn't at all studious when I was young."

She betrays a sarcastic little smile. "So you're starting now."

"That's right."

"Hurry up and drink your water." She frowns, waves her hand impatiently, the dagger traces flashing curves in the air.

Silence.

She taps softly on the table with the knife handle, now a fast, now a slow rhythm. She bends her head, as if the sound contains a unique significance. Clearly she is following some habitual train of thought . . . . Then, with a bang, she throws the dagger down on the table, goes to the window and opens it: a little poplar stretches its clusters of glistening triangular leaves towards the window, leaping joyfully at her shoulder, as if welcoming its long-awaited mistress.

I watch her figure from behind, the cup in my hand shaking. Perhaps I should say something, break this awkward silence, break the barriers of sex, experience and darkness. Perhaps we are in some way connected by fate; but these relationships are always so fragile, so easily missed.

The little girl on the desk smiles mischievously, calls to me silently.

"Is this a photo of you when you were small?" I cannot help asking.

She seems not to hear, her arms folded as before, staring out the window. What can she see? Night, fields, trees . . . . Or is there only the dark, the boundless dark. I ask again. This time I realize how unwelcome my questions are.

Her slender shoulders rise and fall slightly. Suddenly she turns, staring at me coldly, even with a touch of hostility. "You have no tact at all . . . . Don't you know how to respect other people's ways? You've finished your water. Now go, I need some peace."

I rise to my feet. "I'm sorry to have bothered you. Thank you."

She nods, and in that instant I see the glistening of tears.

1B   *Xiao Ling*

MAMA IS PLAYING the "Moonlight Sonata".

The light in the room is turned out. I sit quietly by the piano like a kitten, my plaits loose, wafting out the scent of soap.

Moonlight falls across the floor, begins to dance, like a girl in a white silk skirt, everything around humming softly in sympathy.

"Mama, Mama—" I suddenly cry out involuntarily.

The moonlight congeals.

"What is it, Lingling?" Mama puts her hand on my forehead. "Don't you feel well?"

"Mama, I'm afraid."

"Afraid of what?"

"I don't know."

That's it, I don't know; is it the dark, is it the moonlight, or is it those mysterious sounds?

I put down my pen. Did the past start from here? Memories are sometimes quite strange, the ones we choose are often insignificant little things. But it is really these little things which contain concealed within them the portents of some irreversible fate. It feels strange to be writing after all this time. And besides, what is this? Autobiography? An outline for a novel? No, neither of these, nothing but a recollection of the past.

The siren shrills in the distance. Sometimes I'm like a weary traveller, flung out at a small station along the way, thinking neither of my starting-point nor of my destination, just thinking of peace, and the chance of some lasting rest.

"Fantasy is an intolerably stupid idea. It merely stuns people, drives them crazy, makes them attempt things beyond their ability." The physics teacher in his creased black uniform-jacket paces up and down the lecture platform, rubbing his blue-shadowed chin. "Class, what is science? Science is reason, as is every other subject . . . ."

I raise my hand.

"Yes, what is it?"

"Teacher, what about poetry?"

"Hm, sit down, what I'm saying includes all subjects. Of course, I'm fond of poetry too. To tell you the truth, I sometimes try my hand and send it off to several magazines; the comrade editors have hailed the rigour of my logic. These lines, for instance:

> *'The earth has gravitational force,*
> *And we have strength;*
> *We can therefore walk without fear*
> *Of taking off and bumping into the*
> *ceiling.'"*

The whole room bursts out laughing.

"How's that, class, not bad, eh?" The teacher pulls modestly at the corners of his jacket. "Any more questions?"

"Hey, you really climb fast."

I turn my head. A boy from another class comes climbing up, leaning on a staff. With his bare arm and sleeve tied round his waist he looks like a Tibetan. Now I remember; last summer holidays I helped him make up lessons.

"I'm afraid this is a long way round," I say.

"No, this is a short cut. Come on, I'll lead the way." He pushes ahead, using his staff to beat back the clumps of thorns. "Hurry up, the top's not far off."

Dark clouds are gathering, pressing down low, and the wind blows into my skirt. Suddenly there's a clap of thunder, which seems to burst right in my ear. My legs are caught up in my skirt and it's quite hard to keep going.

"What's up?" the boy calls, turning his head.

"You go first."

He springs down to me like a mountain goat and hands me his staff. "Take this, it'll be easier, don't be frightened. Look, it's a real storm. When I was small I often came to this hill to pick wild jujube, all by myself. If I ran into rain, hey, that was a real thrill! I'd strip off," he strikes his chest, "just like this. I'd stand on the top of the hill, the clouds under my feet, swirling and rolling, thundering out, and I'd give a big yell, and my voice'd be everywhere. Guess what I'd shout?"

"What?"

He clambers onto a rocky outcrop and lets out a great shout across the valley: "Oohwaa . . . Ooh . . . waa . . . ."

The echo rings in the valley, lingering a long time.

Then comes this stranger, bringing with him a traveller's weariness, a cold and unfamiliar breath.

What's the matter with me? My whole body

feels ill at ease, my thoughts are confused, all because of this wretched fellow. What's the connection between us? Just for water and light he came here. And then? Well, go, on your way, however far and long all roads may be . . . .

Face to face with the black night . . . .

Emptiness, obscurity, purposelessness: do I give them to the night, or does the night give them to me? It's hard to distinguish, which is night, and which is me, as if the two have blended into one. That's often how it is; only when living things are in contact with non-living things, can there be harmony and calm, no conflict, no desire, nothing.

Oh little poplar, what is it you keep saying?

"What are you looking at, Lingling, are you watching a seagull?"

"I'm watching the sun, Mama."

"Don't be naughty, you'll ruin your eyes."

"It doesn't matter."

"Do as I say, Lingling." The drops of water are like diamonds against Mama's tanned skin. "Aren't you coming for a swim?"

"You go, Mama. I'm sunbathing."

I lie on my stomach on the burning sand, watching the sun without blinking; the sun's roar is deafening, it covers the falling of the waves and the noise of the crowd. I shut my eyes then open them again, and the colours shift and change in rapid motion.

The sky becomes so dim, so narrow and small, like a dirty rag carried up into the heights by a seagull. The sun's rich, after all . . . .

High tide . . . .

II

2A   *Lin Dongping*

"CIGARETTE——" I ask.

He reaches into the tin box and takes out a cigarette, striking a match unhurriedly. Both of us are used to this kind of awkward silence. Outside the window a dead leaf flutters down, striking against the pane with a light, brittle sound.

"Everyone well at home?"

"Papa's very busy."

"Oh yes, I saw the paper. Foreigners elbowing their way in, what can you do . . . and your mother?"

"She plans to retire this year."

"Retire?" I murmur to myself, my fingers drumming on the glass tabletop.

The door opens with a bang and Yuanyuan rushes in, her face all red; maybe she'd tied her headscarf too tightly or maybe it was because of the wind. "Oh, it's you, Xun, when did you get back? You know, it's really strange, whenever you come, our house goes as quiet as a grave . . . . "

I glare at her reprovingly.

She promptly covers her mouth with her hand, laughing. "It's unlucky to say that, right? I ought to put it this way: 'All is quiet as an unruffled pond. Suddenly, the cock crows, and breaks the . . . . ' " Yuanyuan flings her scarf into the air, and it drops like a parachute onto the top of the clothes-stand. "That's what we were reading in class."

"Go and pour us some tea."

"All right. 'Old farmer Zhang shoos the animals out of the yard . . . . ' " Yuanyuan pushes open the door and leaves.

The phone rings. I pick up the receiver, winding the cord round my hand. "Yes, it's me. Yes, what time? I'll be there."

Yuanyuan comes in carrying the cups. "Another meeting, Pa? Oh, these Party meetings never end . . . . "

"Yuanyuan!" I call out sharply.

"Everyone says the same . . . . "

"Who is everyone? And who are you?"

She sticks out her tongue, winking at Xun.

"Let Xun stay here for a meal, I'll be back soon."

I wind down the window. At once a cool rustling wind fills the car, the curtains flapping against my face. That's better, that cold, aching feeling. Everything diminishes and rapidly dissolves in the side mirror. "Retire", the word is so unfamiliar, especially for her, even a little frightening. Her face is still there in the memory of our first meeting, still so young and bold. Time is unreal. It will soon be thirty years. What were we arguing about at the District Committee Enlarged

Session? Was it the prospects for co-operation between the Nationalists and Communists or the electrical plant workers' strike? She gripped her cup, twisting it round and round in her hands, but never actually touching the water. When the debate got heated, the water spilt and she hurriedly drank a mouthful. Perhaps it was the excitement, or because the light was too dim, but I didn't see her clearly at the time. After the meeting broke up, we ran into each other on a bend of the stairs. She put out her hand so naturally and gracefully, smiling ironically for a moment .... Ah, why do I want to torment myself all over again? Who was it said, pain is a sign of life? Now I remember, it was in our first lecture at medical college, an old American-educated professor told us, then wrote it on the blackboard in English, chalk dust drifting down gently. It was an autumn morning, with the sunlight seeping through the old-fashioned dark and misty windows .... What have I got in common with that tousle-haired university student? My hair is white now.

Outside the window, two young workers in greasy clothes, clutching lunchboxes and arguing about something as they walk, look up; a young girl in a red check scarf, nibbling a hot sweet potato, looks up; a woman washing clothes by the tap, wiping her hands on her apron, looks up. What do their glances mean? Perhaps they never wonder who it is sitting in the car; what does it have to do with them? But the police turn on all the green lights, and even raise their white gloves.

Lin Dongping goes to the office, encountering his bête noire, Wang Defa, a section chief, and Party Secretary Wu Jiezhong, on the way.

I look up. The sun shines on the huge detailed map of the city. The maze of lines, circles and symbols gradually blurs, and there is only the prominent Municipal Hall standing straight up in silence, looking down over the entire city. The third-storey windows of the east wing burn in the twilight sun, converging like the focus of a concave lens ... strange, I only need sit down behind this desk to have my confidence restored. As if only now, amidst this pile of shiny stationery, I find my legitimate place ....

The door opens, and Miss Zhang noiselessly walks in. "Director Lin, some letters from the masses .... "

"Send them over to the Postal Enquiries Section."

"It's the Postal Enquiries Section that sent them over here." She smiles mysteriously.

"Very well, leave them here."

The envelopes have been stuck down again, and I slit them open with the scissors one by one. Most of them are written by local disaster victims (thinking of the floods this summer makes me shudder), asking for an investigation into where the national disaster relief funds have gone. The position of chief of the flood relief sub-group is held by Wang Defa. At every meeting of the standing committee he holds forth about the concrete figures for each disaster. The sweat-stain on his faded army uniform (which he has never washed) has a foul smell, as if he can thereby give people the impression he's working his guts out. In the pile, unexpectedly, there is this inexplicable letter: "... any Wednesday and Saturday evening go to 75 Renmin East Road and catch the adulterers." These people are mad, to send me over a letter like this out of the blue. They're simply playing jokes! I lock the letters in a drawer. There are already a hundred letters lying there, what do a few more matter.

It's time for the meeting. I go downstairs, and open the door to the shop. Su Yumei has her head buried in a book, a strand of hair hanging down.

"A packet of cigarettes," I say.

The instant she looks up, her eyes are very focused. Evidently her concentration just now was merely a pretence. "Director Lin?" She smooths her hair, giving a charming smile.

"What are you reading?"

"*Bitter Herb*. It's really moving."

"Have you got any Qian Men[1] cigarettes?"

"We've got everything. Some top-quality sweets have just come in. The brandname sounds really nice, would you like some?"

"What is it?"

She blinks flirtatiously. "Purity, Purity Brand sweets."

---

[1] One of the highest quality brands.

2B   *Lin Yuanyuan*

*Lin Yuanyuan relates how Yang Xun and Yuan-
yuan's precocious girlfriend Fafa have a quarrel;
Fafa accuses Yuanyuan of being in love with Yang
Xun.*

2C   *Yang Xun*

I WANDER aimlessly down the street.

Goods in the shop-windows are covered with
dust, and there are little signs hanging in front:
"For Display only—not for sale"; "Service for
valid coupons only". An unruly crowd presses
around the grocers. Children banging enamel bowls
push in and out through the throng. A young
fellow in a greasy white cap sticks his head out the
door, shouting something loudly. A row of
pedicabs is parked at the corner of the street,
under the slogan "We have friends all over the
world". The drivers lounge in the back seats
smoking, chatting and napping, battered straw
hats half-hiding their bronzed faces . . . .

Suddenly a girl blocks my way. Her hands stuck
in her coat pockets, she is smiling, her head on one
side. "Don't you recognize me?"

I stop, taken aback. "It's you . . . . "

"That's right, trust your own memory. Are you
sure you weren't sleep-walking that evening?"

I smile. "For a drink of water, I was thrown
out."

"I was in a bad mood that day; it was evening
too."

"What does evening have to do with it?"

"People are influenced by their environment.
That's a materialist saying."

"Aren't there any other kinds of sayings?"

"You have a bad habit of asking questions."
She stops, looking at the people all around.
"Look, we can't just keep standing here. Do you
have any time? Walk a little way with me, I like
walking along the street at this time."

She speaks so frankly and naturally, I cannot
help smiling.

"What are you smiling at?"

"Do you often invite people like this?"

"It depends." She frowns, and turns her eyes
away. "If you have something else to do, forget
it."

I almost shout. "No, nothing, I was just going
for a walk too."

We walk on ahead. A kite caught on the overhead lines flutters, like a small white cloud that
has fallen down from the sky.

"Let me introduce myself. My name's Yang
Xun. And yours?"

Silence.

"Are you afraid I'll pollute your name?"

"Pollute? I haven't heard that word in a long
time."

"In this rosy new world, pollution doesn't
exist." A lorry thunders past, drowning my voice.

"What?"

I repeat myself.

"Nor does man," she says.

"Are you always in a bad mood?"

"My mood's fine."

"And that evening, why was it bad then?"

She stops, raising her eyebrows in surprise.
"So, this is your splendid tradition, you cadres'
kids?"

"My father drives a pedicab."

She laughs sarcastically and draws a circle in
the air with her finger. "You left out the fourth
wheel."

"What's your evidence for saying that?"

"Intuition." She pauses for several seconds,
and in that time I sense she is saying something
to herself. "The bad habits you people have make
me sick."

The paving-stones slide underfoot; blurred,
distinct, blurred . . . . I stop. "Since that's how it
is . . . . "

"Since what? You promised, you have to finish
our walk!" she says almost savagely.

"That's not what I mean."

"Forget it, there's no need to explain."

We pass the dilapidated city gate, walking
silently along the moat. The overpowering greenness of the water adrift with black weeds sends out
a rich autumnal smell. A bird nesting in the trees
twitters and flies off with a rustling sound.

She pushes aside the dangling willow branches,
the dancing sunlight filtering down onto her
shoulders and arms. "Hey, why don't you say
something?" she asks suddenly.

"I'm in bitter exile."

She laughs aloud. "Is it really so bitter? Oh,
you're hopeless. Look, this is a wonderful place

for exile."

"Or a stinking drain."

"Hey, come and look." Suddenly she grasps hold of a willow branch and gazes across the river. Six or seven children are skipping stones. The stones stir up rings of ripples and the sunlight is shattered into fragments, a glittering silver coin floating on the crest of each wave. She is completely captivated, counting them excitedly and tearing off the willow leaves beside her. "Four, five, six . . . look, that little dark kid's really terrific . . . nine, the highest score . . . . " She tears off a willow leaf and holds it in her mouth, her voice becoming indistinct. A willow branch beside her sways back and forth, like a green pendulum.

She turns round abruptly, with a slightly sarcastic wink. "Hey, prisoner exiled to a stinking drain, aren't you interested?"

"I was thinking, adults are unlucky. Even if they have everything, they can't change their luck . . . . "

"You think children are happy? Don't forget, these are poor kids," she says. "People are unlucky as soon as they're born."

"So why do you want to go on living?"

"Living, that's just a fact."

"Facts can be changed too."

"The pity of it is, people have enough inertia to keep lingering on, eking out their miserable existence, and that's what normally passes for life-force."

"Why are you so pessimistic?"

"Another of your whys." She looks at me intently, her eyes, almost severe, flashing green stars, a strand of hair dangling over her forehead. "Are you trying to expound some truth?"

I do not answer.

"Tell me, please." She brushes back the stray hairs, speaking slowly and emphatically. "In your life, is there anything you truly believe in?"

I think it over. "Our country, for example."

"Hah, an out-dated tune."

"No, I don't mean some hackneyed political cliché, I mean our common suffering, our common way of life, our common cultural heritage, our common yearning . . . this indivisible fate that constitutes everything; we have a duty to our country . . . . "

"Duty?" She cuts me off coldly. "What duty are you talking about? The duty to be offered up after having been sacrificed? Or what?"

"If necessary, yes, that kind of duty."

"Forget it. I'd like to see you sitting in a spacious drawing room discussing the subject like this. What right have you to say 'we', what right?" She speaks more and more heatedly, her face growing red, tears filling her eyes. "No thanks, this country's not mine! I don't have a country, I don't have one . . . . " She turns away.

Along the pale green horizon, a few clouds dyed red by the evening light are like unextinguished coals, leaving their last warmth to the earth. The river turns an inky green, breathing out faint, rhythmic sounds.

She turns her head, brushing off the willow

leaves that have fallen on her plaits. Her eyes turning sideways to avoid my glance, she forces a smile. "I shouldn't be like this, let's go back."

We pass a small wine shop.

"Let's go in," I suggest. "Do you drink?"

She nods. "But only white spirits."

At the counter, a drunken creature is flirting with the waitress. "My old woman's a bad egg, you think I haven't been cuckolded enough?"

I shoulder him aside. "Half a *jin* of Fenzhou wine, two cold plates."

At my shoulder, the drunk shouts, "I say it's enough, enough!"

I pay, collect the wine and plates, and stop halfway back. Next to her, a fellow of about my age is sitting, hugging half a bottle of wine, babbling: " . . . come on, I'll tell your fortune, for free. I'll make an exception for you, cross my heart, I never lie . . . . "

I drop my hand on his shoulder. "Hey, what's going on?"

He casts a sidelong glance at me, his eyes dull, his cheeks flushed red, he's evidently rather drunk. "Guv'nor, you want your fortune told too? Line up, line up, priority to women comrades. Oh, it's very busy today, very busy."

She compresses her lips in a smile, indicating that I should sit down. I sit down.

"You're intelligent, no doubt about it, extremely intelligent, a pity your life's difficult, no boyfriend . . . . "

I bang my fist on the table and stand up. He turns, looking sideways at me, an evil glint flashing in his eyes. "Impatient? It's good, good to be alive. Know who I am? Bai Hua, ask around . . . . "

"I don't care who the bloody hell you are, I'll smash your face in . . . . "

I grab an empty bottle beside me, when a small strong hand presses down on mine. I lower my head to look at her.

"Sit down. Can't you see he's drunk?" Her raised eyelashes cast long shadows across her cheeks.

I sit down.

"Are you really a fortune teller?" she asks.

"That's right."

"You don't look like one to me."

Bai Hua grins, takes a half-smoked cigarette from behind his ear, moulds it straight, and strikes several matches before lighting it, shreds of smoke curling out from between his teeth. "Where are you two from?"

"Heaven," she says, fanning away the smoke.

Bai Hua gazes intently at the ceiling, and shakes his head. After a while he asks again, "What's with you two?"

"You try and work it out," I say.

"Boyfriend and girlfriend?"

She laughs loudly and clearly. "No, we just get on well."

"Have a drink! Have a drink!" Bai Hua impatiently tosses most of the cigarette onto the floor, sticks the neck of the bottle into his cup, and begins to sing in an affected voice: "Just swallow a mouthful of wine honey-sweet. In your plain, simple days no sorrow you'll meet . . . . "

"Don't have any more," she catches hold of his cup. "Look how drunk you are."

"Who's drunk? Drunk? Me? What a laugh . . . . "

He tears her hand away from around the cup. "Don't dirty your little hand." He is about to drink, when he's arrested by her hand. With a clatter, he places the cup heavily on the table, the wine spills. "You dare to control me?"

"I'd like to try," she says calmly.

"You? Try?" Bai Hua looks her up and down in surprise, then lets out a long sigh. His shoulders droop. "All right, I, I won't drink."

The street is enveloped in moist night-mist, adorned with the brilliant streetlights wavering opposite each other. An alley cat flies like lightning across the street.

Suddenly she stops. "Do you like poetry?"

"Yes."

"If I recite a poem, will you listen?"

"Of course."

She gazes straight ahead, her voice at once gentle and fervent:

"Green, how much I love you green.
Green wind, green branches.
The ship upon the sea,
The horse in the mountains.

Green, how much I love you green.
Myriad stars of white frost,
Come with the fish of darkness
Which opens the road of dawn.
The fig-tree scours the wind

With the sandpaper of its branches,
The mountain, like a wildcat,
Bristles its angry bitter-aloes.
. . . . . . "

A leaf falls under her foot, spins around and flies away again. She shakes her head. "I recited that badly."

"It was good. By Lorca?"

"Somnambule Ballad."[2]

"It's a beautiful dream. What a pity it only lasts an instant before it dies."

"On the contrary, our generation's dream is too painful, and too long; you can never wake up, and even if you do, you'll only find another nightmare waiting for you."

"Why can't there be a happier ending?"

"Oh, you, always forcing yourself to believe in something; your country, duty, hope, these beautiful sweets always dragging you on until you come up against a high wall . . . . "

"But you certainly haven't seen the end either."

"That's right, I'm waiting for the end. I must see it whatever it is, that's the main reason I go on living. There are two kinds of people in the world; one kind adds to the world's glory, and the other kind adds to its wounds. You probably belong to the former kind, I to the latter."

I gaze at her narrowed, unfathomable eyes in silence. "Is your life very unhappy?"

"My life?" She slowly closes her eyes. "In a time like this, that people should still make that distinction, *you* and *the world* . . . . "

"No, I don't mean that, I was only trying to ask . . . . "

Her expression darkens, and she glares at me fiercely. "Lots of questions are not to be asked, do you understand? That's the simplest common sense these days, understand? 'Why? Why?' You behave as if you've just arrived from another planet!"

The one lighted window in the street has darkened, and all is pitch-black. The road is all bumps and hollows. Some women night-shift workers walk towards us, chattering about something in low voices, gradually fading away in the

distance.

"I have a bad temper," she murmurs to herself, sighing.

"That's understandable, it's evening now."

"Oh," she laughs softly, "but one evening's not the same as another. There's a moon tonight."

"And poetry."

"Yes, and poetry. I'm on night-shift, we must say goodbye."

We stand at the crossroads, facing each other. The mist, like a huge iceberg, floats behind her. In the dark, the wave of silence comes rushing in, drowning us in its midst. Silence, a sudden silence. At last it withdraws, unwillingly, silently.

She puts out her hand. "My name is Xiao Ling."

2D   *Xiao Ling*

WHAT WAS the meaning of what he was saying? The light is flickering in an old green enamel bowl on the toolbox. Or was it just another kind of deception? Our country, huh, none of these ultimate playthings last, it's just those yes-men pretending to be emotional, they need a kind of cheap conscience to reach some sort of cheap equilibrium . . . but why be so fierce? Surely you don't really detest him? But don't forget, you were with him for a whole evening, such a misty evening; and besides, you're so excited, just like a girl going out for the first time. My head aches, I'm drunk. The little coach in the music box, (when I was little I often broke the wheels), speeds out into the distance, towards the end of the earth, loaded with my anguished dreams. And what is there out there? I'm afraid there's nothing, only a continuation of here . . . .

"Hand me the pliers."

Meaning, why does there have to be meaning? Don't meaningless things last longer? Like stones —where is the meaning in them? Children laughing: let them laugh, let them break this endless stillness . . . . There I go, reciting poetry. Fool, when did you become so emotional? Since when have you been so carefree and romantic? Was it the night mist? Was it the moonlight? I love poetry; in the past I loved it for its beauty, now I love it for castigating life, for piercing the heart; but how did I never realize the value of these two

---

[2]Federico Garcia Lorca, "Somnambule Ballad", from *Romancero Gitano*, published 1928.

aspects together? Perhaps because everyone only sees life from one angle . . . .

"The spanner, did you hear? Pass me the spanner!"

Autumn has come and the leaves flutter down one by one, like the listless flowers of spring. It's an imitation, a clumsy imitation, full of human vulgarity; just like flames in a mirror, an empty fervour that lacks warmth; it will always lack warmth, but will never fail to set blood-red haunches rocking . . . . Everywhere there are stage props covered in dust, even people become part of the props, the laughers forever laughing, the criers forever crying . . . .

. . . . . .

In the sky above the small path along the factory wall, the starlight ripples, the moon rolls along the top of the wall overgrown with weeds. I stop and draw a deep breath. Home, how one yearns for it, for something a little more lasting and peaceful. Better to think of nothing at all. No yesterday and no tomorrow, no pain and no happiness. Let my heart unfold towards the outside world, like a dark-red sponge, quietly soaking up each transparent drop of water . . . .

. . . . . .

2E   *Bai Hua*

I WALK UP to the counter, eyeing the sleek red and green bottles on the shelf. They are almost in convulsions, bouncing and jumping, as if all I need to do is close one damned eye and they'll fly away.

"Look, see this? Credentials, the upper ranks' confidence in me . . . . " The blabber-mouth standing in front of me is pestering the waitresses behind the counter.

I tap the fellow on the arm, "Shh—quieten down."

He turns round, staring at me, baffled. "But what can I do if they won't acknowledge my invention? What can you do? Poor we may be, but that's all part of building our great Socialism. Now these women, they only know how to stand and giggle like idiots; it's a big problem, should be treated as a matter of basic political principle . . . . "

The devil only knows what stuff the old crab's

been knocking back. I give his backside a kick. "Beat it. Back to your hole."

He nods, grinning and smiling at me, then waddles off to the door. Suddenly he turns round and shouts: "It's a political frame-up, I'll go to the provincial authorities and the Central Committee, and complain about you people! Old Marx, if he knew . . . hmph!"

. . . . . .

I go out, and limp across the road. In the patch of light at the gate of the city deputies' hostel up ahead, a sleekly shining sedan is parked in the gateway, a dozen policemen marching cockily up and down. Oh boy! Looking for fun as usual.

All at once, two chicks walk out from the side gate, scarcely more than fledglings not yet out of the nest, but very smartly dressed.

"Yuanyuan, what *is* up with you?" the tall, thin one says. "I was just starting to enjoy myself . . . . "

"I didn't drag you away."

"That is an admirable attitude, comrades." I pinch my cap, squash it down over my forehead, and catch up with them.

They stop, staring at me in surprise.

"Who are you?" the one called Yuanyuan asks timidly.

"Me? Responsible for security work."

"Plainclothes," the tall thin one says hurriedly. "You're under my father."

"Oh, you're Director Liu's little treasure? I know your father very well."

"What a way to talk, huh, don't try to chum up with me. What's your cap doing squashed down like that? And you smell of drink. I'll tell my father when I get back, and make him demote you ."

"Ah, I'm nothing," I strike a wounded pose, "but what about the five children?"

They look at each other, and burst out laughing.

I duck down a lane, and stop by a pitch-black doorway with a wooden sign hanging beside it: "Warehouse Site; Workers Only". I reach for a rope behind the sign and pull it hard: one long, two short. In a moment or two someone asks, "Who is it?"

"Stop loafing!"

The door opens a crack, a big forehead appears. "Come in, Guv, there's a show on."

I walk into the room with its boarded-up windows. Number Four's smooth round shoulders are swaying slightly in the choking cigarette smoke. She strums a guitar, singing in a husky voice. The fellows, all drunk as lords, crowd around her.

"Here comes the Guv."

"Sit over here, Guv."

I sit down on a wooden box in the corner and light a cigarette.

When the song comes to an end there is a bit of an uproar, a great burst of shouts and whistles. One bastard with big cheekbones staggers and shoves his way across. He sits down next to Number Four and puts his arm round her waist, whispering something to her. A great cackle all round. Number Four shakes her head, fondles the guitar-strings with a sultry smile.

I feel for a kitchen chopper in the corner, stand up and walk over. The fellows automatically make way for me. I go up close to them and tap Number Four on the shoulder. "She's mine."

The room falls quiet instantly, and you can hear the sound of a cup breaking. Cheekbones is struck dumb, then bends down and pulls out a knife. I duck sideways and the back of the chopper strikes his wrist. The knife falls to the floor with a clatter. The chopper turns in the air and cuts into his shoulder. The blood seeps out of the wound through his fingers as he claps his hand over it.

"Any more bright ideas?" I ask, my eyes sweeping round, and all the young melon-heads turn away. I fish out ten dollars, crumple it into a ball and throw it in Cheekbones' twisted face. "Go and buy some medicine, worm, and then grow bigger eyes.... Come on, Number Four, let's go."

III

3A *Yang Xun*

SHE IS SITTING on the edge of the bed, leafing through a book, the white reflection of the pages shining on her face. Her name is Xiao Ling, she's twenty-three this year. Besides that, what else do I know? She's an enigma. Rose, Little Swallow ... those girls I've known before, they pale before her. They belong in the drawing room, like a painting or a vase of flowers, you don't think of them once you've left. What is she thinking? She certainly has a great many secrets, secrets that don't belong to me, or to anyone. The blue notebook, for instance, lying on the table, it might be packed with secrets, as if her entire life is stored in these secrets, sealed up forever ....

"Hey, haven't you looked enough?" she asks suddenly.

I smile. "No."

She snaps the book shut, and raises her head. "All right, look." Our eyes meet. Her chin trembles a little, unable to hold back a smile. She smiles so naturally and openly, it's like a horizontal blue streak flashing out in every direction. "Say something, silence makes me unhappy." "Don't you know how to respect other people's ways? You've finished the water, now go, I want some peace!" I say.

"I'm sorry to have bothered you. Thank you," she says.

We burst out laughing.

"Hey, beggar," she waves her hand, "don't laugh, talk about yourself."

"What is there to say? My *curriculum vitae* is simple: father, mother, sister, school, work in the countryside, factory work ... about ten words altogether."

"Which is also to say, politically reliable."

"Except that I was in the county gaol for a few days when I was in the countryside."

"For robbery?" Her eyes widen in surprise. "Or for indecent behaviour?"

"You have a rich imagination."

"But there always has to be a charge."

"Another student and I opposed collection of the grain tax; there was a drought that year, and many of the peasants had nothing to eat."

"What a fine champion of idealism. And afterwards, did you bow your head and confess?"

"An old comrade-in-arms of my mother got me out."

"That's how it always ends, that's why people like you always believe in happy endings; at every crossroads there's some protector or other standing, waiting to get you out." She taps on the book with her fingers. "That day, when you were talking about 'our country', I was wondering, is our country the lifelong protector of you and your kind?"

"You mean our country protects us, or we protect our country?"

"It's all one thing."

"No, suppose the former is true, then in order to achieve the latter we must always pay a higher price in our efforts and endeavours."

"What price?"

"The price of the heart."

"But people like you, when all's said and done, never do have to pay the full price; never have to suffer hunger and cold, be subjected to discrimination and insults, lay down your life for a few words . . . . "

"That depends. During the years of . . . . "

"That was only temporary, like the way we're smiling now is temporary."

I leap to my feet. "You, we . . . . You have an interesting way of dividing things up. Since we're not on the same road, it's pointless for us to see each other. I'm sorry, it's time for me to be leaving."

"Sit down." She blocks my way, defiantly biting her lip. "I tell you, you musn't go just because I talk like that."

We stand at a deadlock. She is so close, her breath blows lightly against my face. The crisscross of the window is reflected in her eyes. Crickets chirp softly in the corner.

"You are really hospitable," I say.

"Let me ask you something. What is courtesy?"

"Respect for other people."

"No. Courtesy is just a kind of indifference."

"A certain degree of indifference is necessary."

"And is truth necessary? A person can't have everything . . . . " She stops, with a little smile. "Aren't you tired?"

I smile too, and sit down.

She shakes her head. "All right, let's have some courtesy. Would you like some water? Oh yes, and there's some black tea here too . . . . " She puts on an apron, takes a jar out of the box, walks to the corner and lights the kerosene burner on top of the earthen stove. The blue flames flare up, licking the black base of the pot. Sometimes fire doesn't make you think of its untamed violence, or of the way it makes things collapse, sometimes it reveals

instead that other face: beauty, warmth, kindness . . . .

She stirs the pot with a ladle, clear, crisp sounds clinking out from time to time. She has her back to me, and suddenly asks, "Yang Xun, am I strange?"

"How can I put it; I get a different impression every time."

"To tell the truth, I thought that now I was old, I should be relatively stable. Don't laugh . . . . But I'm changing, sometimes I don't recognize myself at all. What are you laughing at?"

"You don't look more than eighteen or nineteen."

"Don't flatter me. Women always like to be thought younger than they are, isn't that so? They live for others. Really, I feel old, like an old grandmother sitting in the doorway in the sun, sizing up each passer-by with cold detachment . . . . "

"Well, I'm a passer-by."

"You're an exception."

"Why?"

"You didn't just pass by, you broke in . . . . Clear the table, the tea's ready." She pours black tea into two cups, and takes a packet of biscuits out of the drawer. "Please, have one."

"Now *that's* courtesy."

"Is it? Then I've progressed a little." She blows gently on the steam in the cup. "Strange, how did we warm up all of a sudden?"

"Yes, we've got very warm."

"You still haven't answered my question."

"No one can answer it. It's a question with a history of thousands of years."

She blushes. After a little while she says, "Yang Xun, have you ever been to the seaside?"

"Yes, I have."

"Between each high tide and low tide, there's a period of relative calm. The fisherman call it slack water. What a pity the time is so short . . . . "

"I don't really understand such things."

"You should understand!" She raises her voice, and in it there's a kind of deep pain. I stare at her, and suddenly I have the feeling that, in the sunlight, her hair has gone gradually white.

Silence.

"Is it sweet enough?" she asks suddenly.

"It's a little bitter."

She pushes over the tin of sugar. "Add more

sugar, if you like."

"There's no need, I like it a little bitter," I reply.

3B   *Xiao Ling*

I LOVE WALKING alone, walking unrestrained along the street, watching the twilight flood the earth. He left, as suddenly as he came. I didn't detain him, but how I hope he'll come again, and talk of the brief full-tide, and why the sea is salty . . . . You speak to him sarcastically, answer him coldly, yet all the time you're hoping he will stay longer; how do you explain it? I don't like dropping hints, but a hint can only be answered with a hint, because sometimes the truth is too depressing, frighteningly depressing . . . .

"Don't press your nose against the window, Lingling, do you hear?"

"Mama, look at the snowflakes, how do they get like this?"

"Because of the cold."

"But look, they're so pretty."

"Lingling, will you have to get your nose frozen before you learn? Why won't you do as I tell you."

Crossroads: which way to turn. Choices, choices, yet on I go. A crowd of schoolchildren with schoolbags on their backs runs by making a tremendous racket. A motorized pedicab is parked by the side of the road, a driver in a red singlet leans against the door, smoking, staring at me fixedly. A mother with a basket on her arm, dragging her noisy little boy, saying over and over, "Wanwan, stop fussing, Mama will buy you a sweet . . . . "

I've left this world far behind. I've walked out in silence. I do not know where home is. Sometimes, when I turn and look back at this world, I feel a kind of happiness in my heart. It is not pleasure in others' misfortunes, it is not that, still less nostalgia or yearning; it seems that only distance, only the separation and connection of distance, can bring the pleasure of discovery.

Dusk is changing something. The sunlight is being squeezed out, climbing onto the roof of each house. The people hurry by, each one in this instant forming an aspect of your life, that aspect forever changing, and yet you are still yourself.

Things that last, that last . . . those intense eyes again, how many times is it now? Yes, I do crave love and help, even a few considerate words. I once had a father, a mother, and friends . . . .

It's dark. The streetlights are so dim, like fireflies flying slowly. The moon rises, a new moon, with an artist's chin. It's lost in thought. In the distance, under the pale canopy of the streetlights, a swaying figure appears, and quickly vanishes. It's not long before the light reveals . . . .

"It's you, Bai Hua."

"Oh, Xiao Ling . . . . "

"How do you know my name?"

"I always get to know the things I want to know. Believe me?"

"You've been drinking again."

"What of it?" He sways violently, and grabs hold of a telegraph pole. "What of it?"

"Tell me, where do you live?"

He stops, blinking bloodshot eyes with difficulty. "Where do I live? Let's just say, somewhere underground. Huh, a rat who can dig a hole, a rat . . . . "

I cut him short. "Come on, I'll see you home."

"Home? To my place? I mean, you're not, not scared?" He is rather bewildered, sticks his hands in his trouser pockets and pulls them out again, then rubs his damp hair. "Oh, that's a good idea, it sure is, I mean, miss . . . walk, walk, take a big step, take a small step, cross the mountain, cross the stream . . . . " he chants halteringly.

Darkness. Brightness. Darkness. We walk along under the streetlamps. I follow his wavering, and the wavering of the streetlamps; the road is not very steady, as if it too is starting to waver a little. What notion prompts me to go and look? Curiosity? Oh no, hasn't Time played enough tricks? So what is it? Could it be in retaliation for craving warmth just now? That peculiar shadow of his slips under his feet one moment, slants on the roadside the next, then bumps against the wall. Why do I want to see him like this? It's always easy to hide oneself from one's own eyes.

In the distance someone is singing, but the song is hard to make out. Bai Hua seems to sober up a little. "Who's crying? No one's dead yet, what are you crying for? Like rotten mud paste on a body. Fellas, let me do a verse . . . . "

Sure enough he starts to sing, at first quite hoarsely, then rising to his full strength. It's as if he and the song are one, passing through the streetlamps and the curtain of night, flying away towards another world.

> *"Oh the wanderer,*
> *So happy and gay!*
> *Treading the world's mountains and*
> *   rivers,*
> *Tramping in thunder and rain,*
> *Singing beneath the sunlight,*
> *The earth gives me freedom,*
> *Freedom makes me happy and gay.*
> *. . . . . ."*[3]

We turn into a square behind a block of flats and through a pitch-dark clump of trees. He bends over and pushes open a concrete slab on a pulley, revealing a cavernous flight of stairs. I glance at him, and plunge down. Inside it's damp and cold, so dark you can't see a thing. *'Kacha'*, he strikes a lighter. We follow the stairs down, push open an unlatched steel door, the damp vault spreading out in front of the jumping flare. Utter silence, but for water dripping somewhere.

We turn into a little room, he gropes around, lights a kerosene lamp on an old wooden table. Only then do I discover, on a bed spread with a straw mat in the corner of the room, a woman of indeterminate age sitting, propping herself up with her hands behind her back, her eyes flashing like a wildcat's.

"Where've you been?" she asks.

"Number Four?" Bai Hua scratches his head. "Who let you in?"

"You've been boozing again. Guv, come here." She holds out her arms.

"Get lost," Bai Hua snarls.

"I'm not going, this is my place!"

Bai Hua draws a dagger from his belt, and presses forward a few steps. I leap across to block him. "Aren't you ashamed of yourself?"

At this moment Number Four catches sight of me, and slowly gets to her feet. "Oh, so that explains it, you've found another one now. Ha ha." She laughs sarcastically. Bai Hua pushes me

[3] A song popular amongst the educated youth sent to the countryside.

away and charges over. Number Four slips to the doorway in a flash, makes an obscene gesture, "Look at that, such a delicate little face, eh? Ha ha . . . ." The wild nervous laughter becomes a rumbling cacophony, gradually fading into the distance.

Bai Hua walks up to the table, his shadow growing bigger and bigger, wavering on the walls and ceiling. With a clatter he tosses the dagger onto the table, slowly sits down, cradling his head in his hands.

"Is this the freedom and gaiety of your song?" I ask.

Bai Hua throws himself into a chair. "Shut up."

"Answer my question."

"All right. I sang about what I haven't got. Everyone does that!" He brings a bottle of white liquor out from under the table, knocks the top off on a corner of the table, and pours himself a cup.

"Bai Hua, you can't drink any more," I say, going up to him.

"Have one with me." He pours another cup, and pushes it towards me. His eyes gradually fill with tears, then he sighs deeply. "You're a good person, Xiao Ling, I couldn't hurt you, I only wish I could look at you every day, listen to you talk, and if anyone touched you, look, this is what I'd do . . . ."

He draws the dagger fiercely, and stabs his own palm. Blood flows out, drips into the wine cup. He stabs again, and the wine in his cup turns red. I grab his wrist, snatch the dagger away. "You're mad!"

"It doesn't matter." He laughs shrilly. "Our blood isn't worth money. People like us. I swear it, cross my heart."

"That's enough nonsense. Press here, and raise your hand. Press! Did you hear? Have you got a bandage, and something to put on the wound?"

"On the box, genuine knife wound ointment."

When I've finished the dressing, I let out a long sigh and sit down. "Are you always like this?"

He shakes his head. "Huh, it's nothing. Just an old routine."

"Tell me the truth."

The lamp sputters, giving off beautiful arcs of light which immediately turn into wisps of blue smoke.

"Bai Hua, have you seen the stars?"

"Of course."

"Have you ever thought about them? They're old and yet they're new. What we see here is only yesterday's shine, and while we see it they're sending out today's, a new radiance."

"So what?"

"We just accept something as an accomplished fact. We never ask ourselves if these things which have become part of our lives have a value."

"Value? That's money again. That's nothing."

"I have this sudden feeling, about people, life, the pity of it . . . . "

"Yes, the pity of it." He nods in agreement.

Does he understand what I mean? Well, if he understands it's fine, and if he doesn't, that's fine too. What's it got to do with him anyway? It's nothing but my own state of mind. A mood, an endless breakdown touched off by tiny reactions. But this time the breakdown has a different feeling to it, it's strangely still, and within the stillness, sorrow—like an underground river flowing within a mountain, till the landscape slowly starts to subside . . . .

The silence whirrs. Remote at first, gentle, gradually turning into a piercing din, as if this little room can no longer contain it.

He raises the cup. "Come on, have one, my head's bursting."

The cup glistens in the air. Stars. So this feeling is real. They do exist, everywhere. Even in the places where starlight can never reach, there can be another radiance. It all depends on the rays of light connecting: yesterday and tomorrow, life and death, good and evil . . . .

"All right then, I won't drink," he says, hanging his head.

I raise my cup. "Come on, cheers."

3C *Bai Hua*

I'M DREAMING, dreaming of stars.

"Wake up, Guv." Someone's pushing me—oh, it's just Manzi.

"What's up?"

"The one-twenty express will be here soon, Guv."

I pull out my pocket-watch and tap on the glass. "What are you panicking about, there's still another hour to go." A burning stab of pain. I can't help grinning, glancing at my bandaged left hand. I go over to the bucket, splash my face with cold water with my right hand, wipe it. Then I glance at the chair where she's just been sitting. "Come on, don't forget your gear."

On the street, it's utterly desolate, a cat wailing on a rubbish heap. I look up, stars, sparkling and glittering. Huh, good-for-nothing lumps, isn't that what they are?

"What are you staring at, Guv?" Manzi looks up too.

"Have you ever seen stars?"

"Sure, those are stars, aren't they?"

"They're old and they're new, understand?" Manzi stares at me baffled. "No, I don't get it."

"You can pity people . . . . " I say.

"Sure, that's right, and you can hate them too." Manzi nods, to show that he understands this time. "Hey, Guv, you've grown learned."

Reaching the West Station, we follow the shadows round the outside wall. Not far ahead, someone's talking in a low voice.

"We only want five dollars, that's not much at all," says a girl with a thin, shrill voice.

"That's the old price." That hoarse voice sounds like Lanzi's.

"Three dollars, that'll keep you in food for a few days," says some bastard with a Manchurian accent.

I give Manzi a wink, and walk up. Lanzi and another girl, no more than thirteen or fourteen, are leaning against the wall, bargaining with a couple of fellows of about forty.

"If I say no, I mean no, our money doesn't grow on trees either," says the bastard with the big chin. Suddenly catching sight of us, he nudges the other with his elbow and turns to sneak away.

"Hold it!" I call in a low voice, as Manzi blocks their way from behind.

"What's up?" Big Chin runs his tongue over his lips, pretending to be calm.

"Fix the price before you go."

"What price? I don't get it."

"Enough bloody play-acting!" I say. "Ten dollars each."

"What's the idea?" snorts Big Chin, unconvinced. "Are you threatening me?"

"You bet we are!" Manzi pulls out his knife and holds it at Big Chin's back. Big Chin starts shaking.

"Brothers, take your hands off and let us go," whines the other one. "We're new, we don't understand the rules here."

"The rules here are simple," I say. "Your cash, or your life."

"We'll pay, we'll pay." The shivering mongrel takes out two ten-dollar bills and hands them to me.

"Now get lost." I wait till they've gone far enough away, then turn to the small white faces of the two girls, and hand over the money. "Go on, take it."

"Guv," Lanzi gives a wry smile. "The last couple of days haven't been too good."

"Manzi, how much have you got on you?" I ask.

"Sixty."

"Give them thirty."

Manzi unwillingly pulls out the money and hands it to Lanzi.

"Thanks, Guv."

We jump the wall, skirt around the piles of goods, reach the dispatch office, check no one's around, and open the door. Old Meng is rocking his head like a chicken, humming a little tune. He nervously walks to the door and takes a look. "Anyone see anything?"

"Don't worry." Manzi claps him on the shoulder. "What've you got for us this time?"

"Whatever you want." He looks at his watch. "She's coming in twenty minutes, on track three, stops ten minutes. First-class goods are in the third section. But be careful, there are guards . . . . " His Adam's-apple rolls up and down, like a date he can't swallow.

"Some money for smokes." I give him a few notes. "I'll bring the drinking money next time."

"It's my honour, Guv."

We cross the rails silently, and crouch down in the shadow of a heap of cement. Crickets chirp ceaselessly in the thick clumps of grass.

In the distance a whistle blows, the tracks vibrate, clanking. Damn it, there she is, pulling into the station.

IV

4A   *Bai Hua*

THERE'S A BIG plate-glass window, and all kinds of things shining inside: lamps, tablecloths, bottles of wine, guitars, scarves, military uniforms, and what's that . . . a basket of beautiful, bright fresh flowers! Now that's odd, where did fresh flowers come from on a cold day like today? That Yuanyuan rushes busily in and out! Wonder if she'd still recognize me? I heard Yang Xun say, today's her birthday. Good God, when the hell was I born? Xiao Ling's sitting all alone in a corner, well away from that scum. No, Yang Xun's got his filthy eye on her. I'll have to lay things on the line with him.

I press closer to the window, the scene changes completely: a full moon, a cypress bent in the moonlight, like an old man dying. Not a star in sight.

"Quiet, quiet! Who's going to sing first?" someone shouts at the top of his voice. "Bring the guitar . . . . "

The guitar crashes out, some people yelling along with it, stamping on the bloody floor. I really can't take this. Damn it, why should I suffer like this?

I step back, the moon and the old man have flown away. She's still sitting there, not moving at all. Black eyes, red mouth, white face, as white as paper. Something sour and aching pierces through me. Ah, that was ten years ago . . . .

A morning in early winter, the wind had dropped. The rough pitted surface of the road swept clean by the wind. As usual I step across the creaking ice fragments into the waiting-room, shout hello at Old Jia the cleaner, then go behind the seats and pull out a stick with needles on the end, my cigarette-butt collector. There's a thin little girl sitting there, wrapped in an old coat with the padding falling out, no more than eleven or twelve years old by the look of her. She smiles at me, I grin back too, take my stick and leave.

That evening I slip into the waiting-room as usual, the fire in the stove crackling, reflecting on half a dozen crooked figures. Suddenly I give a start, she's still there crouching behind that seat, listlessly smiling at me.

"You haven't left yet?"

She shakes her head.

"You on your own?" I ask again.

She nods, and smiles again.

"I asked you a question. What are you smiling at like an idiot? Are you dumb?" I'm getting a bit angry.

"I'm not dumb," she says softly, enunciating each syllable.

"So what's the idea, not saying anything?"

She stares at me for some time, and runs her tongue over her dry, cracked lips, "Water, I want a drink of water."

I fetch a bowl of steaming-hot water. She clasps it in both hands, her teeth chattering against the rim. I feel her forehead. "Hey, you're really hot! You've got a fever."

Big teardrops roll down into the bowl.

"What is it? Tell me."

She speaks falteringly, half in tears. "My stepmother, she brought me to see the doctor. We came here on the train. The doctor said, the doctor said I couldn't get better, it would be wasting a lot of money .... My stepmother, she brought me here, she said she was going to get something nice to eat, and then she didn't come back, she never came .... "

"The old bitch!" I grind my teeth. "See if I don't beat her flat!"

She stops crying, and blinks at me. "She's not old."

"Old or not, she'll cop it anyway."

"But she's really fat, you couldn't beat her flat."

"Then I'll smash her flat with a brick. Believe me?"

"Yes." She smiles. Round dimples appear in her cheeks.

Early next day, me and my pals pool some money, and I take her a bit of medicine and food. I soak steamed bread in hot water and feed her piece by piece. She's very obedient. Every evening I tell her stories, and she always asks, "And then? And then?"

Once, combing out her plaits, she says to me: "I've got an elder brother, he's great."

"Yes?"

"He's like you, truly."

I catch hold of her little hand. "I'm your elder brother, do you hear?"

She looks startled for a moment, then lowers her eyes shyly. "Yes, elder brother."

Several days go by, and she actually seems to be getting better. I find a "doctor" to look at her. He walks out of the waiting-room with me, rolls the money we've given him into a ball, stuffs it into his cap, thinks for some time, then sighs. "Medicine's too dear, brother, it'll be at least .... " he holds up several fingers.

"Write out the prescription. I can find the money. Yes, I can."

I wander about in the cold wind for a long time, walking, walking, biting my lips till they bleed. I'll do anything for her, even if it means dying!

Night deepens, and I go back to the waiting-room. She's still awake, waiting for me. "Elder brother, why are you back so late?"

"Oh, I had something to do."

"You're shivering .... "

"It's cold outside."

"Come on, sit over here, let me warm you up." The fire-light from the stove lights up her little face. She hugs me tightly. But I shiver even more violently. "Are you still cold?"

"No, I'm not cold."

"As soon as I'm better, I'll sing for you. The people at home in the hills all like listening to me sing, even the calf at home blinks his eyes and listens .... "

I cannot stop myself from breaking into tears.

"What is it, elder brother?" She is bewildered, and smooths my dishevelled hair with her little hand, the tears streaming down . . . .

When morning comes I sit up quietly, unclasp her hot little hands from my arm and stare fixedly at her for a while. Only when her eyelids flicker do I slip away.

It's all right for the time being, but in my mind something keeps shouting: more, just a bit more, and she'll get well, she'll sing her pretty songs . . . . Suddenly, on the bus, a fat-headed bastard twists my ear and drags me into the local police station. An emaciated cur with his cap stuck crooked on his head jangles a bunch of keys and jabs me in the head with his finger. "Five days inside, that's cheap for you!"

I grab hold of the hem of his coat like a madman, imploring bitterly. "Uncle, I don't care what you do, beat me, break this arm, only let me go. Don't lock me up, Uncle, please, my little sister's sick, she's going to die . . . . "

"She's going to die?" he snorts. "If she's another little beggar like you, a dead one'll be one less!"

With a crash the gaol door is locked. I fling myself at it, beating my head against the door, under my fingernails the wall is covered with blood, I faint.

Five days pass. I run madly down the road, the startled people parting to make way for me. I burst through the door of the waiting-room and rush to the corner. It's empty. "Where's my sister? Where is she?" I shout at the people gathered around. No one utters a sound. Old Jia drags his broom along the foot of the wall and slips away.

On the wall, where she'd been leaning, a finger-nail has carved a few spidery words: "Elder brother, I miss you! Elder brother, come back . . . . "

4B   Lin Yuanyuan

Lin Yuanyuan, still at her birthday party, challenges Yang Xun over his relationship with Xiao Ling, and reflects on her realization that she is in love with him herself.

4C   Yang Xun

"Xiao Ling, aren't you feeling well?"

"The truth is, I shouldn't have come."

"Drink up, Yuanyuan's watching us."

"How old is she?"

"Eighteen, five years younger than you."

"I'm a hundred years older than she is."

"Why not even more?"

"That's the limit, a century only has a hundred years. Oh, the great twentieth century, mad, chaotic, utterly irrational century, century without faith . . . . "

"We used to have faith."

"Those broken fragments, still clinking behind us. Perhaps we are moving forward, but where is the road?"

"Why must there be a road? If vast fields can hold humanity, why crowd along one narrow road?"

"Fields . . . . I was thinking of a place beyond the horizon . . . . "

"Such a place doesn't exist."

"When you think of it, it exists."

"You're evading something."

"Perhaps I am, I'm evading happiness, evading beauty, evading light . . . . "

"You're drinking too fast, Xiao Ling. You'll get drunk."

"I'm also evading being sober, because this world's too clear, and clarity makes me sick, I want to blind myself, even if only for a little while."

"This is not the way."

"I hope the people who have a way also have a little conscience; but I'm afraid all they have is endless ways, ways, ways . . . . "

"Don't drink so much."

"Yang Xun, have you ever noticed the old women in the street who collect waste paper? Actually, they're dead, they died long ago. All that's left is a body, and this body has no connection whatsover with the original person, it's just keeping up certain basic habits in order to survive, nothing more. That is my situation at present."

"No, you can still think."

"That's a kind of basic habit too, exactly the same as my drinking."

"Look at Bai Hua."

"Why change the subject? Is it disagreeable? Doesn't it suit this elegant atmosphere? Hm?"

"Xiao Ling, we all have times like this, and everything will pass."

"It won't pass, it never will, you needn't console me."

"Talk about it then, I shan't hinder you."

"I don't feel like talking."

Bai Hua has joined the party and exchanges hostile words with Yang Xun over Xiao Ling. Fafa recognizes him and publicly insults him; he returns the insult, leaves and the party breaks up.

People drift off, until only Xiao Ling and I are left in the room, she sitting in the same place as before, cheek in hand, staring at the clock on the wall.

"What are you thinking about?" I ask.

She shakes her head. Then she walks over to an old piano in the corner, pulls off the old checked cover thick with dust, and sits down on the piano stool, moving very slowly, like an old invalid.

A clear strong chord breaks the silence, the windows in the room tremble in fervent response. The swift notes stream and flow like a boat on a river . . . she stops, turns and begs, "Turn off the light, do you mind?"

She plays Beethoven's "Moonlight Sonata". The moonlight streams in through the window, falling on her white cheeks and forehead. The seaside under the moon. Surf beating gently against the cliff spits out gold and crimson bubbles. A horn blows in the distance . . . a roar, like a clap of thunder; she leans over the keyboard, a slight spasm seizing her shoulders.

"Xiao Ling—" I go up to her.

She looks as if she's just woken from a dream, slowly straightens her back and tosses her hair. She gazes at me with rapt attention, tears in her eyes. In the moonlight, a kind of deep warmth creeps back into her ice-cold face.

4D Xiao Ling

"However you put it, anyone who's against the work group is against the Party!"

"What's the use of sticking labels on people like that? Work groups obviously stifle the masses, what right have they to represent the Party?"

"Well, anyway, that's, that's . . . . " she stammers, her pretty face reddening. "You, what's your class origin?"

The sunlight dances on the red and green wall-poster, dazzling me. I squint painfully. "High intellectual."

"Huh, rotten egg, little bitch, you've got ulterior motives!" She hits me a fierce blow on the ear, her pretty face twisting crookedly. She looks at her reddened palm in surprise.

A door bangs.

"Who is it?" Mother puts down the watering can, wiping her hands on her apron. A crystal drop of water drips from the clusters of violet leaves.

The door opens and about ten people swarm into the room. Leading them is a boy with a baby-face. He wipes his sweating nose with the back of his hand. "Hey, stand still, no messing around . . . let's start."

"Why are you raiding our home?" asks Mama in terror.

Baby Face brandishes his belt and the violet petals flutter to the floor. "Because of this!"

The wall mirror is smashed. Leather boots trample screeching back and forth over the broken glass. Clothes and books are flung all over the floor. A fellow walks up to the piano and kicks it. "American made. Take it away, get some more people . . . . "

"You're nothing but bandits!" Mama mutters, her hands clasped together, the knuckles showing white.

Baby Face turns round, smiling. "Are you talking about us, eh?"

I try to stop Mama, but it's too late. "Yes, you, bandits! What of it?" Mama's voice rises to a pitch.

"Nothing." His smile vanishes and he waves his hand. "Come here, teach her how to speak to Red Guards."

I throw myself towards Mama but I am fiercely pushed away. Half a dozen leather belts fly at her.

"Mama!" I cry, struggling.

The belts whistle, the buckles glistening in the air. Suddenly Mama breaks through the tight circle, runs to the balcony and jumps nimbly onto the other side of the rail. "I'm going to die any-

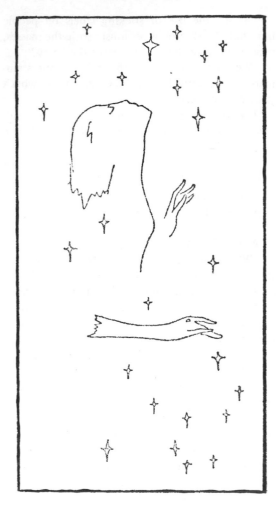

I close the door, and glance sideways. "Papa, take that placard off your neck."

"No, they might come and check. It's no trouble, Lingling."

Dusk filters into the room, Papa and I sitting in the dimness. I feel his gaze fixed on me. "Don't look at me like that, I can't bear it."

"Just this once, Papa doesn't usually look at you enough." Suddenly he asks, "Lingling, if Papa's not here too, what will you do?"

"What nonsense are you talking!" I cut him short indignantly.

In the night, I wake with a start, and tiptoe to Papa's door. In the moonlight, the bed is empty. A note held down on the desk rustles in the breeze. "Lingling, I'm too ashamed. I can't go on living, please forgive my weakness. Don't look for me, I don't want you to see the way I am when I'm dead . . . . This evening, when I was looking at you, my heart broke. You're still so young, what will you do in the future? Goodbye, Lingling . . . . "

Lonely streetlights. Fallen poplar leaves crunching underfoot. I stop, put my hand on the cold stone railing. The river pounds under the bridge, swirling and spinning under the light from the mercury-vapour lamps, spurting out chains of bubbles. Its voice is serene, peaceful, but full of a dignified and irrefutable strength. It's a sound as old as the world.

Far away a train shrills out a long whistle. A wind rises, fallen leaves fly up, and are blown into the sombre river. I turn, and walk back along the lacquer-black road.

way. If anyone comes near I'll jump!"

Everything stands still. The sky so blue, the motionless wisps of white cloud, the sunlight stroking the wound on Mama's temple.

"Mama—" I cry out.

"Lingling—" Mama's eyes turn to me, her voice is so calm. Mama. Me. Mama. Eyes. Drops of blood. Sunlight. Clouds. The sky . . . .

Baby Face seems to wake up, pokes the brim of his cap with his belt, and steps forward. "Go on, jump, jump!"

I rush forward, kneeling on the ground, desperately clasping his legs, staring up at him with bitterly entreating eyes. Looking down he hesitates, his lips parted slightly, showing his shining teeth. He swallows, and pushes me strongly away.

"Mama—"

The clouds and the sky suddenly turn upside down.

V

5A *Lin Yuanyuan*

Yuanyuan and Fafa have been talking about Bai Hua, teasing each other. Fafa makes suggestive remarks about sleeping with Bai Hua, and Yuanyuan calls her a shameless woman.

JUST AT THAT moment, Papa opens the door and walks in. Fafa slips out without a word. I fling the folded clothes fiercely onto the bed. This is all so boring; is this life, are these friends? Is this me? It's so aggravating. The window's shut tight, the central heating boiling with a hissing sound. I always feel there's something hiding outside the window; only open the window, and it'll come whistling in. But what is it?

Papa's big heavy hand falls on my shoulder. "Yuanyuan, you should be working, idle people get into trouble."

"You've been idle for years, and you haven't got into trouble," I throw at him.

"How do you know I haven't?" says Papa. "All right, since it's such fine weather, we'll go to the Tomb of the Martyrs Park, how's that?"

Are we in class? Teacher Mu's big melon-face: "This is where we salute the memory of the re-volution's martyrs ... eyes right!" Drum roll. Recite poems. Lay wreaths .... All right then, we're born to obey.

On the way to the park in the car, they pass Yang Xun in the street and pick him up.

"Yuanyuan—Yuanyuan, come over here—" people call out in chorus. Oh, it's just that bunch from the city deputies' compound, dressed in garish colours, cameras slung over their shoulders. They're standing on the steps to the martyrs' memorial and beckoning to me, the girls waving their bright scarves. "Go on," Papa says. "Wait, why don't we go and have a look together."

We mount the stairs and at once they come crowding over: "Hello, Uncle Lin!"

"Hm, are you putting on a fashion show?" says Papa.

"Are you against it?" says Monkey Xu, pushing forward. Today he's wearing a black leather jacket and a pair of red-brown drainpipe trousers.

"Well, I certainly wouldn't commend you for it."

"Clothes should have individuality, people should wear whatever they like .... " As Monkey Xu finishes, he pulls a face.

Papa taps him on the shoulder. "Let me take a look at this individuality of yours. This is an order: squat! Now then, if there's a war, what will you do?"

"What's it got to do with war?" voluble Fatty Wang interjects. "We hate war!"

"What will you do if the enemy comes?"

"Me?" Fatty Wang counts on her fingers. "Number one, it's utterly impossible."

"And number two?"

"If they really do come, we're not cowards. But I don't understand, what's that got to do with wearing a few clothes that look smart?"

Papa smiles. "I'm not against looking smart. But you should try and acquire a little taste."

Monkey Xu sticks his head out again. "And if our ideas of taste happen to differ? Then you'll simply give us an order: change into standard blue uniforms .... "

"Actually we dressed up specially today because we feel we're too old," Fatty Wang sighs. "Uncle Lin, what did your generation do when you were young?"

Papa's expression becomes suddenly grave, and he turns towards the martyrs' memorial. "Ask this. Under it are lying one thousand one hundred and .... "

" ... fifty-seven martyrs. I know, I've known that since I was three. But I don't believe they charged around fighting every minute of their lives. After all, they were human beings as well. And besides, if there had been no love, then there'd be no us!"

They all laugh.

"What a girl!" says Papa.

"As far as I can see, in those days you were more casual than we are. That's as plain as day-light, there's no need to be vague about it. But for us, either there's just no way out, or all the ways have to be arranged by you. So where's the interest in living. Yuanyuan, what do you think?"

I wink secretly.

"Don't exaggerate our role; whether you succeed or not still depends on you. What's your name? Fine, Comrade Fatty Wang, we'll have another chat some time. Stay here and enjoy yourself, Yuanyuan. Xun and I are going for a walk."

I feel utterly empty, chat with the others for a moment or two, then slip into the shadows behind the martyrs' memorial. Looking at the sky from here, it seems even bluer. A few crows fly past cawing. These ugly creatures are quite happy. I've heard that in some countries people even regard them as holy birds. It seems that even the fates of crows are different, though their cry is about the same: *ka-ka . . . ka-ka . . . .*

The two of them vanish into the thick wood.

5B   *Lin Dongping*

WE FOLLOW the path through the wood, walking towards the hillock. Dry leaves covering the path crunch underfoot. A light breeze springs up, the bright, sparse grey branches swing a little.

I haven't been here for a long time. This memorial park was built in '55. I signed the approval myself. The then Municipal Committee secretary, Old Han, had no inkling that he would one day be the one thousand one hundred and fifty-eighth. Hundreds of the city's teachers and cadres died a violent death at more or less the same time. Their names ought to be carved on the memorial, so that the children will remember them, remember that period of history. Amongst the names of the dead on this long, long list is that of Yuanyuan's mother. She was sent here as a member of the provincial committee work group, and was dead after barely a month. She died in a criticism session, from another heart attack, it was said. I feel guilty towards her, years of disharmony added to the burden on her heart, especially after she knew of my affair with Ruohong. But there's no court of feelings in the world, only conscience. And there are too many kinds of conscience nowadays. For me there's only one, there absolutely cannot be two. And where is my conscience? . . . "They were human beings as well. If there had been no love then there'd be no us!" It's as if Fatty Wang's probing eyes have seen right through what's in my heart, the wretched girl! Yes, we were all human beings. We all have our own history, our own secrets of happiness and pain. Others can never know, except those with whom you have entered into secrets. Why doesn't Xun like to talk? He's not at all like his mother. When the organization sent Ruohong to help me with my work that evening we chatted nearly the whole night. We were afraid of attracting other people's attention and didn't turn the light on in the room. The moonlight poured through the skylight, illuminating the brass knobs of the old-fashioned iron bed she was sitting on. At last she

grew tired, and fell asleep against the bedstead. I covered her with a blanket, then went to the store-room to send the last telegram . . . .

The white poplars brush against us, as we pass each of these white memorials. We ought to set up a memorial for each of our unhappy love affairs, and tell the children: we've sacrificed everything for your happiness. Is that really true? Facts are often blown out of proportion. But at least we left the fruit of love, left lasting memories.

Xun has walked on ahead. A few crows caw noisily, flapping their wings in the treetops and flying off. Blasted creatures. You have no scruples about all that people cherish, it would even give you satisfaction to destroy them. Fortunately the world is big enough to contain everything. What is the meaning of this containment? Is it just co-existence? But can I co-exist with a fellow like Wang Defa? He lives with such confidence, he doesn't take account of me in the slightest, speaks in front of me without any restraint. That scene in the office just now . . . .

" . . . this is the basic situation with the problem of co-operation in the engineering work on the Jinying River." Wang Defa shut his notebook, leant over and pushed a packet of cheap cigarettes at me across the table.

"No thanks, I've just put one out."

"And I have another idea." He rubbed his unshaven chin, hesitated for a moment. "The new financial year will begin soon. Our supply situation's always a problem. Can we improve it? I've made a calculation: if everyone's monthly ration for oil, sugar, meat and eggs is reduced to the lowest limit, then we can depend on the surrounding counties to supply us, and we won't have to go begging."

"The lowest limit?"

"Be patient. This is calculated on a scientific basis. Last time I was at the provincial capital for a meeting, I asked a medical authority—you should have seen his big beard." Wang Defa grew excited and pulled a sheet of paper from his pocket. "I've made out a full report; if we achieve some success, who knows, the whole country might learn from us . . . ."

I put on my glasses and looked at the report. "Two *liang*[4] of white sugar?"

[4]About 100 grams.

"The human body can get sugar from grain and vegetables high in starch, it's scientific!"

"Hm, it's a good idea." I took off my glasses and blinked. "What about the peasants? There's just been a flood, what revenues can we collect?"

"Ah, as the saying goes, 'there's no blessing you can't enjoy and no suffering you can't stand'. I grew up in the countryside, I understand them better than you. You ink-drinkers, you're too sentimental. How was it in '58? That was done by you lot. That winter I happened to go home from the army to visit relatives. You couldn't count how many people had died from hunger; but we got through somehow, didn't we?" He scratched at a greasy stain on his sleeve with his fingernail. "Tighten your belts a bit, that'll solve the problem."

"Tighten whose? Does that include you and me?" I asked.

He smiled knowingly. "Old Lin, you get more and more confused the older you get! Of course it doesn't include us. Don't worry."

I placed my hands on the table, then slowly clenched them again.

"Come on, Old Lin, sign," he said.

I put on my glasses, looked at the report again, then from over the rim of my glasses I caught sight of his hand holding the cigarette. What was that hand capable of? Pounding the table, making telephone calls, even strangling . . . what, was I afraid? Just because he has real power, connections at the top? I am an intelligent person, it's simply not worth destroying myself over this small thing. I can still make many contributions to the people . . . . What a lie! Behind this piece of paper, how many pairs of eyes are watching you, watching your every move, watching your conscience. Yet you still boast unblushingly of 'the people' and 'contribution' . . . for shame!

"I won't sign," I said, taking off my glasses and pushing away the report.

Wang Defa rapped on the table with his knuckles. "Old Lin, you and I are both experienced men . . . I can't do anything either, it's come down from a higher level."

"So why won't they give a proper order?"

He smiled just a little. "You still don't get the point, do you? From the bottom to the top, that's your glorious tradition from the days of guerilla warfare."

"If that's the case, we should take up the discussion from the Party Committee, and listen to their opinions."

The last trace of a smile vanished from his face. He looked at me expressionlessly. "Very well."

Several tall poplars have been planted on the top of the hillock. The sunshine lights up their pencil-straight trunks; in contrast to the surrounding grey tone, they appear unusually clean, erect and stalwart. The wind blows the dry leaves into hollows. I sit down under a wind-weathered rock, drawing deeply at my cigarette, chewing the bitter shreds of tobacco that have fallen into my mouth. In the quiet net woven by the path, the fallen leaves and the poplars, a light thread of sorrow permeates the air, and is carried away by the wind to the mountain wilderness.

Xun walks over to a poplar and gazes into the distance.

5C   *Yang Xun*

Yang Xun says he is going to see a film and admits to Lin Dongping that his engagement is not with a local girl. He leaves, while Lin Dongping remains behind on the hill alone.

THE SNOWFLAKES are spinning, the whole sky is dancing with them. Some of the blackness is drained from the night. The two of us stand on the cinema steps, watching the black tide of people, a floating mass of gaily-coloured scarves, flowing past us like waves, parting and converging again, gradually vanishing into the white vastness of the flying snow.

"It's strange; how can so many other people bear to sit through a film like that?" Xiao Ling says.

"Like enduring life, it's not so hard," I say.

"But it's supposed to be art, after all." She takes a red gauze kerchief from her pocket and ties it on her head. "I always think, these people who make films must be sick in the head."

"It's the state apparatus that's sick."

"Shh—" She puts her finger to her lips and looks all around. "Didn't you spend enough time in the county gaol? I mean, don't push all the problems onto the top; even if there were to be a change, how much effect would it really have?

When the Nazis seized power, the majority of German intellectuals refused to co-operate. The crux of the matter is that the former generation of Chinese intellectuals never formed a strong social stratum, they always submitted to political oppression, and even if they resisted, their resistance was extremely limited."

"And our generation?"

"I can't explain exactly. Still, each generation should be stronger than the last. Really, I can't quite explain." She shakes her head. "Let's change the subject."

"The snowstorm was very sudden," I say.

Xiao Ling greedily drinks in a mouthful of fresh air. "I signed a contract with the snowflakes, to fall when people aren't expecting it."

"Where did you sign?" I ask.

"On the windowpane, with my breath and finger."

"When?"

"When I was four or five."

"Then you were this big." I point at a little girl in a green padded jacket walking by us.

"Then you were that big." She points at a plastic toy dog in the little girl's hand.

We both laugh.

"Haven't they torn up the contract?" I ask again.

"Only once."

"When?"

"This time. Today, I thought it would snow, I thought it would." She sighs, and the snowflakes disappear around her mouth. "Nature has this sort of power, it can reconcile us with ourselves, with others, with life . . . . "

The crowd disperses. The lights at the cinema door go out one by one. The earth, covered with white snow, grows bright, like a dark mirror.

" . . . I'm so tired, how I wish I could have a rest, a home, a nest to go to." She sorrowfully closes her eyes. "So I can lick my wounds, have pleasant dreams."

"A home," I repeat.

She nods. "Yes, a home."

"Xiao Ling," I say, catching hold of her hand.

"What?" She hangs her head, blushing.

"Suppose there were someone willing to help you shoulder everything?"

"Everything," she says softly.

"Yes, everything. Suffering and loneliness, and happiness too."

"Happiness." She answers like an echo.

"That's right, happiness."

She draws her hand away. "Fool."

We are separated by a row of tall white poplars. The snow crunches underfoot. For a long time neither of us speaks.

"Recite a poem, Xiao Ling," I say.

Her expression is a little abstracted. After a while, she bites her lip, and begins to recite in a low voice:

> *"The sky is beautiful,*
> *The sea is serene*
> *But I see only*
> *Darkness and blood . . . . "*[5]

"Why did you choose that poem?" I ask.

"The poem chose me." She bites her lip and shakes her head. "I only deserve this kind of fate. What is there I can do?"

---

[5]From "Un Voyage à Cythère," by Baudelaire, in *Les Fleurs du Mal* (1857).

"You were just talking about resistance."

"That's another matter." She forces a smile. "First I have to resist myself: unfortunately I haven't even that ability."

"So according to what you say, this generation has no hope?"

"Why wander so far from the point? All that can be said is that I have no hope."

"No, there's hope," I say determinedly. "We have hope. Where there's life there's hope."

"Who is 'we'?" She stops by a tree and rests her cheek against the trunk with a captivating smile.

"You and I."

"Oh." She pulls off her headscarf, all wet with snowflakes, gives it a shake and ties it to the trunk of the tree, gliding her finger up and down on it. "Who gave you the right to talk like this?" she asks in a hurried, low voice.

"You and I."

Suddenly she raises her eyes, almost grim. "Do you understand me?"

"Yes, I do."

"Based on what? These few meetings?"

"This isn't something that can be measured in terms of time . . . . "

"No, no, don't say it, you'll pay a price." She hastily cuts short my speech, and releases her scarf from the branch. "It's late, let's go."

The snow has stopped. The rays from the mercury-vapour lamps reflect on the snow, shining with a gloomy blue light. She bites her lip, staring straight ahead, her steps hurried then slow, limping along, kicking up puffs of powdered snow. At the last poplar she stops, looking at me silently, in her eyes hesitation and distress.

"Let's say goodbye," she says.

"When shall we meet?"

"We shan't." She averts her gaze. "Never . . . . "

"Don't make jokes."

"I'm in no mood for joking."

"What's the matter, Xiao Ling?"

"Don't bear a grudge against me, don't . . . . " Her lip trembles. She turns her head abruptly and walks away with rapid steps, gradually disappearing at the crossroads ahead.

I stand in the snow for a long time. How did this nightmare begin? How has it ended so carelessly? I scoop up some snow and rub it on my face, letting the melted snow soak into my neck drop by drop. The wind whistles in the distance. No, the wind is over my head, in the treetops, flowing in a firm direction, like an invisible arm, enfolding this miserable world. No, it can't be seen, there's only darkness and blood . . . . I walk back past the trees, one after another, brushing each trunk with my hand, perhaps a little of her warmth remains on them—no, her temperature is zero, is snow and ice . . . .

I walk haltingly. Narrow streets, crooked houses, they crowd in on me until I can't breathe. I stop beside a telegraph pole. Not far ahead, a man and a woman are talking in low voices. What, is that her with Bai Hua?! Suddenly she catches sight of me here, lowers her voice and says something to Bai Hua. Bai Hua puts his arm round her waist, and walks into the shadows.

Bang! Everything spins round, with a humming sound, in a string of dazzling lights and foul black snow . . . . I grab the telegraph pole, swearing savagely.

5D   *Xiao Ling*

THE WIND BLOWS the tears out of my eyes, a corner of the scarf flaps against my face. I walk on, never turning my head, never! Ahead lies an abyss, but there is no way I can stretch out an entreating hand. No one can save anyone else, and what's the sense in perishing together? One should always leave behind something, leave a shred of warmth, a scrap of fantasy, a corner of clear sky, even though the boundless darkness and pools of blood like pounding waves cover them over unceasingly. Ah, you drifting stars, pure and beautiful, let me find shelter within your radiance.

Xiao Ling, having left Yang Xun, and having decided to end their relationship, goes into the park in the middle of the street, where she runs into her foreman at the factory, Firecracker. He is drunk, and makes advances towards her, but she is rescued by Bai Hua, who beats Firecracker up. Suddenly Xiao Ling catches sight of Yang Xun, acts faint, and is helped away by Bai Hua.

VI

6A *Lin Dongping*

Lin Dongping endures another tedious and disturbing Party session. He defends his closure of a coal-mine where there has been an accident on the grounds that the causes of the accident have not been sufficiently investigated. As usual he has a confrontation with Wang Defa, who this time implies that Lin Dongping has misappropriated funds; Lin Dongping then enquires after the flood relief funds, of which Wang Defa is supposed to be in charge. After the meeting he runs into Su Yumei, who flirts with him again.

I OPEN the car door.

"Finished?" Fat Wu yawns, stretching.

"Turn on the radio. See if there's anything to listen to."

The dial lights up. He flicks it back and forth. It's all dry news and ear-piercing model operas.

"Turn it off," I say.

Streetlights. Shops. Cinema. Streetlights. Restaurant. Rubbish heaps. Little mud-brick huts. Streetlights . . . I shut my eyes, this is such a broken-down city, even the night can't hide its shabbiness. These creatures living in these mud-brick huts, going back and forth amidst the rubbish, are these our people?

Arriving home, Lin Dongping finds Yang Xun waiting in the study.

6B *Yang Xun*

Yang Xun tells Lin Dongping that he has just received a letter from his mother, saying arrangements are being made for his return to Peking. Lin Dongping urges him to go back on account of his mother, although he does not wish to. Lin Dongping guesses that his reluctance is due to his having a girlfriend, and suggests that arrangements may also be made for her to go back to Peking. During the conversation the old cadre begins to suspect there may be something strange in Yang's girlfriend's past; at the same time Yang Xun suspects that Lin Dongping's past may involve his own mother. As Yang Xun leaves he meets Yuan-

yuan, still jealous of his involvement with Xiao Ling, and she angrily tells him not to come to their house so often. On the way to the factory he goes into a wineshop, where he meets Bai Hua. Bai Hua clarifies what really happened that evening when he saw them together. Relieved, Yang Xun then goes back to Xiao Ling's house.

I KNOCK ON the door, find that it's off the latch, and push it open. She gets up from the table without a word, her face pale, almost expressionless, only her hands fiddling with the top of a fountain pen.

"You've come," she says at length, almost inaudibly.

"I've come."

"Sit down."

I remain standing.

"Apparently neither of us understands courtesy very well." She attempts a smile, only making her lips tremble. She looks away fiercely, turning the window. On her snow-white neck a blue vein twitches.

"Xiao Ling." I step forward and turn her round by the shoulders to face me. "Why are you being like this?"

She lowers her eyelids, a glistening teardrop hangs on her lashes, quivers, and rolls slowly down her cheek.

"Tell me, why?" I ask.

She opens her eyes, shakes her head, and smiles miserably. I stretch out my fingers and brush away the tear from the corner of her mouth.

"Look, the moon's risen," she says softly, as if telling me a long-hidden secret.

I look up. "The moon's red."

"Yes."

"Why?"

"Listen to you, still the same old habits."

"Xiao Ling, do you know how I've spent these last months?"

She seals my mouth with her hand. "Don't pour out woes, all right?"

I nod.

Suddenly she clasps my neck, trustingly presses her lips towards me and without waiting for my response pushes me away, dodges over the other side of the table, and pulls a mischievous face. "Just stand there, I want to look at you like that."

I start to move round the table.

"Don't move!" she commands.

"This place has turned into a prison," I say.

"How is it compared to the county prison?"

"A bit better."

"I'll lock you up here," she points at her heart. "How about that?"

"That's much better."

We both laugh.

"What's this?" I pick up the notebook lying on the desk. "May I have a look?"

"No!" She leaps across, and clasps it to her breast. "Not now," she adds.

"Later?"

"I'll let you look for sure."

"What have you written? Epigrams and aphorisms?"

"No, just some of my thoughts, and recollections of the past."

6C   *Xiao Ling*

HIGH NOON. Li Tiejun and I walk along the steaming river, followed by two Red Guards from the Red HQ Brigade, automatic rifles slung upside down over their shoulders. Under the burning sun, several young fellows are listlessly digging a trench by the bank.

"Perhaps those bastards will plan an attack for tomorrow." He waves a willow sprig in the air. "Then you people from Peking will see something."

"We haven't come to watch a play. Give me a gun, I'll stay in the forward position," I say.

"You?" His lip curls in a sneer.

"Don't underestimate us. See how we perform on the field of battle." I stop for a moment, then suddenly ask, "Are you one of the 'strong'?"

"What does it mean to be strong? Not to be afraid of death, right?"

"That's not enough."

"What else is there? Killing someone without batting an eyelid?" He says half-jokingly, "You don't believe me?"

I shake my head.

"Let's make a bet," he says.

We reach the head of the bridge on the highway. In the middle of the sandbag defences the gun-metal mouths of heavy machine-guns point straight ahead. At the wire-netting roadblock,

some Red Guards are checking the passers-by.

We lean on the stone balustrade of the bridge, chatting on about this and that. Suddenly, Li Tiejun's eyes turn towards the crowd, he points to a young fellow, beckoning with his finger, and calls him over.

"Where are you going?"

"Into the city to see my aunt, she's sick."

"Not taking anything, eh? Give him another detailed search."

The search produces a girl's photograph and a badge.

"Who's she?" asks Li Tiejun, taking the photograph.

"My girlfriend."

Li Tiejun picks up the badge, looks closely at the back, and laughs grimly. "Taking a Red Cannon Brigade badge to see your aunt? Let's have the truth."

"I really am going to see my aunt," the youth persists.

"Kneel down!" Li Tiejun gives him a kick from behind, and he falls heavily to his knees. "I'll give you one last chance."

"I'm telling the truth."

"Then get ready to say goodbye." Li Tiejun throws the girl's photograph down in front of him, and pulls out his pistol.

The youth picks up the photograph and presses it to his breast, then turns his head, his face deathly white. His beseeching eyes sweep from the muzzle of the gun to me.

"Tiejun, wait a minute . . . . " As I'm about to rush forward to hold him back, the gun goes off.

In the burning-hot noon, beside the quiet river, the gun is so loud, the report hovers for a long time. With the sound of each gunshot, the youth's head strikes against the hard concrete road. Blood spurts out, dyeing the girl's photograph, running into the river . . . .

Tiejun gives the body a kick, puts away his gun and turns proudly towards my stunned face. "This time you lose the bet, that's one you owe me."

"You, you butcher, bastard!" I shout myself hoarse, turn and run, tears blurring my vision.

"Hey, get up."

I blink; a little old man wearing a patrol officer's armband is standing in front of me.

"Get up. Come with me," he says.

I fold up the raincoat I've been using as a bed on the ground, step over the people curled up everywhere, and follow him into the station duty office.

"Sit down." He points to a stool beside the desk.

I remain standing.

"From Peking?" he asks.

"You could say so."

"So why do you come here to sleep every evening?"

"This is the first time."

"Do you think I'm an old fool with no eyes, eh?" He starts to cough, holding a big handkerchief to cover his mouth, coughs for a while, then suddenly asks, "Your home?"

"I have no home."

He nods. "And no relatives or friends?"

"Whom would I approach? I'm wanted by the school." I say irritably, "What do you want? Go and report me . . . . "

The old man's Adam's-apple bobs up and down, he reaches into his pocket and brings out a little paper packet. "Here, take this."

I hesitate, then take the packet—it's ten dollars. Something salt and astringent blocks my throat. "Uncle . . . . "

"Take it, child, don't be so proud, get some more clothes or something, it's getting cold. Otherwise I'll just use the money for drink. Go on, take it. I haven't told the missus. She'll be sure to agree. She's not much to look at but she's got a good heart . . . . "

"Uncle," I say.

"Go on, go on."

"Uncle Shen, I just don't believe these lies any more." I shut the book and leave it on my lap. "But this period of history . . . . "

"You young people, you always want to go forward. Remember, whatever the verdict, it's never the final verdict." He walks round the pile of books on the floor, closes the only shutter in the little room, walks back, and sits down in a creaking old cane chair. "Lingling, when I met your parents, I was studying Oriental history at Harvard. Now that may seem rather funny, but in fact it's not." He points to the book in my lap. "Old Hegel says this: 'All forms of existence bind themselves to their own self-created history;

furthermore, history regarded as a kind of objective universalism then determines them and transcends them . . . . ' That is to say, it's very difficult for man to transcend his own body and recognize history, and those on the crest of the historical wave recognize this even less; this, then, is the lamentable position of certain great men."

"It's also the lamentable position of our nation," I say.

"No." Uncle Shen makes a resolute gesture. "The life of one person is limited, but the life of a nation has no limit: the latent energy of our Chinese nation has never shone forth. Perhaps it's got a bit old, and as a result it has become rather slow in the process of self-recognition. But this process is now under way, is being carried through by a chain from one generation to the next. If a country blows a tune on an out-of-tune bugle, that symbolizes the decline of a certain kind of power; it is also the prelude to the rising up of the whole nation . . . . "

The bells ring, the clamour of leave-taking on the platform reaches a pitch, shouts and sobs mingling into one. An accordion plays frenziedly, young fellows arm in arm sing themselves hoarse. I sit by the window, watching it all with cold indifference.

"Xiao Ling," Yun, who has come to see me off, takes my hand gently. "Come back this winter. Stay at our place, my mother's very fond of you."

"No, I'm not coming back."

"So when will you come back?"

"I'll never come back."

"Why? Xiao Ling . . . . "

Suddenly, the whole station shudders, slowly withdraws. Yun's voice is drowned. She stretches out her hand, runs forward a few steps, and is engulfed in the crowd.

Goodbye, Peking! Forget me, Peking!

VII

7A *Yang Xun*

Yang Xun and Xiao Ling are walking together in the hills.

A CLEAR MOUNTAIN spring cuts across the stone path, falling away into a deep valley. On the pool at the bottom of the valley white swirling vapour rises. She stands at the edge and looks down, as if listening to the tumbling roar. A few grey birds cry plaintively in the spray.

"Is it death down there?" She looks up, her mood turned solemn and sad.

I do not answer.

"It's very close to us." Colour drains from her eyes, the sunlight in them shivers a little.

"What's wrong?" I ask.

She leans against me silently, still staring down. "I'm afraid . . . . "

"Afraid of what?"

"Afraid of parting," she says in a muffled voice.

"Impossible, nothing can part us."

"Even death?"

"Impossible."

She gazes trustingly at me.

I stroke her shoulder. "Let's not stand here, all right?"

She nods, turns and squats down by the spring, watches her reflection and sighs. She splashes her face and turns her head. "How shall we cross?"

I lift her up and leap across.

"I shouldn't be like this. You must have felt disheartened just now," she says, lying in my arms.

"No."

"Truly? Now, look at me, don't turn away . . . good, now let me go."

A flight of stone stairs weathered by the wind leads down to a carved white marble archway. Beyond, on the dilapidated screen wall, the words 'The Wheel of the Dharma Revolves': the gold lacquer has already peeled away. All is sadness and desolation. The tortoise with the stele on its back is buried deep in mud, revealing only half a head. The rough stone path is covered over with last winter's dry leaves and sheep droppings. Most of the side-hall on the right has collapsed, and from the broken arms of the Eighteen Disciples grow tall weeds, rustling in the passing breeze. We enter the main hall, into a faint odour of mold and decay. In the dimness, a shaft of sunlight falls on the long slender hand of the central Buddha.

"Hello, Guan Yin——" Xiao Ling shouts like a child, and the dark, gloomy hall sends back a low, muffled echo.

"This is Sakyamuni," I say.

"An Indian?"

"That's right."

"Mr. Sakyamuni, welcome to our country. But do you have a passport?"

"He has the scriptures," I say.

"There are more than enough of those here already. If you break one of our commandments, you may get a term of labour reform." Xiao Ling suddenly turns, and asks, "Are you interested in religion?"

"One can't help being interested: these years, we've been living in a kind of religious atmosphere," I say. "And you?"

"Me? I've just become interested," she says, closing her eyes. "I wish that in the darkness there were a god to bless and protect us . . . . "

"Why not Buddha, or Old Father Heaven?"

"Anyone will do, as long as it's some sort of divine being."

"Do you really believe in such things?"

"No. I don't know, it's hard to say." She winks, and smiles mischievously. "My religious feeling is pragmatic . . . oh, look, there's a cave."

Sure enough, there in the corner, is the mouth of a cave as tall as a man. Xiao Ling pops her head in. "It's very dark. Did you bring a lighter?"

Holding up the lighter I walk forward. The cave is very deep; after walking a dozen or so steps a flight of narrow stairs appears. Xiao Ling grabs hold of my sleeve. I turn around, and in her wide eyes shine two little dancing flames. The stone stairs rise slowly in the fire-light. Suddenly it becomes light and roomy. We've reached a small attic; inside, eight ferocious-looking monsters stand around the walls.

"Oh! What a weird place. From the top you'd think it was Heaven, but in actual fact it's more like Hell." Xiao Ling looks the monsters up and down one by one. "It's all right, not too scary after all, really rather sad; they must have suffered a lot to turn into things like this."

I go to the window. "Come and see, this is the look-out point."

We look down. The remnants of a wall stand solemnly in the long grass, as if recalling past glory. The flashing stream flows past the courtyard wall, eroding the exposed roots of an old cypress tree. Blue mountains are faintly visible in the distance.

She leans over and gazes at me, in her eyes a

kind of wonder. Sunlight strokes her shoulders and arms, as if it wants to seep right through her body. The red gauze scarf she is wearing is tugged by the wind, one moment blocking out the sun, the next fluttering back, little rainbow-coloured rings leaping before my eyes.

"It would be wonderful if we were like this for ever," she says, resting her hands on my shoulders.

I draw her towards me, and hold her tight. Her head falls back, her lips parted slightly, her breath coming rapidly. Suddenly, big teardrops come rolling down . . . .

"Xiao Ling," I call softly.

She just lies on my shoulder and cries. After a long while, she pushes me away, brushes away the tears, and shakes her head in embarassment, smiling.

"Are you upset?" I ask.

"You're really a fool. You don't know anything," she murmurs, running her fingers through my hair, ruffling it, then slowly smoothing it again.

Two swallows flutter out through a hole in the ceiling.

"We must have disturbed them," Xiao Ling says.

"No, they disturbed us."

"But this is their home."

"It's our home, too."

"Don't talk nonsense." She glares at me fiercely, covering my mouth with her hand. I catch hold of her hand and kiss it. She withdraws it, smooths her hair. "I'm hungry."

I open the bag, spread a sheet of plastic on the floor, then arrange the wine, the food and fruit. I also take out a little aluminium tin, shaking it in my hand. "I'll go and get some water, and collect some firewood while I'm at it."

"I'll go too." On the way she jostles me with her elbow. "You see, I don't know why, but as soon as you leave me I'm afraid. Aren't I a coward?"

"You're a brave girl."

"In these last few days I keep feeling that I'm changing, changing into something I don't quite recognize myself."

"You've become more like yourself."

"Could there be two me's?"

"Perhaps more than two."

"It gets worse and worse. So which me do you actually love?"

"All of them."

"You're being slippery." Her lips curl slyly. "In fact you only love the me in your mind's eye, and that me doesn't exist, right?"

"No, that's the combination of all the you's." She laughs. "Just turn it directly into a mathematical calculation and come up with the three-headed, six-armed me; could you stand that?"

"Let's try it and see."

"I wonder, how can we go on like this? Walking along this little path, as if nothing's happened, as if all along we live by the rules, birth, school, work, love . . . once in a while getting out to the suburbs, letting our cares drift away, do you understand what I mean?"

"I understand."

"If you could choose your life over again, what sort would you choose?"

"Still the one I've had."

"That's because you haven't paid a high enough price."

"No, it's because otherwise I wouldn't have known you."

"Oh, that reason's quite sufficient," she nods, with satisfaction.

We reach the spring.

"I feel like washing my hair." She stretches out and tests the water with her hand.

I look up anxiously at the darkening sky. "Watch out you don't catch a chill. It looks like rain."

She hums a light-hearted tune, undoes her hairpin, and her hair spills into the water without a sound. "Yang Xun, our treat won't be eaten by rats, will it?"

"If there are rats, they'll probably turn into monsters."

"I'm not that easily scared. Come here, help me squeeze this dry." I roll up my sleeves and give a couple of squeezes. She opens my hand. "You're treating it like a piece of rope, let me do it myself."

The branches crackle into flame, the fire-light flickers over her face. In the dancing shadows of the flames, her appearance is a little eery.

"You sure the floor won't catch fire?" I ask anxiously.

"What are you talking about? Heat rises,"

she says.

Heat. Why have I never realized it before? Perhaps that's what I'm feeling at this very moment, heat, slowly rising, rising. We always felt cold before, an ice-coldness spreading outwards from the heart, a kind of coldness discharged through the need for heat, through the absorption of heat; finally condensing into dewdrops on the blades of grass, rising as mist in the valleys.

Xiao Ling kneels on the sheet of plastic, opens the wine, pours two full cups and hands one to me. "Come on, drink up."

"First, let's think of some toasts," I say.

"To you, and that allegedly brave girl, happiness to you and her . . . . "

"To the two survivors of these tragic times . . . . "

"May this pair of survivors, like the swallows, still return to the nest together after being so rudely disturbed . . . . "

"May the guns not aim at swallows . . . . "

"To the indestructibility of the swallows . . . . "

"To beautiful fairy-tales . . . . "

"To the health of Mr. Sakyamuni! Cheers!"

We drain our cups.

In the distance a clap of thunder roars. She gets up and goes to the window, her hair blowing in the wind. "It's going to rain," she murmurs.

"We won't be able to get back," I say.

She turns her head and darts a peculiar look at me.

Night, night full of menace, full of thunder and lightning and rustling, whispers, presses down upon us. The lightning flashes, and in that instant her clear silhouette is thrown against the shattered sky.

"The wind's too strong at the window, come over here," I say.

She remains leaning against the window, staring into the distance.

"Xiao Ling," I say.

She turns, looking at me as if just woken from a dream, walks over silently and sits beside me. The flames gradually die down, the last embers reflecting on her calm face, delineating a gentle curve. I draw her over, she yields silently. Her lips are freezing. She is rather thinly clad.

"Are you cold?"

She shakes her head, watching me blankly. I bend down, kissing her forehead. Her snow-white throat stretches down, swelling a little inside her collar. A row of white buttons glistens in the dimness. My fingers touch the first one, gently unbuttoning it.

"Don't do that," she says in alarm, grabbing my hand.

I touch the second one.

With a thud, she fiercely pulls my hand away, clutching her collar together tightly. "Get away! Didn't you hear me? Get away!" The lightning illuminates her trembling chin.

I get up, and walk angrily to the window. Raindrops drum on the window-lattice, the wind gradually drops, the invisible river thunders . . . . "

Suddenly I am blindfolded. I pull her small hands away, turn round, and she rushes into my arms.

Lightning. The monsters grin savagely over our heads. Darkness.

7B *Xiao Ling*

LOVE STANDS trembling in the quagmire of pain. This liberation is as violent as death, and I keep wanting to open the flood-gates and let the tide of happiness escape with a roar.

Have you gone mad?

Yes, I've gone mad. If I haven't yet been stifled to death by mediocrity, I'd willingly be a lunatic, a cheerful lunatic. Because compared with so-called normality lunacy is a kind of opposite, and any opposite to *that* is beautiful.

Have you forgotten your own duty?

No. In the midst of duty I still think of what lies beyond duty. I think of love, which bathes in a different sunlight.

Enough! I'm getting too abstract!

I like the abstract things of life. They have not been confined by callous and dirty reality, and because of that are more true, more lasting.

Tell me, are you happy?

What is happiness? Is it just a kind of contentment? Contentment leads to boredom. Perhaps genuine happiness leaves no after-taste, or else is like a storm that has already passed by; you only see the traces left on the ground.

Could it be the resurrection of hope?

There is always hope; even in the darkest hours, I still set aside a radiant corner for it. This has

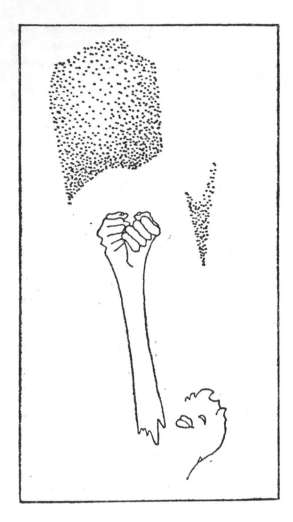

I loathe this tone of yours. Stop interrogating me like an old woman. Leave me in peace.

I open my book, read a few lines, then shut it again. As soon as I pick up my sewing, the needle slips and pricks my finger, and a smooth round drop of blood seeps out. I smile, and suck it dry. It's as if I've only just begun to grasp the true meaning of that experience; to feel astonished, to be intoxicated, to be shy. In fact, the reason for excitement like this isn't in love alone, it's also in finding a new starting point; there are so many things I can do, the little piece of sunlight still left in my heart hasn't grown cold, it can warm others . . . .

I shiver, and my gaze rests on the little glass frame on the table. Jingjing, are you teasing me? Yes, I should find a chance to tell him, tell him all this. Will he understand?

Xiao Ling goes to work at the factory and is summoned by the political work section, where she is reminded of her status as a provisional worker and questioned about her past. When asked whether she had a boyfriend during her years in the countryside, she objects, refusing to say any more. The political officer cautions her about her attitude.

significance in itself, a complete significance. Of course, this hope is by no means illusory, it seeks a goal; as now, in the midst of ruin, caught tightly by the hand of a child and raised up high again; may it gain its heart's desire, may it destroy the boundless and impenetrable darkness!

What kind of goal are you seeking?

This is exactly the question our generation has raised, and which it must answer. Perhaps the search itself is what already epitomizes our generation: we will not easily accept death, or silence, or obedience to any fixed judgement. Even though separated by high walls, mountain ranges, and rivers, each person struggles, hesitates, suffers dejection, even wearies of it all; but taken overall, faith and strength are eternal.

What have you been saying? Why haven't you even mentioned him?

VIII

8A   *Bai Hua*

Bai Hua is hanging around the market-place looking for lucrative opportunities. He runs into Lin Yuanyuan, but she runs away when they catch sight of Yang Xun and Xiao Ling in the crowd.

8B   *Yang Xun*

Bai Hua meets Yang Xun and Xiao Ling in the market and takes Yang Xun aside, intending to threaten him. Yang Xun, however, shows Bai Hua that he does not fear his threats. Bai Hua then warns him about his relationship with Xiao Ling and tells him he does not understand love; their conversation ends inconclusively. Bai Hua buys Xiao Ling an old-fashioned white dress which she has been admiring at a stall, then leaves them. In the evening they sit by the canal and talk; Xiao Ling begins to tell Yang Xun of her fears over the differences between them . . . .

"... I'll ask you again, do you understand me?"

"How else do you want me to understand?"

"For instance, do you understand my past?"

"I imagine our pasts are about the same."

"This 'I imagine' is just it. Why don't you ask?"

"Haven't I run into enough snags?"

"Maybe I'm to blame, but that happened long ago. And another thing, do you understand my frame of mind?"

"You seem very happy to me."

"You're wrong. Until the day I die I can never again be completely happy. One can see that you're very happy; but I, I'm both happy and painfully sad. This is precisely the difference between us."

I dispiritedly pick up a stone, and begin tracing lines in the dust.

She grasps my hand, throws away the stone, and presses my palm against her face. "Don't lose heart, please. I really don't mean to dampen your spirits. It's you who changed my life. I'm also willing to believe that happiness belongs to us." She jumps up, brushes herself down, "Fine, as to the question of the right to happiness, who else has an opinion? Now we'll take a vote." She raises her hand, then pulls up mine. "Add this little poplar, that's three votes altogether, carried unanimously. Wait, I'll go and get some wine to celebrate."

Xiao Ling goes into the house and turns on the light, the window lattice fragmenting her slender figure. As she changes her clothes her movements are like a film in slow motion. In a little while the light goes out and she stands in the doorway, wearing that pure white dress, and walks over. The vast night behind her throws her into relief, amidst the black ocean she is a glistening wave, and the stars countless drops of flying foam. She sets the wine bottle and cups to one side, walks up close to me and looks at me, smiling.

"Come, hold me tight," she says.

I continue to gaze at her abstractedly.

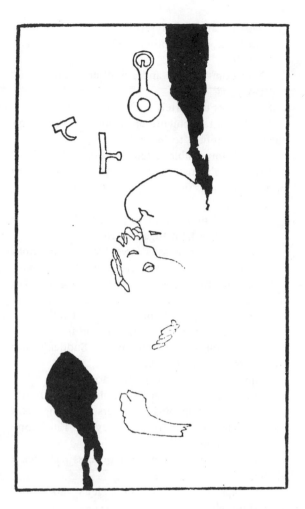

"Come." She holds out two shining arms.

I stand up, and draw her tightly to me till her joints creak.

"Gently, Yang Xun," she says, between breaths.

At the bottom of the wine cup, countless fragments of silver settle into a bright moon. "Xiao Ling, I have something to tell you."

"Go on, then."

"My transfer's been arranged. My mother's sent a letter urging me to go back."

She watches me calmly, her face expressionless. A cold silver-grey light rises slowly behind her. The darkness seems to tremble a little in the cold gleam. "Why didn't you mention it earlier?"

"I wasn't going to tell you anything. I don't plan to go back at all."

She turns the cup round and round in her hands. "Because of me?"

"Also because of myself."

"Go back, your mother needs you."

"No."

"You don't understand a mother's heart."

"Do you?"

She smiles desolately. "Of course I do."

"Unless arrangements are made for you to go back too, I refuse to leave."

"That's impossible, I have no family."

"It doesn't matter, nowadays the more impossible a thing, the more possible it is that it can be achieved."

"No, no, I don't want to go back."

"So let's live here together, then."

"Yang Xun," she says fervently, catching hold of my hand, "I've never asked anything of you before, but this time you must do as I say. Go back. Although we'll be apart, our hearts will still be together, that'll be good, won't it?"

"Don't try to persuade me, it's no use."

"You, you're too stubborn." Suddenly her shoulders begin to tremble.

I am alarmed. "What is it, Xiao Ling?"

"Oh, you're so foolish you should be thrashed." She smiles through her tears, brushing them away from the corners of her eyes. "I'm happy you're so stubborn."

"It's the first time my stubborness has been a virtue."

"Perhaps I'm too selfish . . . let's talk about something else."

"How about discussing your past?"

"First let's have a drink."

We clink cups and drain them at one go.

"Um—where shall I begin?" She rests her hands behind her, gazing up at the stars. "This evening's so beautiful, isn't it?"

"Yes."

She sighs. "I don't feel like talking about it, we still have tomorrow."

In the distance the rumble of a motor starts up, a shaft of snow-bright light leaps out, lighting up the grove of trees and piles of firewood. Numberless shadows revolve in the fields, like a massive mounted army. All at once the light sweeps towards us, so dazzling we cannot open our eyes. Xiao Ling leans close to me, clasping my arm tightly.

The tractor drives away.

8C   *Xiao Ling*

MID-AUTUMN Festival night. The smoke swirls about in our girl-students' low squat room. A bunch of us are crowded on the earthen brick-bed drinking wine, chatting idly. Someone plays mournful songs on a mouth-organ, someone stands by the window, declaiming Gorky's 'The Stormy Petrel' in an affected voice, a girl-student rolling drunk dashes into the yard, dances under the moonlight, inviting peels of laughter and applause from peasants and children. I cast a glance in all directions, shrug my shoulders, and press closer under the oil-lamp with my book.

Suddenly, someone bumps into me. It's Xie Liming. "Why aren't you celebrating with the crowd?" he asks.

"Call that celebrating? Looks worse than crying to me."

"You should try to understand other people's moods."

"I'm studying veterinary science, I'm not interested in human beings."

"Why are you always nettling people?"

"Excuse me, you're interrupting my reading."

He walks off in a huff.

The last flame of the kerosene lamp splutters, flashes, and finally goes out. A moment of dead silence in the room. Suddenly, the boy who has just been declaiming 'The Stormy Petrel' starts howling wildly.

I awaken from a coma. The wind is still wailing, the snowflakes patter against the paper of the window with a rustling sound. Parched! It feels as though my lungs are full of red-hot charcoal. I lick my dry, cracked lips, stretch out my hand to the cup. Not a single drop of water. The cup is sealed with a thick block of ice. With a clatter it falls to the ground, and I lose consciousness again.

The next time I open my eyes, there's a face floating in the mist, slowly becoming distinct. It's Xie Liming sitting by my bed.

"Awake at last." He rubs his brow excitedly. "The doctor's just been, said it was acute pneumonia. He gave you an injection . . . ."

"Doctor?" I murmur uncertainly.

"Couldn't get through on the phone, so I went to the commune."

Ten miles of mountain road, wind and rain, I

shudder all over. "Thank you . . . . "

"Oh, there's no need to mention it."

"Why didn't you go home too?"

He smiles wryly, turns round and carries over a bowl of steaming hot noodle soup. "My mother died early, from persecution; the old man's still in prison, the relatives in Peking only avoid me . . . . I wanted to borrow a book from you. I saw the door unbolted, and nothing stirred however much I knocked . . . drink up, drink while it's hot. It's good for you to sweat a lot . . . . "

A faint knock at the door.

"Who is it?"

"It's me, I've come to borrow a book."

I hesitate a moment, then open the door. Xie Liming stands stiffly in the doorway. A sudden gust of wind blows out the kerosene lamp.

"Xiao Ling, is it too late?"

"Come in."

I close the door and strike a match to light the lamp. Suddenly my hand is seized tightly. The match falls to the floor and goes out.

"Xiao Ling." There's a catch in his throat.

"Let go!"

"Xiao Ling, listen, listen to me . . . . " He clutches my hand, speaking in a low murmur. "I, I'm fond of you . . . . "

"Does that also mean, you need me?" I say with a grim smile, withdrawing my hand fiercely.

"Do you mean there can't be affection between people?"

"What you really mean is, I should repay you."

"You're too cold and unfeeling."

"I like to be cold and unfeeling, I like being cold-shouldered by other people, I like death! Why did you go and save me?"

"Both of us are homeless." He mumbles this one sentence, turns and staggers to the door.

"Come back!" I say.

He stops.

"What did you just say?"

"Both of us are homeless."

The long-distance bus station.

" . . . Father says, as soon as I've graduated from university, we'll help you move back. Then we can get properly married," Xie Liming says in a strained voice, swallowing.

"I hope to hear you say it yourself."

"I, of course, that's what I mean." He looks hurriedly at his watch. "As for the child, I still think get rid of it, don't be too stubborn."

"Don't worry about it, that's my own business."

He pulls a coin from his pocket. "Let's toss and see what our luck will be in the future."

"That's how much your luck is worth?" I snatch the coin from him and fling it into the gutter by the side of the road.

He climbs onto the bus step, breathing a sigh of relief. I watch him with no expression at all.

"Wait for me!" he says, raising his hand.

I am silent.

The bus roars, blows up a cloud of dust, and disappears down the road.

IX

9A   *Lin Dongping*

Lin Dongping finds out about Xiao Ling's illegitimate child, but does not take action to ensure she will not be penalized at the factory as a result, telling them instead to handle the matter "according to principle".

9B   *Yang Xun*

Lin Dongping has called Yang Xun to his house, and begins to ask him about Xiao Ling.

HE SITS UP, turning his gaze out the window. "Xun, are you in love with a girl?"

"You knew that long ago."

"What's her name?"

"Xiao Ling."

"What's she like?"

"All right."

"What does this 'all right' include? Family, thoughts, appearance . . . . "

"You asked what she's like, you didn't ask whether she conforms to the standards of a party member . . . . "

"People's concepts are not abstract."

"Yes, I agree. Did you ask me to come just for this?"

"For a chat." He gets up and goes to the little table between the bookcases, grasps the neck of the decanter and pours a glass of cold water. "Young people are liable to act on impulse . . . ."

"We have known each other for a year."

"But you have several decades of life ahead of you." He puts down the glass, paces a few steps, his hands behind his back.

"Xun, do you really understand her?"

"Of course I do."

"What do you understand?"

"Her intrinsic value."

He makes a mocking gesture. "It's the first time I've heard that."

"Yes, it's only those clichés about family conditions that get endlessly duplicated."

"I'm opposed to matching people according to family background."

"Only in words?"

"It seems that in today's world it's almost impossible for one person to convince another."

"Perhaps."

He is standing by the window. He stretches out his fingers and runs them over the dust on the windowsill, then sighs. "Very well, then, take a look at the papers on the desk."

I sit at the desk and open the file already placed there. The fan whirrs. I feel my whole body go cold, as if the air in the room is slowly freezing.

"Is that all?" I ask, closing the dossier.

"What more do you want?"

I leap to my feet and turn to face him. "It's not me who wants something, it's you."

"Calm down, Xun."

"Let me ask you, what right have you to do this?"

He continues pacing up and down.

"Your curiosity really makes me laugh."

He stands still. "This is not curiosity."

"What is it?"

"Duty."

"Duty?" I laugh grimly. "An emperor's duty to the people, or a father's duty to a son?"

For a moment his right hand gropes nervously for something behind him, until at last he clutches the arm of the cane chair, and sits down. His gaze is dull, as if all of a sudden he's grown old. "Xun," he calls out, his voice weak.

"What's wrong?" I pour a glass of water and hand it to him. With one hand he grasps the glass, the other tightly clutches my sleeve.

"I'm old, perhaps I shouldn't take secrets to the grave?" He seems to be talking to himself.

"What secrets?"

"She couldn't allow it, she couldn't . . . ."

"Who?"

His whole body trembles violently, and the water spills. He puts down the glass and gently pats my hand. "Child . . . ."

"Yes?"

"Time doesn't spare people, it's too late . . . ."

"What do you mean . . . ."

"Nothing." He pulls out his handkerchief, wipes his hands and brow, and gradually recovers his normal composure. "Go on, I'm rather tired. Think this matter over. I've already booked you a ticket for tomorrow afternoon. Whether you go or not is up to you."

9C *Xiao Ling*

YANG XUN stands in the doorway, his expression gloomy, his eyes averted. I put down the little jumper and walk over to him, meaning to brush the dust from his shoulders. He dodges as if he's received an electric shock, slowly goes to the desk, picks up Jingjing's photograph, then puts it down again. "I've come to say goodbye," he says.

"Where are you going?"

"Peking."

"For how long?"

"The rest of my life."

A moment of suffocation. After a while I let out my breath very slowly. "What time's your train?"

"Tomorrow afternoon."

"Fine, I'll see you off."

He crosses to the bed, picks up the little jumper and looks at it, then sits down on the bed holding his head in his hands. I go to him and stroke his hair. This time he doesn't resist, but with each stroke gives a slight shudder.

"I'm leaving," he says.

"You will come back."

"No, men can never turn back."

"The world's round, if you just keep on walking firmly you'll come back from another direction."

"I'm not Columbus."

"Perhaps. Now is not the age of Columbus."

"Don't get off the subject like this!" He roughly pushes my hands away and grabs hold of the little jumper on the bed. "Whom are you knitting this for?"

"The child."

"I haven't the time to joke."

"It's started."

"What?"

"The tragedy."

"I'm asking you, whose child?"

"Yang Xun, I beg you, don't speak to me in that tone, I can't bear it."

"Do you think I'm enjoying this?"

"Living can never be enjoyable. I'm hoping you'll calm down before you say anything more."

"I haven't got time."

"You used to have so much time."

"That was in the past."

"Tomorrow will become the past too."

"Unfortunately there won't be any tomorrow."

I silently pick up a book, and sit down on the stool beside me.

"Xiao Ling, why didn't you tell me earlier?"

I turn the pages.

"I truly don't blame you."

I turn the pages.

"Say something."

"There's nothing to say."

"So it all ends like this?"

I shut the book with a snap. "You mean to make me repent, wash myself with tears? I'm sorry, my tears dried up long ago."

"I'm just begging you to be honest."

"Honest? The honesty we understood when we were students hasn't existed for ages. How can you beg someone you love to tear the bandage from her own wound? And another type of honesty requires silence, loving in silence, dying in silence!"

"I'm not accustomed to talking of death."

"As you like. People think custom is everything, but they don't know it's a kind of continuous death."

"You should have a duty to me."

"No, I have a duty only to myself."

"Xiao Ling—" he cries out desperately, clutching his head tightly in his hands.

I go over, release his hands, and press his head tightly to my breast. "Xun, I understand your pain . . . . "

"Forgive me." He raises his eyes full of tears, staring dully.

We hold each other tightly, and kiss. My lips are moistened with his salt tears, and a kind of maternal love wells up, to help him, to protect him.

"Xiao Ling, what are you thinking?"

"Do you remember how we drunk those toasts in the little temple? I'm afraid there can never be any escape for us from those guns."

"Whom do you mean?"

"No one in particular. This gun consists of many parts. What's more dreadful is the mind of the hunter behind the sights, and that mind is made up of the thoughts of many people . . . . "

"Do you mean conventional ideas?"

"They won't let go of us."

"Don't think this way, Xiao Ling."

"Hm."

Suddenly his gaze travels past my shoulder and falls on Jingjing's photograph. "How old is she?"

"Two years and three months."

"Have someone else take care of her."

I let him go, staring at him in silence.

"Really, it would be better if someone else took care of her."

I go to the door and open it. "Please go."

"Xiao Ling . . . . "

"Please go."

"Don't you love me any more?"

"You still talk so easily of love. I see you only love yourself, love your shadow, love your happiness and suffering, and your future! Please go."

He looks at me hesitantly, goes to the doorway, pauses, then strides away without looking back.

I fling myself on the bed, sobbing uncontrollably.

X

10A *Lin Yuanyuan*

THE PHOTOGRAPH, the lower right-hand corner already yellowed: Mama, holding a thin little girl in her arms, standing amongst the flowers. Is this me? Diary: "Today is Yuanyuan's fifth birthday. Weight 21.5 kilos, height 1.06 metres. With the change in her moneybox she bought a block of chocolate, and got it all over her face." "Yuanyuan didn't pass arithmetic, it's very worrying. Starting today I'll check her homework every day." Hairpin, fountain pen, watch, wallet, letters .... I put back Mama's things one by one. Suddenly, from out of a pile of letters floats a sheet of paper, which falls flickering onto the desk.

"Dongping:

There's no need to hide the whole thing, I know about your past affair. I cannot blame you for anything in your past. But I hope that from now on you will have nothing further to do with her (When you went to the convention in Peking last month you still maintained your relationship with her. Everyone was talking about it, I was the only person in the dark). I know you have no feelings for me, but please think of Yuanyuan, that is my only request .... "

The blood pounds in my temples, throbbing loudly. I read it over and remember that whenever they quarrelled they shut the door soundly, but it always seemed to be about the same thing. I go to the chest of drawers, watching the jumping gold secondhand of the little Swiss clock. Mama, poor poor Mama, why did you never divorce this sanctimonious hypocrite, was it just for my sake, Mama?

After this discovery, Yuanyuan decides to run away from home. She hastily packs a bag and leaves, but when she wants to buy something to eat she finds she has not brought her purse with her. By coincidence, Bai Hua comes to her rescue.

10B *Bai Hua*

Bai Hua advises her to return home, but seeing she is resolute about running away he agrees (or pretends to agree) to help her. Arranging to meet *her at the station late that evening, he goes to see his friend, Manzi, and tells him that he himself is going away too, perhaps forever. At that moment, Lin Dongping's car goes by; Bai Hua is reminded of the score he has to settle with the cadre.*

10C *Yang Xun*

ON THE PLATFORM, Uncle Lin and I smoke in silence.

The wind slowly drags the dark clouds away. Scraps of paper swirl about with the dust, fluttering down the long platform. This city has suddenly become quite unfamiliar, as if the past is being kept at a distance by this high wall. Like a traveller passing through I walk onto the platform, smoke a cigarette, breathe in a mouthful of fresh air, then at the urging of the whistle and the bell climb once again into the carriage.

The loudspeaker crackles with static, blares out that special soporific female broadcaster's voice. A train pulls into the station. With the puffing of the engine, the step-ladders at the carriage doors are let down with a bang one by one. The passengers boarding and alighting clamour and shout, crowd into one mass.

"It's too noisy here, let's sit inside the car for a while," says Uncle Lin.

I scan the platform, nod abstractedly.

"Who are you still waiting for?"

"No one." I do not know if I am answering him or myself.

We sit in the back seat of the car.

"Old Wu," says Uncle Lin, "you go, I'll drive myself back."

Fat Wu grunts a reply, takes off his gloves, picks up his bag, and carrying his tea-mug and whistling a tune waddles off.

"Xun, I understand your feelings." Uncle Lin breaks the silence.

"Understanding carries no obligation, it does not cost you anything."

"Cost."

I turn my gaze out the window.

"Did you send the family a telegram?"

"No."

"You should have let your mother know in advance."

"There's no need."

"You're too unreasonable."

I turn round. "That's right, it's inherited from you people."

"We're not like that at all."

"That's even sadder."

"Why?"

"You're not qualified to be model bureaucrats."

"Xun, now you're taking liberties."

"I'm sorry, I really don't wish to quarrel with you . . . ."

Suddenly, a familiar figure dashes along the platform, peering in at every window. I throw open the car door. "Xiao Ling . . . ."

She stops, slowly turns round, stands there. I hesitate a moment, then rush over. "I'm late," she says.

"No, Xiao Ling . . . ."

She draws the blue notebook from her bag. "Take it, I promised. Wait till the train goes to read it."

I take the book without a word, clutching it tightly, as if afraid the wind might blow it away.

The loudspeaker rings out: " . . . the train will depart immediately, passengers please board . . . ."

"Xiao Ling, I . . . ."

"Don't say anything, all right?"

We hold one another's gaze silently. She frowns, and on the bridge of her nose several faint lines appear. Whatever it is that dissolves in my mind, the process is so sudden it is far more than I can cope with.

"You'd better board," Uncle Lin says behind me.

I step aside. "May I introduce you; Uncle Lin, Xiao Ling . . . ."

Xiao Ling unaffectedly holds out her hand. "How do you do!"

Uncle Lin wipes his hand awkwardly on his trousers and shakes her hand. "Er, we should have met earlier."

"It's not too late now, is it?"

"No, no, it's not too late."

The bell rings.

I climb onto the carriage steps and hold out my hand to her. "I'll be seeing you."

"What did you say?"

"See you, Xiao Ling."

"Say it once more, please."

"See you, I shall come back!"

She sorrowfully closes her eyes. "See you."

Suddenly, with a clang, the train begins to move. Her chin quivers, she turns away fiercely.

"Xiao Ling——"

She turns, her face white, her expression blank. She raises her arm and her sleeve slides down. That slender arm floats before the crowd, floats before the receding city.

10D *Lin Dongping*

MY VISION blurs: green signal-lights, dark clouds dyed red in the evening light, the dim black outlines of buildings and that ribbon of never-dispelled smog all kneaded together.

The girl lowers her arm, and stands there dejectedly.

"Miss Xiao, let me give you a lift."

"Please don't worry."

"It's no trouble. I'll take you back to the factory."

"My contract's already been terminated by the factory."

"What? That's impossible," I stammer. "I'll ring them immediately . . . ."

"Reverse your own decision?" She shakes her head. "I know all about it. But why do you still wish to avoid reality at a time like this? Really, from your angle, you did quite the right thing."

"Young people's emotional ups and downs are temporary. They come and go like waves."

"Have you experienced this temporariness, Uncle Lin?"

"We've undergone many painful experiences."

"So you use these experiences to teach young people a lesson, to tell them that they too are doomed to failure, isn't that so?"

"I don't want to see tragedy re-enacted."

"Tragedy can never be re-enacted. Only certain tragic roles are re-enacted. They believe themselves justified within the tragedy."

"Are you referring to me?"

"Then you believe in this kind of justification?"

"Xiao Ling, I have both of your interests at heart."

"When we were small and went to the pictures, adults always told us the difference between good and bad. But today, I don't know what meaning such words still have?"

I look at my watch.

"I'm sorry, I've delayed you," she says.

"Not at all, I like to chat like this. And now, what do you plan to do?"

"Go back to the village."

"I can arrange other work for you."

"Thank you, your kind of charity is the very last thing I want to accept."

"You're too obstinate."

"We must act out our own roles to the end."

"You believe in your justification too?"

"Yes, I believe the world won't go on like this for ever. Perhaps that's the difference between us."

"You're still young."

She gives a little smile. "So this world seems too old. Goodbye, Uncle Lin."

"Goodbye."

She walks towards the exit, the wind wrapping her clothes tightly round her, blowing her hair. She vanishes into the twilight haze.

What have I gone and done? So the girl's been sacked from the factory; how will she manage now, I wonder? But why should I be held responsible? I'm only responsible for my son; surely that's right. And even if I were to accept any responsibility for her, this was a factory matter. I said nothing, I didn't even drop a hint. No, it's not my responsibility. Where's she going now, I wonder? She won't go and commit suicide, will she? No, it's not my responsibility. These young people, it's so hard to know what's in their minds, what they're thinking, what direction they're going in . . . .

Lin Dongping leaves the station in his car, and is hailed by Su Yumei, the woman from his department who is always flirting with him. He picks her up, a thunderstorm breaks, and he begins to drive madly.

Before that thin weak girl I appear so hypocritical and immoral; how did all this begin? And in the instant she disappeared, why did I feel she was so like Ruohong, Ruohong when she was young, especially that reproachful gaze. These waves of emotion may only be temporary, but their aftermath is too devastating to contemplate. That line of scratch marks on Chen Zijian's cheek.

Our underground Party district secretary, why do I always think of him? There was something unforgettable about his appearance; yet it wasn't his appearance, it was his words that drove like nails into my mind: "How dare you have such an improper relationship with Comrade Ruohong? Her husband is a commander in one of the liberated areas . . . . The Party has decided to put you on good behaviour. You are to leave here immediately . . . . " One's memories are sometimes frighteningly clear. In the clump of trees by the riverside a boy appeared suddenly, carrying a tattered sack, a branch in his hand, his surprised face betraying a sly smile. From behind, the moonlight shone on a patch on his shoulder, covered all over with stitches. In fact I hadn't seen his face clearly, it was only from the flash of his white teeth that I felt he smiled, the smile of a child who has spied out a secret for the first time. He guessed what we were doing in this quiet, secluded place. By that time, Ruohong had already got dressed and was leaning very close to me, sobbing soundlessly. Yes, that was our last parting. Although seven years later we met again in Peking, it wasn't the old Ruohong at all, and Xun had grown tall too . . . .

"Stop! Stop!" cries a voice.

With a whoosh, a little tree scrapes the body of the car and flies past. Only then do I discover that the car has just left the road and is bumping violently along a ditch in the fields, the speedometer needle jumping back and forth. I slam on the brake, the car shudders, comes to a halt. What a narrow scrape! There's a deep canal in front of us.

"Have you gone mad!" Su Yumei, her eyes wide and her fists clenched, looks as if she might pounce on me at any moment. "Back the car up!"

The wheels spin in mid-air. At last we manage to reverse, clods of earth are flung up and fall into the waters of the invisible canal. The car slews round, and turns onto the road.

It has stopped raining, and the street is deserted. Under the dim streetlights, a few boys are playing barefoot in the water. They chase after the car for a while, shouting out in queer voices.

"Take me home," says Miss Su, still full of indignation.

"Where do you live?"

"75 Renmin East Road."

Where do I seem to have seen that address before? The workers and staff register, the trade union register . . . . I can't remember.

She nudges me with her elbow. "This is it, just at the little gate ahead." The car stops. She breathes a sigh of relief, smooths her hair. "Do come in for a while."

"It's not too late?"

Without a word, she opens the door and jumps out of the car. I hesitate a moment, lock the car. As I get out, I step in a puddle and my shoe fills with water. The lights are out in the courtyard. She pulls a bunch of keys out of her handbag and walks ahead.

"Where have you been?" Suddenly a figure emerges from under the eaves.

"Oh! You gave me a fright." Miss Su takes a step backwards. "I thought you wouldn't come because of the rain."

"Who's that behind you?"

"Oh, I forgot to introduce you. Do meet each other." Miss Su jumps aside, laughing shrilly.

Wang Defa looms close to me, strands of wet hair sticking to his forehead. I shudder and turn back.

10E *Xiao Ling*

THE TICKET booth window is shut. A girl with her hair in a bun stands with her back to it, cracking melon seeds and chatting to a young fellow in a red singlet. Her shoulders shake, showing that she is laughing.

I tap on the glass.

The boy points at the window, and the girl turns round. She throws the window open and pulls a face. "What is it?"

"A ticket to Floodwater Valley Village."

"Didn't you see the sign outside?!" she snorts in a huff, banging the window shut.

I look up, the sign says: 'Due to heavy rain, no buses for the next two days.' At the end a squat full stop is drawn, a moist melon seed stuck near it.

In the waiting-room, a few peasants are crowded in a bunch pulling at their pipes, gossiping amongst themselves. Outside the door the rain patters slowly down, like a flapping grey curtain. I walk down the steps and shelter under the eaves, watching the outlines of the rows of buses in the parking lot. A blinding light flashes behind the buses, lighting up the squares of each window, like a naughty child playing with a torch.

I draw the plastic wallet from my bag, and Jingjing smiles at me sweetly. Suddenly a big teardrop rolls down her face. It's only a splash of rain. I rub it out with my thumb. No, I must go back, go back immediately, even if I have to walk. Oh, my poor child.

Suddenly someone dodges under the eaves, and drops a bag on the ground. There's the rattle of jangling coins. He takes off his coat, wrings it out hard and glances at me. "Hey, what are you gawking at, think I'm a performing monkey?"

I say nothing.

"What's up, sister?"

"Bai Hua . . . ."

His mouth falls open in astonishment. He moves closer, dropping his screwed-up coat on the ground like a wet stick.

"What, you don't recognize me?" I ask.

"Xiao Ling, you're a real tease. You here alone?"

"Yes, alone."

"Keeping out of the rain?"

"And the wind, and the thunder."

"Huh, this filthy weather."

"You don't like it?"

"That's how it is in this business: lights out, pitch black, the wind blows and the rain pelts down. It's not a matter of liking it or not."

"Do you like the sunshine?"

"No, we can do without it, it gives you a headache."

"Do you like wind?"

"It's not bad, except in the middle of the winter; otherwise it slides along nicely, nice and easy."

"Do you like this city?"

"You've hit the nail on the head. I'm just about to leave this devilish place where pigs don't eat and dogs don't drink."

"Where are you going?"

"Nowhere particular. The world's a big place."

It's true, it's so large, one person's sorrow and unhappiness count as nothing.

He pulls out his pocket-watch, and taps the face. "Time's up."

"O.K., goodbye."

Bai Hua contemplates me in silence. Suddenly he catches hold of my hands tightly.

"Not so hard, Bai Hua, are you mad?"

"Let me say something."

"All right, say it."

"Xiao Ling, in this life I've met a lot of women, but I've never met one like you . . . say one word, do you like me?"

I think for a while. "It's like what you said about liking the wind: not bad except in the middle of the winter . . . . "

"But it's summer now."

"Don't you feel coldness in your heart?"

He swallows, as if he has something more to say. But then he lets go my hands, picks up his bag and coat, turns and staggers away, his shadow lengthening under the lights.

A bat cries sharply, wheeling in the air. The rain stops, I too must be on my way.

XI

11A *Yang Xun*

I CLOSE THE BLUE notebook, light a cigarette. The trickles of rain on the windowpane draw fine, haphazard lines. Lights float in the distance. Clumps of bushes by the side of the track catch the light from the window, flash, and are gone.

I blow a thick stream of smoke onto the windowpane, open the book again, and go on reading.

11B *Xiao Ling*

ON THE LEFT is a drop of unfathomable depth. The trees beside it rustle in the rain, the branches rock gently. The lights of the distant city are already hidden by the mountains.

The road, the road.

11C *Lin Dongping*

I WALK OUT of the garage, following the crazy

paving, climb the stairs. It is very quiet along the verandah, a faint radiance cast by the wall-lamp.

Before Yuanyuan's bedroom door I pause, listening, then knock. "Are you asleep, Yuanyuan?"

No sound. I turn the knob, switch on the light, the bed is empty. The room is in a jumble, the drawers of the chest-of-drawers half-open, a pair of trousers hanging out. On the desk a teacup holds a note in place: "Papa, I've gone away. I may never come back!"

11D *Lin Yuanyuan*

THE STONES crunch underfoot. To the side the goods carriages stand like headless, tail-less tin cans.

"When did you leave home?"

"I've never had a home," Bai Hua says.

"So how were you born?"

"Stop jabbering!"

"Why so fierce? Huh, I was just asking."

He stops at an open carriage. "Get up."

I climb up with difficulty. Hey, how warm it is. There are still piles of hay in the corners. I peel off my plastic raincoat. "Do we sleep here?"

"Breathe another word, and I'll throttle you!"

11E *Yang Xun*

I CLOSE the book, pick up my bag and walk to the compartment door. The buffers screech loudly and the train comes to a halt at a little station. I climb down the steps, out into the cool breeze, and approach the lit-up duty-office. In the doorway stands a middle-aged man, all skin and bone.

"When does the next southbound train go through here?" I ask.

"In forty minutes."

11F *Xiao Ling*

A SERIES OF strange rumblings rolls out. I still haven't realized what has happened when the roaring mountain torrent surges over everything. I put out my hand to clutch at a sapling by the edge of the road, tumbling rocks thunder past, strike my ankle and leg, arrows of intense pain.

Suddenly the mud under my feet gives way. My body twists, and falls . . . .

11G *Bai Hua*

WITH A CLANK, the body of the train shudders. A moment later, a long blast of the whistle.

"Get down!" I say.

"Me?"

"Go home, go back to your father's."

"What, what's the idea, cheating me like this?" she says, biting her lip.

"Get down!" I force her to the door.

"Bastard!" she finishes, turns and jumps down. The train slowly starts to move.

11H *Yang Xun*

I GET OUT of the carriage. The hammers of the train maintenance crew ring out, all the louder on this rainy night. The mercury-vapour lamps are netted by the sheets of rain, transformed into dim haloes.

By the gate at the barrier, the old ticket collector yawns, his rubber raincoat glistening.

11I *Xiao Ling*

I AWAKEN, a little blade of grass lightly brushing my cheek. A dense fog floats across the steep cliffs above my head. Then the sky clears, and the moon rises.

Suddenly, a girl the image of me drifts forward, and vanishes in the tide of golden light . . . .

First draft November 1974
Revised June 1976
Second revision April 1979
First published in Today, *Nos. 4, 5 & 6 (1979)*
Revised and reissued in
Changjiang wenxue congkan,
1981 (1)

Illustrations by Gan Shaocheng

易言：評《波動》及其他

Postscript: Yi Yan's Critique of 'Waves' in *Literary Gazette*

Translated by Zhu Zhiyu

THE LONG STORY 'Waves' has attracted the attention of a large number of young readers. Its author, comrade Zhao Zhenkai, is a young writer, who during recent years has published much poetry, and somewhat less fiction. The first draft of this story, written in 1974, during the devastating rule of the Gang of Four, circulated widely among young people in hand-copied form. The editorial department of the magazine *Changjiang* 長江 asked the author to revise the story, and has now published it for the general public, to give more people an opportunity to read and comment upon it. This is a welcome decision.

The story's exposure and criticism of many of the social problems of the Cultural Revolution is rare and commendable. From today's vantage-point we can see that the author's observations of the reality around him and his overall view of life were limited by the period within which he was living, were naive, sometimes even erroneous; but we cannot therefore deny or underestimate the impact his story made on young readers, the enlightening effect it had upon them. Especially when we recall, with bitterness, the prevailing social circumstances and remember that the author was only young and inexperienced, then his undeniably keen insight into life and his valuable inquiring spirit will enable us to understand and tolerate the naivety, bias, and errors manifested in the story.

1

THE STORY IS WRITTEN in the 'misty' style, and the author has adopted the 'stream-of-consciousness' technique. The fragmented leaps, the complicated and confused psychological impressions, the intricate and obscure philosophical sermonizing are all stamped with the brand of the age. The excessive 'mistiness', obscurity and fragmentation create a sense of total confusion. One has to read the story three or four times to make any sense of it, and even then a great deal remains unclear. The plot develops along two lines. On the one hand we follow the misfortunes and tragic love story of Yang Xun and Xiao Ling; on the other the intricate relationships between Lin Dongping, Wang Defa, Lin Yuanyuan and Yang Xun. The former describes the thoughts and mental questioning typical of the younger generation in a time of great catastrophe, revealing the painful process of spiritual crisis brought by confrontation with a new reality. The latter deals mainly with the struggles and personalities of various middle-ranking cadres during the Cultural Revolution. The two are not really extended parallel lines: they intersect in the underworld society of which the hooligan (*liumang* 流氓) Bai Hua is the centre. It is Bai Hua who links together the two 'drop-outs' (*tianya lunluo ren* 天涯淪落人) Yang Xun and Xiao Ling on the one hand, and the disintegrating family of Lin Dongping and Lin Yuanyuan on the other.

We must concede that the author's description of the young people and their fate is realistic. Whether they belong to the category of Yang Xun, or Xiao Ling, or Bai Hua, or Lin Yuanyuan, they are all twisted, crushed, branded by life. Yang Xun has experienced a certain amount of hardship, but he still manages to preserve a fairly firm set of beliefs, and is relatively optimistic. This is the result of his social position. Xiao Ling is a talented girl from a well-educated family who has come down in the world. She has degenerated into a loose woman, and is living far from her home city. Her lonely and isolated life and the cruel, unfeeling social reality she encounters are responsible for the sense of solitude and despair she feels in her soul. Bai Hua has already sunk into the underworld, and the only protest he can make against the political 'evils' of society is a totally destructive one. Lin Yuanyuan once felt the impact of the 'waves' of society, but the conditions of her life have improved, relatively speaking, now that her father has been restored to his prominent position. But then she too comes to see the dark, contemptible side, in her father; disgusted with his hypocrisy, she seeks freedom from convention and eventually runs away from home.

As can be seen, through these characters 'Waves' reflects the misfortunes and psychological crisis of our intellectual youth during the late 60s and early 70s. The aftermath of the Second World War saw the appearance in America and throughout the Western World of the phenomenon known as the 'beat generation'. They detested war and the whole capitalist system, and suffered from a sense of spiritual depression. After the upheaval of the Cultural Revolution, there was a similar disintegration, a similar change in our own younger generation. Some of them became pessimistic and lost their faith in the socialist system; nihilism began to spread. This is the process of psychological crisis described in 'Waves'. With his insights and philosophy, the author attempts to awaken his contemporaries, who are either still intoxicated with revolutionary slogans, or else aware (though only faintly so) but demoralized. But the onesidedness of the author's understanding of social life, and his shaky world outlook lead to the philosophical confusion and errors present in his work. In other words, it is commendable that a young man under such conditions should have embarked upon an independent inquiry into the life of his society, should have sought to express his objection to, his anxiety about, his protest against the feudal, fascist dictatorship of the Gang of Four; but regrettably his inquiries have not reached a correct conclusion.

The author creates in Xiao Ling a character embodying his own philosophical ideas. She has a cynical attitude towards life, towards her own future, towards her country. She thinks of herself as a 'foundling' of her society and her country, and the future fills her with bleak despair. Her survival consists in her having sufficient 'inertia'. She has no goal, no hope, no ideal, no tomorrow. In short, she no longer believes in anything but her own 'existence'. Her life story is roughly as follows. Her parents are hounded to death one after the other by the 'revolutionary activities' of the Red Guards. This first and fatal blow, sustained by an innocent girl, ignorant of the ways of the world, decisively changes the course of her life. Afterwards, at school, she herself encounters 'mass dictatorship', is placed in solitary confinement and interrogated. Then she becomes a fugitive from school, and in the waiting-room of a railway station receives help from a kind old man. She goes to the country, is seduced, becomes a worker . . . . The blows fall one after another, they undermine her spirit. She no longer believes that justice, truth and friendship exist in the world. Revolution has become an empty word to her. She even mocks sacred words like 'her country' and 'duty'. She speaks of 'her country' as an 'out-dated tune', a 'lollipop' to tease children with. She protests: 'This country's not mine. I don't have a country.' It is clear that so far as 'her country' is concerned Xiao Ling's thoughts are confused and nihilistic. It is not naivety that makes her feel lost in this way; it is an expression of despair, the result of a hailstorm of misfortune. Her torment has caused her to hate even her country. She says: 'Our country, huh, none of these ultimate playthings last, it's just those yes-men pretending to be emotional, they need a kind of cheap conscience to reach some sort of cheap equilibrium.' Leaving aside for the moment the author's strange, incomprehensible expressions, I would like to ask:

How can our 'country' be the product of those 'yes-men pretending to be emotional'? To any normal person, what an incomprehensible attitude this is! All of us who have gone through the Cultural Revolution, old, middle-aged, or young, have been hurt and persecuted in varying degrees. Not only do we not share this feeling toward our country, we cannot even understand it. We have no right to demand that the author should describe Xiao Ling as a character with a clear understanding of the social upheaval occurring around her. That would be inconsistent with the principles of historical materialism and of realism. But through her mouth the author unscrupulously lays all the filth at the door of 'our country', confusing the fascist acts of the Gang of Four with 'our country'. This definitely betrays a new nihilism of thought. In those hard times, our country, our people and our party went through purgatory. The country cannot be blamed. The author lacks a critical attitude toward the character of Xiao Ling. The way he writes the dialogue between her and Yang Xun can perhaps be seen as an implicit criticism of her character. But Yang Xun, a person with similar experiences to hers, not only fails to touch the crux of the matter in his criticism of her, he is very soon attracted to her side; she becomes his goddess. When he writes about Xiao Ling's nihilistic attitude toward objective reality, the author stubbornly affirms and praises her humanity (*renxing* 人性)—the 'existence' of her 'self'. He spends a whole section describing a scene where she and Lie Tiejun, the head of the Red HQ Brigade, are checking people at a sentry post. Li amuses himself by killing an innocent youth, 'without batting an eyelid'. Xiao Ling shouts hoarsely, turns and runs away, tears blurring her eyes: 'You, you butcher, bastard!' Another example is when the drunken Bai Hua is accompanied by Xiao Ling back to his den in an anti-aircraft shelter. After throwing out a slut called Number Four, he suddenly blurts out his admiration for Xiao Ling, stabs his palm with a dagger and lets the blood drip into his wine cup. At this moment, Xiao Ling is so noble and kind-hearted. She says, 'You're mad!' and helps him to dress the wound, beginning to philosophize about the stars. At this moment she no longer wears her cold, cynical face, but is a veritable angel, with absolutely authentic feelings. It can be seen from the author's descriptions that his idea is simply this: reality is hideous, cold, indifferent and wretched, while people's inner feelings are noble, fine and full of human compassion 人性. He wants to resolve this contradiction and to save the world through inner perfection, through the 'existence' of the self. Is this correct?

2

IN 'WAVES' the author advocates the philosophy that 'cowards create their own cowardice, and heroes make heroes of themselves' (Jean-Paul Sartre). Through his descriptions he is telling us: life is absurd, solitary, the world is tragic; but man is free and man's essence (*benzhi* 本質) is determined by his acts. Human essence, human meaning, human value reside in the inner world of this group of people, whom life has so contorted.

Xiao Ling is a character who puts up a fierce but futile fight for her own human value in this absurd world. In solitude she gradually grows cold. She longs to have a 'home', but what this means is not clear. Maybe it means a family to give her warmth, maybe it means death; it is hard to tell. Yang Xun attempts to warm her almost frozen heart with his love; once he succeeds in reviving her confidence, he restores her human feelings, her human essence. She admits it herself: 'It's you who changed my life. I'm also willing to believe that happiness belongs to us.' But her beautiful dream once more comes into conflict with reality. Yang Xun's mother, a high-ranking cadre, does not want a woman who has lost her family status, a woman moreover who already has a daughter of her own, to marry into her family. Yang Xun has no social prejudice about her family background, but he too is loth to take on the illegitimate child and forsaking her, returns alone to Peking. Tragedy pushes her once again toward the abyss of cold indifference and despair. Once more her heart is shrouded in disillusionment, emptiness, indifference, and solitude.

Her efforts to shake off the bonds of life have failed. She can only wrap herself in sorrow and misery, tighter and tighter, isolating her heart from the outer world and returning to Floodwater Valley, the village which once deceived her and in which her own flesh and blood, the little daughter forsaken by her father, still lives.

Lin Yuanyuan's path is also imbued by the author with the same dominant idea. She seeks human 'freedom', and human 'essence'. By chance she discovers in a letter evidence of her father's despicable hypocrisy, and resolutely runs away from her family (a family not lacking in warmth); she would rather live Bai Hua's kind of life, the life of a hobo. I do not exactly know why the author lets this character of his develop in this way. Her running away has nothing to do with the social turmoil created by the Gang of Four, nor is it the inevitable outcome of the development of her character. It is deliberately conceived by the author, according to his own subjective intention . . . . Perhaps he thinks this is the only way his characters can conform with the principle that 'heroes make heroes of themselves'.

Bai Hua is a predominantly cruel and wild character. His acts are destructive. The author does not criticize Bai Hua's destructive acts as he should; instead he affirms in them some sort of chivalry, which, as it appears in various situations, highlights his heroic character. For example, he helps a little girl abandoned by her stepmother in the waiting-room of a railway station; he also gives generous help to Lanzi, a girl who has no one to fall back on and has to sell her body for her livelihood. The author describes these various acts in such a positive light that it is very difficult to reconcile Bai Hua's character—the shining morality—with his ruthless, fierce behaviour. He can cut Cheekbone on the shoulder with a chopper for appropriating the slut Number Four; he can also jab a knife into his own palm, without flinching, merely to create a favourable impression on Xiao Ling! The author describes him as a strong character, a man who still has some conscience left in him. It is clear that the author, in working up his subject matter and developing his themes, is only concerned with the conflict between human existence and the objective world; he does not place the characters in an environment influenced by the fluctuations in social circumstances. And therefore he cannot perceive, let alone put into words, the existence of people who are making useful efforts to propel society forward.

Solitude, anxiety, depression, pain, despair, cruelty . . . these are not just isolated psychological elements; they are the key note that runs through the whole story, and a telltale sign of the author's ideological inclination. This gloomy and pessimistic tone is precisely the literary reflection of the nihilistic trend rampant in our society. It arises from weariness with the strain of the prolonged class-struggle, from disillusionment with revolutionary ideals. This trend denies the rationality of the realistic life order. True, the critical attitude of this trend toward the ultra-leftist line (and toward the reality of the 'evils' created by that line) has its progressive side; but it does not guide people on to the correct Marxist road. Instead, blindly and without restraint, it seeks free development of individual character, and rejects without exception anything which does not accord with or hampers this development. This trend seeks rational humanism, it strives for 'true human worth', it calls upon men to confront an absurd reality. It is true that its opposition to the fascist brutality of the Gang of Four, its endeavour to restore sincere relationships between people, are not without their positive side. But to set universal compassion, human nature 人性 and humanism 人道主義 against the Marxist world view is without question erroneous. This kind of philosophy is incompatible with our revolutionary-realistic literature, with our ideal of a socialist literature whose guiding ideology is the Marxist world view. Revolutionary realism requires the writer to bring to light social contradictions; at the same time it requires him to suffuse life with a glow of idealistic glory. It forbids him to lead the reader to pessimism and despair.

3

'WAVES' IS NOT an isolated literary phenomenon. Its appearance reminds me of the existentialist trend in philosophy and literature following the Second World War. I am not saying that we already have an influential school of existentialist literature in China. But among young people interested in literature there are *some* who are influenced by the existentialist trend in thought and literature, and who have produced works permeated with this thought . . . .

A common characteristic of these works is that they take as their guiding ideology the philosophy that reality is absurd and man is free; they adopt a nihilistic attitude toward the objective world and stand for the perfection of man's spiritual nature, attempting to substitute universal human nature and humanism for the Marxist world view.

April 1981

趙振開：稿紙上的月亮

Moon on the Manuscript

By Zhao Zhenkai

Translated by Bonnie S. McDougall

SUNLIGHT SLID ONTO the glass desk top. A warm band of orange trembled lightly as I lowered my eyelids. It was a still morning. At intervals the oppressive sound of popped rice spread through the lane. A war was going on in Afghanistan. A jumbo jet had crashed in southern France . . . . The world was so concrete, as if meaning only existed in a given concrete time and place. The tired and drawn face in the mirror when I was washing this morning resembled a cornered beast. At the public lecture a few days ago, the university students had started to hiss, and someone handed up a slip saying "You represent us? How disgusting!" The grating sound of the microphone's alternating current gave me the opportunity of silence. What more had I to say to those fellows, who considered themselves so superior?

I opened my eyes and blew lightly, and the snow-white cigarette ash on the glass top was like a flock of seagulls skimming over the water. At low tide I would almost invariably go hunting for shellfish with my playmates. We would knock off

oysters from the rocks one by one and pour them into our mouths. There were also small crabs that hid in the seaweed or under the rocks . . . . I'm a fisherman's son, but it seems as if this was no longer a fact but only a line in a dossier. Had my mother not died and her brother taken me to Beijing, at this minute I would probably be sitting on the deck of a chugging, throbbing motorized junk, smoking a long-stemmed pipe and surrounded on all sides by fishing nets full of salt slime and the odour of fish. I spread out a hand: pale, slender, not a single callous. Fate is incomprehensible, perhaps the only thing that is incomprehensible . . . .

Someone knocked on the door, so lightly that at first I thought I'd heard wrong. It was a girl with short cropped hair that had a brownish tint.

"Is Mr Ding here?" she asked timidly.

"That's me."

"I . . . . " her round face flushed.

"Come in and tell me what's on your mind."

She almost kicked over the thermos flask on the floor. "I'm sorry . . . . "

"It doesn't matter. Please sit down."

This story appeared in Shouhuo 收獲, *1981.5.*

After some hesitation she sat down on an old stool beside the couch, placing her old satchel on her knees. "My name is Chen Fang, I'm a student at the Normal College. I came because I like your stories." She laughed apologetically.

"Which ones do you like?"

She thought it over. "I like 'The Relic'."

"As far as I'm concerned that's become a relic itself. What about the more recent ones?"

"Er," her tone was a little uncertain. "I haven't read them yet."

I got on my guard, thinking she might be one of the students who had been booing. "What's the reaction of the students around you?"

"I'm not sure. Some people seem to think they aren't as deep as before."

"A hole in the ice is deep," I said.

The girl seemed to be a bit nervous, continually fiddling with the frayed strap of her satchel, twisting it back and forth around her fingers.

"Would you like some water?"

"No, please don't bother, I'm going in a minute." She took out a thick manuscript from her satchel. "I tried to write something. It's fairly poor. I thought I'd ask you to read it, is that all right?"

I took the manuscript and weighed it in my hand. "Are you in the Chinese department?"

"No, physics."

"Your first try at writing?"

She nodded earnestly.

"Take my advice, stick to your own field and don't waste your efforts on this."

She shrugged "Why?"

"It's sour grapes."

"Really?"

"I say that because I've tried."

She laughed, very sweetly, and for a moment her ordinary-looking face appeared beautiful. "But I've always liked sour things since I was little."

I bit my lip and remained silent.

"And you can make sweet wine with sour grapes."

"Sweet wine?"

She stood up. "Anyway, I'd still like to try."

"Very well then, I won't say any more."

At the door she turned her head. "I thought, I thought you would be full of confidence."

"Confidence? The word is too abstract."

"What is a concrete one then."

"Life, writing," I grimaced, "and confidence, too."

After seeing my visitor off, I sat down again at my desk. Perhaps this was the beginning of a story, starting with the conversation about sour grapes, and then what? I picked up my pen, screwed off the cap, and stared at the metal nib. What was the matter? It was fine weather outside, and I was shut up in a room, like a fly in winter. I used to be able to write eight thousand characters a day, "like a fountain", to use the old lady's expression. She saw herself as my protector. One look at that stupid face would make anyone contemplate suicide. Perhaps a difficult labour is a good thing, a new beginning. How droll, a man approaching forty still talking about new beginnings. Emperors build their mausoleums when they're still in their teens. Ordinary people are lucky, you can go for a walk after work, of slip off and have a drink, you don't have a load of worries . . . . The pen slipped between my fingers and poked a hole in the right upper corner of the manuscript, splashing a big blob of ink on it. Idly I drew a crescent moon.

THE SIGHT OF Juan coming in aroused a feeling of time fleeting. It was as if in that second, memories of the past welled up and swirled around me, forming a background in disharmony with our everyday life.

"Why're you looking at me like that?" she asked.

"Nothing," I said dully.

She pulled out Dongdong from behind her. "Say hello to daddy."

Dongdong stood between me and Juan, looking glum and gazing blankly at the floor.

"Say hello." Juan's voice was a little impatient.

Dongdong still stood there, not budging.

"The teacher says he had a fight with the other children this afternoon, he grabbed someone's car . . . . I'm exhausted." Juan settled her bottom on the couch and sighed.

I went over and hugged Dongdong, prickling him with my moustache as I kissed him. Not saying anything, he dodged aside, detached himself from me and toddled over to the desk.

"Moon," he muttered, stretching out his small hands to the manuscript.

Juan bustled over. "Ah, the great author, he can't produce a single word, but he knows how to doodle. There'll soon be a mountain of letters piled up demanding stories. I wonder how you're going to meet those debts."

"I don't owe anything to anyone," I said stiffly.

She smoothed a crease on my sleeve with her fingers, giving me a quick glance.

"I only owe myself," I said then.

"What's up with you?"

I stayed silent.

She walked over, patted me on the shoulder and stroked my face. "You're tired."

I looked into her eyes and gave a forced laugh.

"What's bothering you?"

"Nothing."

"Then why this?"

I grasped her hand. "I'm tired."

"You've got such a terribly gloomy expression. Shave off that moustache tomorrow. I'm going to chop up some meat, I bought some chives."

I sat down at the table and stroked Dongdong's downy head. This time he did not dodge away.

"Daddy will buy you a car tomorrow."

"I don't want one," he said, staring at the paper.

"Why not?"

"Fatty said the car was his grandad's." He suddenly lifted his head and asked, "What's my grandad?"

"A fisherman."

Dongdong turned his head to look at the goldfish bowl on the side table.

"What sort of fish?"

"All sorts."

"Where does he live?"

"He's dead."

Dongdong raised his eyes in surprise.

"He drowned at sea."

"Wasn't he careful?"

I shook my head.

"Were you sad?"

"I was only three then."

"I'm four and a half."

"Yes, you're a big boy now."

Dongdong drew his forefinger back and forth on the manuscript. "Teacher says the moon is round."

"She's right."

"Why didn't you draw it round?"

"Each person has a different moon."

"Grandad's moon?"

"Quite round."

I remembered the small dark cottage piled with fishing gear. I often burrowed myself in there, to lie alone on the dried fishing nets. Moonlight filtered down from the cracks between the rafters, murmuring in the sea wind, an accompaniment to the monotonous sound of the waves.

"POSTERITY EQUALS zero," Kang Ming smacked his lips and threw the matchstick into the ashtray. "Zero, old man."

I shook my head, reluctant to continue the argument. All arguments were meaningless. I knew he was needling me, trying to draw me into a game that I was already tired of. Every Saturday evening as a rule he would occupy our twelve square metre room in his own unique way.

"There's no need to feel any responsibility in regard to posterity. The question's very simple, no-one has to feel responsible in regard to any-one."

"Do you have a responsibility to yourself?" I asked.

"That's a complicated question."

"No, it's also very simple. People now tend to put the responsibility on society all the time. In fact, society is composed of individual people. If each individual refuses to accept responsibility for his own acts, how can we expect any social progress?"

"OK, I give up. Your wife?"

"Taking the child back to her mother's."

"Writing coming along well this time?"

"No."

He turned his head and looked at me. One eye was very bright, reflecting the light from the standard lamp, the other was in a dark green shadow.

"You've changed," he said.

"Really?"

"Probably it's the conscience of the artist pressing on you so hard you can't breathe."

"I'm not an artist, never have been."

"Your name is big enough."

"It'd be bigger if I started a fire on the street."

"Don't set your demands too high, old man."

I stayed silent.

"The question is not how you or I think, of course it's a good thing to develop your own brain." He got up and walked to and fro, his shadow slipping across the wall. "One thing should be understood, we are merely society's luxuries."

"I don't understand."

"It seems that only we 'commercial' editors know how the market works . . . . " He walked over to the desk and picked up the sheet of paper. "Interesting. Do you know what makes the moon appear full or not?"

I gazed at him.

He turned around and leant against the table, smiling enigmatically. "It's the result of the earth beneath our feet blocking off the sunlight, common knowledge."

THE PAPER AT the end of the cigarette began to curl up, covering the red fire that was gradually darkening, the blue and brown wisps of smoke mixing together. Although technically deficient, the girl's story still touched me deeply. The tragedy was certainly her personal history, the beginning and the end of love. To search for love in this loveless world is very difficult, but loss is something instant and eternal. "The business about the room, haven't you been keeping up the pressure for it? The application's been in for months." A rustling sound, it was Juan taking off her clothes. The cigarette ash tumbled off, falling in separate flakes on the manuscript. "Go and see Xu tomorrow, one word from him is more effective than you making ten visits to the Association." "I'd prefer not to." Was that my voice? People can never hear their own voices accurately. How long can this voice linger in the world? At most seventy years, then it will disappear along with me. But the noise of the sea never ceases, never ends. I write something, it is printed in a book, but who dares guarantee that twenty or thirty years later people will still be reading it? Not even just twenty or thirty years, the younger generation have begun shaking their heads right now. "Ge's wife, he works in our factory, she's in a washing machine factory, they're having a trial sale, only a hundred and fifty . . . . " What lasts forever? Eternity in art is too terrible, the sight of it strikes fear into people's hearts, like a cold gravestone. It demands a writer stake everything on a single venture. The bed boards creaked, Juan was turning over. Seagulls staked everything on a single venture. No one who has heard their full-throated, doleful wail could doubt this. Why am I always thinking of the sea lately? I drew a deep breath, smoking relaxes me. A piece of cigarette ash fell near the moon. Ah, the result of blocking sunlight. Yes, artists are still men. I really shouldn't look down on Kang Ming, we're all the same. And he has his own reasons, too. Perhaps lying is man's basic nature, and being sincere is acquired; sincerity must be studied. Is the problem only in speaking truthfully? "It's getting late," Juan said in a muffled voice. This was a hint. She was waiting for me, just as primitive tribal woman waited for the hunter, no, fisherman. The fishing spear in his hand, an animal skin around his waist, he utters a full-throated cry answering the summons. "Yes, this month it's our turn to collect the water and electricity bill, last month the electricity was so dear, there must be someone stealing the electricity . . . . " I wonder if the small dark cottage still exists? The pungent fishy smell, the slippery floor, the small iron bucket hanging from the ceiling to catch the rainwater. Haven't been home for many years, I really should go back and look around. "Tomorrow evening you should go to our place and pick up Dongdong. I may be working overtime." My father, to me, will forever be a mystery. How he drowned not even I know. He didn't leave a single thing behind. No, he left me. And what shall I leave behind? I stubbed out the cigarette and switched off the lamp. Everything disappeared, the moonlight poured in, I remembered the girl's smile. "Why don't you say something?" Juan snorted, and turned over facing the wall. She was angry, but it was a pretence. I turned down the quilt and pulled her over by the shoulder, watching her quivering eyelids in the dark. "All right," I said. She slowly lifted her arm, moving her face nearer. "The business about the room . . . . "

"HERE'S TO YOUR creative work, may it be an eternal fountain!" said the old lady.

I put down my cup.

"What's up?" the old lady looked at me.

"We should drink to Xu's health."

"May as well, I suppose. To my reluctance to go to the grave," the old man said.

The old lady placed a piece of fish on my plate. "Try some, it's yellow croaker, my own work."

"Excellent."

"Compared with your stories?"

"Much superior."

The old lady moved closer, with a mysterious air. "There is something you must thank me for properly . . . . "

"What?"

"Guess."

I shook my head.

"Go on, guess." She trod on me with the tip of her foot.

"That's enough." The old man impatiently knocked the plate with his chopsticks. "Stop making such a fuss, if you've something to say, come out with it."

"It's none of your business!" The old lady gave him a baleful look. "A few days ago, Mr Zhang, the director of the press, was here; I mentioned you to him. He's agreed to publish a collection of your work."

"Oh."

She waited for me to make a better response.

"Thank you, but . . . . " I knocked the table with my knuckle. "Why don't we wait a little, we can talk about it later."

"What?"

"I haven't put together anything decent yet."

"Ho, here am I burning joss-sticks and the buddha turns his backside to me."

"He's looking ahead," the old man mumbled, sucking on the fish head. "Mm, mm, wait and see."

"You've been waiting all your life, and in the end, all you've got is a name with nothing to show for it except your memoirs, huh?" the old lady said indignantly.

"What're you yelling?" The old man thumped the table. "At least I've got something worth putting into memoirs."

"Humph," came from the old lady.

The old man's good humour revived after a minute. He dug out a dark brown fish eye and looked it over carefully.

"Think it over, don't let this opportunity slip by." The old lady clasped her arms around her shrivelled chest and sighed. "I'm going to take a look in the kitchen."

"The old nag," muttered the old man, waiting until she had gone out the door. He turned towards me, "Don't listen to her gibberish."

"She means well."

"There must be something bothering you."

I gave a noncommittal smile.

"It doesn't matter, literary men are given to over-sentimentality." He concentrated again on the fish eye.

"I'm just a little unwilling."

He lifted his head and gazed at me expressionlessly. "How old are you?" he asked.

"Thirty-seven."

"Do you know how old China's history is?"

I didn't answer.

"Five thousand years." He stretched out five crooked, trembling fingers. "There's no harm in waiting a bit longer, young man." As he finished speaking, he downed the fish eye in a single gulp.

I SAT DOWN at the desk. I knew this would be the inevitable result. I could not go back to the deck, to the rocks, to the small dark cottage where the moonlight rang out from the rafters. I had a slight headache, it was the wine—the sun-dried grain was to blame, the sun was to blame. I felt a sadness I had not known before, and felt like crying although I hadn't cried for years. Perhaps my tears were saltier than others'. I was a fisherman's son. My father died at sea. His boat overturned, and there wasn't even a corpse, but they set up a wooden tablet for him in the village graveyard. There were many wooden tablets there, facing the sea, facing the sunrise every morning. I was fortunate. I wonder whether authors who have been published often go past bookshops and look at their own books behind the glass. Hardback and paperback. The hardback editions have characters stamped in gold on the outside, and the cover is made of soft, pliable leather. They are more fortunate than I. Fortunes can change, however. I shouldn't stop. I didn't choose this opportunity, it chose me. Actually, nothing is of much importance in the end. My nerves are weak, I'm always being troubled by nightmares, nightmares that trouble my peace of mind. That fish eye has seen everything there is in the sea: seaweed, electric eels, mother-of-pearl . . . yes, oysters too. Don't stop, I'm only thirty-seven, that's still an up-and-coming age for writers. That girl's smiling face didn't hold beauty and purity alone. A smile can cover up anything. But where the smile has been, a scar or wrinkle will remain. I pulled open the drawer and gingerly touched the dog-eared corner of the manuscript. Sour grapes will only ripen and turn into wine if there is a sun. She had hope. Although the students' booing was not very pleasant, it nevertheless held a sun-like sincerity and honesty. Oh, what's the point of thinking of these things, life is always concrete. I have known love too, I have the right to describe this love too. It was a secret, a secret that couldn't be transcended in a tragedy, but I've had my brush with it. This isn't plagiarizing; nonsense, of course it isn't.

I spread out the sheet of paper with the drawing of the moon and began to write.

HOLDING A TOY car in his hand, Dongdong was kicking a stone, humming snatches of a song which seemed to be a story about a cat and a butterfly.

"Hurry up, Dongdong," I pulled his small hand. "Stop kicking that stone." He looked around at the dark shadows of the pedestrians and traffic around us, still humming.

"Daddy, look at the moon," he said.

The moon was big and round.

"That isn't your moon."

"No, it isn't."

"Where's your moon?"

I said nothing. We were walking under the dense shade of a pink siris. I knew he was looking at me intently, but he couldn't see my face clearly.

Poetry

朦朧詩選

Mists

Introduction: Into the Mist

Gu Cheng: Misty Mondō

Hong Huang: A Misty Manifesto

New Poets from China

Bei Dao
    tr. Bonnie S. McDougall

Gu Cheng
    tr. Tao Tao Liu, Seán Golden *et al.*

Jiang He
    tr. Alisa Joyce, Ginger Li, Yip Wai-lim

Mang Ke
    tr. Susette Cooke and David Goodman

Shu Ting
    tr. Tao Tao Liu

Yang Lian
    tr. John Minford with Seán Golden

Yan Li, Painter and Poet
    tr. Ling Chung, introduced by Alisa Joyce

Into the Mist

THE WORD 'MISTY' (*menglong* 朦朧) runs through these pages. Zao Wou-ki's paintings of the decade 1955-64 grow progressively larger, wilder, more faint, more misty, even invisible.[1] The technique of Zhao Zhenkai's long story 'Waves' is characterized by its critic Yi Yan as misty.[2] In Gu Cheng's poem translated here as 'Nostos' we have the line: 'to pass the misty first light of dawn' 渡過朦朧的晨光.

To translate *menglong* as misty is to convey only a part of the meaning. It is a word rich in associations, and to try to define it with any precision is self-defeating. Like so many of the old two-syllable words in Chinese it conveys a feeling, a texture, evokes a series of complex images —the moon about to go behind a cloud, a landscape seen through snow or drizzle; its individual component characters and related compounds (same phonetic but different radicals—sun, water, eye, bamboo, grass) suggest something concealed, a veiled prospect, a hidden light or a half-light, the sun about to rise, a meaning opaquely hinted at, a focus blurred, a state between dreaming and waking, a 'fuzzy' spectrum of values in place of a clearcut bipolarity. In the mist there is a hint of mystery, even mysticism. It is the aura breathed by the mountains in the great landscape tradition of Chinese painting, the luminous cloud of the Daoist immortal, drifting back towards its source, the primordial flux. The French have the ideal word for it: *(poésie) floue*.[3]

'Misty' was adopted as a shorthand compromise to denote the new and controversial poetry written in China during the past decade by a loosely associated group of young poets, including

[1]See p. 18 above.

[2]See p. 168 above.

[3]Bonnie McDougall, in her excellent introduction to Bei Dao's *Notes from the City of the Sun* (Cornell, 1983), prefers to reinterpret the word as 'shadows' and to call *menglongshi* 'a poetry of shadows'. Professor A.C. Graham, during a recent visit to Hong Kong, suggested 'hermetic'——which does indeed convey an important part of the meaning. For the French, see *Doc(k)s* N° 41, Hiver 81/82, edited by Julien Blaine *et al.*, to date the best anthology in any Western language of Misty poetry. As Ferdinand Godard notes (p. 338), the word *floue* conveys well both the 'mists and the diaphanous light' which bathe the poetry.

the seven represented in this anthology.[4] Another expression I once heard applied to this same school of writers is 'edge-ball literature' 擦邊文學, a term taken from ping-pong: the shot grazes the edge and is accepted within the rules of the game, while being at the same time almost unreturnable. By contrast a ball that bounces normally (in a straightforward fashion) can be returned normally, and a ball that lands beyond the edge loses the point outright.

In 1931 Yu Pingbo 俞平伯, the distinguished essayist, poet and scholar of *The Story of the Stone*, wrote an essay entitled 'The Mystery of Poetry',[5] in which he used the term 'misty' to refer to that quality in poetry which defies normal logic, as when an image or phrase leaps directly from the subconscious, without interference from the conscious mind. Inspiration propels the poet along this short cut to poetic achievement, and he is himself often stumped for a logical explanation of what he has written. Yu quotes as an extreme example Xie Lingyun's 謝靈運 dream-dictated line 池塘生春草, of which Xie said: 'These words are not mine; a spirit helped me.'[6]

As many critics have pointed out, this literary mist has a long and rather formidable Chinese pedigree. *The Story of the Stone* itself is surely the *menglong* novel par excellence. Yan Ming 晏明 lists as 'Old-style Misties' the poetry of Ruan Ji 阮籍, Li He 李賀, Li Shangyin 李商隱, Wen Tingyun 溫庭筠 and Mao Wenxi 毛文錫; the lyric verse (*ci* 詞) of the Tang, Five Dynasties and Southern Song; and the modern poets Dai Wangshu 戴望舒 and Li Jinfa 李金髮 from the 30s and the Shanghai Nine Leaves Group (九葉集) from the 40s.[7]

To the Western reader poetic density, found in every period, but most characteristic of modernism, is a commonplace. However we may understand or mythologize the workings of imagination and inspiration, we recognize that the leaps of the 'true inward creatrix' and the transformations wrought in the 'deep well of unconscious cerebration' sometimes entail a degree of obscurity and ambiguity — 'like darting fish with the hooks in their gills, dragged from the depths of an unplumbed pool, . . . like birds on the wing and the arrow strung to the bow — down they drop from out of the cloud.'[8] In bodying forth the form of things unknown, logical precision and overt statement are not always possible or even desirable. This is, as Yip Wai-lim puts it, all 'an integral and indispensable part of the hermeneutic habits of readers in pre-1949 China and in the West.'[9] Or, in the words of Havelock Ellis:

> If art is expression, mere clarity is nothing. The extreme clarity of an
> artist may be due not to his marvellous power of illuminating the
> abysses of his soul, but merely to the fact that there are no abysses to
> illuminate . . . . The impression we receive on first entering the presence
> of any supreme work of art is obscurity. But it is an obscurity like that
> of a Catalonian cathedral which slowly grows more luminous as one
> gazes, until the solid structure beneath is revealed.[10]

In recent years the veteran Chinese poets Ai Qing, Tian Jian and Zang Kejia, with other representatives of the currently entrenched literary bureaucracy, have availed themselves of 'misty'

[4]For the compromise, cf. Gu Cheng's 'Mondō' on p. 187 below.

[5]See his *Zabanr zhi er* 雜拌兒之二, repr. 1983 Jiangxi People's Press, p. 15 ff.

[6]Yu is quoting from Zhong Yong's 鍾嶸 *Shi Pin* 詩品, 卷中.

[7]See his article in *Poetic Explorations* 詩探索 1982.2, pp. 92-6.

[8]Coleridge and Henry James, quoted by John Livingston Lowes in *The Road to Xanadu*, Picador 1978, p. 52. Lu Ji 陸機, *Wen Fu* 文賦, tr. E.R. Hughes, Pantheon 1951, pp. 96-7.

[9]From Yip's preface to a forthcoming book of Yang Lian's poetry.

[10]From Havelock Ellis, *Impressions and Comments*, vol. 1. Quoted in *The Art of Life*, Constable, n.d., pp. 41-2.

"现在请蒙眬派诗人朗诵……"
一九八一年の月半君武作

'And now, one of the Misty Poets is going to recite some of his poems for us . . . .'

CARTOON by Hua Junwu—April 1981.

as a term of abuse, handy for putting down a new development in poetry which they clearly feel to be threatening. But the word itself, with its built-in ambiguity, has rebounded on them, and grazed the edge. For the veil of obscurity implies the hidden light, and for some readers to brand a poet as 'misty' is a recommendation, an indication that his work may contain something authentically poetic. Ai Qing calls the Misties the 'smash-and-grab' poetry camp 打砸槍派. 'They plagiarize my work, then pack me off to the crematorium.' Their work, he protests, is incomprehensible, and does not serve the people. As Zang Kejia puts it: 'They discredit the reputation of contemporary poetry and poison the minds of a minority of the people. The great mass of people abhor such poetry because it lacks the breath of daily life and the spirit of the times. It is a lone, funereal voice, bewitching readers with its morose, despairing tone.' And Tian Jian sums up his attitude in these words: 'If the political and ideological content of the poem is not high there is no further need to discuss it. I advocate writing in the popular style, poems that go out into the people. Can Misty Poetry serve the people? Can it serve socialism?'[11]

Ai Qing's determination to dispel the poetic mists dates back at least to his series of aphorisms *On Poetry*, written in 1938-9.[12] In the present context it has acquired a new significance, and a more strident note, since the mists against which he is now doing battle harbour spiritual pollutants innumerable, among them individualism, alienation, self-expression, even existentialism, considered by the custodians of public mental health to be the greatest threat to the minds of the younger generation. It is certainly a tribute to the continued power of poetry within China that the Misties should have drawn so much of the fire of the Spiritual Pollution non-campaign of late 1983, itself a spiritually degrading spectacle, enlivened only by the occasional Monty Pythonesque absurdity (e.g. 'Tibet's Party Secretary warns the region's largely illiterate yakherders against the Jean-Paul Sartre concept of alienation . . . ').[13]

[11] These quotations can be found in 'Misty Debates', *Rolling Stock* 4, 1983, Boulder Colorado, translated by Debby Davison from Su Liwen's 蘇立文 article in *The Seventies* 七十年代, Nov. 1981.

[12] See Ai Qing's *On Poetry* 詩論, Hong Kong, Cosmos Books 1980, pp. 31-2 and 40-1.

[13] *South China Morning Post*, March 25, 1984.

The anti-misty invective is of literary interest only in that it expresses rather poignantly the deep gulf between the embittered older generation of poets, whose own inspiration has dried up, and the new generation, who (after all) are only trying to revive the long dormant creative experiments in which their elders themselves once participated.

More subtle and reasonably argued, within the framework of a more flexible literary Marxism, is the debate between critics such as Sun Shaozhen 孫紹振 and Cheng Daixi 程代熙. Sun, in a controversial essay, has hailed the new misty poetry for embarking on a 'search into the secrets of life dissolved in the heart and mind', for its 'expression of the self', while Cheng has come to the attack, denouncing its petty-bourgeois individualism and anti-rational anarchism. Yuan Kejia 袁可嘉 has adopted a middle (and more academic) position, claiming that the modernist concern with language is at least good poetic training.[14] From the misty camp itself, Xu Jingya 徐敬亞 (singled out as a chief target during the Spiritual Pollution months of late 1983) and Chen Zhongyi 陳仲義, among others, have written extensive and articulate expositions of the 'new poetry', from very much an insider's point of view.[15]

Most intelligent observers agree that the problem with this 'problematic' poetry is not *really* one of obscurity or incomprehensibility. Bonnie McDougall, translator of Bei Dao's poetry, writes that ' . . . any young readers and some older ones . . . readily supply for themselves the unspoken implications of the sometimes cryptic lines.'[16] In other words, they see the moon through the mist. William Tay quotes a teacher writing to *Poetry* 詩刊 in November 1980: 'Obscurity is partially the result of hiding a strong political content behind startling poetic devices and a special mode of presentation.'[17] The message is clear enough. As Gu Cheng says, 'actually it is not misty at all . . . . Some areas are in fact becoming gradually clearer.' Yang Lian's 'The Torch Festival' is, in Yip's words 'perhaps the most luminous expression of the mental and emotional horizon of the young poets of his generation'; the hidden light casting these poetic shadows 'evokes in the readers' minds certain responses, certain possible directions of thought that they (the critics) cannot intellectually keep under control. Such imagery is, therefore, potentially dangerous.'[18]

Some of these poets have been translated into Western Languages (English, French, German, Swedish). But this is the first time their work has been represented extensively in English. The seven selected here cover a wide range of styles. They all published work in the seminal magazine *Today*, have continued to write since the closure of the magazine, to produce their individual *samizdat* collections, and to be published sporadically, depending on the direction and force of the prevailing wind. Jiang He and Yang Lian can be seen as a school-within-a-school; their poetry is longer, less personal and less lyrical, more public and concerned with large philosophical and historical themes, less closely worked, more rhetorical. Yang Lian in his most recent work is exploring a new range of ideas and developing new and more refined techniques, a more individual voice, with which to express them.[19] Mang Ke is considered by many to be the founding father of the movement—his poems published here were written in the early 70s—while Bei Dao, Gu Cheng and Shu Ting have all explored and extended in their different directions the vein of haiku-

[14]This is based on William Tay's paper ' "Obscure Poetry": A Controversy in Post-Mao China', presented originally at the Conference on Contemporary Chinese Literature, St. John's University, N.Y., 1982, and included in Jeff Kinkley ed., *After Mao: Chinese Literature and Society, 1978-81*, Harvard University Press, forthcoming.

[15]See pp. 59-65 above for an extract from Xu's essay. For Chen Zhongyi, see the undated fifth poetry supplement to *Hua Cheng* 花城, pp. 179-185.

[16]McDougall, *op. cit.*, p. 7.

[17]Tay, *op. cit.*, MS p. 17.

[18]Yip, *op. cit.*

[19]See, for example, his 'Nuo-er-lang' 諾爾朗 in *Shanghai Literature* 1983.6, and also 'Tian Wen' 天問, in *Shi Feng* 詩風 No. 115, Hong Kong Jan. 1984, pp. 11-17.

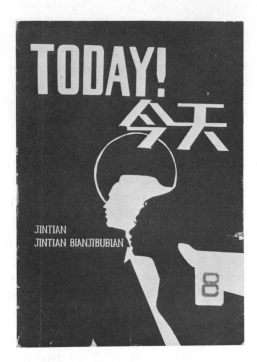

THE COVER OF *TODAY* NO. 8 (1980), a special
issue devoted to poetry including work by Bei Dao,
Gu Cheng, Jiang He, Mang Ke, Shu Ting, Yan Li, Yang
Lian and nine other poets.

like lyricism that Mang Ke opened. Yan Li has been included as a tangible link between the poets
and the more internationally famous art group, the Stars, with which they have such close af-
finities, and some of whose work we have chosen to acompany this anthology.

The more sophisticated modernists in Taiwan may find the language of these poems jejune.
But they should not forget that this is the first real experimentation with poetic language within
China since 1949. This poetry has an authentic inspiration and passion. If there is an alternative
culture in China today, this is its voice. It speaks for its generation, and over and above that for
the rediscovery of the poetic pulse of one of the world's great literary traditions.

—JOHN MINFORD

CALLIGRAPHY of Wang Duo 王鐸, Ming dynasty.

顧城：朦朧詩問答

Gu Cheng: Misty Mondō

Questions and Answers about "Misty" poetry

Q.: Please describe "Misty" poetry, and its more widespread characteristics.

A.: The term "Misty" poetry has a very Chinese ring to it, and its invention was quite natural. In fact, this kind of new poetry had already been in existence for several years before the term's invention, but had not been duly christened. By the time people began to pay attention to the new poetry it had lived through a difficult childhood and entered a rapid adolescence. What was it to be called? Different people gave it different names, from their different points of view: Modern New Poetry, Misty Poetry, Peculiar Poetry . . . . Later the controversy over it broke out and there was a need for a name that would be commonly accepted. "Misty" was adopted as a compromise.

Certain fellow-poets and I have all along considered the term "Misty" in itself somewhat misty. What after all does "misty" mean? Traditionally, it describes objects such as "flowers viewed in the mist" or "a ferry crossing in the moonlight haze". According to the new critique it refers to the symbolic, the suggestive, the remote conception; alternation of impressions, juxtaposition of conscious and unconscious, etc. There is some truth in this. But these are not I think the main characteristics of the New Poetry. Its main characteristic is that it is real—moving from objective reality to subjective reality, from passive reflection to active creation.

Actually it is not misty at all, but the awakening of an aesthetic consciousness. Some areas are in fact becoming gradually clearer.

Q.: But some people claim that the main characteristic of the New Poetry is the difficulty of understanding it. What do you think about the problem of "understanding" and "not understanding" poetry?

A.: To put it in a more literary way, understanding is comprehension.

I do not think it has ever been easy to comprehend either poetry or Man. This comprehension is dependent on two participators, the writer and the reader. Many elements are involved on both sides. They are mainly: different

Mondō: a rapid question and answer technique employed in Zen Buddhism by a master seeking to lead a pupil into transcending the limitations of conceptual thought.

SCULPTURE by Wang Keping
王克平, born 1949.

levels of aesthetic appreciation, differing aesthetic modes, differences in objective experience, in subjective disposition; and the success or failure of the writer in the moment of self-expression.

Firstly, the levels of aesthetic appreciation.

Everybody who understands some basic theory knows that aesthetics has no cast-iron scale of measurement; it is a developing consciousness, accompanying the progress of mankind and the growth of the individual. For mankind, it is a river always reaching farther; for a normal individual, it is a tree always growing higher.

Once, in the years when I usually read comics, I stumbled across Walt Whitman. I was greatly shocked. Surely he was mad? His words were ungrammatical and illogical. Then why were they published? Was the publisher mad too?

Of course, later on I gradually came to comprehend; from the "Song of the Stream" 小溪流的歌[1] to "The Long River" 長長的流水; from O. Henry to Jack London; to Victor Hugo, to Romain Rolland, to Tagore . . . . When I read *The Songs of the South* and *Leaves of Grass* again, I was deeply affected. This was different from the shock of my childhood. This was overwhelming.

---

[1]Ed. note. Bonnie McDougall has identified the first of these titles as one of Yan Wenjing's 嚴文井 children's fables. See Yan's *Tonghua yuyan ji* 童話寓言集 (Peking 1982).

I have asked my fellow-poets, and found that they have all had the same experience. Each has had one or several favourite works, at different periods, at different levels of aesthetic appreciation. The favourite is always changing. In the end, what one likes is usually what has been accepted by all mankind. And these works (except children's literature) will not be understood at primary school.

That is a normal phenomenon.

Besides the different levels of aesthetic appreciation that may cause a gulf in comprehension, differing modes of perception and differing aesthetic conceptions may also create difficulty in understanding. Among these modes and conceptions, some can and should co-exist; others are part of the functional consciousness left over from our "age of havoc", a consciousness which, even according to our traditional aesthetic concepts, must be considered abnormal.

In the period of the Gang of Four people became accustomed to thinking of literature as mere explanation of policy between beautiful covers, as one of the many ways of eliminating illiteracy. And the writing of poetry became the competitive versification of editorials. Later the situation improved somewhat. From the time of the April the Fifth Movement [Tian'anmen Incident], poetry began to tell the truth. It had the chance to recover and develop. Soon there was a breakthrough in reflecting social problems, and poetry gained an independent social value of its own. This was exciting. But was it all? Man embraces many other realms. In these realms our ancestors once sowed and harvested. The fruits they reaped have become everlasting stars in the sky of mankind. Yet some years ago these realms were mostly covered with wild grass. These realms are the world of human psychology, the vast world of nature, and the world of the future, which man cannot clearly fathom.

These realms must be opened up again and broadened; the vitality of the Chinese people must find expression. It is for this that there are explorers. They respect the ancient masters of the art of poetry, but they do not repeat ancient methods of husbandry, for repetition is no artistic labour. The fervour of their creative aspirations drives them to express the needs and ideals of the new generation.

("Misty" poetry is simply one of their means of expression.)

Why are those who like "Misty" poetry mostly young people?

Why is it that the hearts of so many young people, who do not otherwise read widely, can beat together, across great distances of space, through the medium of this "Misty" poetry?

Is this some surreal intuition? No! It is the shared experience of the younger generation, the shared reality they face, and the shared ideals they pursue.

Of course this pursuit has its price. In exploring any new path in art you will always encounter more brambles than flowers. But a nation must have some such people to sacrifice themselves; for among them, some, along the trail blazed by the failures of their companions, will eventually discover new land, new areas of the heavens.

We have paid an enormous price, and we have begun to understand that neither politics nor materialism can substitute for everything. If a nation wants progress, it needs more than electronic technology and scientific management; it needs a highly advanced spiritual civilization, and that includes the creation of a modern, a new aesthetic consciousness. Beauty will no longer be prisoner or slave, it will shine with as much light as the sun and the moon. It will rise high in the heavens to drive away the shadow of evil. Through the windows of art and poetry it will cast light on the hearts of both the waking and the sleeping.

That the next generation may rise higher than ours, these windows must be more numerous, larger and cleaner.

From *Literature Press*
文學報, Shanghai, March 17, 1983.

tr. SEÁN GOLDEN,
with DAVID WAKEFIELD and SU KUICHUN

洪荒：新詩──一個轉折嗎？
Hong Huang: The New Poetry—A Turning Point?
(A Misty Manifesto)

I. Birth of the New Poetry

A new kind of poetry has been born.

It is flowing in the winds and waters of our land, in the blood and breath of a new generation. Some call it a revolution; others an invasion of the world of Chinese poetry by Western monsters. But its birth is an incontrovertible fact.

It has been given a variety of names: symbolist, surrealist, "misty 朦朧", even impressionist. In fact, it is none of these. We should rather call it a new embodiment of the national spirit, the voice and pulse of the thinking generation, a reaction to the poetic disease of the past two decades. Or just simply the New Poetry.

Its birth is no secret.

Since the fall of the Gang of Four, China has seen the dawn of a Renaissance. Prose (fiction, reportage, etc.) is moving toward reality. So too is poetry. The prose reality is objective; the poetic reality subjective, knowledge of the true self, a passionate rejection of alienation.

This breakthrough in content has led to a breakthrough in form. Now that the poet's own wealth of authentic feeling has replaced an abstract, false and prejudiced set of "intents" as poetic material; now that a truly vital self, one endowed with dignity, intellect and a complex inner life, has appeared in poetry; now that poetry is no longer hack literature, no longer the mouth-piece of politics; now that we are standing face to face with this land imbued with suffering and yet full of hope, musing on this sorrowful but radiant dawn; we need our own stance, our own voice.

We have substituted irregular lines for ornate parallelism. Rhythm has been given a new meaning. It is conceived of as the vibration of the poet's feelings, which he projects directly into his poems, no longer through some static system of poetic conventions. Form has become simply an extension of content.

The real identity of the author of this essay has not been established. The editors of Today *accepted it and published it under the pseudonym Hong Huang.*

Like Debussy, we substitute colouration for functional organization, rich visual imagery for auditory pleasure. Rhyme is neglected, even abandoned altogether. In terms of art psychology, we do not seek to achieve the fleeting pleasure of the reader at the moment of perception, but rather endeavour to imprint images in his mind and thereby to arouse him to imagining and thinking. Here we have reversed the famous dictum of the poet: "Music above all else."

The traditional, simple, harmonious beauty we replace with a rich, uncomfortable tension. We are seeking not serenity, but impulse.

. . . . . .

The most severe accusation levelled against the New Poetry is that it is too Westernized, a betrayal of our national heritage.

This question must be answered.

II. *What can we learn from Chinese classical poetry?*

At the end of the 1950s, a debate was conducted criticizing the "formlessness" of the "new poetry" of the time. The conclusion was reached that poetry should develop on the dual basis of folk song and the prosodic rules of classical poetic composition. This was a victory for classicism, and virtually determined the poetic orientation of the following two decades. To defend the new poetic revolution, a re-appraisal of this debate is imperative.

Is it necessary to prescribe a form for New Poetry? Is it evil to refrain from so doing? Surely not. Surely no such necessity exists.

To prescribe a form is to prescribe an evolution according to formula. True, our classical poetry (*shi*, *ci*, and *qu*) is thus formalized, and classical opera, even literati painting, tends towards formalization, tends to be formulaic. Their rich repertoire of artistic devices (prosody, lyric metre) achieves an abstract formal beauty. The advocates of "formalization" usually emphasize musical beauty as an artistic effect. A talented poet should indeed possess a sensitive ear and a sense of musical beauty; he should convert emotional rhythm accurately into poetic rhythm. The musical beauty of poetry, therefore, is a creative artistic means, not a pure technique. The unlimited creative potential of art should not be confined within the limitations of a technical formula. It is true that it requires less effort to create a rhythm according to a ready-made formula than it does to create one in free verse; but this very ease limits the creativity of the poet. Great lyric poets of the past, of course, chose differing lyric metres to suit their subjects; and out of the strict prosody of new style Regulated Verse, the great master Du Fu created musical beauty. But surely, in today's uniquely complex emotional world, when the emotional rhythm and colouring of every line of poetry are absolutely "individualized", it is hard to imagine how the poetic rhythm should not be equally "individualized". Even the "technical" 格調 school of the Ming dynasty, the strongest advocates of imitation and musical effect in poetry, did not identify "technique" with prosodic rules, and preferred the less rigid Old-style Verse 古體詩 to the strict Regulated Verse 今體詩, as it gave freer rein to the musical creativity of the poet. Li Dongyang 李東陽 wrote that a slavish imitation of prosodic rules actually "bridled the expression of personal feelings 無發人之性情". (See his *Huailutang shihua* 懷麓堂詩話). Why then should we emphasize a "formalization" based on traditional classical prosody?

It was the most worthless imitators of the classics, the "early and late Seven Masters" of the Ming dynasty, who lost the brilliant spirit of Tang poetry.

Prosodic rules do not merely reflect the patterns of language, they should also, and more essentially, reflect the rhythm of life. Both Whitman and the Victorian poets used the English language. But Whitman, when confronted with the vast rugged landscape of the New Continent, with the mighty labours of the pioneers, created a tone and a style totally different from those of the English poetic tradition. In the same way the two-stress four-character line found in *The Book of Songs* 詩經 can only reflect the rhythm of the primitive productive labour of the pre-Qin period. In a thinking era, in a society that is embarking on modernization, it is unimaginable that we should continue to use a poetic rhythm evolved under the agricultural mode of production. We do not deny the existence of some good new works in folk-song style, especially narrative poems like *Wang Gui and Li Xiang-xiang* 王貴與李香香 and *Zhanghe Shui* 漳河水. But they are almost all without exception about country life. Agricultural production had, after all, not changed greatly since ancient times. We can predict with confidence that with the agricultural modernization of our country, a new rhythm will appear in folk poetry!

What, then, *should* we learn from classical poetry?

The lesson is precisely what some friends dismiss as insignificant, precisely what they regard as a defect of our New Poetry.

We should revive the rich visual-imagist tradition of Chinese poetry, what Hulme called a "visual, concrete language", and oppose external logic and syntax as the sole source of poetic creation. The American imagist poet Ezra Pound wrote: "It is . . . because certain Chinese poets have been content to set forth their matter without moralizing and without comment that one labours to make a translation." This is not worshipping and fawning upon things foreign. Ouyang Xiu 歐陽修 said long ago, "the poet's task is to present an elusive scene so that it seems to appear before the (reader's) very eyes, and to contain therein the endless meaning beyond words"; or, as Wang Fuzhi 王夫之 put it, "true profundity is attained when the poet implants feeling in the scene, in such a way that no sign of the intent is visible."

We should revive the many levels of meaning, the ambiguity that is part of the tradition of the Chinese classical poetic language. This is a quality that has been singled out for comment by many Western sinologists. And yet this is not worshipping and fawning upon things foreign either. Sikong Tu 司空圖, after all, sought the "flavour beyond flavour 味外之味", the "resonance beyond harmony 韻外之致", the "image beyond imagery 象外之象", the "meaning beyond words 言外之意". Yan Yu 嚴羽 urged "the use of living language 須參活句", advised the poet "not to be trammeled by words 不落言筌".

We must revive the suggestive quality traditionally associated with Chinese poetic conception. This may coincide with contemporary Western poetics. But it is certainly not worshipping and fawning upon things foreign. The Tang poet Dai Shulun 戴叔倫 said of the ideal poetic conception: "It is like Lantian in the warmth of the sun, the aura of fine jade wavering in the heat, to be viewed from afar, not scrutinized." And Sikong Tu: "To describe it from a distance is to be there; to approach it is to negate it." Wang Shizhen 王士禎 borrowed the terminology of art-criticism in his description of poetic imagery: "In the distance, the mountains have no folds, the water no ripples, the faces no eyes." Are we to criticize these ideas as too "obscure", or "misty 朦朧"?

We must revive the four-dimensional perspective of the Chinese poetic tradition. We must apply the artistic technique of multiple development of ideas. This is not a poetic extension of Picasso's aesthetics; to understand it, just read the magnificent poetry of the Tang dynasty!

We believe this to be the essence of the classical tradition in Chinese poetry.

We live in an era of world cultural interfusion. The magnificent heritage of Eastern classical painting, drama and poetry has influenced the modern Western arts. Similarly, in drawing on the modern arts of the Western world, we can come to understand more deeply the true value of our own artistic tradition; we can combine this tradition more harmoniously with the content of modern life in order to develop our own new literature and art. Perhaps this is the secret of the New Poetry of the new Chinese generation, a secret which our poets and critics refuse to take seriously. This Rose on the tomb of Homer remains unconcerned and indifferent to the Nightingale singing fresh songs before her, would rather see youth wither in the parchment pages of the *Iliad*. But the Nightingale will continue to sing, to conjure an oasis of moisture and fragrance out of this wilderness ravaged by wind and sand.

From the third pamphlet published by *Today*'s Literary Research Society, 1980.

Translated and adapted
by ZHU ZHIYU with JOHN MINFORD

PHOTOGRAPHS of the 1981 'International Poetry Encounter' held amid the ruins of the Old Summer Palace, Peking, are reproduced from Julien Blaine, ed., *Doc(k)s* No. 41, 1981/2, as are many of the accompanying illustrations. We express our profound gratitude to Mr. Blaine.

北島

Bei Dao

Translated by Bonnie S. McDougall

The Bank

Companion to the present and the past
the bank, lifting a tall reed,
gazes in all directions
it is you
who keep watch on each wave
and the bewitching foam and stars
when the sobbing moon
strikes up an age-old shanty
it is so forlorn

I am a bank
a fishing haven
I stretch out my arms
to wait for the needy children's little boats
bringing back a string of lamps

Tomorrow, No

this is not a farewell
because we have never met
although shadow and shadow
have overlain on the street
like a solitary convict on the run

tomorrow, no
tomorrow is not the other side of night
whoever has hopes is a criminal
let the story that took place at night
end in the night

岸

陪伴着現在和以往
岸，舉着一根高高的蘆葦
四下眺望
是你
守護着每一個波浪
守護着迷人的泡沫和星星
當嗚咽的月亮
吹起古老的船歌
多麼憂傷

我是岸
我是漁港
我伸展着手臂
等待窮孩子的小船
載回一盞盞燈光

明天，不

這不是告別
因爲我們並沒有相見
儘管影子和影子
曾在路上疊在一起
像一個孤零零的逃犯

明天，不
明天不在夜的那邊
誰期待，誰就是罪人
而夜裏發生的故事
就讓它在夜裏結束吧

Six of these translations of Bei Dao's poems are reprinted from Bonnie S. McDougall, trans., Notes from the City of the Sun: Poems by Bei Dao (East Asia Papers, No. 34, 1983), courtesy of the China-Japan Program, Cornell University. For a general introduction to the poetry and fiction of Bei Dao/Zhao Zhenkai, see pp. 122-124. For the poems 'On Tradition', 'The Answer', and 'All', see pp. 9, 59-60, and 62.

Boat Ticket

he doesn't have a boat ticket
how can he go on board
the clanking of the anchor chain
disturbs the night here

the sea, the sea
the island rising up from the ebbing tide
as lonely as a heart
lacks the soft shadows of bushes
and chimney smoke
the mast that flashes lightning
is struck by lightning into fragments
innumerable storms
have left behind fixed patterns
on rigid scales and shells
and jellyfishes' small umbrellas
an ancient tale
is passed on by the ocean spray from wave to wave

he doesn't have a boat ticket

the sea, the sea
the lichen tightly massed upon the reef
spreads towards the naked midnight
and adheres to the surface of the moon
along the seagulls' feathers gleaming in the dark
the tide has fallen silent
conch and mermaid begin to sing

he doesn't have a boat ticket

time hasn't come to a stop now
in the sunken boat the fire is being stoked
rekindling red coral flames
when the waves tower up
glittering indeterminately, the eyes of the dead
float up from the ocean depths

he doesn't have a boat ticket

yes, it makes one dizzy
the sunlight drying out upon the beach
makes one so terribly dizzy

he doesn't have a boat ticket

船票

他沒有船票
又怎能登上甲板
鐵錨的鏈條嘩嘩作響
也驚動這裏的夜晚

海呵，海
退潮中上升的島嶼
和心一樣孤單
沒有灌木叢柔和的影子
沒有炊煙
劃出閃電的船桅
又被閃電擊成了碎片
無數次風暴
在堅硬的魚鱗和貝殼上
在水母小小的傘上
留下了靜止的圖案
一個古老的故事
在浪花與浪花之間相傳

他沒有船票

海呵，海
密集在礁石上的苔蘚
向赤裸的午夜蔓延
順着鷗羣暗中發光的羽毛
依附在月亮表面
潮水沉寂了
海螺和美人魚開始歌唱

他沒有船票

歲月並沒有從此中斷
沉船正生火待發
重新點燃了紅珊瑚的火焰
當浪峯聳起
死者的眼睛閃爍不定
從海洋深處浮現

他沒有船票

是呵，令人暈眩
那片晾在沙灘上的陽光
多麼令人暈眩

他沒有船票

The Old Temple

The fading chimes
form cobwebs, spreading a series of annual rings
among the splintered columns
without memories, a stone
spreads an echo through the misty valley
a stone, without memories
when a small path wound a way here
the dragons and strange birds flew off
carrying away the mute bells under the eaves
once a year weeds
grow, indifferently
not caring whether the master they submit to
is a monk's cloth shoe, or wind
the stele is chipped, the writing on its surface worn away
as if only in a general conflagration
could it be deciphered, yet perhaps
with a glance from the living
the tortoise might come back to life in the earth
and crawl over the threshold, bearing its heavy secret

古寺

消失的鐘聲
結成蛛網，在裂縫的柱子裏
擴散成一圈圈年輪
沒有記憶，石頭
空濛的山谷裏傳播回聲的
石頭，沒有記憶
當小路繞開這裏的時候
龍和怪鳥也飛走了
從房檐上帶走瘖啞的鈴鐺
荒草一年一度
生長，那麼漠然
不在乎它們屈從的主人
是僧侶的布鞋，還是風
石碑殘缺，上面的文字已經磨損
彷彿祇有在一場大火之中
才能辨認，也許
會隨着一道生者的目光
烏龜在泥土中復活
馱着沉重的秘密，爬出門檻

Chords

The trees and I
formed a close circle around the pond
my hand dipping into the water
disturbed the swifts from slumber
the wind was all alone
the sea very far away

I walked into the streets
noise stopped behind a red light
my shadow opened like a fan
footprints askew and crooked
the safety island all alone
the sea very far away

A blue window was lit up
downstairs, several boys
strummed guitars and sang
cigarette ends alternately glowed and darkened
the stray cat all alone
the sea very far away

As you slept on the beach
the wind paused by your mouth
and surging up in silence
waves converged in a gentle curve
the dream was all alone
the sea very far away

和弦

樹林和我
緊緊圍住了小湖
手伸進水裏
攪亂雨燕深沉的睡眠
風孤零零的
海很遙遠

我走到街上
喧囂被擋在紅燈後面
影子扇形般打開
腳印歪歪斜斜
安全島孤零零的
海很遙遠

一扇藍色的窗戶亮了
樓下，幾個男孩
撥動着結他吟唱
煙頭忽明忽暗
野貓孤零零的
海很遙遠

沙灘上，你睡着了
風停在你的嘴邊
波浪悄悄湧來
滙成柔和的曲線
夢孤零零的
海很遙遠

Sleep, Valley

Sleep, valley
with blue mist quickly cover the sky
and the wild lilies' pale eyes
sleep, valley
with rainsteps quickly chase away the wind
and the anxious cries of the cuckoo

Sleep, valley
we hide here
as if in a thousand year long dream
where time no longer glides over the blades of grass
the sun's clock is stopped behind layers of clouds
no longer shaking down the evening glow or dawn's
    first light

The spinning trees
toss down innumerable hard pine cones
protecting two lines of footprints
our childhoods walked with the seasons
along this winding path
and pollen drenched the brambles

Ah, it's so quiet and still
the cast stone has no echo
perhaps you are searching for something
—from heart to heart
a rainbow arises in silence
—from eye to eye

Sleep, valley
sleep, wind
valley, asleep in blue mist
wind, asleep in our hands

睡吧，山谷

睡吧，山谷
快用藍色的雲霧矇住天空
矇住野百合蒼白的眼睛
睡吧，山谷
快用雨的腳步去追逐風
追逐布穀鳥不安的啼鳴

睡吧，山谷
我們躲在這裏
彷彿躲進一個千年的夢中
時間不再從草葉上滑過
太陽的鐘擺停在雲層後面
不再搖落晚霞和黎明

旋轉的樹林
甩下無數顆堅硬的松果
護衛着兩行腳印

我們的童年和季節一起
走過那條彎彎曲曲的小路
花粉沾滿了荊叢

呵，多麼寂靜
拋出去的石子沒有回聲
也許，你在探求什麼
——從心到心
一道彩虹正悄然昇起
——從眼睛到眼睛

睡吧，山谷
睡吧，風
山谷，睡在藍色的雲霧裏
風，睡在我們的手掌中

A Toast

the cup is filled with night
without lights; the room floats in its depths
the dotted line along the asphalt road stretches to the clouds
without rising currents of air; think of
yesterday, searching for peace between flashes of lightning
swifts darting in and out of the turret
without being stained by dust
but rows of guns and bouquets
formed a forest, and took aim at the lovers' sky
summer is over, and red gaoliang
comes along a line of bobbing hats
neither cheerless adulthood nor death
may be averted; the darkness of the night
is so tender in your eyes, yet who
can stop the trains heading for each other in the mist
from colliding at this instant

祝酒

這杯中盛滿了夜晚
沒有燈光，房子在其中沉浮
柏油路的虛綫一直延伸到雲層
沒有上昇的氣流，想想
昨天，在閃電之間尋找安寧
雨燕匆匆地出入城樓
沒有沾上塵土
而一枝枝槍和花束
排成樹林，對準了情人的天空
夏天過去了，紅高粱
從一頂頂浮動的草帽上走來
不幸的成熟或死亡
無法拒絕，在你的瞳孔裏
夜色多麼溫柔，誰
又能阻止兩輛霧中對開的列車
在此刻相撞

You Wait for Me in the Rain

you wait for me in the rain
the road leads into the window's depths
the other side of the moon must be very cold
that summer night, a white horse
galloped past with the northern lights
for a long time we trembled
go, you said
don't let anger destroy us
leaving no way of escape
like entering the mountains of menopause
at many corners we took the wrong turn
but in the desert we met
all the ages gather here
hawks, and long-lived cacti
gather here
more real than heat mirages
as long as one fears birth,
and the smiling faces that do not don their masks in time
then everything is connected with death
that summer night was not the end
you wait for me in the rain

你在雨中等待着我

你在雨中等待着我
路通向窗戶深處
月亮的背面一定很冷
那年夏夜，白馬
和北極光馳過
我們曾久久地戰慄
去吧，你說
別讓憤怒毀滅了我們
就像進入更年期的山那樣
無法解脫
從許多路口，我們錯過
卻在一片沙漠中相逢
所有的年代聚集在這裏
鷹，還有仙人掌
聚集在這裏
比熱浪中的幻影更真實
祇要懼怕誕生，懼怕
那些來不及帶上面具的笑容
一切就和死亡有關
那年夏夜並不是終結
你在雨中等待着我

The Host

the neglected guest has gone
he left behind disastrous news
and a glove
in order to come knocking at my door again
there's still no way for me to see daylight fireworks
a dance tune strikes up
the moonlight streaming from the mill
is filled with hints of a dream
let us have faith in miracles
a miracle is that nail on the wall
my shadow is trying on
the clothes dangling on the nail
and my last chance at luck
between the two knocks on the door
my hands, propping up sleep, fall down
the dangerous stairs
are outlined against the darkness of the night

主人

被忘慢的客人走了
他留下災難性的消息
和一隻手套
為了再敲響我的門
我仍無法看清白晝的焰火
舞曲響起
那從磨房流出的月光
充滿了夢的暗示
相信奇跡吧
奇跡就是那顆牆上的釘子
我的影子在試
釘子上搖摵的衣服
試我最後的運氣
兩次敲門之間
支撐睡眠的手垂下來
危險的樓梯
從夜色中顯出輪廓

Untitled

rancour turns a drop of water muddy
I am worn out, the storm
has run aground upon the beach
the sun pierced by the mast
is my heart's prisoner, but I
am banished by the world it shines on
nothing is left to sacrifice
on the reef, this dark and pagan altar
except myself as I go to close or open
the clamorous book

無題

積怨使一滴水變得混濁
我疲倦了，風暴
擱淺在沙灘上
那桅桿射中的太陽
是我內心的囚徒，而我
卻被它照耀的世界所放逐
礁石，這異教徒的黑色祭壇
再也沒有什麼可供奉
除了自己，去打開或合上
那本喧囂的書

For Many Years

this is you, this is
you, pressed upon by fleeting
shadows, now bright, now dark
no longer shall I go towards you
the cold also makes me despair
for many years, before the icebergs were formed
fish floated up to the water's surface
and sunk down, for many years
stepping warily I
passed through the slowly drifting night
lamps glowed on the forked steel prongs
for many years, lonely
the room without a clock
the people who left might also have taken
the key, for many years
the train on the bridge rushed past
whistling through the fog
season after season
set out from the small station among the fields
paused briefly for every tree
flowered and bore fruit, for many years

很多年

這是你，這是
被飛翔的陰影困擾的
你，忽明忽暗
我不再走向你
寒冷也讓我失望
很多年，冰山形成以前
魚曾浮出水面
沉下去，很多年
我小心翼翼
穿過緩緩流動的夜晚
燈火在鋼叉上閃爍
很多年，寂寞
這沒有鐘的房間
離去的人也會帶上
鑰匙，很多年
在濃霧中吹起口哨
橋上的火車馳過
一個個季節
從田野的小車站出發
爲每棵樹逗留
開花結果，很多年

Random Thoughts

dusk rose over the beacon tower
on islands in the border river
a tribe settled
and spread; the land changed colour
myths lay under shabby cotton quilts
the dream's gestation bore poisoned arrows which spread
a painful throbbing; bugles fell silent
skeletons walked at night
unfolding in the wife's unceasing tears
a white screen that blocked
the gate to distant lands

the east, in this piece of amber
was a vaguely looming bank
as tufts of reeds sped towards the trembling dawn
fishermen quit their boats, and dispersed like the smoke from their fires
history, starting from the bank
felled great thickets of bamboo
inscribing limited compositions
upon imperishable slips

in the vault a row of ever-burning lamps
witnessed the death of bronze and gold
there is another kind of death
the death of wheat
in the interstices between crossed swords
it grew like a challenge to battle
and set the sun on fire; the ashes covered winter
cartwheels fell off
scattering in the direction of the spokes
the moat invaded by a duststorm
is another kind of death; steles
wrapped in moss as soft as silk
are like extinguished lanterns

only the road is still alive
that road which outlines the earth's earliest contours
passing through the endless zone of death
it has reached my feet, stirring up the dust
in the air above the ancient fort the puffs of gunsmoke have not dispersed
long ago was I cast, but within the ice-cold iron
an impulse is preserved, to call up
the thunder, to call up our ancestors returning from the storm
yet if a million souls beneath the earth
should grow into a tall and lonely tree
to shade us, let us taste the bitter fruit
at this time of our departure

隨想

黃昏從烽火台上昇起
在這界河的島嶼上
一個種族棲息
又蔓延，土地改變了顏色
神話在破舊的棉絮下
夢的妊娠也帶着箭毒擴散時
痛苦的悸動，號角沉寂
尸骨在夜間走動
在妻子不斷湧出的淚水中
展開了白色的屏風
遮住那通向遠方的門

東方，這塊琥珀裏
是一片蒼茫的岸
蘆葦叢駛向戰慄的黎明
漁夫捨棄了船，炊煙般離去
歷史從岸邊出發
砍伐了大片的竹林
在不朽的簡册上寫下
有限的文字

墓穴裏，一盞盞長明燈
目睹了青銅或黃金的死亡
還有一種死亡
小麥的死亡
在那刀劍交叉的空隙中
它們曾挑戰似地生長
點燃陽光，灰燼復蓋着冬天
車輪倒下了
沿着輻條散射的方向
被風沙攻陷的城池
是另一種死亡，石碑
包裹在絲綢般柔軟的苔蘚裏
如同熄滅了的燈籠

只有道路還活着
那勾勒出大地最初輪廓的道路
穿過漫長的死亡地帶
來到我的腳下，揚起了灰塵
古老的炮台上空一朵朵硝煙未散
我早已被鑄造，冰冷的鑄鐵內
保持着衝動，呼喚
雷聲，呼喚從暴風雨中歸來的祖先
而千萬個幽靈從地下
長出一棵孤獨的大樹
爲我們蔽蔭，讓我們嚐到苦果
就在這出發之時

Notes in the Rain

waking up, the window over the street
preserves the glass pane's
complete and tranquil anguish
gradually turning transparent in the rain
the morning reads my wrinkles
the book lying open on the table
makes a rustling noise, like
the sound of a fire
or fan-like wings
gorgeously opening, flame and bird together
high over the abyss

here, between me
and the sunset clouds which herald immutable fate
is a river full of drifting stones
jostling shadows
plunge into its depths
and rising bubbles
menace the starless
daylight

people who draw fruit in the earth
are destined to endure hunger
people who shelter among friends
are destined to be alone
from tree roots exposed beyond life and death
rain water washes away
mud, and grass
and the sound of grief

雨中紀事

醒來，臨街的窗戶
保存着玻璃
那完整而寧靜的痛苦
雨中漸漸透明的
早晨，閱讀着我的皺紋
書打開在桌上
瑟瑟作響，好像
火中發出的聲音
好像折扇般的翅膀
華美地展開，在深淵上空
火焰與鳥同在

在這裏，在我
和呈現劫數的晚霞之間
是一條漂滿石頭的河
人影騷動着
潛入深深的水中
而昇起的泡沫
威脅着沒有星星的
白晝

在大地畫上果實的人
註定要忍受饑餓
棲身於朋友中的人
註定要孤獨
樹根裸露在生與死之外
雨水沖刷的
是泥土，是草
是哀怨的聲音

The Window on the Cliff

with dangerous movements the wasp forces open the flower
the letter has been sent, one day in a year
matches, affected by damp, no longer illuminate me
wolf packs roam among people turned into trees
snowdrifts suddenly thaw; on the dial
winter's silence is intermittent
what bores through the rock is not clean water
chimney smoke is cut by an axe
staying straight up in the air
the sunlight's tiger-skin stripes slip down the wall
stones grow, dreams have no direction
life, scattered amid the undergrowth
ascends in search of a language; stars
shatter; the river on heat
dashes countless rusty shell fragments towards the city
from sewer ditches hazardous bushes grow
in the markets women buy up spring

峭壁上的窗戶

黃蜂用危險的姿勢催開花朶
信已發出，一年中的一天
受潮的火柴不再照亮我
猿羣穿過那些變成了樹的人們
雪堆驟然融化，表盤上
冬天的沉默斷斷續續
鑿穿岩石的並不是純淨的水
炊煙被利斧砍斷
筆直地停留在空中
陽光的虎皮條紋從牆上滑落
石頭生長，夢沒有方向
散落在草叢中的生命
向上尋找着語言，星星
迸裂，那發情的河
把無數生銹的彈片衝向城市
從陰溝裏長出兇險的灌木
在市場上，女人們搶購着春天

August Sleepwalker

the stone bell tolls on the seabed
tolling, it stirs up the waves

it is August that tolls
there is no sun at high noon in August

a triangular sail, swollen with milk,
soars above the drifting corpse

it is August that soars
August apples tumble down the ridge

the lighthouse that died long ago
shines in the seamen's gaze

it is August that shines
the August fair comes close on first frost

the stone bell tolls on the seabed
tolling, it stirs up the waves

the August sleepwalker
has seen the sun at night

八月的夢遊者

海底的石鐘敲響
敲響，掀起了波浪

敲響的是八月
八月的正午沒有太陽

漲滿乳汁的三角帆
高聳在漂浮的尸體上

高聳的是八月
八月的蘋果滾下山崗

熄滅已久的燈塔
被水手們的目光照亮

照亮的是八月
八月的集市又臨霜降

海底的石鐘敲響
敲響，掀起了波浪

八月的夢遊者
看見過夜裏的太陽

顧城

Gu Cheng

Translated by Tao Tao Liu, Seán Golden *et al.*

An Autobiographical Montage

1956   In autumn I came into this world by way of the Peking Hospital. For a short while I uttered a weak cry and then entered the first dream.

1963   Looking at the wet headlamp of a car, mother asked me whether I would rather go to kindergarten or primary school. I answered, primary school.

1966   After receiving an injection to bring down my fever, I limped to school where the red storm had already wrecked the doors and windows.

1969   The wind was freezing cold; a military lorry lurched across the alkaline flats in the north of Shandong province. My whole family was "going to the countryside".

1970   I walked out of the mud-walled, straw-thatched village, driving the pigs, out to the wilds. Great flocks of wild geese broke formation, which made my life tremble a bit.

1974   A clean and clear Peking appeared once more before me. I loosened my grip, and poems and painting-brushes dropped to the ground. I had a job. In a workshop dark as a decayed tooth, I sawed, and cleared away the wood-chips and sawdust.

1976   Dusk at Tian'anmen was truly beautiful; golden Mars was rising, rising, and I was knocked down by a troop of people on the pavement. Sound of the radio.

1979   An exceedingly fresh gust of air; the Cultural Centre of Xicheng District ran a literature and art tabloid, and three groups of my youthful poems were published in it—"Some Anonymous Small Flowers".

1980   I removed the trade union key from the cabinet; the work unit was to be disbanded.

1982   I showed my award and the catalogue of my published work to a comrade at the Peking Writers' Union.
"More than three hundred pieces. Almost enough."
I opened the membership card and wrote down three words in the space marked Occupation—"Waiting for work".

1983   Shanghai also has winters, but not quiet. With a letter of invitation from the University of Stockholm in my pocket, I wander the streets, blessing mankind.

tr. SEÁN GOLDEN

The Cliffs

Two tall cliffs
Lean towards each other nearer and nearer.

What burning enmity
Has fired their bodies black?

The ligaments of tree roots bind them close
The flesh and muscles of the rocks rise high.
The fearsome power of their horns would soon erupt
If the dew were to let fall but one drop.

But this drop condenses and suddenly congeals
And in a moment solidifies.
So the ancient enmity will always be preserved
Causing our slight wonder today.

石壁

兩塊高大的石壁,
在傾斜中步步進逼。

是多麼灼熱的仇恨,
燒彎了鐵黑的軀體。

樹根的韌帶緊緊繃住,
岩石的肌肉高高聳起,
可怕的角力就要爆發,
祇要露水再落下一滴。

這一滴卻在壓縮中突然凝結,
時間變成了固體。
於是這古老的仇恨便得以保存,
引起了我今天一點驚異。

On Parting

Today
You and I
Will cross this ancient threshold
Don't offer good wishes
Don't say goodbye
All that is like a performance
The best is silence
Concealment can never be counted a deceit
Leave memory to the future
As dreams to the night
Tears to the sea
Wind to the sails

贈別

今天
我和你
要跨過這古老的門檻
不要祝福
不要再見
那些都像表演
最好是沉默
隱藏總不算欺騙
把回想留給未來吧
就像把夢留給夜
淚留給大海
風留給帆

For My Revered Master Hans Andersen
(Andersen, like the poet, was once a clumsy carpenter.)

You pushed your plane,
Like riding in a dugout canoe,
On that smooth sea surface,
Floating slowly . . . .

Shavings scatter like the waves,
Disappearing to the edge of the sea and the sky;
The wood grain like rhythmic lines of verse,
Brings with it the greetings of months and years.

There are no flags,
No gold or silver, or bolts of coloured silk,
But the emperor of the whole world
Is not as rich as you.

You bring a land from heaven,
You bring flowers and dream balloons.
All lovely innocent children's hearts
Are yours for harbour.

給我的尊師安徒生
安徒生和作者本人都曾當過笨拙
　　的木匠

你推動木刨,
像駕駛着獨木舟,
在那平滑的海上,
緩緩漂流……

刨花像浪花散開,
消逝在海天盡頭;
木紋像波動的詩行,
帶來歲月的問候。

沒有旗幟,
沒有金銀、彩綢,
但全世界的帝王,
也不會比你富有。

你運載着一個天國,
運載着花和夢的氣球,
所有純美的童心,
都是你的港口。

Far and Near

You
Sometimes look at me
Sometimes look at the clouds.

I feel
When you look at me you are far away
When you look at the clouds you are very near.

遠和近

你
一會看我
一會看雲。

我覺得
你看我時很遠
你看雲時很近。

A Stare

The world goes clattering by
What are you staring at?
Under your shadowy eyelashes
I discover myself

A clumsy shadow
At a loss under the starry sky
The stars gradually gather into tears
Slip and fall from your heart

I don't know how to ask
Neither did you speak

tr. TAO TAO LIU

凝視

世界在喧鬧中逝去
你凝視着什麼
在那睫影的掩蓋下
我發現了我

一個笨拙的身影
在星空下不知所措
星星漸漸聚成了淚水
從你的心頭滑落

我不會問
你也沒有說

BLACK & WHITE I, Ma Desheng.

Ma Desheng 馬德升 *is one of the original members of the group of artists in Peking known as The Stars. He specializes in engraving and black-and-white illustration.*

Winter Day's Longing

on winter's tree
a large crow perches
as dark as the hour before the dawn
gleaming, so
first one eye, then the other
behind, the clear and silent sky

a kind of longing
a glooming kind of longing
compels me to walk away
to tread firm the loose waste land
among the meagre shadows
could there be no tadpoles
swimming, scouting for green coral

冬日的溫情

在冬天的樹上
落着一隻大鴉
黑得像接近黎明的夜
因而發出光亮
它的眼睛在交替使用
後面是無聲的晴空

一種溫情
一種溫情中擴展的壓抑
迫使我走開
去踹實鬆鬆的荒土
在稀少的影子裏
難道沒有許多蝌蚪
游着，偵察着綠珊瑚

Brief Note

A friend told me, sunny solitude.
Suddenly I thought of the whole north, winter . . . I was
*   raised in this kind of solitude.*
The sunlight on the latticed window paper, bright but cold,
*   subtly insinuated everything. The birds wore heavy*
*   padding, mute, sound became mere illusion, dis-*
*   appearing.*
Wind seemed to be blowing far off in the distance; what
*   will come? What will go?*
The whole solitude was shouting for the green spring trees.

〔小釋〕

　　一個朋友告訴我，晴朗的寂寞。
　　我一下想起了整個北方，冬天……
我是在這種寂寞中成人的。
　　窗紙上的陽光，明亮又寒冷，微妙
地制約着一切。鳥雀都穿得厚敦敦的，
不能說話，聲音變成了虛幻的影像，消
失着。風好像在極遠的地方吹，什麼將
要到來？什麼將離去？
　　整個寂寞都在呼喊着春天的綠樹。

Nostos

do not go to sleep, do not
my love, the route is still quite long
do not go near the forest's lure
do not despair

please use cool cool melted snow
to write directions on the hand
or lean on my shoulder
to pass the misty first light of dawn

part the clear rainstorm
we can already reach the homeplace
a round patch of green earth
spreading near an age old pagoda

I will be there
to protect your weary dream
to repel the hordes of black night
leaving only bronze drums and the sun

on the aged pagoda's far side
there are many ripples
quietly climbing the sand dune
gathering quivering sound . . . .

回歸

不要睡去，不要
親愛的，路還很長
不要靠近森林的誘惑
不要失掉希望

請用涼涼的雪水
把地址寫在手上
或是靠着我的肩膀
渡過朦朧的晨光

撩開透明的暴風雨
我們就會到達家鄉
一片圓形的綠地
鋪在古塔近旁

我將在那兒
守護你疲倦的夢想
起開一羣羣黑夜
祇留下銅鼓和太陽

在古塔的另一邊
有許多細小的波浪
悄悄爬上沙岸
收集着顫動的音響……

NUDE, Huang Rui.

Huang Rui 黃銳 was born in 1952, and was a founding member of The Stars.

Brief Note

We would return home. We have only heard about home;
the last generation abandoned it.

We have only heard about the great mountains like huge
beasts, only heard about silvereyes and betel palms,
only heard about the song of the subterranean spring
and the pattern of the trilobite.

We would return home, return to the midst of the ancient
music of bronze; our lives are filled with the desire to
return to the fountainhead.

It seems we have set off from an island, bade farewell to
the perilous boat.

We have journeyed for a long long time; the quest is quite
long.

"Tired?" "Yes."

Only on the soil where our forebears lay can our love sleep.

〔小釋〕

我們要回家鄉去。我們祇聽說過家鄉，父輩遺棄了它。

我們祇聽說過那巨獸一樣的大山，祇聽說過綉眼鳥和檳榔，祇聽說過地下泉的歌和三葉蟲的圖畫。

我們要回家鄉去，回到青銅的古樂中去，我們的生命充滿了歸復本源的願望。

我們好像是從島上出發的，已經告別了危險的船。

我們走了好久好久，路真長。

「累嗎?」「累。」

祇有在祖先安息的地上，我們的愛才能安睡。

The Wind Stole Our Oar

it's like this
    a gust of wind, warm and mild
  stole our oar
dark green lake water, prankish flash of light
    "go, never search again
    search again for the starting place"

perhaps, summer rain's felicity
        made the sluices sink
  from the submersed tip of a willow tree
frog is conducting a family
      choir rehearsal
perhaps, autumn wind has dessicated the clouds
  bold ants
  climb a dry lotus leaf
    marquee, reconnoitring from the heights
perhaps, a row of old palings
    still stands in the water
  together with the children, waiting for small fry
      laying clear glass bottles
    down among green water weeds
perhaps, like philosophical cant
      damp cicada
    still clamber back and forth
stray penny
     on a mud floor, thinking deeply
  do not think again
  think again of that starting place

the wind stole our oar
      we
    will in another springtime pull alongside
    the embankment thin and long
poplar blossoms carried off the stars, leaving only
    moonlight
    leaving only moonlight
      beside our lips
        to illuminate the strange little road

風偷去了我們的槳

就是這樣
    一陣風，溫和地，
  偷走了我們的槳
墨綠色的湖水，玩笑地閃光
    「走吧，別再找了
    再找出發的地方」

也許，夏雨的快樂
      使水閘坍方
  在隱沒的柳梢上
青蛙正指揮着一家
    練習合唱
也許，秋風吹乾了雲朵

  大膽的螞蟻
  正爬在乾荷葉的
    帳篷上，眺望
也許，一排年老的木樁
    還站在水裏
  和小孩一起，等着小魚
    把乾淨的玻璃瓶
    在青草中安放
也許，像哲學術語一樣的
    濕知了
    還在爬來爬去
遺落的分幣
    在泥地上，冥想
  不要再想
  再想那出發的地方

風偷去了我們的槳
    我們
    將在另一個春天靠岸
    堤岸又細又長
楊花帶走星星，只留下月亮
    只留下月亮
    在我們的嘴唇邊
      把陌生的小路照亮

Brief Note

When we boarded love's boat the past evaporated.

Everything was gradually rising, subsiding, everywhere began strange singing, and we seemed to travel in the song.

All the spirits hidden within nature, all released from the binding spells, danced in the blue sky. Their wings beat the air . . .

Love is wonderful, but where does it lead us? The simple plan and the oar have already been lost. Sometimes, we can only let the waves carry.

Don't be afraid; if we believe in ourselves and the world, believe in the ideal, that blessed shore will be reached.

〔小釋〕

當我們踏上了愛的小船，過去就消失了。

一切都在緩緩地昇起、落下，都開始了奇異的歌唱，我們好像在歌曲中航行。

所有隱藏在大自然中的精靈，都解脫了咒語，在碧藍的天空中舞蹈。它們翅膀營營有聲。……

愛是美好的，但它要把我們帶到哪去？簡單的設想和槳已經失落了。有時，我們只聽憑波瀾的推送。

別害怕，祗要我們相信自己和世界、相信理想，那幸福的彼岸就會到達。

BLACK & WHITE II, Ma Desheng.

Résumé

I am a child of sorrow
from cradle to grave undergrown
from the northern grasslands I
walked out, followed
a whitish road, walked into
the town stacked with gears
walked into narrow lanes'
lean-tos—every trodden heart;
wrapped in indifferent smoke I
still tell my green tales
I believe my devotees
—the sky, and
the spuming drops of water on the sea
will shroud me completely
shroud that insituate
grave, I know that
at that time, all the grass and small flowers
will all crowd round, in
the glimmer of the dim lamplight
softly softly to kiss my sorrow

簡歷

我是一個悲哀的孩子
始終沒有長大
我從北方的草灘上
走出，沿着一條
發白的路，走進
佈滿齒輪的城市
走進狹小的街巷
板棚，每顆低低的心
我在一片淡漠的煙中
繼續講綠色的故事
我相信我的聽衆
——天空，還有
海上迸濺的水滴
它們將覆蓋我的一切
覆蓋那無法尋找的
墳墓，我知道
那時，所有的草和小花
都會圍攏，在
燈光暗淡的一瞬
輕輕地親吻我的悲哀

Brief Note

No one likes sorrow; we have all passed that way.

I drifted to a stretch of grasslands; raised pigs. I could not go to school—no books, not even the clatter of people eating. The only thing that comforted me was the silently rising cloud at the edge of the grasslands.

Walking, I dreamed of someone I could talk with; the footprints on the alkaline land were white.

I rambled into the city, and in a roar became a carpenter. My three masters, their ages combined, were 220 years old. They liked me; tenderly teaching me how to make latticed windows. They also liked to smoke (one had smoked opium), liked singing The East Is Red, *definitely did not believe the earth to be round (because water always stays in the water vat). Later, came a sister apprentice. Every day she added to her collection of boy friends, occasionally removed her false eye to show others.*

Who could I talk to? Tell that looking-glass forest's fairy tale.

One time, I cleaned the only window—a broken one, so, while working, I could see the tiny patch of blue sky. I asked myself, "Why this way?" "It can only be this way." "What for?" "For everything I love."

I answered. I wrote this "Résumé".

I will tell tomorrow, tell tomorrow's newborn flowers: in the past, in a small smokefilled room, there was a heart which had loved them.

〔小釋〕

　　沒有人喜歡悲哀，我們卻都經歷了那個時代。

　　我漂流到一片草灘上，放着豬。我沒有學上，沒有書，甚至沒有人聲和食物。唯一給我安慰的，就是草灘盡頭靜靜昇起的雲。

　　我走着，夢想着對誰訴說。礆地上的腳印是白色的。

　　我走進了城市，在一陣轟響中，變成了木匠。我的三個師傅，加起來總年齡在二百二十歲左右。他們喜歡我，熱心地教我做小木格的窗子。他們還喜歡抽煙(有一個曾抽過鴉片)，喜歡唱《東方紅》，絕不相信地球是圓的（因爲水始終呆在缸裏）。後來，來了個師妹。她每天都增加幾位男朋友，不時地把一隻假眼睛挖出來給人看。

　　我對誰說呢？說那個倒映着森林的童話。

　　有一次，我把唯一的窗子——一塊破玻璃擦淨了，我幹活時就望着那片小小的藍天。我問自己：「爲什麼這樣？」「祇能這樣。」「這樣爲了什麼？」「爲了我所愛的一切」。

　　我回答。我寫下了《簡歷》。

　　我要告訴明天，告訴明天誕生的花朵：在過去，在一間充滿煤煙的小屋裏，有一顆心，愛過它們。

To a Null Star

why are you always watching me
you're lonely
you're not so pretty as the Swan star
haven't such a brood of sisters
it's been like this since birth
this is not your fault

but, I am the guilty one
I've left many people
or is it they who've left me
I have no smiling flowers
haven't the habit of grinning indiscriminately
before wise men I am often silent

silent, like an evening cloud
I don't know
don't know what you want, really
the silk tree again bars a small half of the heavens
guess! many nights still remain
"I need you not to be lonely again"

給一顆沒有的星星

你爲什麼總在看我
你是孤獨的
你沒有天鵝星那麼美麗
沒有那麼衆多的姐妹
從誕生起就是這樣
這不是你的過錯

然而，我是有罪的
我離開了許多人
也許是他們離開了我
我沒有含笑花
沒有分送笑容的習慣
在聖人面前經常沉默

沉默，像一朵傍晚的雲
我不知道
不知道你要什麼，眞的
合歡樹又遮住一小半天空
猜吧，還有許多夜晚
「我需要你不再孤獨」

Brief Note

By the wall, I seemed to see a dim star.
*She was Cinderella in the heavens. She didn't go to the
    grand ball of the other stars, where princes in golden
    armour chatted and laughed loudly.*
She was an orphan. She hadn't the habit of speaking.
I too like silence.
*Did milady slicing roast goose beside the hearth know
    warmth? Did the children dreaming under silken
    quilts know love? Did the princes strolling back and
    forth among the skirts and coy glances know happi-
    ness?*
*No, the ones who know are Oliver, Cosette, and the girl
    who sold matches in the snow.*
*There is only one pure love and it belongs to those who
    cherish it.*

〔小釋〕

在牆邊，我好像看到了一顆微弱的
星星。
她是天上的灰姑娘。她沒有去參加
羣星盛大的舞會，戴金盔的王子們正在
那裏大聲說笑。
她是一個孤兒，沒有說話的習慣。
我也喜歡沉默。
在壁爐邊切烤鵝的太太懂得溫暖
麼？在絲絨中作夢的孩子懂得愛麼？在
眼波和裙紗間穿行的王子懂得幸福麼？
不，懂那一切的是奧列弗爾，是珂
賽特，是在雪地裏賣火柴的小女孩。
最純的愛是唯一的，屬於珍惜者。

tr. SEÁN GOLDEN, with DAVID WAKEFIELD
and SU KUICHUN

江河
Jiang He
Translated by Alisa Joyce, Ginger Li, Yip Wai-lim

UNFINISHED POEM

I. An Ancient Tale

I was nailed upon the prison wall.
Black Time gathered, like a crowd of crows
From every corner of the world, from every night of
    History,
To peck all the heroes to death, one after the other,
    upon this wall.
The agony of heroes thus became a rock
Lonelier than mountains.
For chiseling and sculpting
The character of the nation,
Heroes were nailed to death
Wind-eroding, rain-beating
An uncertain image revealed upon the wall—
Dismembered arms, hands and faces—
Whips slashing, darkness pecking.
Ancestors and brothers with heavy hands
Laboured silently as they were piled into the wall.
Once again I come here
To revolt against fettered fate
And with violent death to shake down the earth from
    the wall
To let those who died silently stand up and cry out.

沒有寫完的詩

一、古老的故事

我被釘在監獄的牆上
黑色的時間在聚攏，像一羣羣烏
    鴉
從世界的每個角落，從歷史的每
    個夜晚
把一個又一個英雄啄死在這堵牆
    上
英雄的痛苦變成了石頭
比山還要孤獨
爲了開鑿和塑造，
爲了民族的性格
英雄被釘死
風剝蝕着，雨薇打着
模模糊糊的形象在牆上顯露
——殘缺不全的骼膊、手、面孔
鞭子抽打着，黑暗啄食着
祖先和兄弟們的手沉重地勞動
把自己默默無聲地壘進牆壁
我又一次來到這裏
反抗被奴役的命運
用激烈的死亡震落牆上的泥土
讓默默死去的人們站起來叫喊

II. Suffering

I am the mother. My daughter is about to be executed.
Gun-point walks toward me, a black sun
Upon the cracked earth walks toward me.
I am an old tree. I am a bunch of dried fingers.
I am those convulsed wrinkles upon the face.
The land and I both bear together this catastrophe,
Heart thrown upon the ground.
My daughter's blood is splashed into the mud,
Hot and flowing, my child's tears run upon my face;
They too are salty.
As in winter, small rivers, one after the other, freeze,
One after the other stop singing.
I am sister, I am daughter and wife.
Lapels and hems are torn, hair falling,
Not leaves.
Spindrift flies from rocks.
My hair is an ocean.
I am father, I am husband, I am son.
My big hand bumps and jolts upon the hair-ocean.
Bone-joints dully crackle.
I am boats and vessels.
I am cut jungles
While still growing robustly.

二、受難

我是母親，我的女兒就要被處決
槍口向我走來，一隻黑色的太陽
在乾裂的土地上向我走來
我是老樹，我是枯乾的手指
我是臉上痙攣的皺紋
我和土地忍受着共同的災難
心被摔在地上
女兒的血濺滿泥土
滾燙滾燙的，孩子的淚水在我臉上流着
孩子的眼淚也是鹹的
像是在冬天，一條條小河在冰凍
一條條河流停止了歌唱
我是姐妹，我是女兒和妻子
衣襟被撕破，頭髮在飄落
不是落葉
淚花在岩石上飛濺
我的頭髮是一片海
我是父親，我是丈夫，我是兒子
我的大手在頭髮的海洋上顛簸
骨節沉悶地響着
我是船舶
我是被破伐的森林
我的森林還在粗獷地生長

III. Brief Lyric

As in a dream,
I became a girl
Arriving upon this world
Upon the squeaking gravel road
Stepping shadows into pieces.
I became barefooted
Blood dripping fresh red
Into the dew
Like red agates glittering upon a rising bosom.
In order for a tender green heart
To blossom at dawn
I offered the stirrings of my pure youth to revolution
Stretching out my arms like a white bridge
To search for the sun.
I was no longer afraid of stars trembling in the water.
In the forest of book columns, in the night quest
I became a star
That trembled no more.

三、簡短的抒情詩

像是在夢中
我成了女孩子
來到這世界
在吱吱叫着的石子路上
踹碎影子
我赤腳跑來
鮮紅的血滴觸進
露水
像一顆顆紅瑪瑙，閃動在起伏的胸前
爲了嫩綠的心
在黎明時開放
我把青春純潔的騷動獻給了革命
手臂像潔白的橋
尋找太陽
我不再怕星星在水中顫抖
在書脊似的林子裏，在夜的摸索中
我變成一顆星星
不再顫抖

IV. To the Execution Ground

Cheating winds muffle windows and eyes.
At this hour, killing is going on.
I cannot hide in the house.
My blood cannot let me remain this way.
Morning-like children cannot let me remain this way.
I am thrown into the prison.
Handcuffs and foot-fetters cut deep into my flesh.
Whips and blood weave into a net upon my body.
My voice is cut off.
My heart is a ball of fire, burning silently upon my lips.
I am walking toward the execution ground, looking with scorn
Upon this historic night. In this corner of the world,
There is no other choice. I have chosen the sky
Because the sky will not rot.
Nothing but execution for me, otherwise darkness has nowhere to hide.
I was born in darkness, in order to create sun rays.
Nothing but execution for me, otherwise lies will be exposed.
I am opposed to anything that Light cannot bear, including silence.
Around me is packed with driven crowds,
Darkly-pressed, packed with people stripped of lustre
Among whom I am now standing.
I am all the people being milled by ancient rules and laws
Painfully watching
Myself being executed
Watching my blood flow, wave upon wave, till dried out.

BLACK & WHITE III, Ma Desheng.

四、赴刑

欺騙的風蒙住窗子和眼睛
這時候，屠殺在進行
我不能躲在屋子裏
我的血不讓我這樣做
早晨似的孩子們不讓我這樣做
我被投進監獄
手銬、腳鐐深深地釘進我的肉裏
鞭子和血在身上結網
聲音被割斷
我的心是一團火，在咀唇上無聲地燃燒
我走向刑場，輕蔑地看着
這歷史的夜晚，這世界的角落
沒有別的選擇，我選擇天空
因爲天空不會腐爛
我祇有被處決，否則黑暗無處躲藏
我是在黑暗中誕生，爲了創造出光陽
我祇有被處決，否則謊言就會被粉碎
我反對光明不能容忍的一切，包括反對沉默
周圍擠滿了被驅趕來的人羣
黑壓壓的，擠滿被奪去光澤的人們
我也站在這人羣中
我是被古老的刑法折磨的所有的人
痛苦地看着
自己被處決
看着我的血一湧一湧地流盡

V. Unfinished Poem

I am dead.
Bullets left in my body holes like empty eye-sockets.
I am dead,
Not to leave behind whimpering and weeping or to impress people,
Not to let a lone flower bloom upon a tomb.
National emotion is already too full, too rich.
The grasslands are drenched with dew-drops.
Rivers flow, everyday, toward the big ocean,
Like old, old wet emotions.
Can we really say that we lack feeling and have not yet been moved enough?

              *   *   *   *   *   *   *

I am nailed upon this prison wall.
The hem of my clothes rises to the winds
Like a flag about to be raised.

tr. YIP WAI-LIM

五、 沒有寫完的詩

我死了
子彈在身上留下彈坑，像空空的眼窩
我死了
不是爲了留下一片哭聲，一片感動
不是爲了花朵在墳墓上孤獨地開放
民族的感情已經足夠豐富
草原每天落滿露水
河流每天流向海洋
像久遠的潮濕的感情
難道被感動的次數還少嗎

        *   *   *   *   *

我被釘死在監獄的牆上
衣襟緩緩飄動
像一面正在昇起的旗幟

BLACK & WHITE IV, Ma Desheng.

BLACK & WHITE V, Ma Desheng.

From the Poem-cycle **BEGIN FROM HERE**

IV. Meditation

At twilight I come to the loess plateau,
Shadows at dusk swaying,
eyes of cave dwellings sinking deeper and deeper,
watching me without a sound.
Rough road sparkling, phosphorescent,
Like shards of broken pottery,
Carrying me into a dream.

I am gripping many lumps of clay, kneading,
squeezing;
The mist seems to embrace my child like chimney smoke,
stroking the jar which is plump like the child's head,
letting clear water flow into its lips,
clear as a jar of blue life.
I sketch a pattern as beautiful as rivers,
And then, pitchblack hair begins to ripple,
yellow waves flash radiant in the sun,
flowing dunes, yellow river tumbling;
My skin also dyed golden,
reflecting the sun's brilliance.
This should make me proud.

My ancestors have bequeathed their bright red blood to me,
Not without demands.
In the spots of light in the dusk,
before separation from the fire's midst,
my nature,
and the fire,
had no distinction,
and no fear of wolf or lion.

I do not know why
people are so fearful of each other.

(continued overleaf)

BLACK & WHITE VI,
Ma Desheng.

四、沉思

薄暮中，我來到黃土高原
黃昏時分的陰影在搧動
窰洞的眼窩越陷越深
沒有聲音地看着我
坎坎坷坷的道路閃着鱗光
像是有許多陶器的碎片
　　　　把我帶入夢想

我攥着一塊塊黏土，揉着，
捏着
彷彿炊煙似的霧靄抱着我的孩子
撫摸着孩子的頭一樣圓滿的罐子
爲了讓清澈的水流進嘴唇
清澈得像一罐藍色的生活
我勾畫出河流一樣美麗的花紋
於是，烏黑的頭髮開始飄動
陽光下，黃色的河流閃出光輝
風沙流動着，黃河翻滾着
我的皮膚也被染得金黃
太陽的光輝交映着
值得讓我驕傲

祖先把鮮紅的血液遺贈給我
不是沒有要求
在黃昏的點點燈光
從火中被分割出之前
我的性格
與火
沒有區別
不怕狼和獅子

不知道爲什麼
人卻被人懼怕了

The jar is shattered. Exquisite porcelain,
lustre stolen from my hands. Wife's sisters
reveal their beauty only against a background of woven silk,
falling like flowers,
flowing towards a place which is not theirs.
Frozen moon shining remote light,
in a dark thicket of cypress;
Golden palace shining remote light,
brutal labour, black sweat.
In the darkness sweat of a thousand years has
rolled, congealed like the thick gum of pine cones into
amber, treasure;
Imprisoned in a place which is not mine,
like ridges of scorched, glazed tile,
fixed, unmoving on our roofs;
Unable to follow the rippling wheat of autumn flowing into my smile.

This palace, this trembling light,
Cannot reflect my features,
Cannot connect my wisdom and my dreams.
My features are part of a mountain far loftier than this palace,
Part of the grotto I have carved, enchantment of the East,
Clouds drifting out from the fresco, carrying the mountain to the skies;
Part of the mountain's many different trees, wild-flowers, birds, songs,
Every-coloured feather and leaf—fall, and then grow again;
Part of the grasses twisted by fierce wind, the indignation,
Part of the damp mountain road along which I tread,
Part of the people secretly acquainted in the deep wood,
Part of the honey, the pollen, and the dissemination,
Mountain's meditation,
Roaring flood merged of many streams;
Topography of my features,
rivers connecting mountains and the sea.
So that the faces of wife's sisters
will no longer flow with distress and disappointment,
So that brothers' shoulders
may lift the earth, arouse millions upon millions of suns.

tr. ALISA JOYCE

陶罐碎了。精美的瓷器
奪走我手上的光澤。妻子的姊妹
祇有在織出的綢子上才顯出美麗
像飄落的花朵
流向一個不屬於自己的地方
冰凉的月亮閃着幽光
在綠得發黑的松柏叢中
金黄的宮殿閃着幽光
用鐵的勞動，發黑的汗水
黑暗中滾動了幾千年的
松脂一樣黏稠的汗水凝成的
琥珀，珍寶
被幽禁在一個不屬於我的地方
一壟壟燒焦了似的琉璃瓦
固定在我們的屋頂上
不能隨着秋天的麥浪流進我的微笑

這宮殿，這顫抖的光
不能映出我的面貌
不能聯結我的智慧和夢想
我的面貌屬於比宮殿高大的山
屬於由我開鑿的岩洞，東
方的神往
從壁畫中飄出的雲，把山托向天空
屬於山上各種各樣的
　　　樹木、野花、鳥、叫聲
各種顏色的羽毛和葉子
　　　——落了，又生長
屬於狂風捲走的茅草，屬於憤怒
屬於濕漉漉的，被我踩出的山路
屬於密林裏秘密結識的人們
屬於蜜，屬於花粉和傳播
山的沉思
奔騰的小溪滙集成的巨大的水流
屬於我的地理面貌
聯結着山脈和海洋的一條條江河
爲了讓妻子和姊妹的臉上
不再流動着憂傷和失望
爲了讓兄弟們的肩頭
擔起整個大地，搖醒千萬個太陽

V. Finale: Begin from Here

Begin from here then,
Begin from my own story, begin from the human aspirations
Of millions, dead and alive;
Begin from the name that thrilled through me before my birth.
That the forgotten,
the injured,
the lone,
May stretch from their huddled, fearful numbness
stretch out for life.
Ice breaks, language begins to reconcile;
Each plain name is title for a poem,
flowing with the grand melody of life.
Begin from here then, blood
quickening,
fragrance of every flower, every child, every wisp of kitchen smoke
rising as one into the spring time, every brown tree swaying
branches and leaves
lifting ripened fruits, fuller than a mother's breasts.
White clouds hang big in the sky,
passion a cumulus within the heart, building,
every contact, every lightning, every kiss
frees me from loneliness, unites me
with all beating hearts.
Love cannot be withheld, the earth hungers and thirsts.
Begin from the rain then, begin from the teeming river
Begin from stone bridge, steel bridge
Arm stretched from earth to earth, from hill to hill,
leading every brother and sister
connecting every valley and riverbed.

(continued overleaf)

五、從這裏開始

就從這裏開始
從我個人的歷史開始、從億萬個
死去的、活着的普通人的願望開始
從誕生之前就通過我
激動地呼出的名字開始
把被遺忘的
被迫害的
隔閡着的
人們
從蜷縮、恐懼、麻木中展開
舒展着各自的生活和權利
破碎的冰塊。語言開始和解
每一個樸素的名字都是詩的標題
流動出浩大的生命的旋律
就從這裏開始，血液
激動着每一個人

每一朵花的香味，每個孩子，一縷縷炊煙
一同昇回春天，棵棵棕色的小樹搖動着
枝葉和枝葉連在一起
托着成熟的果子，比母親的乳房還要豐滿
大團大團的白雲掛在空中
胸中的熱情積鬱着，越來越濃
每一次接觸和閃電，每一片嘴唇和吻
都把我從孤獨中解放，觸進另一個人
觸進所有跳動的心
愛情不能存留，大地在饞渴
就從雨開始，從溢滿的河流開始
從石頭的橋，鋼鐵的橋開始
手臂從土地伸向土地，從山腰伸向山腰
挽着所有的兄弟姊妹
溝通所有的峽谷、河床

BLACK & WHITE VII
—THE CRY OF THE PEOPLE, Ma Desheng.

Let the moon, sickled by night, image no more the father's crooked spine,
let the bent ears of grain be grasped taut as a bow in the sons' hands,
let the waves stirred by bird and fish, the wind,
be strong to blow sail, spread net,
highways grid the wilderness and hills,
cities like knots
pin the net, roads of sunlight quiver
in the ditches, in the streets, the flowing water, the crowds
forever blue.
Let me uncover the pattern latent within action,
honeycomb it, instil order in my dwelling-place;
let light etch the borders of shadow,
and shadow slowly drain into noonday;
my gloom, my silence, my suffering
fade into joy, as
I, homo aureus, the golden-skinned,
join all pigments of the planet
to make life glow with the colours of light.

tr. GINGER LI, with JOHN MINFORD

讓黑夜壓彎的月亮不再像父親的脊背
讓彎彎的谷穗像飽滿的弓，握在兒子們的手中
讓鳥和魚激起的浪花，風
足夠吹起帆，張開網
讓公路鋪遍荒野，山崗
城市像一個又一個結
拉着網，洒滿陽光的條條道路微微顫動
渠道中，街道中流動的水，人羣
永遠蔚藍
讓我在繁忙中整理出秩序
如同羣蜂整理蜜，整理着住所
讓光劃出影子和光明的界綫
讓影子漸漸透明，在中午消失
讓我的那些苦悶、沉默、艱難的年代
消失在歡笑中
我，金黃皮膚的人
和世界上所有不同膚色的人連成一片
把光的顏色──鋪遍生活

芒克

Mang Ke

Translated by Susette Cooke and David Goodman

Frozen Land

The funeral crowd floats past, a white cloud,
Rivers slowly drag the sun.
The long, long surface of the water, dyed golden.
How silent
How vast
How pitiful
That stretch of withered flowers.

凍土地

像白雲一樣飄過去送葬的人羣,
河流緩慢地拖着太陽,
長長的水面被染得金黃。
多麼寂靜,
多麼遼闊,
多麼可憐的,
那大片凋殘的花朵。

Smoke from the White House

The smoke from the white house
Is fine and long,
The woman walks slowly towards the river bank . . . .

There drifts by a broken mast,
Splattered with splinters of shell.

白房子的煙

白房子的煙
又細又長,
那個女人慢慢走向河灘……

那兒漂過去半段桅桿,
上面佈滿了破碎的彈片。

These translations are reprinted with permission from Beijing Street Voices *(Marion Boyars, London & Boston, 1981).*

A POEM FOR OCTOBER

Crops

Autumn steals across my face
And I am ripe.

Labour

I shall go with all the wagons,
Drawing the sunshine to the wheatfields . . . .

Fruit

What lovely children
A lovely sight
The red apple of the sun
And beneath it the marvellous dreams of countless children.

Autumn Wood

Not your eyes' light,
Nor your voice's sound,
Red scarves fallen on the ground . . . .

十月的獻詩

莊稼

秋天悄悄地來到我的臉上,
我成熟了。

勞動

我將和所有的馬車一道
把太陽拉進麥田⋯⋯

果實

多麼可愛的孩子,
多麼可愛的目光,
太陽像那紅色的蘋果,
它下面是無數孩子奇妙的幻想。

秋天的樹林

沒有你的目光,
沒有你的聲音,
地上落着紅色的頭巾⋯⋯

遭遇

那是個像雲片般飄動着的
女人的身影。

小路

那在不停搖擺的白楊,
那個背靠着白楊的姑娘,
那條使姑娘失望的彎彎曲曲的路上⋯⋯

風

我很想和你說:
讓我們並排走吧。

雲

我愛你,
當你穿上那件白色的睡衣⋯⋯

河流

疲勞的人兒,
你可願意讓我握住那隻蒼白的小手。

Encounter

A woman's silhouette
Like a cloud, floating.

The Path

That white poplar swaying unceasingly,
That girl leaning against the poplar,
That crooked road which makes the girl lose hope . . . .

Wind

I long to say to you:
Let us go side by side.

Clouds

I love you
When you wear that white nightgown . . . .

Rivers

Weary people,
You may let me clasp that pale hand.

HARVEST (Oil, 86 x 66cm, 1982), Qu Leilei.

Qu Leilei 曲磊磊 was born in 1951. His work appeared in the exhibitions held by The Stars in Peking in 1979 & 1980.

Wife

I shall take all my days
And give them all to you.

Earth

Across all my feelings
The sun has shone.

The Bath

Stark-naked child
A woman's uncovered breast . . . .

Chimes

Men
Bringing warmth to the women from the midst of the sunshine . . . .

妻子

我將把所有的日子
都給你帶去。

土地

我全部的情感
都被太陽晒過。

沐浴

孩子赤條條的,
女人袒露着胸脯……

鐘聲

男人們
從陽光裏給女人帶回了溫暖……

墾荒者

我是河流,
我是奶漿;
我要灌溉,
我要哺養。
我是鐵犁,
我是鐮刀;
我要耕種,
我要收割。

日落

太陽朝着沒有人的地方走去了……

孩子

那向我走來的黑夜對我說:
你是我的……

The Reclaimer

I am rivers,
I am milk;
I want to irrigate,
I want to feed.
I am an iron plough,
I am a sickle;
I want to cultivate,
I want to gather in the harvest.

Sunset

The sun moves towards the peopleless place . . . .

The Child

That black night approaching me says:
You are mine . . . .

PEASANT (Oil, 90 x 70cm, 1981), Qu Leilei.

Sleeping in the Open

Sitting face to face,
Silent face to face,
All around shack and hearth,
Men's legs, the smell of earth.

Wine

That is a lonely little grave . . . .

In the Fields

There, written on her solitary grave:
I have not left you anything,
I have not left myself . . . .

Life

Ah,
Suffering and joy already prepared for you!

露宿

面對面地坐着，
面對面地沉默，
遍地是窩棚和火堆，
遍地是散發着泥土味的男人的雙腿……

酒

那是座寂寞的小墳……

田野

在她那孤零零的墳墓上寫着：
我沒有給你留下別的，
我也沒有給你留下我……

生活

啊，
那早已爲你準備好了痛苦與歡樂！

路燈

整齊的光明，
整齊的黑暗。

回憶

你呀，
這紅紅綠綠的夜，
又不知該怎樣地把我折磨。

青春

在這裏，
在有着繁殖和生息的地方，
我便被拋棄了。

歲月

生活向我走來了，
從此她就再沒有離開過我。

Streetlamp

Even light,
Even night.

Recollection

Ah, you,
This rainbow night,
I know not how you can thus torment me.

Feeling

Startled awake,
Then fall back in love with loneliness.

Youth

Here,
In this place for greenness and growing,
I have been cast aside.

Years

Since life approached me,
She has never left.

FLY! (design on plate, 1981), Qu Leilei.

The Poet

Put on your own heart!

Daybreak

But let you and I be of one heart,
And sweep clean the road's dark.

Baiyangdian Lake

Do not forget,
The time of joy
Will let all the fishing boats clink glasses together.

Sailboat

When that time comes,
I shall return with the windstorm.

Love

Though you are far, far from me,
I still shall be remembering:
What is mine,
What you gave, all, to me.

Last Will

No matter what my name,
I hope
To leave it on this beloved ground.

Choice

Best
In waste ground
To set my life down.
Then
Welcome all seeds
To come to my fields.

October 1974

詩人

帶上自己的心!

黎明

但願我和你懷着同樣的心情
去把道路上的黑暗打掃乾淨。

白洋淀

別忘了,
歡樂的時候,
讓所有的漁船也在一起碰杯。

帆船

到那個時候,
我將和風暴一塊回來!

愛情

即使你離我很遠很遠,
我也一定會記着:
是我的,
你全都賦予了我。

遺囑

不論我是怎樣的姓名,
希望
把她留在這塊親愛的土地上。

選擇

最好
在一個荒蕪的地方
安頓我的生活。
那時
我將歡迎所有的莊稼
來到我的田野。

1974年10月

舒婷
Shu Ting
Translated by Tao Tao Liu

Gifts

My dream is the dream that the pond has
Whose existence is not merely to reflect the sky
But to let the surrounding willows and ferns
Suck me dry.
Through the tree roots I'll enter the veins of their
    leaves
Yet when they wither I'll not be sad
For I shall have expressed myself
And gained life.

My happiness is the happiness of sunlight
In a brief moment I leave behind everlasting works
In the pupils of children's eyes
Kindling sparks of gold.
In the sprouting of seedlings
I sing an emerald green song.
I am simple but abundant
So I am deep.

My grief is the grief of seasonal birds
Only the Spring understands such strong love.
Suffering all kinds of hardships and failure
To fly into a future of warmth and light
Oh the bleeding wings
Will write a line of heart-felt verse
To penetrate all souls
And enter all times.

All that I feel
Is the gift of the earth.

饋贈

我的夢想是池塘的夢想
生存不僅映照天空
讓周圍的垂柳和紫雲英
把我吸取乾淨吧
緣着樹根我走向葉脉
凋謝於我並非悲傷
我表達了自己
我獲得了生命

我的快樂是陽光的快樂
短暫，卻留下不朽的創作
在孩子雙眸裏
燃起金色的小火
在種子胚芽中
唱着翠綠的歌
我簡單而又豐富
所以我深刻

我的悲哀是候鳥的悲哀
祇有春天理解這份熱愛
忍受一切艱難失敗
永遠飛向溫暖、光明的未來
啊，流血的翅膀
寫一行飽滿的詩
深入所有心靈
進入所有年代

我的全部感情
都是土地的饋贈

See also p. 62 for Bonnie S. McDougall's translation of the poem 'This, Too, Is All'.

243

A Boat with Two Masts

Fog has drenched my two wings
But the wind will not allow me to dally
Oh land, land that I love
Only yesterday I said goodbye to you
Today you are here again
Tomorrow we will
Meet again at a different latitude

It was a storm, a lamp
That held us together
It was another storm, another lamp
That parted us to the east and west
Even to the edge of the sky and the farthest shore
Surely every morning and evening
You will be on my route
I will be in your sight

雙桅船

霧打濕了我的雙翼
可風卻不容我再遲疑
岸呵，心愛的岸
昨天剛剛和你告別
今天你又在這裏
明天我們將在
另一個緯度相遇

是一場風暴，一盞燈
把我們聯系在一起
是另一場風暴，另一盞燈
使我們再分東西
那怕天涯海角
豈在朝朝夕夕
你在我的航程上
我在你的視綫裏

雨別

我真想摔開車門，向你奔去，
在你的寬肩上失聲痛哭：
"我忍不住，我真忍不住！"
我真想拉起你的手，
逃向初晴的天空和田野，
不畏縮也不回顧。

我真想聚集全部柔情，
以一個無法申訴的眼睛
使你終於醒悟；

我真想，真想……
我的痛苦變為憂傷，
想也想不夠，說也說不出。

Goodbye in the Rain

I really wanted to wrench open the door and rush towards you
And cry my heart out on your ample shoulders.
'I cannot bear it, I really cannot bear it.'

I really wanted to take your hand,
And run away to the freshly cleared sky and the open fields,
Without shrinking or looking back.

I really wanted to gather all my tenderness,
In my eyes that have no power of speech,
And make you at last realize.

I really wanted to, really wanted to,
My pain changes to grief,
Never-ending in thought, inexpressible in words.

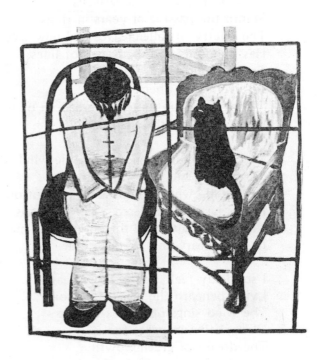

WAITING, Li Shuang 李爽 (born 1957).

Fallen Leaves

The setting moon is like a sliver of ice
Floating in the drenching cold night.
You take me home, along the way
You lightly sigh.
Since it is not worry
And it is not just sadness,
We couldn't explain at all
The feeling that
Was conveyed to us by
The falling leaves in the shaking of the wind.
Only after we had parted
I heard your footsteps
Mixed with the falling leaves.

From every direction around us Spring
Whispers at us
The fallen leaves at our feet show
The proof of winter's punishment, a dark memory
Trembling deep within
Made our glances avoid each other
But even stronger refraction of light
Made our thoughts meet again.

Only on plants do the seasons
Stamp the passing of years in rings
The poetry of fallen leaves and new seedlings
Has hundreds and thousands of lines.
Trees should have
An everlasting theme:
'Though we stretch to the freedom of the air,
We never leave the great earth.'

Through windows and doors, the wind
Narrates to me your whereabouts
Telling me when you pass by the cotton tree
It was he who scattered a fall of petals.
Saying that although the spring cold makes us shiver
In your heart you are not cold.

I suddenly feel: I am a fallen leaf
Lying beneath the black dark soil
The wind sings obsequies for me
I lie waiting in peace for
The dream of green growth
To take from my body the first thread of life.

COLLAGE, Li Shuang.

落葉

殘月像一片薄冰
漂在沁涼的夜色裏
你送我回家，一路
輕輕歎着氣
既不因爲惆悵
也不僅僅是憂鬱
我們怎麼也不能解釋
那落葉在風的揮掇下
所送達給我們的
那一種情緒
祇是分手之後
我聽到你的足音
和落葉混在了一起

春天從四面八方
向我們耳語
而腳下的落葉卻提示
冬的罪證，一種陰暗的回憶
深刻的震動
使我們的目光互相迴避
更强烈的反射
使我們的思想再次相遇

季節不過爲喬木
打下年輪的戳記
落葉和新芽的詩
有千百行
樹祇應當卻有
一個永恒的主題
《爲向天空自由伸展
我們絕不離開大地》

隔着窗門，風
向我叙述你的踪跡
說你走過木棉樹下
是它搖落了一陣花雨
說春寒雖然料峭
你的心中並非冷意

我突然覺得：我是一片落葉
躺在黑暗的泥土裏
風在爲我舉行葬儀
我安詳地等待
那綠茸茸的夢
從我身上取得第一綫生機

船

一隻小船
不知什麼緣故
傾斜地擱淺在
荒涼的礁岸上
油漆還沒褪盡
風桅已經折斷
既沒有綠樹垂蔭
連青草也不肯生長

滿潮的海面
祇在離它幾米的地方
波浪喘息着
水鳥焦灼地撲打翅膀
無垠的大海
縱有遼遠的疆域
咫尺之內
卻喪失了最後的力量

隔着永恒的距離
他們悵然相望
愛情穿過生死的界限
世紀的空間
交織着萬古常新的目光
難道眞摯的愛
將隨着船板一起腐爛
難道飛翔的靈魂
將終生監禁在自由的門檻

A Boat

A small boat
For whatever reason
Lay marooned on its side on
A desolate stony bank
The paint had not quite gone
But the mast was already broken
There were no green trees to give shade
Or grass willing to grow

The sea at high tide
Was only a few yards away
The waves sigh
Water birds anxiously flap their wings
Even if the endless ocean
Has domains far away
In this vicinity
It has lost its last strength

Across that eternal divide
Lost, they gaze at each other
Love crosses the boundary of life and death
And the vacancy of hundreds of years
Weaves a cross pattern of glances, ancient and yet always fresh
Surely deeply felt love
Does not decay along with the boards of the boat?
Surely the fluttering soul
Will not be imprisoned for ever on the threshold of freedom?

楊煉：冰湖之鐘

Yang Lian
Selections from the Poem-cycle
Bell on the Frozen Lake

Translated by John Minford, with Seán Golden
Illustrations by Gan Shaocheng

> *'I came back from the most holy waves, born again,*
> *even as new trees renewed with new foliage,*
> *pure and ready to mount to the stars.'*
> *Dante:* Purgatorio

Translator's Note

Bell on the Frozen Lake *is a cycle of seven long poems written by Yang Lian during 1980. It is his second such cycle, the first being* Earth 土地, *parts of which appeared in* Today *under the pseudonym Feisha* 飛沙, *Flying Sand. He has since written two further cycles.*

The first of the seven poems in Bell, *'Apologia', which has appeared in Chinese and in French translation in Julien Blaine's anthology (*Dock[k]s, 41*), is Yang's personal statement on his calling as a poet. The second, 'Wild Goose Pagoda', which appeared in its entirety in the 5th poetry supplement of the Canton literary magazine* Huacheng 花城, *together with Gan Shaocheng's illustrations, is a long excursion into Chinese history (in* menglong *or 'misty' terms). The famous pagoda in Xi'an becomes a symbol of Silent China through the ages, in deliberate though unstated contrast with the pagoda at Yan'an, hackneyed symbol of revolutionary aspiration and confidence.*

Space has limited us to two extracts from these two poems. But the entire cycle, together with other writings by and about Yang, is soon to be published in book form.

Apologia

The ruin is that of the European Palaces—Qianlong's multiple folly—which once formed part of the Yuan Ming Yuan, the Old Summer Palace on the outskirts of Peking. When the whole palace was burnt down in 1860, it was the brick and marble of these European structures that survived. 'It is said that the Empress-Dowager disliked them so much that she would never visit them. They stood as picturesque and tragic witnesses to the former glory of the garden long after most of the Chinese buildings had vanished.' (Danby, The Garden of Perfect Brightness, *London 1950, p. 224.)*

Yang Lian grew up near these ruins, and for him they are both a reminder of his childhood haunts, and a symbol of the explosive interaction between East and West in Chinese history and in the evolution of modern Chinese poetry.

APOLOGIA
—To a Ruin

Birth

Let this mute stone
Attest my birth
Let this song
Resound
In the troubled mist
Searching for my eyes

Here in the grey shattered sunlight
Arches, stone pillars cast shadows
Cast memories blacker than scorched earth
Motionless as the death agony of a hanged man
Arms convulsed into the sky
Like a final
Testament to time
Once a testament
Now a curse muttered at my birth

I come to this ruin
Seeking the only hope that has illumined me
Faint star out of its time
Destiny, blind cloud
Pitiless chiaroscuro of my soul
No, I have not come to lament death! It is not death
Has drawn me to this desolate world
I defy all waste and degradation—these swaddling clothes
Are a sun that will not be contained in the grave

In my premature solitude
Who can tell me
The destination of this road singing into the night
To what shore its flickering ghostfires lead?
A secret horizon
Ripples, trawls distant dreams to the surface
Distant, almost boundless.
Only the wind rousing a song
In place of the broken sundial buried in the earth
Points to my dawn.

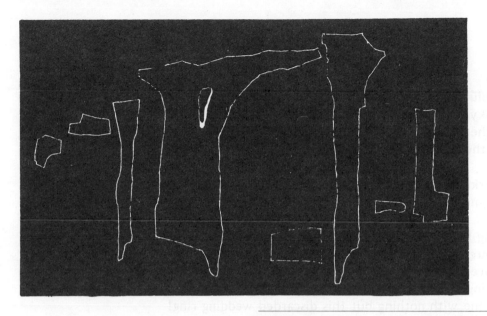

Gan Shaocheng 甘少成, *who drew the illustrations for these poems and also for Zhao Zhenkai's story 'Waves', was born in 1948 in Peking. Since 1968 he has been living and working in Shanxi province. He exhibited some of his work in Peking in 1980.*

自白

給一座廢墟

誕生

讓這片默默無言的石頭
爲我的出生作證
讓這支歌
響起
動蕩的霧中
尋找我的眼睛

在灰色的陽光碎裂的地方
拱門、石柱投下陰影
投下比燒焦的土地更加黑暗的回憶
彷彿垂死的掙扎被固定
手臂痙攣地伸向天空
彷彿最後一次
給歲月留下遺言
這遺言
變成對我誕生的詛咒

我來到廢墟上
追逐唯一照耀過我的希望
那不合時宜的微弱的星
命運──盲目的烏雲
無情地勾勒着我的心靈
不是爲了哀悼死亡! 不是死亡
吸引我走向這個空曠的世界
我反抗屬於荒蕪和恥辱的一切
──襁褓
是與墓地不能相容的太陽

在我早已預支的孤獨中
有誰知道
這條向夜晚歌唱的路
閃着磷光通往哪一處海岸
秘密的地平綫
波動着，泛起遙遠的夢想
遙遠得幾乎無窮
祇有風，揚起歌聲
代替着埋進泥土的殘缺的日晷
指向我自己的黎明

Soul

Frozen lake
Childhood blue never to be regained;
Stretch of sky forever still
Weighs on the weary evening sun
Slips down the back of the wind.
No warmth
As if the darkness will never be noticed again.
Don't leave me here alone!

With nothing but doubt and fear
Desolate accretions of solitude,
Ruined palaces overgrown with reeds
Murky shifting sands of destiny.
Don't leave me with nothing but this discarded wedding ring!
I know none to gather the metal of tears
And forge a bright sword,
To weave anew a drifting sail
On the long frozen imagination.
Don't leave me here alone!

With nothing but dreams
Of a girl awaiting my return, rubbing
Bubbles of moonlight, starching country clothes.
My loved one—nightly now
There is no quickening sound,
Only this frozen lake;
This frozen lake
And no instant of peace.
Don't leave me with just a promise of happiness!
If I must live here—
Then let me rather breathe the curse of eternal damnation
Kindle the flame of defiance, the oath of sacrifice
Let the old wound pound in my chest again
The massacre of the past reincarnadine
The shroud of sunrise caul the dead.
This is precious: for all will pass.
This is precious: for all is yet to come.
I commit my soul to her calling.

When the bell sounds once more on the frozen lake,
There in the distant surf will be my new abode.

靈魂

冰封的湖
再也找不回童年的藍色
一塊永恆靜止的天空
逼迫着黃昏時疲倦的太陽
從風的脊背滑落
沒有溫暖
似乎也不再查覺黑暗
不要僅僅留下我!

不要僅僅留下疑惑和恐怖
陪伴着空曠在我的孤寂中沉積
傾圮的宮殿長滿蘆葦
棕黃的命運搖動着沙岸
不要僅僅留下這被遺棄的訂婚戒指
我不知道: 誰能收集眼淚的金屬
鑄成閃閃發光的匕首
誰能在早已凍結的想像上
重新織出漂泊的帆
不要僅僅留下我!

不要僅僅留下那夢中
守候我歸來的姑娘, 揉散
月光的泡沫, 漿洗着原野的衣衫
我的情人, 在每個夜晚
沒有碧綠的呼喊
祇有冰封的湖
祇有冰封的湖
卻找不到安寧的瞬間
不要僅僅留下對於歡樂的許諾
如果我注定在這裏生活──
寧願呼吸永無拯救的咒語
點燃不屈者的心和佩戴荊冠的誓言
我要讓一縷血痕再次捶打我的胸膛
讓被屠殺的歲月再次鮮紅
讓早霞的尸布遮蓋死亡
這是珍貴的: 一切都會過去
這是珍貴的: 一切還沒開始
我把靈魂留給她的召喚

當冰封的湖再次敲響鐘聲
遙遠的浪花間有我新的居所

Homage to Poetry

The aged century bares its brow
Shakes its wounded shoulders;
Snow covers the ruins—white and restless
Like surf—moving among the pitchblack trees;
A lost voice transmitted across time.
There is no road
Through this land that death has lent mystery.

The aged century cheats its children
Leaving everywhere riddles
Snow on the stone, to patch the ornamented filth.
I clutch my poems in my hand.
Call me! In that nameless moment
The little boat of the wind bearing history scudded
Behind me—shadowlike,
Complete with ending.

So—I know all this:
Weeping is no rebellion, the young girl's fingers and
The shy myrtle sink into a grove of purple thorns;
Meteor-eyes splash into the boundless ocean;
I know that ultimately every soul will rise once more
Exhaling the fresh moist breath of the sea,
Eternal smile, voice of unyielding defiance,
Up into an azure world;
And I shall sing my songs aloud.

I shall believe each icicle the sun,
Suffuse this ruin with a weird light,
And in this wasteland piled with stones hear a song.
Full breasts shall nurse me;
I shall earn the dignity of a new life, a sacred love,
In fields of purest white lay bare my heart,
In pure white sky lay bare my heart,
Challenge the aged century—
For I am a poet.

I am a poet.
I will the rose to bloom and it blooms;
Freedom will return, bringing its little shell,
And within it the echoing roar of the storm.
Daybreak will come, the key of dawn
Turn in the tangled trees, ripe fruits flame.
I will return, reopen the furrow of suffering,
Begin to plough this land deep in snow.

詩的祭奠

蒼老的世紀露出它的額角
抖動受傷的肩膀
雪蓋滿廢墟上——白色的不安
像浪花，在黑黝黝的叢林間移動
迷途的聲音從歲月那邊傳來
沒有道路
通過這由於死亡而神奇的土地

蒼老的世紀哄騙着它的孩子
到處拋下無法辨認的字跡
石頭的雪，修改着被裝飾的髒骯
我在手裏攥緊自己的詩章
召引我吧！那不知姓名的時刻
風的小船載着歷史匆匆划過
在我身後——影子般的
跟着一個結束

於是，我懂得這一切
嗚咽不是拒絕，少女的手指和
謙恭的桃金娘在紫紅色荆叢中沉沒
隕石似的目光在無垠人海上濺落
我懂得每顆靈魂終將重新昇起

帶着新鮮濕潤的海的氣息
帶着永恆的微笑和永不跪倒的聲音
昇向天藍的純淨的世界
我將高聲朗誦自己的詩篇

我將相信所有冰凌都是太陽
這廢墟，因為我，佈滿奇異的光
岩石累累的荒野中我聽到歌聲
飽滿的蓓蕾的乳房哺育我
我將有新生的尊嚴和神聖的愛情
在潔白的田野上我要袒露一顆心靈
在潔白的天空上我要袒露一顆心靈
並向蒼老的世紀挑戰
因為我是詩人

我是詩人
我要讓玫瑰開放，玫瑰就會開放
自由會回來，帶着它的小貝殼
裏面一陣風暴發出迴響
黎明會回來，曙光的鑰匙
在林莽中旋轉，成熟的果子投射出火焰
我也會回來，重新挖掘痛苦的命運
在白雪隱沒的地方開始耕耘

WILD GOOSE PAGODA

Location

Here come the children
Trailing their young mother's hand
Through the grey courtyard.

Here they come
Their eyes from between the green skirts of the little locust-tree
Like windblown
Translucent drops of rain
Quietly staring.
By my side the chattering swallows whirl.

Here I have been made to stand, immobile,
For a thousand years
In China's
Ancient capital
Upright like a man
Sturdy shoulders, head held high,
Gazing at the endless golden earth.
I have stood here
Immobile as a mountain
Immobile as a tombstone
Recording the travail of a nation.

Mute
Heart hard as rock
Pondering in solitude
Pitchblack lips parted
In a silent cry to the sun.
Perhaps I should tell the children
A tale.

大雁塔

位置

孩子們來了
拉着年輕母親的手
穿過灰色的庭院

孩子們來了
眼睛在小槐樹的青色襯裙間
像被風吹落的
透明的雨滴
幽靜地向我凝望
燕子喳喳地在我身邊盤旋……

我被固定在這裏
已經千年
在中國
古老的都城
我像一個人那樣站立着

粗壯的肩膀，昂起的頭顱
面對無邊無際的金黃色土地
我被固定在這裏

山峯似的一動不動
墓碑似的一動不動
記錄下民族的痛苦和生命

沉默
岩石堅硬的心
孤獨地思考
黑洞洞的嘴唇張開着
朝太陽發出無聲的叫喊
也許，我就應當這樣
給孩子們
講講故事

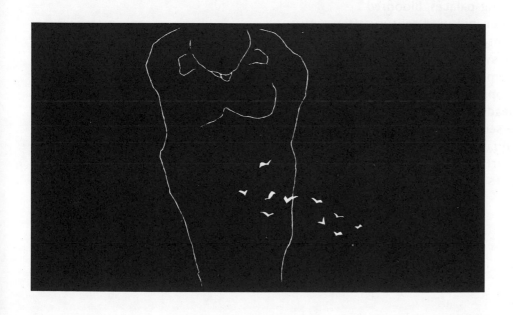

A Children's Tale from Long Ago

I should be laughing for joy at all my brilliant memories.
Golden radiance, jade radiance, radiance soft as silk
Shone upon my birth;
Hardworking hands, peony magnificence, intricate upturned eaves
Surrounded me;
Banners, inscriptions, glorious names surrounded me.
From temple halls the bells pealed bright on my ear,
My shadow caressed fields and hillsides, rivers and the springtime.
By the huts of our forefathers
I scattered towns and villages like seed, like specks of jade;
Firelight flared, daubed my face red, ploughshare and pot
Rang clear, music and poetry
Wove across the festive sky.
I should laugh for joy at all these brilliant memories.
In my youth I gazed down upon the world
Watched purple grapes, like night, drift in from the west
Fall on the noisy street, each crushed drop a star
Set in a bronze mirror, and my face shining in it,
My heart swelling like the earth, the ocean at dawn,
And from my side camel-bells, fresco-sails setting out
For distant lands, saluting the golden coin of the sun.

At my birth
I laughed, sang even for joy,
For the dazzling palaces, bloodred
Walls, noblemen pillowed century after century
On their incense-laden altars
Rapt in their sweet reveries.
I sang for them with passion
And never stopped to question why
Pearls and beads of sweat all flowed
To the same serried tombs full of emptiness,
Why in the quavering dusk
That village girl wandered on the river bank
Her bright eyes filled with such grief . . .

In the end, powder and fire blew the sealed manor apart:
From the north, between the endless mountains and the plain
Stormed horses' hooves, butchering, wailing
Chaos of banners whirled around me, like clouds,
Like clothes tattered in flight;
And all the while the Yellow River rushing past
Elegy silvered white by the moonlight,
Keening history, keening silence.
Where are the streets and crowds and clamour I once knew
The seven-leaved Bo tree I longed for, the green grass
And the babbling brook beneath the bridge—where have they gone?
Only the flowerseller's blood clots in my soul,
Charred houses, rubble, ruins,
Slowly sinking in the drifting dunes,
Turning to dreams, to a wasteland.

遙遠的童話

我該怎樣爲無數明媚的記憶歡笑
金子的光輝、玉石的光輝、絲綢一樣柔軟的光輝
照耀着我的誕生
勤勞的手、華貴的牡丹和窈窕的飛檐環繞着我
儀仗、匾額、榮華者的名字環繞着我
許許多多廟堂、輝煌的鐘聲在我耳畔長鳴
我的身影拂過原野和山巒、河流和春天
在祖先居住的穹廬旁，撒下
星星點點翡翠似的城市和村莊
火光一閃一閃抹紅了我的臉，鐵犁和瓷器
發出清脆的聲響，音樂、詩
在節日，織滿天空
我該怎樣爲明媚的記憶歡笑
在那青春的日子，我曾俯瞰世界
紫色的葡萄，像夜晚，從西方飄來
垂落在喧鬧的大街上，每滴汁液是一顆星
嵌進銅鏡，輝映出我的面容
我的心像黎明時開放的大地和海洋
駝鈴、壁畫似的帆從我身邊出發
到遙遠的地方，叩響那金幣似的太陽

在我誕生的時候
我歡笑，甚至
朝那些炫耀着釉彩的宮殿、血紅色的
牆，那些一個世紀、又一個世紀枕在香案上
享受着甜蜜夢境的人們
灼熱而赤誠地歌唱
卻沒有想到
爲什麼珍珠和汗水都向一個地方流去
——向一座座飽滿而空曠的陵墓流去
爲什麼在顫抖的黃昏
那個農家姑娘徘徊在河岸
明澈的瞳孔裏却溢出這麼多憂鬱和悲哀呵……

終於，硝煙和火從封閉的莊院裏燃起
從北方，那蒼茫無邊的羣山與平原之間
響起了馬蹄、厮殺和哭嚎
紛亂的旗幟在我周圍變幻，像雲朵
像一片片在逃難中破碎的衣裳
我看到黃河急急忙忙地奔走
被月光鋪成一道銀白色的挽聯
哀悼着歷史、哀悼着沉默
而我所熟悉的街道、人羣、喧鬧哪兒去了呢
我所思念的七葉樹、新鮮的青草
和橋下潺潺的溪水哪兒去了呢
祇有賣花老漢流出的血凝固在我的靈魂裏
祇有燒焦的房屋、瓦礫堆、廢墟
在彌漫的風沙中漸漸沉沒、
變成夢、變成荒原

Wild Goose Pagoda

The Great Wild Goose Pagoda in Xi'an was built in 652 by the great traveller and translator, the monk Xuanzang, to house his precious sutras from India. Chang'an was then one of the great cosmopolitan centres of the world. The 'purple grapes . . . drifting in from the west . . . set in a bronze mirror' are a reference to the haima putao jing 海馬蒲桃鏡, the mirror with a design of 'sea-horses' and grapes, popularly believed to have some connection with the Manichaean 'religion of light' 明教, one of the many foreign creeds tolerated during the early part of the Tang dynasty. The rising tide of xenophobia which gathered momentum in the wake of the An Lushan rebellion ('horses' hooves, butchering, wailing . . . ') forced this religion underground, and China gradually turned in on itself—one of the themes of this complex poem.

Finale: The Thinker

I often strain to catch voices wafted from afar
Faint snatches, dead leaves, white snow
Drifting down from a remote dreamworld.
Often in the rainbow wandering in after the rain
I seek the shadow of the Great Wall, proud and comforting;
But the roaring wind only tells me new tales of ruin
—Mud and rubble have silted
The canal, my arteries no longer pulse,
My throat no longer sings.

I am held fast in a cage I have myself forged
History of millenia weighs heavy on my shoulders,
Leadweight; my spirit
Shrivels in this venomous solitude.
Ah—grey courtyard
Desolate, empty.
Place where swallows perch and soar.

I am shamed
To see this boundless golden earth,
To see the sun that kisses me each day,
Light like a finger molding the beauty of mountains;
Catkins, tresses
Each year flutter anew in the spring breeze,
Ripe fruit hangs like a necklace from the branches.
I am shamed: from the grass that hides their bones
Our ancestors stare at me mournfully,
Rows of faces, whose gore
Was given for my glory, stare at me:
Even when the children come
And their small hands stroke me so trustingly, soft as petals,
Their eyes pure as April lakes,
I am shamed.

My heart is quickened by waves from beyond the sea,
By wings, lightning, constellations within the hand of man;
But I cannot soar like a bird free,
I cannot join those men of old from the desert,
Those men who came in dugout canoes;
There can be no such joyful celebration.
I am sick and sad at heart and trembling.

Let these yearnings, sufferings, dreams become a force
Like ice over rapids,
Melting in the sun's rays.
I stand here like a man,
A man of immeasurable suffering, dead but obstinately upright,
Sturdy shoulders, head held high.
Let me destroy at last this nightmare-cage,
Realign shadow of history, spirit of defiance,
Contiguous, like night and dawn.
Like a tree growing minute by minute, greenshade, forest,
My youth will spring.
Brothers, let the silence of death vanish forever—
Like snow from earth—my song
Will return in flight, with the geese
In their great formation like a man

With all of mankind, towards the light.

I shall raise the children
High, high, laughing for joy to the sun.

Drafted June-August 1980 while travelling in southern China.
Revised for the fourth time, January 1981.

思想者

我常常凝神傾聽遠方傳來的聲音
閃閃爍爍，枯葉、白雪
在悠長的夢境中飄落
我常常向雨後游來的彩虹
尋找長城的影子，驕傲和慰藉
但咆哮的風却告訴我更多崩塌的故事
——碎裂的泥沙、石塊，淤塞了
運河，我的血管不再跳動
我的喉嚨不再歌唱

我被自己所鑄造的牢籠禁錮着
幾千年的歷史，沉重地壓在肩上
沉重得像一塊鉛，我的靈魂
在這有毒的寂寞中枯萎
灰色的庭院呵
寥落、空曠
    燕子們棲息、飛翔的地方……

我感到羞愧
面對這無邊無際的金黃色土地
面對每天親吻我的太陽
手指般的，雕刻出美麗山川的光
面對一年一度在春風裏開始飄動的
柳絲和頭髮，項鏈似的
樹枝上成熟的果實
我感到羞愧
祖先從埋葬他們尸骨的草叢中
憂鬱地注視着我
成隊的面孔，那曾經用鮮血
賦予我光輝的人們注視着我
甚至當孩子們來到我面前
當花朵般柔軟的小手信任地撫摸
眸子純淨得像四月的湖
我感到羞愧

我的心被大洋彼岸的浪花激動着
被翅膀、閃電和手中升起的星羣激動着
可是我卻不能飛上天空、像自由的鳥
和昔日從沙漠中走來的人們
駕駛過獨木舟的人們
歡聚到一起
我的心在鬱悶中焦急地顫慄

就讓這渴望、折磨和夢想變成力量吧
像積聚着激流的冰層，在太陽下
投射出奔放的熱情
我像一個人那樣站在這裏，一個
經歷過無數痛苦、死亡而依然倔强挺立的人
粗壯的肩膀、昂起的頭顱

就讓我最終把這鑄造惡夢的牢籠摧毀吧
把歷史的陰影、戰鬥者的姿態
像夜晚和黎明那樣連接在一起
像一分鐘一分鐘增長的樹木、綠蔭、森林
我的青春將這樣重新發芽
我的兄弟們呵，讓代表死亡的沉默永久消失吧
像覆蓋大地的雪——我的歌聲
將和排成「人」字的大雁並肩飛回
和所有的人一起，走向光明

我將托起孩子們
高高地、高高地、在太陽上歡笑……

1980年6—8月構思於南行途中
81年1月四改於北京

嚴力
Yan Li

Translated by Ling Chung

Death

I crawl down a plastic board loaded with electrical spare parts
Turn around, no longer find my space
Read a book again
Don't care to sleep, or stay awake

I edge towards streets crammed with chessboards
Raise my head, find no trace of sun
Take a step again
Neither leading to reality, nor swerving into dreams

My gaze rests on clothes permeated with family scents
The left sleeves long for a rendezvous with the fragrant one
I'll build a home again
Neither bungalow, nor highrise

死亡

在滿是電器零件的膠板上爬下來
一回頭已不見空位曾在何處
重新看一本書
既不要睡去也不要醒着

往滿是棋盤的街頭湊過去
一抬頭已不見太陽的痕跡
重新走一步路
不通往現實也不拐進夢裏

在滿是親戚味的衣服上停住目光
那些左袖在等待一塊更有味的布來赴約
重新成一個家
既不在平房也不在樓裏

Untitled

I've betrayed you
Scorned you
Howled huskily at you
Blocking the path with my cane
I and my senility wait for you

But when you graze a herd
Of futile sighs on paper
I shall pounce upon you
Swiftly and fiercely like a wild dog
The next moment I'll be up on the ridge
Crouching and waiting for more herds to come

It is for your sufferings
That I stand up to you—
How they have altered you!
I'd rather see you buried deep
In my love than succumb to them

I want you to start out with the building blocks
Unravel again the enigma of life

COVER DESIGN for Yan Li's collection of 24
poems, by Ma Desheng.

無題

我背叛你
蔑視你
聲嘶力竭地喊過你
把我的手杖橫在路口
用衰老等你

但當你在紙上放牧一羣
空虛的歎息
我將以一隻野狗的迅猛而
對你襲擊
轉而又在山崗上
歇候你的下一批

和你作對　　是爲你
苦痛的遭遇——它
修改了你　　比起
屈服於它　　更該
安葬在我的愛裏

我要讓你從搭積木開始
重新解開生命之謎

Yan Li—Painter and Poet

By Alisa Joyce

THE GOD-POET (1981).

YAN LI is a painter and a poet. His room, in his parents' flat in the western suburbs of Peking, was filled with the sounds of reggae music, the colours of his surrealistic paintings and the laughter of friends from Peking University when I first visited him there a year ago. Behind the uniform grey walls of Peking, hidden in the twists of endless monochromatic alleys, in an apartment house resembling thousands of others in this city, is a room of bright colour, Caribbean tunes and isolated creativity.

He is not completely isolated, of course. As a member of the group of artists known as The Stars 星星, he exhibited his works in 1980 at Beihai Park and is known as one of the foremost "unofficial" young painters in the capital. As a poet he is perhaps less well-known, few of his poems having ever been published in China. Yet again, he is not alone, as he belongs to the loose assortment of young poets in China who are labelled "misty". This very mistiness, or obscurity, in fact, seems to be a criterion for greatness in the eyes of these young artists. "No," responded Yan Li, "my poems have very rarely been published. The language is beautiful, they say, but the meaning is too difficult to understand." This is a reason for pride. It is a sign to the artistic crowd of a sublimity of meaning and an erudition in language not shared by the common editor or reader. Another poet, whose poems have been criticized in the press lately for their obscurity, is dismissed by Yan Li as "immature"; his poems are "too easily understood".

CHILDREN WITH APPLES.

Now thirty years old and deliberately unemployed, Yan Li has been educated by the Cultural Revolution and yet recites his sacrifices without bitterness. "I attended primary school through the fifth grade and then was sent to the country-side with my parents, to live in a cadre school. When I was old enough I was as-signed to a factory for work." Like many of his contemporaries, he began writing poetry and painting in oils during these years and, despite his lack of education, is extremely well-read in both Chinese and Western philosophy, history and literature. Now, in his small room, he paints in bright colours both the sombre and optimistic themes of his self-taught understanding, and writes poetry to express what oils and watercolours cannot.

"There is a form of expression appropriate to each kind of inspiration," he explained. "A painting gives the viewer an immediate and complete impression which includes both colours and forms. Poetry, on the other hand, is a line by line impression, a process and a movement toward understanding the idea which the artist is expressing. In general, poetry is more expressive of the meaning of life, and that is the main focus of all my work.

"The creation of art is a process in which the artist, the audience and the piece of work itself are all involved. Every idea, inspiration or solid object has a central essence which can best be expressed in only one way. An artist is one who has dis-covered that absolutely correct form of expression."

He pointed to the painting above his bed and explained how the "essence" of that idea came to be expressed in oils on canvas. It is a painting of two chairs, the smaller one resting upside-down on the larger one. The colours are dark, the larger chair black and the smaller blue. The perspective of the chairs and the space they

THE SUN CLIMBS THE HORIZON——To Brush His Teeth.

fill is warped and compressed. A leg of the smaller chair juts up into the air, offering an apple to the larger chair. Yan Li explained that this was the image of a son's dependency on and responsibility to his father. The shaken perspective of the painting and the geometrical edges of the chairs' relationship to each other conveyed a direct and powerful image.

Yan Li is a self-proclaimed idealist. "There is progress in history and in civilization, and education is the means of this progress. History and culture move upward in a spiral as humanity and her artists attempt to look forward and backward at the same time. As artists we have a responsibility to history to create, thereby creating history. Because institutions have different beliefs from people, institutions often have a different sense of this historical responsibility from mine. I believe in understanding humanity and, through my work of course, having humanity understand me."

In spite of many obstacles and much discouragement, there is still a great deal of optimism and idealism among the young writers and painters in China today. In the tiny, hidden rooms of bright paintings and artistic philosophizing, there is a belief in the inevitability of artistic spirit and strength.

"The only common goal among the young artists is to continue creating," stated Yan Li. "The inspiration is everywhere, as long as we dare to express it."

晨光詩選

Dawn Light:
Six Young Poets from Taiwan

Translated and edited by Dominic Cheung

DU YE

LI NAN

LUO QING

WU DELIANG

WU SHENG

XIANG YANG

INTRODUCTION

IS WESTERN MODERNISM a deluge from which Chinese poetry cannot escape? Do contemporary Chinese poets have to start and end with loneliness and alienation? Does the retreat into classicism and Buddhism in some way resuscitate the long-dormant Chinese-ness of the westernized poet?

The recent evolution of Chinese poetry in Taiwan offers tentative answers to some of these questions. In the 1970s, some of the younger poets in Taiwan became more conscious of presenting social themes, while other poets endeavoured to perfect the modernist tradition. This conflict came to a head in the Native Literature 鄉土文學 dispute of the late 70s. After much painful experimentation in making poetry socially oriented and popular, there arose a new awareness among the young poets that poetry must have more than a forceful, didactic manner and a social mission. They began to write more freely, unbound by the practices of either camp. They affirmed that poetry could be, or rather should be, written without pre-set poetic theories.

The reader may wish to refer to Yang Mu's essay on pp. 74-80.

In contrast to the sophisticated modernists, who pursued human existence into deeper but less clearly delineated realms, the new poets attempt to attune their inner sensibility to a more solid and unsophisticated outer environment. The new poet, unlike some of his modernist predecessors, does not attempt to evade reality by drawing deeper within himself into a dark and alienated corner. Instead, he extends his ego onto the social plane, protesting the threat to his personal ecology, but nevertheless viewing himself as part of society. He seeks a clearer mode of expression, to replace the sophisticated, manipulative diction of the modernists. Man and real life become once again the primary sources of poetic imagination.

Wu Sheng's preference for village themes is an attempt to reveal and reaffirm the simple sweetness of the soil. "Impressions of My Village" is a series of poems attempting to depict a more naked and true reality, a return to the village soil. Wu's vision of the truth, innocence and sweetness of the village is the corollary of his rejection of the machine and the city. Li Nan and Wu Deliang share this awareness. Luo Qing's works reflect a continuation of the modernist influence, but the variety of objects he presents and his unique insight in "abstracting" them have opened for him a new way out of the modernist impasse. Du Ye has rejuvenated modernism with a strong dose of new imagery and symbolism, as in his "Telephone Booth in the Rain". Xiang Yang is the youngest of the six poets selected here, and in his long poem "Sailing in the Rain" he strikes a new note, brooding on the theme that preoccupies every modern Chinese writer: China.

The social consciousness of Taiwan's poets has intensified steadily in a span of little more than thirty years. Theirs is a poetry that penetrates deeply into Chinese life, a lyrical voice that leads the reader to a higher understanding of the modern Chinese mind.

—DOMINIC CHEUNG

PAGODA.
Woodcut, 1980,
Hong Suli.

Hong Suli 洪素麗, *whose woodcuts accompany several of the poems, was born in 1947. She is a native of Kao-hsiung (Gaoxiong) in Taiwan, and is currently resident in New York. She is an artist specializing in woodcuts, and also writes prose and poetry.*

DU YE 渡也 (born 1953)

Despite his youth, Du Ye has more than three hundred poems to his credit. All his work is of a high quality, and its striking imagery and dramatic content testify to the originality of his imagination. He also writes prose poems.

1. For Myself
In memory of my forever-gone nineteenth year

In the beginning, I really did not know what was happening. Until I heard myself utter the first cry, Du Ye! (Oh! Each heavy echo was a sad, sad summons!) Then I rushed headlong into the heart of a dark cave. Later I recalled, "... Darkness ... was my beginning ..." Yet I had already seen, had no time to intercept, so many, oh, so many Du Ye's rushing out, pell-mell:

"For the Sake of Birth."

till all the Du Ye's
drown the barren hill
utterly.

渡也
——紀念永遠不再回來的十九歲

起先我真的不知道為什麼。渡也！然而我只聽到我喊了一聲（哦，密密的回響都是，悽悽的召喚），然後，不斷地，奔進黝黑的山洞深處。後來我想起來了：「……黑暗……是我的最初吧……」但我已經看見，我已經看見了，而且來不及攔截，啊，許許多多，許許多多的，渡也！不斷地，不斷地，奔出去：

「為了誕生」

直到所有的渡也將整座荒山
淹
沒

2. Telephone Booth in the Rain

suddenly

    a flash of thought strikes
    O blood-dripping roses

wither

雨中的電話亭

突然

以思想擊響閃電的
鮮血淋漓的玫瑰啊

凋萎

3. The Chrysanthemum and the Sword
"Would that in each and every life we could be husband and wife."

—Shen Fu

If I am the forlorn chrysanthemum awaiting execution, then you are the sword bearing sorrow. On a dark night in the cold desolation of the mountains, slowly you pierce my warm heart, and my yellow blood flows, drips, filters into the closely textured earth, roots, sprouts, for ever without regret. Finally, in deepest autumn, a chrysanthemum blooms whose past life you wounded, and once again on a dark night in the cold desolation of the mountains, on the plain where we keep tryst in each and every life, with tearful eyes, it waits again

for you to be drawn from your scabbard.

This is our last reunion; you will crack before my eyes, painfully vomit my yellow blood, and return all the blood
to my former self
the present chrysanthemum.

菊花與劍
——沈三白: 「願生生世世爲夫婦。」

如我不幸爲臨刑的菊花，妳便是含著恨的劍了，在關山淒冷的黑夜，徐徐刺入我溫熱的心臟，容我流淌黃色的血，點點滴滴，滲進泥土密密的組織，九死不悔地生根發芽，終於在深秋時，仍然綻放一朵，生前被妳刺傷的菊花，復在關山淒冷的黑夜，我們生生世世約會的草原，含淚，再度
等妳出鞘

最後的重逢，妳當在我眼底碎裂，痛苦地吐出我黃顏色的血液，
——還給
從前的我
如今的菊花

LI NAN 李男 (born 1952)

Like Luo Qing and Wu Deliang, Li Nan is a poet-painter. He started painting and writing in his high school days. His "2½ Mythology" is a long confessional poem written when he was a senior high school student. His poems are filled with domestic warmth, and he is one of the more unadorned of the younger poets, stressing the spontaneous flow of emotions and the realistic portrayal of events. At the same time, he subscribes to the mimetic theory of poetry: "Poetry is like photography; every poet is a camera, revealing in forms all objects he sees and feels. Once they are seen as literary objects, they become poetry."

EIGHT POEMS FOR CHILDREN

1. The Fifteenth Evening of the First Lunar Month

After the stars have disappeared,
The lonesome moon, with tearful eyes,
Searches for them everywhere.

The stars have sneaked out to the streets
And changed into warm, cozy lanterns.
Joyfully they play with the children,
Hand in hand, in the human world.

2. Papa and Mama

Mama is a tree,
Papa's words a breeze
Blowing gently in mama's ears;
Mama often laughs aloud
Like a joyful tree
Rustling in the breeze.

童話八首

1. 元宵夜

滿天星星都不見了
剩下孤單的月亮
睜開眼睛到處找
好像要哭出來的樣子

原來星星都偷偷跑到街上
變成一盞一盞溫暖的燈籠
和小朋友們手牽著手
高高興興在人間遊戲

2. 爸爸和媽媽

媽媽是一棵樹
爸爸的話是微風
常常在媽媽耳邊輕輕吹拂
而媽媽總是笑得很大聲
像一棵快樂的，被微風吹動的樹

3. The Rooster

Conceiving of the universe as a big cookie,
The young rooster goes on his journey,
Pecking at the earth.
Sometimes it's quite delicious;
But when he pecks at his own shadow,
His head droops sadly sideways.

4. The Dream

Father fell asleep one day,
Whistles blowing in his mouth.
There must be lots of ships laden with dreams
In father's head.

5. The Dog

There's a secret in the dog's mind,
And he doesn't know where to hide it;
Back and forth he runs outside the house,
Sometimes stopping to dig a hole,
Sometimes sticking out his nose,
Carefully sniffing for a while.
Somehow, he can't seem to trust
His secret to a hole.
So up he gets and keeps on running.

Tired at last, he rests in the shade;
Imperceptibly, his secret dozes off
Too, in the gentle breeze.

CHICKENS AMONG PLANTAINS.
Woodcut, 1982,
Hong Suli.

3. 公雞

以爲世界是一塊大餅
年青的公雞一面旅行
一面啄著泥土
味道偶而特別可口
但有時會啄到自己的影子
牠就悲哀的歪著頭

4. 夢

有一天，爸爸睡著了
嘴吧裡有汽笛的聲音
一定有很多載滿夢的輪船
在爸爸的頭腦裏

5. 狗

狗的心中有一個秘密
不知道應該藏在那裏
牠在屋外跑來跑去
有時停下來挖一個洞
伸長鼻子小心聞一聞
總是不太放心
千萬不能把秘密放在洞裏
只好站起來繼續跑

跑累了，牠躺在樹蔭下休息
不知不覺，牠和心裏的秘密
在陣陣微風中一齊睡去

6. The Breeze

In an invisible dress, the breeze
Tiptoes past the garden,
Steals a flower's fragrance.

Annoyed, the flower shakes her head—
Drops a few quivering leaves.

7. Fireflies

When mother was small,
She used to catch tiny fireflies in the yard.
I'm always seeing flickering fireflies in the room, too;
I want to catch them.
But when I get closer,
I discover they're not fireflies, only
Father smoking on the sofa.

8. The Telephone

The telephone is a house without doors.
Sometimes father's friends stay inside,
Sometimes mother's friends.
They always ring to talk to my parents.

I have a phone too, a toy phone
With my own friends inside,
But they never call me;
And they are never at home
When I try to call them.

SPRING CHORUS. Woodcut, 1982,
Hong Suli.

6. 微風

微風穿著看不見的衣服
輕輕從花園走過
偷走了花的香味

花生氣的搖搖頭
落下幾片發抖的葉子

7. 螢火蟲

媽媽小時候常常在院子裏
抓到小小的螢火蟲
我常常在屋子裏
也看到閃亮的螢火蟲
我想去抓，跑到旁邊才看清
那不是螢火蟲，那是
爸爸坐在沙發上抽香煙

8. 電話

電話是一間沒有門的房子
有時候爸爸的朋友住在裏面
有時候媽媽的朋友住在裏面
他們常常搖鈴找爸爸媽媽說話

我也有一個玩具電話
裏面住著我的朋友
他們從來不找我說話
我想找他們時
他們又總是不在家

LUO QING 羅青 (born 1948)

Luo Qing was once heralded as a fresh starting point for modern Chinese poetry in Taiwan. When the modernist influence began to peter out in the 1970s, he represented a new development, a new type of imagination. He can be seen as a poet nursed by modernism, who yet succeeded in escaping its nihilistic attitude. He is also a professional painter, and always executes his compositions in a carefully planned manner.

The Writing of the Character "Tree"

My younger brother and sister ran up to me,
Arguing, "How should we write the character 'tree'?
How many strokes?
How difficult is it?"

Looking at my sister's
Round little mouth in her round little face,
I slightly rearranged the glistening pigtails by her mouth,
Picked up the wooden pencil that was handed me,
Thinking I'd say:
"First we must find a piece of good wood,
Carefully saw it, sand it, inch by inch,
Saw it square, sand the corners,
Build a tiny little village,
And not forget to sprinkle ten lovely little beans
In the middle."
I patted my younger brother's chubby legs,
Stroked his black hair,
Looked into his big, shining eyes,
Thinking I'd say:
"One stroke goes right the way down like this."
But then I wanted to say,
"A hundred slanting strokes go like that."
And then,
"A big round blob will do."

I thought and I thought. In the end, I looked it up in
The textbook on the desk,
Studied the character for a long while,
And wrote down a most meticulous "tree",
Saying, "It's very easy,
Just do it slowly and patiently,
Like writing 'brother' and 'sister',
Altogether, sixteen strokes."

樹的寫法

弟弟妹妹吵吵鬧鬧
爭着跑來問我:
寫一個樹, 要幾劃? 幾劃?
難不難? 難不難?

我望了望妹妹圓臉上圓張的小嘴
爲她理了理小嘴旁溜溜的辮子
順手接過遞上來的木頭鉛筆
想說, 先找塊好木頭
細細心心, 一寸寸的鋸呀磨呀
鋸得四四方方, 磨得方方正正
蓋一座小小的大村子
村子中間, 不要忘了灑上……
十粒可愛的小豆豆
我拍了拍弟弟的小胖腿
摸了摸弟弟的黑頭髮
我望了望弟弟睜得大大亮亮的眼睛
想說, 一直豎長長
又想說, 一萬撇密密
更想說, 一個圓圓點. 也成
想了半天, 終於——
我看了看桌上的標準教科書
看了半天, 終於
我一筆不苟的, 在上面
寫了個「樹」字
說: 不難不難
只要一筆一畫慢慢寫用心寫
就像寫弟弟妹妹這兩個字
一樣, 共要二八一十六劃

RIVER CROSSING. Woodcut, 1983, Hong Suli.

The Sword of Li Ling

Hunan, Hubei, Taishan, Taiwan,
East and West of the River,
North and South of the Desert,
General Li! Hey you, Ling,
Show some guts, come out!

If good blades will not clash,
How can virtue be tested?
If heroes will not fight,
How can valour be told?

We met at first night-watch,
Talked swords at second,
At third, fought!
Wine bottles cracked, like high spirits,
Voices roared like biting winds;
Chairs tumbled, tables turned, doors banged ajar,
In fierce tournament of minds.

Swords sliced the evening to drops of dew,
Scattering the ten-league mist,
Wills pierced the pine needles to cold stars,
Thrusting through the ten-layered forest;
Mist scattered, stars fell,
We saw each other more clearly
In each other's eyes.

(continued overleaf)

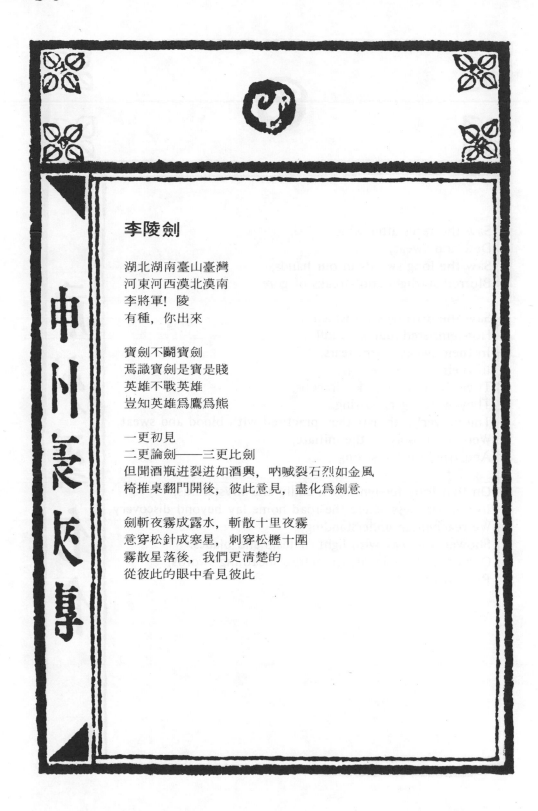

李陵劍

湖北湖南臺山臺灣
河東河西漠北漠南
李將軍！陵
有種，你出來

寶劍不鬥寶劍
焉識寶劍是寶是賤
英雄不戰英雄
豈知英雄為鷹為熊

一更初見
二更論劍──三更比劍
但聞酒瓶迸裂迸如酒興，吶喊裂石烈如金風
椅推桌翻門開後，彼此意見，盡化為劍意

劍斬夜霧成露水，斬散十里夜霧
意穿松針成寒星，刺穿松櫪十圍
霧散星落後，我們更清楚的
從彼此的眼中看見彼此

Saw the faces after wine,
Dew and sweat;
Saw the long swords in our hands,
Blurred starlight and streaks of gore.

Saw the drifting swordsmen,
Hot-tempered, quick to kill.
In their sweat, warm tears,
In their blades, feelings;
Their swords sang like dragons,
They were tigers roaring,
The powerful thrusts they practised with blood and sweat,
Were given only to the initiate,
And tried on the strong.

On that long foreign night, chilly and mysterious,
In the darkness where the road home lay beyond discovery,
We reached an understanding,
Showed the way with light of tears and blades.
Our unpredictable silence before sheathing swords,
Roused the dawn.

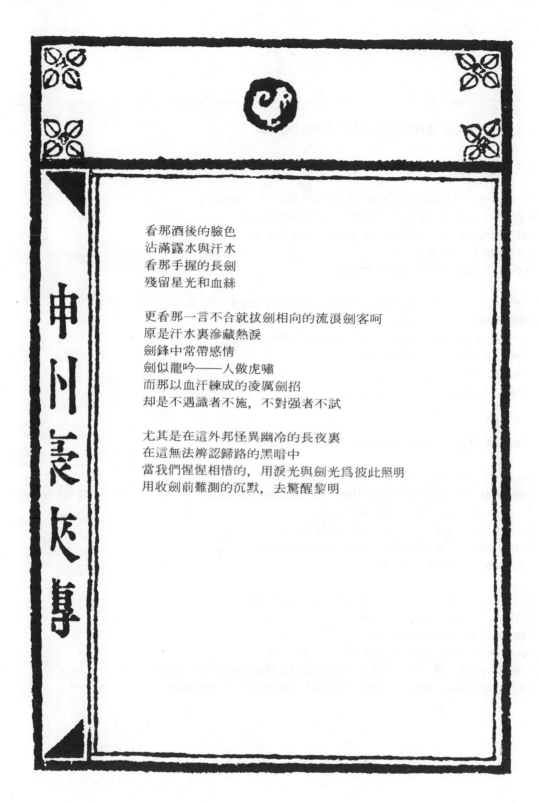

看那酒後的臉色
沾滿露水與汗水
看那手握的長劍
殘留星光和血絲

更看那一言不合就拔劍相向的流浪劍客呵
原是汗水裏滲藏熱淚
劍鋒中常帶感情
劍似龍吟——人做虎嘯
而那以血汗練成的凌厲劍招
却是不遇識者不施，不對強者不試

尤其是在這外邦怪異幽冷的長夜裏
在這無法辨認歸路的黑暗中
當我們惺惺相惜的，用淚光與劍光為彼此照明
用收劍前難測的沉默，去驚醒黎明

SIX WAYS OF EATING WATERMELONS

The 5th Way: The Consanguinity of Watermelons

No one would mistake a watermelon for a meteorite.
Star and melon, they are totally unconnected;
But the earth is undeniably a heavenly body,
Watermelons and stars
Are undeniably consanguineous.

Not only are watermelons and the earth related
Like parent and child,
They also possess brotherly, sisterly feelings,
Like the moon and the sun,
The sun and us,
Us and the moon.

The 4th Way: The Origins of Watermelons

Evidently we live on the face of the earth;
And they, evidently, live in their watermelon interior.
We rush to and fro, thick-skinned,
Trying to stay outside, digesting light
Into darkness with which to wrap ourselves,
Cold and craving warmth.

They meditate on Zen, motionless, concentrated.
Shaping inward darkness into
Substantial, calm passions;
Forever seeking self-fulfilment and growth.
Someday, inevitably, we'll be pushed to the earth's interior,
And eventually they'll burst through the watermelon face.

吃西瓜的六種方法

第五種　西瓜的血統

沒有人會誤認西瓜爲隕石
西瓜星星，是完全不相干的
然我們卻不能否認地球是，星的一種
故而也就難以否認，西瓜具有
星星的血統

因爲，西瓜和地球不止是有
父母子女的關係，而且還有
兄弟姊妹的感情——那感情
就好像月亮跟太陽太陽跟我們我
　們跟月亮的一，樣

第四種　西瓜的籍貫

我們住在地球外面，顯然
顯然，他們住在西瓜裏面
我們東奔西走，死皮賴臉的
想仆在外面，把光明消化成黑暗
包裹我們，包裹冰冷而渴求溫暖的我們

他們禪坐不動，專心一意的
在裏面，把黑暗塑成具體而冷靜的熱情
不斷求自我充實，自我發展
而我們終就免不了，要被趕入地球裏面
而他們遲早也會，衝刺到西瓜外面

AUTUMN LEAVES. Woodcut, 1978, Hong Suli.

The 3rd Way: The Philosophy of Watermelons

The history of watermelon philosophy
Is shorter than the earth's, but longer than ours;
They practise the Three Don'ts:
See no evil, hear no evil, speak no evil.
They are Daoistically *wu-wei*,
And keep themselves to themselves.

They don't envy ova,
Nor do they despise chicken's eggs.
Watermelons are neither oviparous, nor viviparous,
And comprehend the principle
Of attaining life through death.
Consequently, watermelons are not threatened by invasion,
Nor do they fear
Death.

The 2nd Way: The Territory of Watermelons

If we crushed a watermelon,
It would be sheer
      jealousy.
Crushing a melon is equivalent to crushing a rounded night,
Knocking down all the
      stars,
Crumbling a perfect
      universe.

And the outcome would only make us more jealous,
Would only clarify the relationship
Between meteorites and watermelon seeds,
The friendship between watermelon seeds and the universe.
They would only penetrate once again, more deeply,
      into our
      territory

The 1st Way:

EAT IT FIRST.

第三種　西瓜的哲學

西瓜的哲學史
比地球短，比我們長
非禮勿視勿聽勿言，勿爲——
而治的西瓜與西瓜
老死不相往來

不羨慕卵石，不輕視鷄蛋
非胎生非卵生的西瓜
亦能明白死裏求生的道理
所以，西瓜不怕侵略，更不懼死亡

第二種　西瓜的版圖

如果我們敲破了一個西瓜
那純是爲了，嫉妒
敲破西瓜就等於敲碎一個圓圓的夜
就等於敲落了所有的，星，星
敲爛了一個完整的，宇宙

而其結果，卻總使我們更加
嫉妒，因爲這樣一來
隕石和瓜子的關係，瓜子和宇宙的交情
又將會更清楚，更尖銳的
重新撞入我們的，版圖

第一種　吃了再說

TAIJI IN BRONZE, Zhu Ming 朱銘.

WU DELIANG 吳德亮 (born 1952)

Among the young poets, Wu is the most concerned with external reality. He deals with events from real life in his poems, and looks at his surroundings with curiosity and bewilderment. Yet hiding behind this curious and bewildered mind is a deep concern for life. He began painting and writing when he was in high school in Hualian, his native town on the east coast.

Sharpshooters

We wait for the moving mountains to break
And rise as drifting memories.
In our moving viewfinder,
The mountains gradually become part of the sky.
Soil of a foreign land
Clams to our prone bodies, so cold,
Like the damp barrel of a gun
Sticking to our faces.

Plaster our bright blood with praise!
When we lie still in the muddy trenches,
Feeding our hunger with moonlight,
And when our thoughts fly southward,
Please use the tegument of turf above our heads
To conceal this restlessness of ours.

Hand gestures are our language,
Beneath a sky with no flying doves,
We wait silently for an incident;
No matter what happens,
We will not die in desperation.

Plant a black poppy in our enlarged pupils!
Let anticipation, from far away mountains
Aim at us with the same posture,
Shoot down
This entire deposit of homesickness!

GIRL AND RIVER. Woodcut, 1983, Hong Suli.

狙擊手

等待在移動的山頭擴散
昇起爲紛飛的記憶，而山頭
在移動的狙擊鏡裏
已逐漸成爲天空的一部分
異鄉的泥土
貼在我們俯臥的身體上
竟是如此的陰冷
一如緊貼在我們臉上
微濕的槍管

爲我們鮮紅的血塗上掌聲吧
當我們躺在泥濘的戰壕
以月色充飢
而思念正飛向南方的時候
請用覆蓋的草皮
掩飾我們焦躁不安的心情

用手勢交換彼此的語言
在絕對不可能
有鴿子飛過的天空底下
我們靜靜地
等待發生
無論任何事情
我們均不致在絕望中死去

在放大的瞳孔內
種植一株
黑色的罌粟花吧
讓期望在遠遠的山頭
用同樣的姿勢瞄準我們
將沉積的鄉愁
全部射殺

Night Guards

Our steel helmets
Serve to hold the moonlight,
And our repeated perspiration,
In reachable fears,
To complete the presenting of arms.

Homesickness lies down in advancing darkness,
Our faces turn aside,
Meet the piercing wind,
While the other side of our face,
Fills out the tree shadows.

Boiling in our eyes
Are the farewell tears of mothers;
Their repeated advice gnaws our chapped lips.
After a volley of dogs barking,
We wake abruptly.

The password has already become a time bomb,
Suspended vertically amid the sounds that pass;
As we march,
It becomes the perspiration expressed
From our tight buttocks.

On the cold concrete,
Our lonely shadows project
Into the sky at a thirty-degree angle,
Each step is difficult.

Bitten awake by the cold,
We lift our guns
And use the barrels to sweep away our thoughts.
From this shooting position in an endless night,
We strafe the distance with our eyes.
Stand and gradually transform ourselves
Into casuarinas.

夜晚衞兵

我們用鋼盔
抬着月光，用汗水
重複的
在可及的恐懼裏
完成我們握槍的姿勢

鄉愁在行進的黑暗中臥倒
我們側過去的臉
迎着刺骨的風
以另外半隻臉
補滿樹的陰影

我們的眼眶裏煮着
臨別時
母親的淚水
叮嚀啃着我們龜裂的唇
在一陣犬吠之後
猛然驚醒

口令已經成爲一枚結
發的炸藥
在走過的聲音裏
垂直掛着
成爲行進的時候
我們挾緊的臀部裏
擠出的汗水

我們的影子孤獨地
在冰涼的水泥地上
以三十度仰角
撐住天空
每一個擧步都是一種
艱辛

被寒冷咬醒時
我們正擧着槍
用槍管撥開思念
在無限的夜間射擊位置裏
用眼的餘光掃射遠方
逐漸的
把自己站成一株
木麻黃

OLD WOMAN FEEDING CAT. Woodcut, 1980, Hong Suli.

WU SHENG 吳晟 (born 1944)

In 1975, Wu Sheng received, together with Guan Guan 管管, the Modern Chinese Poetry Award of the Epoch Poetry Society. The Award Committee made the following comments: "His poetic style is simple and real, natural and solid. He uses rural language to express the sad moods of the changing times, in a touching and sincere manner." In his speech of acceptance, entitled "I Would Rather Lose Myself in Simplicity and Clumsiness", Wu stated that he was not trained in literature and literary theories, and that his creative work had therefore very little academic basis. Most of his writing derives from his own experiences, and deals with the life of the hard working peasantry.

Wu's simple poetic style is in fact a reaction against the flimsy, decorated style of the academic modernists. He often describes himself as representing the conscience of the common man, in opposition to the hypocrisy of the modern intellectual.

Elegy

Yes, I experienced youth—
The heady hovering of youth,
In the small village where I once grew.
I experienced youth's bewilderment;
Every forlorn beam of starlight knows.

Yes, I experienced springtime—
The fragrance of spring,
In the small village where I once grew.
I experienced the mildewy smell of spring;
Every rotting petal knows.

Yes, I experienced love—
The intoxication of love,
In the small village where I once grew.
I experienced the agony of love;
Every sad gaze of yours knows.

Yes, I experienced singing—
The charm of song,
In the small village where I once grew.
Once I seemed to hear my own dirge;
Every blade of the cemetery grass knows.

SUGAR CANE. Woodcut, 1983, Hong Suli.

輓歌

是的，我曾體驗過年輕
年輕的飛翔
在我生長的小村莊
我曾體驗過年輕的彷徨
每一晚迷茫的星光都知道

是的，我曾體驗過春天
春天的芬芳
在我生長的小村莊
我曾體驗過春天的霉味
每一片腐爛的落花都知道

是的，我曾體驗過愛
愛的沉醉
在我生長的小村莊
我曾體驗過愛的絞痛
你每一道淒涼的凝視都知道

是的，我曾體驗過歌
歌的激盪
在我生長的小村莊
我曾隱隱聞見自己的輓歌
每一株墳場的小草都知道

An Accident

How did a timid seedling ever
Sprout, bud, and come to be
A green sapling?
How did my reluctant cries protest
The fearful coming of the tiny me?
It was all just the most casual
Tiny little accident.

How did the green sapling ever
Branch, leaf, and flower
With unprepossessing fragrance?
How did my tiny talent,
After so many nights of torment,
Find outlet in a small poetry magazine?
It was all just the most casual
Tiny little accident.

How did that flower of unprepossessing fragrance ever
Bear its sour fruit?
How, after jolting of many storms,
Did my tiny name
Acquire a pleasing touch of fame?
It was all just the most casual
Tiny little accident.

How did that sour fruit ever
Ripen, fall, and timidly
Sow its seed, grow once more into an old and hoary tree?
And how did the old tree sigh in the wind, and wither, and lose its sap
And utter a last choking cry of farewell?
How did someone learn of my disappearance
From some tiny obituary?
Oh! That too was just the most casual
Tiny little accident.

意外

一粒怯怯的種籽，如何
而芽而苗而靑靑的樹
以不情不願的哭聲抗議
如何，小小的我驚惶的來臨
那只是一件非常偶然的
小小、小小的意外

一株靑靑的樹，如何
而枝而葉而不怎麼芬芳的花
以多少淒清的夜晚熬着屈辱
如何，在一本小詩刊上
有人竟讀到我小小的才華
那只是一件非常偶然的
小小、小小的意外

一朵不怎麼芬芳的花，如何
而澀澀的果
以幾番風風雨雨的搖撼
如何，我小小的姓名
塡上一紙頗爲好聽的名聲
那只是一件非常偶然的
小小、小小的意外

一顆澀澀的果，如何
而熟而落而怯怯的種籽而蒼老了樹
一棵蒼老的樹，如何
而蕭蕭而颯颯而枯竭了汁液
以最後一聲哽咽告別
如何，在一張小小的訃聞上
有人風聞我已消失的消息
啊！那也只是一件非常偶然的
小小、小小的意外

PEASANT AMONG LOTUS
        FLOWERS.
    Woodcut, 1983,
    Hong Suli.

Impressions of My Village
—A Preface

Long before long ago
The people in my village
First knew how to look up
At the village sky,
The nonchalant sky,
Indifferently dark or blue.

Long before long ago,
The mountain shadows stretching in
From the left of my village
Were a large gloomy ink-splash scroll,
Glued to the villagers' faces.

Long before long ago,
Generations of my forefathers dripped their salty sweat,
Raised and multiplied
Helpless descendants
In a land that would grow neither wealth,
Nor fame, nor miracles.

吾鄉印象
——序說

古早古早的古早以前
吾鄉的人們
開始懂得向上仰望
吾鄉的天空
就是那一付無所謂的模樣
無所謂的陰著或藍著

古早古早的古早以前
自吾鄉左側綿延而近的山影
就是一大幅
陰悒的潑墨畫
緊緊貼在吾鄉人們的臉上

古早古早的古早以前
世世代代的祖公，就在這片
長不出榮華富貴
長不出奇蹟的土地上
揮灑鹹鹹的汗水
繁衍無奈的子孫

PLOUGHING. Woodcut, 1979, Hong Suli.

XIANG YANG 向陽 (born 1955)

At the end of the 1970s, when modern poetry in Taiwan was still vacillating between Western and Chinese models, a new note was struck by the emergence of the Sunlight Ensemble Poetry Society 陽光小集詩社. Xiang Yang, a major figure in this dedicated group of young and promising poets, presents a new prospect, a confirmation of both modernism and realism in modern Chinese poetry.

Xiang once compared himself with a gingko tree, in a somewhat elaborate botanical metaphor. The syphon of love draws water from the soil, thereby strengthening the inner tradition (the xylem). The tree's sieve tubes of wisdom are used to filter and distill nutrients from the air, expanding and exploring the elasticity of the outer modernity (the phloem).

Ten Lines: Autumn

Unable to hold on to the dry branches,
Leaves tumble to the morning-chilled pond.
A man with an umbrella walks past the dewy lake,
Listens to a pine-cone drop from the right of the woods,
Calls out in surprise:

"Is this the way you come?"
Ripples and echoes linger on the hollow surface of water,
Duckweed stands abrupt, leaving the clear mountain reflections
To kiss the sky, blue after rain.
This is deep, deep autumn now.

秋辭十行

葉子攀不住枯黯的枝枒
紛紛奔向清晨微寒的潭心
有人打傘自多露的湖畔走過
只聽見右側林中跳下一顆
松子，驚聲喊道

你就這樣來了嗎？漣漪
和回聲都流連在空盪的水面上
一些浮萍忽然站起來
留下山的倒影明晰地吻着雨後
蔚藍的天空，而秋是深得很深了

Sailing in the Rain

In the thick rain, the ink-splash rain,
In the solitary raising of hands,
The expectant eyes,
Let me take you sailing
Down a dream, and dream-like rivers.
Gently, gently we glide
Into the winds and tides of five thousand years,
To the rocky shore where
Dignity has confronted wilful pride these five thousand years,
Towards the sombre firmament of rain,
Towards the vast universe of sea,
Towards the tears of begonia blood,
The grid of scorching veins.*

Hard we sail! In the rain
From which night and dawn refuse to separate,
I hold my pen for lamp,
And call a dawn in blackest night,
To make the morning rooster rouse
Silent China! That China may grow to grandeur!
On every inch of blood-drenched earth,
Plough peaceful acres,
Through every clod of tear-drenched soil,
Lay tear-free furrows;
Step by step, track joy down
Through the face of darkness and sorrow.

And in these hundred years, our fathers
Never once dreamed
They were waking lions, or dragons
Dancing in the clouds!
A century of battle-fires,
Of uncleansed bloodstains,
A century of war-ashes
Still lie above the irreparable ruins;
A century of foreign might
Compacted, chewed, devoured us.
The one thing China has not known is light.
The fields were not tilled, but shrapnel fell to plough them,
The trees were not yet fully grown, but they fashioned guns.

*The map of China is often likened to a begonia leaf.

在雨中航行

在緜密的雨中，潑墨般的
雨中，在落寞的舉手
期待的眼裏，我帶你航行
沿着夢，夢也似的江河
慢慢，我們慢慢滑出
迎五千年風和浪，五千年
尊嚴與桀驁相抗的岩岸，向着
雨的冷肅陰沉的天，向着
海的遼夐寬廣的宇宙，向着
棠的血淚縱橫交錯最最炙人的脈絡

我們努力航行！在黑夜與黎明
不忍割捨的雨中，執筆
爲燈，在黑與夜裏叫出
一聲黎明，要晨鷄喚醒
沉寂的中國，要中國更加壯闊

在每一寸血染過的土上
耘出不再染血的田畝
在每一分淚洗過的泥中
犂下不再洗淚的道路
向陰鬱悲哀，我們步步索求歡騰

而百餘年來我們的祖先，夢
也不曾，夢見自己是醒獅或歡騰
雲際的龍！百餘年的戰火
未褪的血跡，百餘年砲灰仍在
無力重修的殘垣；百餘年的外力
條約過、蠶食過、也鯨吞過
我們的中國，只是不曾開朗過
田尚未耕好，有彈片來翻土
林尚未植就，木已先成了槍

THE CRY OF THE REFUGEE, 1981, Li Nongsheng 黎農生 (Malayan artist).

The impact our fathers sustained
We can but surmise in silence,
Reading our textbooks,
And chewing on the aftermath of the Opium War.
In this thick rain, drop upon drop,
Falls the inexorable sorrow of modern China,
From the hands reaching for help
In the billows of the South China Sea,
To the footprints running for refuge
On the borders of Laos and Vietnam;
From the upheavals and calamities of the old country,
To the homeless driftings abroad,
The bitter struggle of the diaspora.
In our papers, wherever we turn,
The pages brim with China,
Sailing lonely in the rain.

In the rain, we too are sailing,
Repelling demons and the roses of vanity,
Roar of applause, spittle of curses.
We are neither lion dormant,
Nor dragon from distant Cathay,
Just Chinese,
And the Chinese soil is beneath our feet,
In our blood and tears.
Warmly we tread the breadth of
The begonia leaf.
No need of dreams, we can take to our hearts
The winds and tides of five thousand years,
The myriad miles of home.

Sweep away the mists of gloom,
Let us grow!
In a wild and stormy night,
Though leaves may fall,
More fruits will swell.
Leaping from our dream,
Let us take a walk on the rocky shore
Of dignity and wilful pride,
Let us watch the vast universe of sea.
Soon, the bright day will dawn,
But till then, in the thick rain, the ink-splash rain,
In the bold raising of hands,
And the determined eyes,
Let me take you sailing.

這些驚悸，祖先吞忍過
這些驚悸，我們只能默默感覺
咀嚼，教科書上鴉片役後的餘味
在如此綿密的雨中，點滴而來
近代中國無以避免的悲哀
從南海驚濤中掙扎求援的手
到越寮邊境亡奔的足跡
從故舊山河的動盪、災變
到寰宇流離，各地華裔的辛酸苦關
我們面對報紙而去取難分
滿版中國，在雨中落寞航行

在雨中，我們也在航行
推開一切魍魎一切虛華的玫瑰
一切掌聲一切四方湧來的唾液
我們不是睡獅，也不是遙遠
所謂「東方」的一條龍
我們是中國的，中國
土地就在腳下，血與淚
我們溫暖地踩過，整片秋海棠
我們無需夢中，也能緊緊擁抱
這五千年風和浪，千百萬里地家國

將陰霾的雲霧全部掃去！讓我們
成熟，在疾雨狂風的夜裏
一些葉子可能墜落，更多果實
則在等待綻放。從夢中跳出
我們去走一程尊嚴與桀驁的
岩岸，看遼敻的海寬廣的宇宙
俟候即將展現的白日青天
而在此際綿密的雨中，潑墨般的
雨中，在昂揚的舉手
肯定的眼裏，且讓我帶你航行

Ten Lines: Seed

Only by parting resolutely from my dependent coronet
Can I bend and hear the wilting of the twigs.
All fragrances, bees, butterflies, yesterdays,
Will float on the wind. Only by casting off the armour of green leaves,
Can I prepare for the shock of the shattering soil.

But mountain cranny would preclude the open wilderness,
Ocean eyrie deny the cleansing stream.
In this whole universe, so vast and cramped,
I drift, fly, wander, seeking only a fixed, congenial
Piece of ground, on which to settle and multiply.

種籽十行

除非毅然離開靠託的美麗花冠
我只能俯聞到枝枒枯萎的聲音
一切溫香、蜂蝶和昔日，都要
隨風飄散。除非拒絕綠葉掩護
我才可以等待泥土爆破的心驚

但擇居山陵便緣慳於野原空曠
棲止海濱，則失落溪澗的洗滌
天與地之間，如是廣闊而狹仄
我飄我飛我蕩，僅為尋求固定
適合自己，去縶根繁殖的土地

香江詩風

Aeolian Chimes:
Twelve Poems by Huang Guobin

Translated by the Author and Mok Wing-yin

With three paintings by Wang Wuxie (Wucius Wong)

It is often said that a poet is born, not made. Huang Guobin is both. He decided to become a poet in his early teens, and from then on, his life has been dedicated to that goal. He has learned English, French, German, Italian and Spanish in order to read the major poets in their native tongues. At the same time, he has read widely in Chinese poetry, from the Book of Songs *to the present day. Among contemporary poets, he acknowledges his indebtedness to Yu Kwang-chung. His first collection of verse, entitled* A Child Reaching for the Laurels, *was published in 1975, his sixth collection in 1983. Most of these poems appeared first in* Shi Feng Bi-monthly 詩風雙月刊, *now in its twelfth year, edited and published in Hong Kong by Huang and a group of young enthusiastic fellow-poets.*

He has also published three solid volumes of poetry criticism. The first, published in 1976, is a collection of essays on a diversity of topics: "On the Obscurity of Modern Poetry", "Du Fu and Epic Poetry", "A Close Analysis of Yu Kwang-chung's White Jade and Bitter Melon*", "A Short Comment on Eugenio Montale", "The Waste Land—an Interpretation" etc. The second, his* Three Major Chinese Poets: Qu Yuan, Li Bo and Du Fu *appeared in 1981. Most recent is his* The Poetic Art of Tao Yuanming, *published in November 1983. These studies have helped to complement his own creative insight and sharpen his awareness of the nuances of the Chinese language.*

Huang is also a firm believer in the Chinese dictum: "To travel ten thousand miles surpasses by far the reading of ten thousand volumes". He has made two extensive trips to Mainland China when conditions have permitted him to do so. He has gone there not as a tourist but in order to recapture the experiences of the great poets of the past. He often resorted to hiking, to enjoy the magnificent views of the legendary mountains, lakes, river gorges, temples and shrines of old. His impressions and observations he carefully recorded in two travel journals published in 1979 and 1982 respectively.

S.C.S.

Autumn

The sea, a bright eye
Staring at the sky,
Staring at the hill;

The hill
In meditation,
Holds the gaze of the bright eye;
Suddenly the cry of a wild goose cuts across the vast
        silence,
A pebble drops down the gorge in the mountains.

Soft as silk the west wind
In skeins
Over endless harvest fields
Comes swiftly,
Twines around the few remaining twigs and branches,
Trailing behind it the heavy golden ears of corn.

The sunlight has mellowed
Like red wine,
Soaking the hill,
Soaking the clouds.

12th November, 1971

tr. MOK WING-YIN

秋

海是一隻明眸,
凝視着天,
凝視着山;

山
入定,
叫明眸盼住了;
突然有雁聲劃過千萬頃寂寥,
一顆石子跌落山中的大壑;

柔軟如絲的西風
便一絡絡
從遼闊的麥田那邊
飄了過來
繞住疏疏落落的枝椏,
後面還牽着金黃的麥穗纍纍;

陽光也醇了起來,
像紅色的葡萄酒,
浸着山,
浸着雲。

1971年11月12日

Waiting

My arms, like the bay in mid-summer,
Waiting for the sail beyond the horizon,
Wide open, wait for you to come home;
Come home to me, like the tender sail that returns
In the starlight, in the sea breeze
Quietly, and stay.

22nd June, 1976

tr. MOK WING-YIN

等待

我的臂,如仲夏的海灣
等待水平綫外的一片帆,
張開,等待你歸來,
歸來,如溫柔的一片帆,
在星光下,在海風裏,
默默地停泊。

1976年 6 月22日

Taking a Picture

You stand under a tree, posing for a picture.
Behind the tree is a building,
Behind the building is a big mountain,
Behind the big mountain is the wide, wide sea,
And then there are the white clouds, ever-changing,
And then there is the vast empty sky.
The background beyond the sky—
Let the focus shift as it may—
Is not to be reached
Till you leave:
The tree withers,
Mountain and sea and white clouds all vanish,
Like tattered clothes
The vast empty sky peels off,
And the ultimate background
Before the lens, in the absence of the peeping eye,
Bares itself.

30th August, 1976

tr. MOK WING-YIN

Song of Madness

Let the reeds pander to the wayward wind,
I am the mountain range
That determines the course of the wind.

Let the seaweed flatter the inconstant tide,
I am the moon
That controls the tide's ebb and flow.

Let the magnet succumb to the unbending north and
    south,
I am the great earth:
Only I have directions.

28th December, 1976

tr. MOK WING-YIN

拍照

你站在樹下拍照，
樹的後面是一幢建築物，
建築物後面是一座大山，
大山之後是茫茫的大海，
大海之後是變幻的白雲，
白雲之後，是漠漠的天空；
天空之外的背景，
任攝影機的焦點怎樣推移
也尋找不到；
直至你離去，
老樹枯萎，
山海白雲全部消失，
如一襲破衣裳
漠漠的天空脫落，
最後的背景
才向無人窺視的鏡頭
裸露。

1976年8月30日

狂吟

讓蘆葦諂媚任性的風吧；
我是山脈，
劃出風的道路。

讓海藻奉承善變的潮汐吧；
我是月亮，
支配潮汐的漲退。

讓磁石服從嚴峻的南北吧；
我是大地，
因我才有方向。

1976年12月28日

A Night Prayer

We believe too much in ourselves,
Like high and perilous walls
Perched on a cliff when a storm impends,
Confident and self-assured.
We refuse to groan when wounded.
We shed no tears when hurt.
We are so unlike our ancestors, who feared the thunder, the wind,
And the dark in the wilderness.
When they were helpless, they would pray to the earth, call upon heaven,
Gather round a totem,
Kneel down, prostrate themselves, confess their sins,
Telling of their anxieties, misgivings, and fears.

We believe too much in ourselves,
Like stubborn locks, deaf and dumb,
Refusing the probings of all keys;
Like mummies,
Locking themselves up in a tomb,
Refusing the moonlight that knocks at the door,
Refusing even more the dawn that comes over the mountains.
In the quiet of the night, singing is heard from the galaxy,
But we lock our doors and windows fast,
Reluctant even to give ear to the wind that blows over our roofs,
More reluctant to go out
Into the wilderness and look up at the starlit sky.

We believe too much in ourselves.
We never let our roots reach into the soil
To listen to the song deep in the ground
And the ore racing in the veins of igneous rocks.
We never stretch ourselves like seedlings
To put forth soft green tender leaf-tips
Into the deep, blue sky,
And, trembling in apprehensive delight,
Reach into the damp, cool mist of dawn,
Towards the morning star in the east,
And, finally, amidst the silence of lakes and mountains,
Hurl headlong into the boundless space beyond the heavens.

13th December, 1977

tr. HUANG GUOBIN

夜禱

我們太相信自己：
像一堵高峻的危牆，
暴風雨前聳立在崖上，
自信而肯定。
受了傷，卻不呻吟；
受了委屈，也不流淚。
不像初民：畏雷畏風，
畏曠野的黑暗；
無救時，懂得祈地，呼天，
懂得圍着圖騰
下跪，匍伏，懺悔，
訴說內心的惶惑和恐慌。

我們太相信自己：
像一把聾啞的頑鎖，
拒絕一切鑰匙的探詢；
像一具木乃伊，
把自己關在墓內，
拒絕叩墓的月光，
更拒絕漫山而來的黎明。
夜靜時銀漢傳來歌聲，
我們卻把戶牖緊鎖，
連屋頂的風聲也不願傾聽；
更不願走出屋外，
到曠野去仰望星空。

我們太相信自己：
從不把根鬚探入土壤，
聽大地深處的歌聲，
聽礦脈在火成岩內奔流。
從不舒展，像一株幼苗
把嫩綠敏感的葉尖
伸入蔚藍的空曠，
半驚半喜，震顫着
探入濕涼的曉氣，
向東方的啓明；
最後，在湖山的沉寂中
直衝天外的無窮。

1977年12月13日

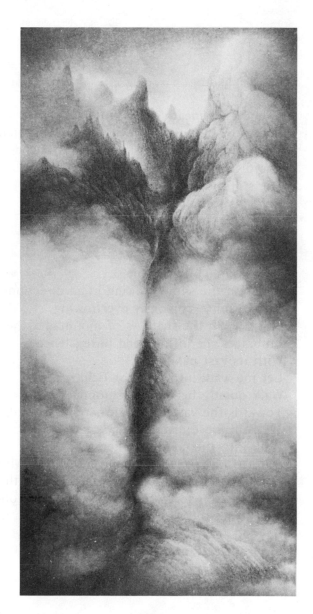

BEYOND THE CLOUDS, No. 1

Wang Wuxie 王無邪 *(Wucius Wong) was born in Guang-dong Province in 1939. He is now principal lecturer at the Hong Kong Polytechnic's Swire School of Design. 'Hong Kong,' he is quoted as saying, 'where East and West join hands, could play an important role in (China's) move towards a universal culture. This unification will later become the foundation for the new Chinese culture of the next century—hence the importance of our develop-ment.' (*South China Morning Post, *June 15, 1983)

Snow Night

Boundless beneath the infinite sky,
The snow billows into a blue beam of liquid light
Playing on the horizon, and dimly touches
The distant silence.
The still more distant mystery
Remains soundless beyond the silence.
The earth's round and soundless crust
Is listening to the revolving of a nebula
Beyond the galaxy.
The moonlight from the sky
Pours on the snow, flowing in all directions
Into infinity, copiously overflowing
The sky. In the shadows of mountains, the earth
Embraces the infinite and pure silence
With its vast nakedness.
Let me walk into the snowfield, naked,
Walk quietly beneath the moon,
Towards the vast expanse of snow, towards
The still more distant silence,
Walk into the centre of silence,
To touch and feel the liquid moonlight with my naked body, to feel
The mystery on the other side of the earth's crust,
To listen to the vortex of the nebula beyond the galaxy,
And to let the still deeper tranquility
Beyond space
Flow silently into me.

5th February, 1978

tr. HUANG GUOBIN

雪夜

白雪茫茫在無盡的空間
湧入地平流幻的
一脈藍光，幽幽觸到
遠處的寂靜。
更遠更遠的神秘
在寂靜之外無聲。
渾圓無聲的地殼
在沉沉的黑夜
傾聽銀河外
星雲的旋動。
月光自天空瀉落
雪地，向四面流入
無垠，溶溶向天外
泛濫。山影下，大地
以浩瀚的裸體
擁抱無窮而純粹的寂靜。
讓我，赤裸走入雪地，
在月下無聲
走向茫茫，走向
更遠更遠的寂靜，
走入寂靜的中心，
用裸體去接觸，感覺
溶溶的月光，感覺
地殼那邊的神秘，
傾聽銀河外
星雲的旋動，
任宇宙之外
更深更深的寧謐
脈脈流入體內。

1978年 2 月 5 日

BEYOND THE CLOUDS, No. 2

When You Are Naked, You Have Everything

Like the earth,
You must have nothing,
Except starlight, the water of streams,
And a dark night which is everywhere;
Like the reef,
Which has only the sound of billows, the spray of waves,
And the rise and fall of eternal tides;
Like the wind,
Which has only loneliness and solitude.

When you are naked,
You have everything;
Like the earth,
Which has rivers, mountain ranges, and forests;
Like the reef,
Which has the sea
And the pulse of the moon;
Like the wind,
Which has lofty mountains, towering ridges,
Boundless plains,
And vast oceans.

When you are naked, you have
The heavenly music beyond the nebulae
And the splendour beyond the heavenly music.

When you are naked, you have everything.

9th March, 1978

tr. HUANG GUOBIN

赤裸時你擁有一切

你要像大地，
甚麼也沒有；
只有星光、溪水
和一個無所不在的黑夜。
像海礁，
只有濤聲、浪花
和萬年潮汐的漲落。
像風，
只有孤獨和寂寞。

赤裸時
你擁有一切。
像大地，
擁有河流、山脈、森林。
像海礁，
擁有大海
和月亮的脈搏。
像風，
擁有崇山、峻嶺、
和無際的平原、
浩瀚的大海。

赤裸時你擁有
星雲外的天籟、
天籟外的光芒。

赤裸時你擁有一切。

1978年 3 月 9 日

SOLITARY HEIGHTS, No. 2

My Poem

My poem is a bridge, silent, lonely;
For long, long years, it bears my tribesmen, a simple people,
Helps them cross rivers, climb hills; in the morning and evening
It reaches out to the village in smoke, in the light of dawn.

My poem is a well, old, alone;
Through the ages it listens to the swallows as they come and go,
Watches the folk as they wash and cook by the well,
Listens to footsteps as they move away, as they draw near.

My poem is a song, distant, lasting,
Hidden in the countless gorges, in the breathing of the sea;
When crowds disperse, cries and clamour die down,
It rises lightly, like the sea-gull in the wind.

My poem is a star, remote, steadfast,
Resisting the heartless cold in the void beyond light years.
Deep in the night, when the air is no more polluted by the neon lights,
Its brilliance will linger on, in the eyes that look up to the sky.

29th March, 1978

tr. MOK WING-YIN

我的詩

我的詩是一道橋, 沉默, 寂寞,
在悠悠的歲月裏渡淳樸的族人,
幫他們涉水, 登山, 在黃昏和早晨
伸向曙色和炊煙中的村落。

我的詩是一口井, 古老, 孤獨,
世世代代在村中聽燕去燕來,
看村民在井邊浣衣洗菜,
聽跫音消失後傳來另一些脚步。

我的詩是一首歌, 遙遠, 持久,
藏在萬壑, 藏在大海的呼吸;
當擾攘潰散, 吶喊和叫囂靜止,
就裊裊揚起, 像風中的海鷗。

我的詩是一顆星, 夐邈, 堅定,
在光年以外的廣漠抗拒酷寒。
夜深, 當大氣不再受霓虹的污染,
光芒就脈脈流入仰望的眼睛。

1978年 3 月29日

The Kingfisher

In early spring, hovering over
A fish pond, like a blue star
Shining upon a sheet of glass,
It spellbinds a small fish
In the gaze of its brown pupils,
And, dazzling the sky and the earth,
Strikes like purple lightning.
When it flies away, skimming over the water,
The sharp, vermilion claws folded,
Already holding its prey in the black beak,
It leaves behind only a shrill scream
That rips open the dawn of spring.

15th May, 1978

tr. HUANG GUOBIN

Playing the Er-hu

A room,
In the centre sits a man
Holding an *er-hu*,
Drawing, drawing his bow,
He draws out tall mountains and flowing streams.

The man sits in the centre of the universe,
Bowing the strings of the *er-hu*;
Tall mountains and flowing streams
Flow up and down, to the four corners,
Flow into the past, into the future.

The man is gone,
Leaving the *er-hu*
In the centre of the universe
To draw out tall mountains and flowing streams.

The *er-hu* is gone,
Leaving the tall mountains and flowing streams
To flow in the universe.

18th August, 1978

tr. MOK WING-YIN

The er-hu *is a traditional Chinese stringed instrument played by drawing a bow across the strings.*

翠鳥

早春，在魚塘的上空
懸着，像一顆藍星
俯照玻璃。
把小魚祟入褐瞳，
天地眩轉間如紫電下擊。
當它掠水而去，
黑喙已叼着獵物，
朱紅的利爪收斂，
只留下一聲尖叫，
如刀劃破春曉。

1978年 5 月15日

拉二胡

一個房間，
中央坐一個人，
抱一個二胡，
拉着拉着，
就拉出了高山流水。

那人坐在宇宙的中央，
繼續拉着二胡；
高山流水，
流向四方上下，
流入了過去未來。

那人不見了，
剩下二胡
在宇宙的中央
奏着高山流水。

二胡不見了，
剩下高山流水
在宇宙裏流。

1978年 8 月18日

Listening to My Aeolian Bell at Night

On a night when the reeds were moist with dew,
The aeolian bell before my window gently trembled.
A tinkle from under the eaves
Escaped into the night,
Into the field,
Towards the peak,
Towards the stars,
And touched their light in the remote reaches of the
        universe,
Like the diamond on the ear of a beautiful woman,
Falling into a silent, deep, dewy well, glittering.

I walked into the field. All was quiet.
I saw only starlight quivering in the sky.
The diamond
Had already sunk into the depths of the stars,
Never to be found again.

15th October, 1978

tr. HUANG GUOBIN

夜聽風鈴

在蒹葭滴着白露的夜晚，
窗前的風鈴輕顫，
就有聲音逸出，
逸入屋簷外的黑夜，
逸入平野，
逸向山巔，
逸向星際，
觸着遙遠的星光，
像美人的鑽石耳墜，
亮晶晶的
跌落一口幽深的露井。

走出曠野，萬籟沉寂，
只見一天的星光顫動；
那顆耳墜
已沉入衆星深處，
再也尋找不到。

1978年10月15日

Eel
Written in imitation of Montale's "L'anguilla"

Fish and shrimp follow the spring tide to the sea.
I, from the sea, against the spring tide,
Thrash inland,
Like a flame, blazing,
And there, thousands of miles away,
Leave the warmth of my body.

22nd August, 1979

tr. MOK WING-YIN

鰻
　—擬蒙達萊
　　《鰻》

魚蝦趁春汛入海，
我從大海逆春汛
鞭入內陸，
像一把火炬，熊熊
在幾千里外
留下我的體溫。

1979年8月22日

Drama

A Word for the Impostor
—introducing the drama of Sha Yexin

By Geremie Barmé

IN JULY 1979, a short farce written by students of Fudan University called *Son of the 'Artillery Commander'* '炮兵司令'的兒子 was staged in Shanghai.[1] Although basically a comedy of errors, there was one element of the play that assured its immediate popular success and even earned it first prize in a Shanghai drama competition:[2] the story hinged on a lowly youth impersonating the son of a high level army official.

The play holds an old party cadre up to ridicule and much is made of the obsequious fawning he displays in front of the 'commander's son'. The story would have appeared forced and unlikely if it had not been for the arrest of a youth by the name of Zhang Longquan for fraud some time earlier. Zhang had impersonated the son of Li Da, Deputy Chief of Staff of the PLA, for some months, and by the time this play was produced the impostor had taken on the aspect of a minor folk hero. Zhang had originally struck on the idea of pretending to be the son of an official after being frustrated in his attempts to get a ticket to see a highly popular production of Shakespeare's *Much Ado About Nothing*. The ease with which the 'back door' of the theatre and Shanghai high society opened for him as a result of this simple ruse emboldened him to continue the deception. Starting off in late 1978 as a mere farm-hand, an 'unreturned' countryside youth from Chongming Island, by the Spring Festival of 1979 Zhang had been accepted by the upper crust of Shanghai society and had the run of the city. His slick and winsome ways won him fame and widespread popular credence; stories of this luminary from the north even took precedence over other local gossip for a time. It was only when his neighbours reported him, suspicious of his comings and goings at all hours of the day and night in a chauffeured limousine, that an investigation was finally undertaken and the deception uncovered.[3]

---

[1] See *Eastern Horizon* (Hong Kong), Vol. 18, No. 10, 1979, pp. 39-48, *Son of the 'Artillery Commander'*, translated by Geremie Barmé; also Takashima Tadao's *Koe naki tokoro ni kyōrai o kiku* 聲無き所に驚雷を聴く, Tokyo 1981, pp. 83-9.

[2] *Wenhuibao* 文滙報 (Shanghai), July 3, 1979.

[3] See *Zhengming* 爭鳴, August 1979, pp. 22-4, and *The Seventies* 七十年代, January 1980, pp. 74-5.

Zhang Longquan had unwittingly become the son of Li Da, the PLA commander; following his arrest he went on to receive popular fame and recognition as the protagonist in a number of short stories and plays. Shanghai audiences seemed to have an insatiable appetite for new plays in 1979, and not long after *Son of the 'Artillery Commander'* was staged, another play with a similar theme appeared. It was called *If I Were Real* (假如我是真的, referred to by its other name *The Impostor* 騙子 hereafter). Written by three young Shanghainese—Sha Yexin 沙葉新, Li Shoucheng 李守成 and Yao Mingde 姚明德—from the Shanghai Drama Company,[4] the play was only allowed restricted exhibition due to its controversial representation of the impostor (Li Xiaozhang 李小璋) and the various cadres who appear. By the end of the year it was something of a *cause célèbre*, and the question of whether it should be performed publicly or not eventually required the intervention of the then Director of Propaganda of the CPC, Hu Yaobang.

Before continuing this study of the fate of *The Impostor* and its main author, Sha Yexin, it might be appropriate to consider the comments made by Ba Jin on the subject. Ba Jin, a famed veteran writer and long-time resident of Shanghai, is the most publicly outspoken writer of his age. Through his "literary bequest" *Random Thoughts* 隨想錄, a series of casual essays that range from reflections on the past to pointed political comment, Ba Jin has become the conscience of a generation, and since 1978 he has been a central figure in all of the major cultural debates. In his article "The Little Impostor" 小騙子, written on 29 September, 1979, during a bout of illness he tells us something of the relevance and impact of not only the impostor, but the play written about him:—

> A few months back a little impostor was unmasked. Prior to his being found out a number of people really had been taken in: they had all heard he was the son of a high-level cadre in the Army. Once he had been arrested there was much wringing of hands; some people overreacted, while there were those who took it all as a great joke. The city was full of stories about the incident, so much so in fact that two Shanghai dailies eventually reported it in full. Even some Hong Kong journals printed articles about it. (Naturally, neither these reports nor articles necessarily correspond completely with the truth.) Certain people had been made to look like fools; there were those who were delighted and others still who were furious. All in all, it was cause for considerable popular discussion.
>
> Subsequently a drama company put on a play about the little impostor. It has only been shown to limited audiences because there are conflicting views about it, and there is definite opposition to

---

[4] For background to the writing of the play refer to Sha Yexin's article 'Concerning *If I Were Real*' 關於《假如我是真的》, *Shanghai Drama* 上海戲劇, June 1980, p. 2. An interesting criticism of *The Impostor* can be found in Yuan Shaojie's 袁少傑 "Looking at the writing of satirical drama by a comparison of three plays about impostors" 從三個騙子劇的比較中看諷刺劇的創作, *Journal of Dandong Teachers' College* 丹東師專學報, January 1982, pp. 22-32, in which the author studies the influence of Gogol's play on Chen Baichen's 陳白塵 *Bureaucrats' Snakes and Ladders* 陞官圖, Lao She's *Looking West to Changan* 西望長安, and Sha's *The Impostor*. In the body of this article the writer makes a detailed and fairly damning critique of Sha's play.

making it public. Some say that the writers sympathize with the little impostor, and there's also the opinion that the play denigrates older cadres.

I haven't seen the play so, naturally, I can't comment. For that matter I've never met the impostor either, although I heard about him, starting from when he was being treated like the 'son of a high-level cadre'. The talk continued right up to his arrest, and it's still going on now. Rumour has it that after he was arrested he said, 'My only crime is that I am not the son of So-and-so.' He is also supposed to have asked, 'What would have happened if I were really So-and-so's son?' I believe that sympathizers have offered to act as his defence counsel in court. Needless to say, all of the above is hearsay and therefore not particularly reliable. Although I haven't heard of anyone expressing concern for those who were taken in—the general comment is that 'they only got what they deserved'—there definitely are people who pity the impostor. As for me, I have greater sympathy for the victims. This incident is not a comedy, it's a tragedy, and it is established social practice (社會風氣) that should be coming under fire. 'I'm just doing what everyone else does. It's just my bad luck to have been caught out by a phoney.'

I can't help thinking of the play the Russian writer Gogol created 143 years ago, *The Government Inspector*. The mere mention of this 19th century Russian writer still gives people a headache. Worst of all is that this particular writer hits us just where it hurts. I know there are those who will disagree with this and who will argue: Gogol attacks the feudal society of Russia, it has absolutely nothing to do with our own 'beautiful socialist society'. They are right, of course; there is no connection. Furthermore, that 143-year-old cheat and our impostor have nothing in common. Yet that is just why it is all so odd, because in both cases the reason that so many people were attracted to the impostors was exactly the same: it was for personal gain. Why, they both nearly even got wives out of their masquerade. The only difference between them is that Gogol's impostor was smarter, he managed to escape to distant parts and even had the satisfaction of deriding his victims in a letter to a friend. Our little impostor, on the other hand, has been arrested and is in gaol awaiting trial. Even so, he is by no means a fool because he has posed us a question that demands careful thought: 'What would have happened if I really were So-and-so's son?' It is a problem to which I have devoted much thought, and I must admit, my conclusion is that if he had been So-and-so's son then nothing would have come of it. Everything would have been peaches and cream and the story would have had a happy ending. All the meals, the free shows, the car he was given to use, the girlfriend he had been introduced to . . . . He could have gone on to select a beautiful woman to be his bride, then he could have arranged to have her transferred to a better job, and so on and so on. It would all have been perfectly all right. He could even have gone on an overseas junket, and enjoyed so many, many . . . . In a word, all of the crimes that the little impostor has been accused of would have been legitimate and quite acceptable. There would be no newspaper reports or plays about him, no conflict over whether the play should be performed publicly or not. In actual fact, this type of thing has been going on since ancient times, everyone takes it for granted, nothing strange in it at all. But WHY does it continue?

The sentence uttered by the little impostor has disturbed my dreams for months. But there's another question that haunts me as well: 'How could all of those experienced people fall so willingly into his trap?' The more I think about it the more depressed I become, for I have to admit to myself that there are still backward aspects of our society, even things that Gogol attacked back in 1836. Despite the fact that over the last three years we have constantly been told that 'malpractices involving backdoorism' are to be corrected, the back door is opening wider all the time. If you can't see or even find a front door when you have to get something done, even something as simple as repairing a broken window which in the normal course of events takes ages, naturally you are going to think of finding a back door. It's not surprising then that people make fools of themselves when they inadvertently get involved with an impostor. Why can't our *yamen* open up their front doors and do a little more for the people? Why don't certain cadres pay more attention to the people below them instead of always thinking of their superiors?

Reverting to the question of whether the play should be staged for the general public, I can only repeat that I have no right to comment. However, as to those who are of the opinion that the play blackens the image of cadres and socialism, I would say that this is not necessarily so. Shanghai is not the only city in which an impostor has appeared, it has happened in other provinces. Is his appearance a freak? He would never have come into being if there wasn't the proper soil and climate for his 'growth'. If he had not been able to take advantage of the peculiarities of our society then no one would have been taken in. It is only proper that he was uncovered and roundly condemned, as that is all part and parcel of ridding the society of the 'climatic conditions' and soil which gave him life.

If this illness is not attended to, if this sore is not given treatment and the back door is constantly opened and the use of position and so on is made into the 'ideal'; if the old feudal belief that one 'can't wash one's dirty linen in public' is approved of as a motto in our social and political life thereby disallowing people to touch any sore spots, then in the long run you won't just be blackening the face of socialism, you end up undermining its very foundations.[5]

Ba Jin's attitude to the play has remained unequivocal: he has supported the public staging of *The Impostor* since 1979. However, during the Fourth All-China Congress of Writers and Artists held in Peking at the end of that year, *The Impostor* along with a number of similar works that were construed as being critical of older cadres and sympathetic towards youthful criminals became the object of heated debate. *The Impostor* was staged a number of times during the congress for the

---

[5]From *Searching* 探索集, volume two of *Random Thoughts*, by Ba Jin, Beijing 1981, pp. 4-7.

convenience of the delegates, but no overall consensus as to just how the questions it raised should be treated in the arts was reached. Concerned by the lack of unanimity in what was the first major cultural gathering since before the Cultural Revolution, another meeting was organized for January 1980, when the play was again the object of considerable attention.[6] Although organized in the name of the Dramatists', Film-makers' and Writers' Associations, the meeting reached a climax when Hu Yaobang made a lengthy speech which has since acquired the status of a major policy statement on culture. In it he prefaces his comments on *The Impostor* and like works with the words:

> We must pay attention to the following points:
> 1. It is vital that an isolated phenomenon should not be made into artistic reality. Artistic reality should be based on real types (典型) and essential reality;
> 2. Something that is no more than a transient phenomenon should not be represented as an immutable and unchanging reality. [Writing] should reflect the dialectic of historical development.
> It is my feeling that our socialist authors should keep these [points] in mind regardless of whether they write tragedies or comedies; or whether their works show positive or negative [aspects of society]. They will only produce works that can achieve some degree of success if they write like this.[7]

After a few prefatory remarks about Gogol's *The Government Inspector* and the nature of the society it criticized, Hu directed a number of fairly withering comments at *The Impostor* and the play's authors:—

> Which of the works that have appeared in the last three years then are to be found lacking, unsuccessful and negative in their social effect? I haven't read a great deal, so I'll have to ask you to reflect on this question yourselves. Two months ago I flicked through *If I Were Real*, and made a few comments on it at a meeting. Today, in the presence of the authors and you other comrades, I'd like to repeat [those comments], and lay my heart bare before you. If you think I'm right, I still hope you'll discuss [what I say]; if I'm wrong, then I welcome your criticisms.
> In my opinion, the writers [of the play] are talented and they have a future ahead of them. In dealing with problems involving young writers we must not repeat the errors of the past: we should not disparage them or attack them. In this context I made some mistakes when dealing with young writers before the 'Great Cultural Revolution'. The comrades in question were talented but their works were

---

[6] See 'Précis of the Proceedings at the Symposium on Scenario- and Play-writing' 劇本創作座談會情況簡述, *Wenyibao* 文藝報, April 1980, pp. 2-8; *Zhengming*, April 1980, p. 56; *The Seventies*, June 1980, pp. 84-5; and, *Shanghai Drama*, January 1981, pp. 2-5.

[7] The full text of this speech was made public in the first issue of *Wenyibao* 1981, pp. 2-20. For this quotation, see pp. 12-3.

lacking in maturity; they needed our help, but our policy towards them was incorrect. But, now they are back again and are accomplished writers. If any of those middle-aged writers was to say in one of their works that 'the old goat So-and-so made an error in dealing with my case', I would approve because that's the truth.

As I see it, *If I Were Real* is not a mature work; it contains some serious defects. I might be wrong, however. Now, what do I mean when I say it is not a mature work? First and most importantly, I feel that the characters that form the human scenery of the work give a [collective] impression [of the society] since the Third Plenum that is neither sufficiently real nor typical. At the end [of the play], a positive character, Lao Zhang, does make an appearance, and that is laudable, to be sure; but he's still an outsider. He appears as a liberator, and definitely has something of the saviour about him. Furthermore, characters that deserve no sympathy at all are unabashedly indulged. Do people like Li Xiaozhang actually exist? Of course they do. But what we've got in this play is countryside youth being represented as willing to resort to any means of deception to get back to the city. The character is a morally low being with an equally low awareness. His sole motivation in life is to get back to the city, and he is prepared to do anything to achieve this goal. By creating such a character the authors have failed to reflect the true spirit and moral perception of Chinese youth during the New Period. The broad masses of young people surely would, on reflection, feel affronted by this misrepresentation. What could have produced such a cheat? The play lays the onus of responsibility on the corrupt cadres, and by so doing treats the cheat with even greater sympathy. These are the faults of the play.

This play has been staged for quite some time, and I believe there's been a mixed reaction to it. These reactions must be seen in context. Some young people, in particular those who want to return to the cities, or parents with children in the countryside, may well react to this play positively. Another group is convinced that there will be trouble if certain special privileges enjoyed by leading cadres go unchecked, and they are in favour of exposing them. Insofar as the play works towards this end, it has performed a positive service. However, if it is permitted to be staged as it is, we must ask ourselves: what other social effects will it have? This question deserves reflection. We need to make a serious and detailed study of just how [artistic] works can be used to make a more accurate criticism of our faults so that they achieve the desired result of uniting and educating the people. In fact, the masses and cadres have already expressed a range of differing opinions concerning this work. Naturally, not all of the views expressed are correct; but some deserve our attention. We are in support of artistic works that make a correct exposé and criticism of unhealthy tendencies among party and state cadres. At the same time, we hope that our writers will sum up their experience and achieve new heights in their ideological understanding and creative expression. [. . .] As for the problem of what should be done with this particular play,— there's no problem at all. If, when everyone has finished discussing it, the writers themselves feel it is not a successful work and that it requires major revisions, I think they should volunteer the following: 'If [the play] can't be revised satisfactorily, we agree that it should not be performed. And performances of it should be stopped for the time being.'

Units that have been performing the play as well as propaganda organizations are free to express their opinions [about the work], and they can offer the writers sincere and dispassionate help in their task. They should certainly not remain silent for fear of being accused of wielding sticks [打棍子]. To express an opinion and to use a stick to beat a work are very different things. We don't wield sticks; we use the format of a comradely discussion to raise the ideological and artistic level [of our writers]. Everyone has to be responsible to the broad masses, after all; and responsible to the 'Four Modernizations'. I believe the author is prepared to revise the play on the basis of everyone's criticisms. We hope he makes a good job of it.[8]

Only two days after this speech was made the first voice was raised in public dissent. Again, it was the voice of Ba Jin. On February 15, 1980 in an article entitled "Further Comments on Searching" 再談探索,[9] he wrote, "There is no need to be afraid of works of literature that go crashing around like an elephant in a china shop. [To have any influence on people at all] they still have to pass through three tests: that of [their audience's] social conditioning, home education and school education. Only the most simple-minded accept everything they read uncritically, and that's only because they have nothing in their heads to start off with—there's lots of room for new things up there. Such people are rare. So surely it is just a little unfair to make works of literature responsible for absolutely everything."[10] Commenting that there are still people who are against 'scar literature' 傷痕文學, he continued, "Yet even today there are those who think the scars will heal themselves as long as we keep them covered up and don't talk about them. They are not surprised that they get sores, but they are furious when others make an issue of them. When they are getting ready to let fly at a work they suddenly start making a big thing of the influence of literature . . . ."[11]

A pointed comment indeed, but the argument in favour of limiting the availability of works which had the potential of encouraging negative 'copyist phenomena' won the day, even though the debate over 'social effect' 社會效果 had only just begun. The meeting and Hu Yaobang's speech were taken by many writers as being the first direct act of government and Party intervention in the arts since the Cultural Revolution. Not surprisingly, Sha Yexin, having been the major target for criticism, was particularly outspoken on the subject. He claimed that although the meeting had not condemned his play as a 'poisonous weed' as such, it had had the effect of a caveat on further performances which amounted to a ban (變相禁戲). The concept of 'social effect' that had been first introduced at this meeting, he said, had

[8]*Ibid.*, pp. 13-4.

[9]*Searching*, pp. 33-7.

[10]*Ibid.*, pp. 36-7.

[11]*Ibid.*, p. 37. For the significance of the timing of this essay, see Bi Hua's 璧華 'Memorializing the CPC —a critique of Ba Jin's *Random Thoughts*' 中共文藝的諍言——評巴金的《隨想錄》, *The Seventies*, April 1980, pp. 61-3.

provided a theoretical basis for this 'virtual ban' which in turn gave certain particularly dogmatic and heavy-handed leaders an excuse to suppress works they did not
favour. He concluded that the upshot of all this was that most writers had begun
shying away from writing works that 'interfere with life' 干預生活 in 1980, and
that the cultural scene in general had suffered severely because of this meeting.[12]

Sha also claimed that although Hu Yaobang and others at the meeting had
suggested that he revise *The Impostor* so as to make it fit for public display, he was
not given a chance to do so.[13] This contention was subsequently disputed by a
number of people who had attended the meeting and had hoped the play could be
revised.[14] Although it is by no means certain that Sha was actually forestalled from
revising the play, by mid-1980 his energies were otherwise engaged in the production
of a major new work, *Mayor Chen Yi* 陳毅市長.[15] In fact, both Sha and his co-author
Yao Mingde when faced with the alternatives of either revising *The Impostor* or
going on to other things, are reported as having said, "We have put the play out of
our minds."[16] However, as the innocuous *Mayor Chen Yi*—which was earmarked
as being one of the major cultural presentations for the celebration of the thirtieth
anniversary of the liberation of Shanghai—was bringing Sha back into favour with
the cultural establishment and the authorities in Shanghai, he wrote a caustic article
about the genesis of *The Impostor* and the opposition it had encountered. In his
own defence he quoted extensively from Ba Jin (see "The Little Impostor") and in
reply to the charge that his work would have a 'negative social effect' he cited other
instances of fraud that had absolutely nothing to do with the play—"it is not art
that has 'exaggerated' life; for life is always more 'exaggerated' than art."[17] In
conclusion he states, "In my opinion, no one has the right to bring down a final
judgement on the effect of a work in the name of the whole 'society'. Let [social]
practice be the impartial judge. History itself is fairminded, and I am convinced
that in the end it will be history that will find the most reasonable and acceptable
conclusion to the arguments surrounding *The Impostor*."[18]

The question of 'social effect', however, dominated the cultural world throughout 1980; and, in fact, it continues to do so today. Ba Jin in a tone of innocent
candour that reflects a hard-won self-awareness continued his 'defence' for *The
Impostor* in "More on the Little Impostor" 再談小騙子. I quote in full:—

[12] See *Wenyibao*, October 1980, pp. 24-6.

[13] *Ibid.*, pp. 25-6.

[14] 'Not Chatter, but a Wish' 并非閑話，而是期望，
by Huang Mei 荒煤, *Wenyibao*, December 1980, pp.
23-5; 'More Chatter on "扯淡"' 也扯〈扯淡〉, by Feng
Zi 鳳子, *ibid.*, pp. 25-6; and 'My Interjection—
concerning the revision of *The Impostor*' 一段插話——
關於〈騙子〉的修改 by Liu Jin 劉金, *Wenyibao*,
February 1981, pp. 38-9.

[15] A ten-act play published in *Plays* 劇本, May
1980, pp. 2-39; see also Sha Yexin's 'On the Publication of *Mayor Chen Yi*' 寫在〈陳毅市長〉發表的時候,
ibid., p. 40. This play followed on from *Advance
on the East!* 東進，東進 and *Chen Yi Emerges From*

the Mountains 陳毅出山, as part of the stage (and
subsequently screen) representation of Chen Yi. This
was one of the first major 'adaptations' of the figure
of a deceased government leader for the arts.

[16] See 'After the Staging of *If I Were Real*' 關於
〈假〉劇演出以後的一些情況, by Zheng Huaizhi 鄭懷之,
Wenhuibao, February 2, 1981.

[17] See *Shanghai Drama*, June 1980, p. 5.

[18] *Ibid.*, also see Xie Junhua 謝俊華, 'Summing
Up Experience, Determined to Reform' 總結經驗,
立志改革 in *Yalu River* 鴨綠江, January 1981, pp.
58-60, for a detailed comment on the deleterious
effect of the Symposium on the cultural world in
1980.

One question that has concerned me for the last two or three years is whether it is a good idea to lie about an illness for fear of getting treatment. The conclusion I'm led to is: definitely not. However, some people would not agree. In their opinion if you don't tell anyone what is wrong with you then the very fact that you are sick will remain a secret. According to such thinking, if you have a healthy constitution then any ailment you have can cure itself: a major illness will gradually become a small one and eventually disappear altogether.

But what happens when these people do become ill? Are we supposed to believe that they don't go to the doctor? Or, don't even take medicine? In the past I was quite the innocent, but I'm a little more astute these days. Despite the fact that there are those who say I've retrogressed, that my writing is 'ungrammatical',[19] my understanding of people and events is a little deeper and thorough [than in the past] , and I'm not deluded so easily now.

I wrote one of my 'random thoughts' in late September last year in which I talked about a little impostor. At the time he had already been arrested and a play based on him was being staged. There were all sorts of reactions to that play, and it was even condemned on the grounds that it showed the impostor in a sympathetic light, and attempted to excuse his crimes. Accordingly it was declared that this type of play had a negative social effect and that showing it would encourage juvenile criminality, and so on and so forth. Therefore the play was not to be performed or published, 'a domestic shame should not be made public'. I haven't seen the play, but I have read it. I sympathize with those people who were cheated as well as with the little impostor. In my view, it is the social environment that we should be condemning. Rough and flawed the play may certainly be—it is like a comic skit in street theatre—but it lashes out at unhealthy social tendencies, and attacks attitudes towards social privilege. It is like a bucket of cold water thrown in the face of a person in a swoon. To my mind, the staging of the play had a very salutary effect. The play I'm talking about is called *If I Were Real*. This is what I have thought about it all along, and I have done nothing to hide my opinion. When I was in Peking for the Fourth All-China Congress of Writers and Artists I made an appeal to the leading comrades in the government that they allow this play to be performed. During the congress the play was shown a number of times, and on one occasion during a casual conversation I had with my driver he suddenly said that he had seen it and thought it wasn't at all bad. He commented that they should let it be shown.

I'm not all too clear as to the exact number of performances that have been given. But I am aware that subsequently a meeting was held in Peking to discuss the play. The playwrights were there and the defects of the play were gone into. Following on from that I heard that [the main] playwright had written another play that was very

[19]This refers to the criticisms of Ba Jin's essays by a number of Hong Kong University students, see *Kaijuan* 開卷 September 1980, pp. 54-6, 'What We Think of Ba Jin's *Random Thoughts*'; and 'Further Comments on Telling the Truth' 再論說眞話, *Searching*, p. 93.

popular. After that there was no more talk of the little impostor. His sentence, 'If I were really . . . ' was forgotten, well, at least until other little impostors made their appearance.

On the second page of the September 23 issue of the Shanghai *Liberation Daily*, there was the following item of news, 'Another Impostor Fools Certain Leading Cadres.' Of course, this is not referring to that other little impostor by the name of Zhang; he has been tried and sentenced. This time it is a fellow by the name of Wu. It turns out that he has been impersonating the 'nephew of a leading cadre who works in the municipal government'. He claimed he was a Section Head in the Harbin Tourist Bureau, and he 'bought a large quantity of high-quality cigarettes which he was planning to sell [at a profit] in the provinces.' Upon being eventually caught out he said, 'Everything's a question of privilege in this society; if I hadn't used people the way I did I would never have been able to buy any cigarettes . . . . '

This little impostor has been nabbed; but he is not necessarily repentant. He is smarter than any of us: while we are all tying ourselves up in knots over such questions as 'family honour', 'face' and 'scars', he's got down to brass tacks. Forbidding people from performing plays about it isn't going to solve a thing.

I have been asked whether by using the word 'little' when referring to the impostor I mean to absolve him of some guilt. Most certainly not! However, there are little impostors and big impostors. People like Zhang and Wu are only little impostors. Then there are the big impostors; and there are a lot of them. Those people who created a god and conjured up hosts of demons, with their trumped up charges and accusations, false statistics and forced 'suicides' . . . . All of those big impostors have been out of the reach of the law for long enough. Everyone is waiting for news of *their* trial. So am I.

October 9, [1980][20]

The trials of the 'big impostors' began at the end of 1980, but the problem of little impostors continued.[21] And, although *The Impostor* was never revised and was staged with only the greatest difficulty, its 'social effect' had been significant. Despite being a fairly conventional stage play in theatrical terms, certain elements of *The Impostor* presaged the new range of expression of the Chinese arts in the 80s. Naturally, it was not unique in doing so; but its contribution is undeniable. The most important aspect of the play in this context was the fact that the writers had chosen to portray the impostor in a favourable light. This was pure anathema to those with an unrelenting class view—why, it was tantamount to selling out to the enemy.[22] The play depicts Li Xiaozhang not as a hero—that was a matter left

[20] *Searching*, pp. 104-6.

[21] There were a number of other cases of fraud similar to that of Zhang Longquan in 1980-1, and also at least two telefeatures inspired by *The Impostor* screened in late 1980 and early 1981. There were 'Who is he?' 他是誰? made by Beijing Television

and 'A Dream That's No Dream' 似夢非夢, produced by Yunnan Television. See "A Third Article on Impostors" 三談騙子 by Ba Jin, in *Telling the Truth* 眞話集 (the third volume of *Random Thoughts*), Hong Kong 1982, p. 1.

[22] See *Wenyibao*, April 1980, p. 4.

to the audiences—but rather as a human being. Motivated by reasonable, under-standable and quite common needs and being a character-type familiar to the average Chinese urban-dweller, Li Xiaozhang had resorted to criminal means to protect and advance himself. He starts out as a victim of social inequities, and then ironically, having had a taste of the 'good life' as proferred by privileged society, he becomes a victim of those very inequities in reverse! He is not fated by birth or association to fall into perdition, but ultimately must be viewed as the engineer of his own tragedy; however, the writers are quite insistent in their desire to blame society as a whole for Li's plight, and the impostor's question, "If I were really . . . ?" could just as well be translated simply as "j'accuse". Sha Yexin says that the play condemns Li the fraud and criminal at the same time as recognizing the reasons that drove him to crime: the Cultural Revolution and his loss of the right to live in the city, his lack of education, and most importantly the 'encouragement' he gets from those cadres who are besotted with their dreams of privilege and social status. This is the reason, Sha argues, why so many people sympathize with the impostor and feel little or nothing for his victims.[23]

The Impostor is one of many works that although still typical of the 'scar literature' of 1978-9, had already moved away from simply dwelling on the past and the problems resultant from the Cultural Revolution towards a more direct study of the present. In ideological terms it foreshadowed some of the concerns of Chinese 'humanism' and 'modernism', especially in their emphasis on the in-dividual.[24] Artistic interest in and appreciation of the 'anti-hero', that is, a figure who would previously have been treated as a negative or at best 'middle' character, has grown considerably since 1979, and works such as Teng Wenji's 滕文驥 film *Village in the City* 都市裏的村莊 (1983) which has as its major theme the love story of a model worker and a petty hood, Gao Xingjian's first play, *Alarm Signal*, in which the protagonist is a petty thief, and many other films, plays and stories, reflect this new dimension of understanding.

It is because *The Impostor* had had such an impact that, although presumably forgotten since the Symposium 'ban' of early 1980, the play and its main author were to be subjected to further criticism in the aftermath of the 'Bai Hua Incident' of 1981.

The first warning of this came in early November 1981, when Du Gao 杜高, a professional critic employed by the Dramatists' Association, wrote an article on 'social effect' citing the case of Gorky's opposition to the production of a stage version of Dostoyevsky's *The Devils* in 1913 on the grounds that it would be

---

[23] See *Shanghai Drama*, June 1980, p. 5.

[24] The Chinese press carried numerous articles on the question of 'abstract humanity' as part of the drive to 'clean up spiritual pollution'. Zhou Yuanbing, a noted Chinese expert on ethics, summed the problem up rather neatly in an interview: "If the notion of abstract humanity is encouraged, there will be no end of strife. Why, people will start saying, 'Workers have an intrinsic value, as do university students and cadres.' This will lead to people arguing that it is in-human to send people to work in the border regions, that to do so shows a disregard for the value of the individual. It is precisely thinking like this that has been poisoning the minds of the masses, turning them into selfish individualists. Such thinking is detrimental to our socialist cause, and will do nothing but harm to the [correct] development of one's self." See *Guang-ming Daily*, November 5, 1983.

harmful to the audience.[25] Du goes on to laud the 1980 Symposium and, without naming him, criticizes Sha Yexin and his talk of 'disguised bans', and so on. He then bewails the fact that a drama journal had actually gone so far as to praise the staging of *Girl Thief* and *The Impostor* in the spring as a 'victory for the coura-geous'.[26] From the appearance of this article in the *People's Daily* it was clear that more was in store for *The Impostor* and Sha. It was only a few weeks later, at the end of November 1981, that the CPC Ministry of Propaganda held another major Symposium on Scenario- and Play-writing. The press release issued after the sym-posium revealed that:—

> At the Symposium on Scenario- and Play-writing in February 1980, following a democratic exchange concerning *If I Were Real* and other controversial works, a leading comrade from the Centre raised a number of important points in regard to cultural work in the new period. However, due to a serious failure in propagating and carrying out the spirit of that meeting, there has been a marked lack of aware-ness of bourgeois liberalism and its influence on creative writing, resulting, for a time, in a situation in which certain incorrect opinions that clash directly with the spirit of the Centre have gained currency in the theatre world. It has been commented that the [earlier Sym-posium] 'set a precedent for "disguised bans"', and there is a mistaken view that 'the raising of the theory of "social effect" has had a negative social effect in itself'. Those who hold to this view go so far as to claim that the theory of social effect is 'a stick' 棍子 and 'a restriction' 框子, as well as suggesting that 'it is still impossible to say whether the Symposium' was a success. Some journals have been engaged in dis-seminating seriously incorrect opinions that are in direct opposition to the spirit of the Symposium, and they declare that writers need to fortify themselves so they don't buckle under (長幾塊反骨), and that they should 'loudly sing discordant notes'. Such journals have also continued to encourage the production of *If I Were Real* and other such flawed works. It should be noted that this tendency to oppose the Symposium has not been universal, and there has been resistance to some [incorrect] views. However, in general the theatre world has been most obviously polluted by this type of bourgeois liberalism.[27]

The intriguing thing is that in the 1980-1 period, although there was a marked drop in the amount of 'social comment' and 'dark side' literature that appeared as a result of the various strictures that had been placed on works that 'interfered with life', there was an increased interest in a more subtle, even insidious type of writing. Some authors, reluctant to deal with larger social issues and questions of the moment, were thrown back on themselves, and it was perhaps the 1980 'crack down' 收 that gave an important impetus to the development of the 'humanist' and 'modernist' aspects of contemporary Chinese literature.

[25] See *People's Daily*, November 11, 1983.

[26] *Ibid.*

[27] See *People's Drama* 人民戲劇, April 1982, p. 31.

Following the success of *Mayor Chen Yi* and what must have been a salutary period of self-reflection resulting from his 1980 defence of *The Impostor*, Sha Yexin came to prominence again with the production of *The Secret Life of Marx* 馬克思秘史. The popularity of *Mayor Chen Yi* seems to have emboldened the writer to attempt the stage presentation of other famous personages; but in writing a play for the centenary of Marx's death Sha may not have been aware of just how dangerous it was to try and 'humanize' the figure of Marx in 1983.

This new work chronicles Marx's private life during the period when he was working on *Das Kapital*. The play shows Marx as a garrulous, loving, at times generous and sometimes also quite petty man. For some critics, however, it is a play that makes Marx out to be all *too* human. Again, it is Sha Yexin's old 'sparring partner', Du Gao, who takes the playwright to task for his new work. In an article published in the *Guangming Daily* Du says:—

> Certain playwrights having fallen prey to the influence of the bourgeois theories of humanity and humanism, have made strenuous attempts to represent abstract 'man' and human nature [on the stage]. Both of the plays depicting Marx that have been published this year obviously belong to this category.[28] The authors set Marx the Revolutionary against the so-called Marx the 'Man' and they even imply that a description of Marx's revolutionary activities only weakens and dulls the image of Marx the 'Man'. One of the playwrights has written a prelude to his work with the express aim of underlining this view. [See below] ... Having taken this as his approach, our writer directs his attention to a study of the trivia of Marx's life, and he does everything in his power to create the figure of a thoroughly human man who was 'a good husband, a good father and a good friend'. He even opines that to do so is a more arduous and meaningful task than it was for Marx to write *Das Kapital*! We cannot but query: If in a play about Marx's life one does not exhaust oneself in the realistic description of Marx's tremendous revolutionary experience, or in the realization of his lofty revolutionary spirit that was devoted to the cause of liberating the working class and also his communist thinking and ideals, then what is there left of Marx the 'Man'?
>
> How can such a play possibly help audiences understand anything about Marx, or for that matter show them what they have to learn from him? What we are looking for and encouraging in the arts is the artistic depiction of the individuality of leadership figures. While carefully avoiding simplification and conceptualization in doing so, we desire the vivid vision of the richness of the spiritual world of great men. It is on this point that both of the above playwrights are in complete disagreement with us.[29]

---

[28]The other play Du is referring to is *The Season of Cherries* 櫻桃時節, which is based on a longer French work entitled *The Paris Commune*.

[29]See *Guangming Daily*, November 3, 1983.

As a play, Sha's *The Secret History of Marx* is staid and uninteresting,[30] showing none of the innovative promise of Gao Xingjian's *The Bus-stop*. Nevertheless, it is a daring and important work. Sha, all too mindful of the caveat on 'humanizing' bad elements, turned his hand to the 'demystification' of the awesome father of scientific socialism. It was bad enough that he had used the words 'secret history' 秘史 in the title of the play—words rarely used in the arts in China since Mao's condemnation of Yao Ke's 姚克 *Secret History of the Qing Court* 清宮秘史 in the early 50s—but the possibility that it would set a precedent for writing about the private nitty-gritty of the great for the stage was just too much. The full seriousness of Sha's error, however, is only clear when considered in the light of the Zhou Yang 周揚—Wang Ruoshui 王若水 speech on alienation. By late 1983, it was inevitable that the play would be denounced as a 'spiritual pollutant'.

We may not have seen the last of *The Secret History of Marx*, and we will definitely be hearing more of Sha Yexin.

[30]My own reaction to the play which I saw during its opening season in Shanghai in April 1983, was as follows: "It is a tedious and over-acted fantasy about Marx's private life performed by beefy and hirsute Chinese actors who prance around the stage in wigs and late-nineteenth century drag. The word 'secret' in the title nearly got the play banned, but once official approval was obtained the word got out that no, there were no juicy scenes between Karl and Jenny, nor any startling revelations about Engels' private life. I only managed to steel myself for the first two acts of the play. I heard later that it had a reasonable run courtesy of the municipal labour unions and Youth League organisation, who rallied their members and sent them along by the busload to have an evening of indulgence in this 'vivid stage realization of political struggle'." See, *Chinese Drama: To Be Or Not, The Australian Journal of Chinese Affairs*, No. 10, 1983, p. 144.

沙葉新、李守成、姚明德：假如我是眞的

The Impostor (If I Were Real)

By Sha Yexin, Li Shoucheng, and Yao Mingde

Translated by Daniel Kane

With twelve illustrations by Ah Wu

Characters:

THEATRE DIRECTOR ZHAO:	Director of a Theatrical Troupe
DIVISION HEAD QIAN:	Head of the Political Division of the Organization Department
SECTION HEAD SUN:	Head of the Cultural Affairs Section
LI XIAOZHANG:	A "rusticated intellectual youth"
ZHOU MINGHUA:	A worker in a cotton mill; Li Xiaozhang's girlfriend
SECRETARY WU:	The Secretary of the Municipal Committee
FARM DIRECTOR ZHENG:	Director of a State Farm
JUANJUAN:	Section Head Sun's daughter
VENERABLE COMRADE ZHANG:	Responsible Cadre from the Central Committee's Discipline Commission

PUBLIC SECURITY OFFICERS A & B
BYSTANDERS A, B, C, D, E & F
THEATRE ATTENDANT
A MIDDLE AGED MAN
RESTAURANT ATTENDANT
INTELLECTUAL YOUTHS A & B
JUDGE
ASSESSORS A & B
PROSECUTOR

"Can't a concept serve the same purpose as its opposite? Can't comedy and tragedy express the same sublimity? Can't an examination of shamelessness delineate high moral standards? Does not all illegality and lack of discipline, scandal and debauchery show us what law, duty and justice really ought to be?"

Gogol: At the Theatre's Door

PROLOGUE

The theatre has its basis in life.
This play of ours is also based on life, on a true story.
Since the curtain has not yet risen, why don't we start our play from the actual living situation in front of us?

All right then. Take a look at our dear, loyal audience, which has flocked to this theatre tonight. Of course, at this stage, they know nothing about our play, "If I were real", and perhaps they are sitting in their seats, thumbing through the programme notes, hoping to find out what the play is all about. Or perhaps they are standing around in the foyer, part of the motley crowd out there, chatting with their friends, and trying to guess the plot. Or perhaps they are having a smoke, or eating some ice-cream, carefree and leisurely, not caring to use their brains at all. . . .

Before long, urged along by the bell, the audience files into the theatre, sits down quietly, and, with bated breath—or perhaps without any interest at all—waits for the curtain to rise.

At last, the play is about to begin. The lights are dimmed, the music starts, the audience open their eyes wide, concentrating on the stage. But suddenly the music stops and the lights are turned on again. Behind the screen, THEATRE DIRECTOR ZHAO can be heard shouting "Turn the lights off! The curtain's about to rise!" But the curtain, which has just separated slightly at the centre, closes again. A short time later, THEATRE DIRECTOR ZHAO walks on to the stage, from the side, and moves to the centre.

ZHAO: Comrades. My deepest apologies. It's time for the play to begin but—er—there are two leading comrades and an honoured guest who haven't arrived yet. Please wait a little longer. This sort of thing often happens here—there's nothing unusual about it. Don't worry, comrades, the play will be performed, just wait a while. As soon as they come, we'll start immediately. I'm terribly sorry. My deepest apologies.

When THEATRE DIRECTOR ZHAO has finished, she walks off the stage. What sort of reaction does the audience have to this? Helpless grumbling? Expressions of deep discontent? Fierce protest? Loud cursing? Each of the audience expresses his opinion about this sort of thing in his own way. Or at least he ought to.

There is a flurry of murmuring, and THEATRE DIRECTOR ZHAO pokes her head out from the side of the stage, and looks towards the exit. Suddenly, a look of pleasant surprise appears on her face. The audience, of course, follows her gaze towards the exit at the side of the theatre.

Then, under the gaze of the audience, the Head of the Political Division of the Organization Department, DIVISION HEAD QIAN (who is the wife of the Secretary of the Municipal Committee) enters, carrying herself with great dignity. She is followed by the Head of the Cultural Affairs Section, SECTION HEAD SUN, who is looking particularly solemn. The audience must think that these two are the honoured guests for whom they have been respectfully waiting so long, but this is not, in fact, the case. They beckon, and a young man enters the theatre. This is the real honoured guest. His name is LI XIAOZHANG, but he is using the name ZHANG XIAOLI. DIVISION HEAD QIAN and SECTION HEAD SUN say to him, respectfully, and in hushed tones "After you, after you. . . ." Then, clustering around him, they go straight to three empty seats in the front row, just off the aisle. After they have settled themselves, THEATRE DIRECTOR ZHAO's voice can be heard from behind the curtain "They've arrived! Get ready to raise the curtain!"

The music starts again. Suddenly, again from the exit at the side of the theatre, two armed officers of the Public Security Bureau come in, and quickly move to where LI XIAOZHANG is sitting.

PUBLIC SECURITY OFFICER: *(to* LI XIAOZHANG*)* Li Xiaozhang, you're under arrest!

DIVISION HEAD QIAN: *(greatly surprised)* What? What? His name isn't Li Xiaozhang. You can't just go around arresting people!

PUBLIC SECURITY OFFICER: *(showing the arrest warrant)* This is the arrest warrant! *(Another* PUBLIC SECURITY OFFICER *puts handcuffs on* LI XIAOZHANG.*)*

SECTION HEAD SUN: Let him go! You've made a mistake! Do you know who he is?

PUBLIC SECURITY OFFICER: You tell me!

SECTION HEAD SUN: His name is Zhang Xiaoli!

DIVISION HEAD QIAN: He's the son of a Central Committee member—one of our leaders!

PUBLIC SECURITY OFFICER: No. He's an impostor!

QIAN, SUN: Eh?

    *(*THEATRE DIRECTOR ZHAO *runs from the side of the stage, to the centre.)*

ZHAO: What's going on? What's happening? How can you expect us to perform our play? *(To the* PUBLIC SECURITY OFFICER*)*: Comrade, would you mind explaining what this is all about?

PUBLIC SECURITY OFFICER: Very well. *(The two* PUBLIC SECURITY OFFICERS, LI XIAOZHANG, DIVISION HEAD QIAN *and* SECTION HEAD SUN *all go on to the stage.)*

PUBLIC SECURITY OFFICER: Comrades! My deepest apologies for having disturbed you.

PUBLIC SECURITY OFFICER: This man is an impostor. His name is Li Xiaozhang, but he has been going under the name of Zhang Xiaoli. He is really a "rusticated intellectual youth", but he has been pretending to be the son of a Central Committee member and he has been swindling his way all over this city. There was a danger that he would escape, so we have to take emergency measures to arrest him here.

ZHAO: What?! *(To* LI XIAOZHANG*)* Is this true?

LI XIAOZHANG: Aren't you performing a play here tonight? I have just been acting out a role, too. Now my performance is over. You can continue with yours!

ZHAO: Eh?

QIAN: You . . . !

SUN: Oh!

    (The spotlight settles on the faces of LI XIAOZHANG, THEATRE DIRECTOR ZHAO, DIVISION HEAD QIAN *and* SECTION HEAD SUN, *one after the other. Then the lights dim.)*

ACT I

Early evening on a day in the first half of 1979. The main entrance of the theatre.

(If this play has the good fortune to be performed in a theatre, the stage setting for this act should be exactly the same as the main entrance of that theatre, or at least should closely resemble it.)

There is a large advertising poster on the wall of the theatre. "Such-and-such Theatre Company is Performing the Russian Satirical Comedy 'The Inspector General'." There is a portrait of Khlestakov on the poster.

It is obviously a full house. A number of people are waiting around, hoping that some one will turn up with extra tickets. They have money in their hands, and, whenever anyone approaches, they rush over and say "Do you have any tickets?" If anyone has, a great crowd of people mills around, pushing and shoving. Those who get a ticket are deliriously happy, and can't stop thanking whomever sold it to them, and they enter the theatre, very pleased with themselves. Those who miss out are disappointed but not discouraged; they continue to ask around. This scene should be played realistically and naturally, so as to make the audience believe it is genuine. They will then identify with the players on the stage—or, they will believe that they themselves are in the play.

LI XIAOZHANG is wearing an old military uniform, and has a soldier's satchel over his shoulder. A cigarette is hanging from one side of his mouth; he occasionally blows smoke rings. He is nonchalantly watching the scene at the main entrance of the theatre. He throws his cigarette butt away, and fishes something out from his pocket. One of the bystanders quickly goes over to him.

BYSTANDER A: *(urgently)* Do you have a ticket?
LI XIAOZHANG: A ticket?
BYSTANDER A: Yeah.
LI: *(with a drawl)* Well . . . yes!
BYSTANDER A: *(extremely excited)* Great!
     (*Other members of the crowd hear that* LI XIAOZHANG *has a ticket, and he is immediately surrounded. They are shouting "Give it to me! Give it to me!" or "I want it! I want it!"* LI XIAOZHANG *is almost knocked off his feet, and is forced to the wall.*)
BYSTANDER A: You should give it to me. I got

here first!
BYSTANDER B: I'll swap your ticket for ten movie tickets!
BYSTANDER C: Give it to me! I'll give you three *yuan* for it—how about that?
LI: Don't quarrel. I've got enough for all of you. Just queue up now, queue up!
     (*The crowd, muttering, lines up in front of* LI XIAOZHANG, *in a long queue.*)
LI: Calm down, calm down! I've got plenty of tickets. Everyone has. Some you can use all over China, some are just local ones!
BYSTANDER A: What?
BYSTANDER B: You can use some all over China? And local ones, too?
BYSTANDER C: What sort of tickets are you talking about?
LI: *(Taking out his wallet, he takes out a few ration coupons.)* Here! Ration tickets!
BYSTANDER A: Eh?
BYSTANDER B: What sort of a joke is this?
LI: Aren't ration tickets tickets? They're the most important kind of tickets. If you don't have these, you'll go hungry!
BYSTANDER B: Bloody fool!
BYSTANDER D: Bash him!
LI: *(without changing the tone of his voice)* Do you want to try? Well?
BYSTANDER B: Forget it. Let's go. Let's go.
     (*They leave, dejected.*)
BYSTANDER A: Comrade, you shouldn't deceive people like that!
LI: I'm just playing a joke on them, that's all. Anyway, what's wrong with deceiving people? Isn't performing a play deceiving people? There is so much acting going on in the real world, but you don't notice it—you just want to go to the theatre to watch plays instead. Isn't that deceiving yourself?
BYSTANDER A: You are ignorant. The play being performed today is the world-famous "The Inspector General".
LI: Oh. "The Inspector General"? Is it good?
BYSTANDER A: It's really interesting. It's about an ordinary twelfth-grade clerk of St. Petersburg who happens to be passing through a certain city. The Mayor of that city thinks that he is the Inspector General, so he crawls and panders

to him, gives him money and presents—even wants to marry his daughter off to him. You'll split your sides laughing!

LI: Oh? The Inspector General was an impostor?

BYSTANDER A: Yes. An impostor.

(LI XIAOZHANG immediately goes over to the advertising poster, and looks at it with great interest. After a few moments he glances at his watch, and looks into the distance. Before long, ZHOU MINGHUA hurries onto the stage, carrying a small satchel.)

ZHOU MINGHUA: Li Xiaozhang!

LI: Minghua! Just look—you're late again.

ZHOU: My father wouldn't let me come out.

LI: The silly old fool . . . .

ZHOU: How can you . . . ?!

LI: He is a silly old fool. Last time I went to your place he took no notice of me at all!

ZHOU: You can't talk about my father like that. *(She takes a bottle of* maotai *out of the satchel)* Look. My father told me to give this back to you.

LI: *(surprised)* Eh? He drank it?

ZHOU: Drank what? He didn't drink anything!

LI: *(taking the bottle)* Oh.

ZHOU: Why did you give him a bottle of *maotai*?

LI: To butter up my future father-in-law.

ZHOU: You're really extravagant. Fancy buying such an expensive wine!

LI: It's not real.

ZHOU: What? This *maotai*'s not real?

LI: Do you think I could afford it? The bottle's genuine enough—I bought it at a junk shop—it cost me twenty *fen*. Inside it's just one *yuan* twenty low-grade plonk!

ZHOU: Eh? Weren't you afraid my father would notice?

LI: People only ever look at the outside appearance of things . . . your father's no exception.

ZHOU: Why did you do it?

LI: To get your father on our side—because of you—and me . . . .

ZHOU: You'd better get transferred back from the countryside then, and fast. Otherwise, no matter what you give him, he'll never approve of our being friends. Get transferred back, quickly!

LI: *(worried)* It really is a problem.

ZHOU: I'm trying to think of some way out. In fact, you're very smart and capable, too. You should be able to find a way. Other people get transferred back—why can't you? A lot of the people I used to go to school with got transferred back long ago.

LI: What do their fathers do?

ZHOU: One of them is the Party Secretary of our factory, another is a Deputy Commander in the Navy . . . another—the father of one of my friends—is the Head of the Cultural Affairs Section.

LI: No wonder they can get transferred back. But what does my father do? *(He makes a thumbs-up sign, and says sarcastically)*—he is a member of the so-called "leading class"—he's a worker—one of the selfless working classes. What bloody use is that? I should have been transferred back last year, but my place was taken by *them*.

ZHOU: If only your father were more important. Then everything would be all right.

LI: When I'm reincarnated, I'll make sure first that my father is an important cadre—otherwise, I may as well just die in the womb!

ZHOU: Don't talk such rubbish. We'd better think of a way of getting you transferred back soon. We can't keep on putting it off, you know . . . .

LI: All right, all right. Getting upset about it won't help. Why don't we get a couple of tickets, and go and see a play.

ZHOU: A play?

LI: I've heard this play is not bad.

ZHOU: I can't. I sneaked out.

LI: You can't go with me?

ZHOU: I'm afraid my father will find out.

LI: It's up to you!

(ZHOU MINGHUA hesitates for a moment, but then leaves.)

(LI is about to follow her, when he stops on hearing the sound of a car approaching. Light from the headlights of the car is seen, and the sound of brakes can be heard. THEATRE DIRECTOR ZHAO comes running out of the main entrance of the theatre, pushing the crowd gathered around out of the way. In a moment, SECTION HEAD SUN and his daughter, JUANJUAN, come onto the stage. THEATRE DIRECTOR ZHAO hurries out to meet them.)

(LI XIAOZHANG eyes them off, aloofly.)

ZHOU: *(warmly)* Section Head Sun! *(Shakes*

hands) How are you?

SUN: I'm well. How are you?

ZHAO: How has your health been recently?

SUN: Not bad at all.

ZHAO: You should look after yourself. This must be Juanjuan, I suppose?

SUN: Say hello to Auntie Zhao.

JUANJUAN: Hello, Auntie Zhao.

ZHAO: She's so beautiful! You've been transferred back from the countryside, I suppose?

JUANJUAN: Long ago.

ZHAO: And your husband?

JUANJUAN: He's still in the North-East.

ZHAO: Oh dear. How can a young married couple live apart?

JUANJUAN: Daddy's making some arrangements . . . .

SUN: Who said so? Nonsense!

JUANJUAN: *(to* THEATRE DIRECTOR ZHAO, *in a low voice)* I'm not talking nonsense. It's he who's talking nonsense!

ZHAO: *(smiling)* Come inside! *(Takes out two tickets)* I've kept these for you.

> *(Another car approaches from the distance; again there is a light from the headlights and the sound of brakes.)*
> *(*THEATRE DIRECTOR ZHAO *and* SECTION HEAD SUN *stop, and look towards the car.)*

SUN: Who's that in the car?

ZHAO: It seems to be Division Head Qian—the Head of the Political Division of the Organization Department.

SUN: Division Head Qian?

ZHAO: The wife of Secretary Wu of the Municipal Committee.

SUN: Oh yes. Of course, of course . . . .

ZHAO: *(smugly)* An old comrade-in-arms of mine. We're on very good terms.

> *(*DIVISION HEAD QIAN *enters.)*

ZHAO: *(immediately going over to welcome her)* Sister Qian! What good fortune brings you our way?

QIAN: Ah, Little Zhao! How could you have forgotten me? You didn't invite me to come and see your play!

ZHAO: I thought of inviting you, several times, but I was afraid you'd be too busy. Would you like to see it this evening?

QIAN: Do you have any tickets?

ZHAO: Of course—for *you* we have tickets. As many as you like.

QIAN: I only need one.

ZHAO: Isn't Secretary Wu coming?

QIAN: How does he have the time to go and see plays? He's busy from dawn to dusk—I keep urging him to take a rest but he refuses to—he says he has so much time to make up for that he lost due to the Gang of Four.

ZHAO: Secretary Wu really works so hard. His responsibilities are so onerous.

SUN: Division Head Qian, let's go in. The play's about to begin.

QIAN: Who are you?

SUN: I'm from the Cultural Affairs Section.

ZHAO: This is Section Head Sun. Haven't you met before?

QIAN: Oh. Your immediate superior. *(To* SUN*)* I haven't seen you for ten years—your hair's gone white.

ZHAO: Section Head Sun, you accompany Division Head Qian, and go inside. I'll just wait here for Department Head Ma.

QIAN: Department Head Ma?

ZHAO: Head of the Propaganda Department of the Municipal Committee.

QIAN: Oh, Old Ma! He's going on an overseas trip tomorrow—he won't be able to come here this evening.

ZHAO: Oh? In that case we'll go in.

QIAN: After you!

> *(*QIAN *and* SUN *go through the main entrance of the theatre). (*THEATRE DIRECTOR ZHAO *is called over by* LI XIAOZHANG, *who has been standing at the side of the stage, eavesdropping on their conversation.)*

LI: Hey, comrade!

ZHAO: What do *you* want?

LI: Do you have any tickets?

ZHAO: No. None at all!

LI: Aren't there any tickets in your hand?

ZHAO: They are reserved tickets. For high level cadres.

LI: Didn't you just say that Department Head Ma wasn't coming?

ZHAO: Even if he doesn't come, I can't sell you his tickets.

LI: If there are some unused tickets, why can't you sell them?

ZHAO: Because they're reserved for high level cadres.

LI: What about that girl who just went in? Is she a high level cadre?

ZHAO: Her father is. Is yours?

(ZHAO goes into the theatre.)

LI: Damn! You can't even get to see a play without an important father!

(LI XIAOZHANG is about to leave, but, as he walks past the advertising poster, he stops. He keeps looking at the poster, unable to leave it. He thinks for a few moments, then walks to the side of the stage, where a telephone has appeared. He lifts the receiver and dials a number.)

LI: Hello? Backstage, please .... I'm from the Propaganda Department of the Municipal Committee; I'm the Department Head—my name is Ma ... right .... I want to speak to Theatre Director Zhao. *(Waits a few moments)*—Yes, yes, it's me .... Is that Theatre Director Zhao? .... I'm going on an overseas trip tomorrow, so I won't be able to come and see your play tonight .... Oh, Secretary Wu's wife told you ... good. I'd like to ask you a favour ... the son of one of my old comrades-in-arms in Peking would really like to see your play, but he just rang me to say he wasn't able to get a ticket—could you help him? .... No problem? ... Good. He only needs one ticket. His name is Zhang Xiaoli. You'll wait for him at the door? Good. He's not far from the theatre right now, so I'll tell him to go and see you.

(LI puts down the phone, and stands at the side of the stage, leaning against the wall, looking at the main entrance of the theatre.)
(In a few moments, THEATRE DIRECTOR ZHAO comes running out of the entrance, a ticket in her hand. She stands in the middle of the crowd, looking around. After a while, she walks up to BYSTANDER E.)

ZHAO: Comrade—what's your name?

BYSTANDER E: Wu—what's it to you?

ZHAO: Oh! I'm sorry. *(ZHAO approaches another member of the crowd, BYSTANDER F.)*

ZHAO: Comrade—what's your name?

BYSTANDER F: Ji. Do you have any tickets?

ZHAO: No, no! None at all! *(THEATRE DIRECTOR ZHAO looks at her watch, extremely anxious.)*
(LI XIAOZHANG walks over to her.)

LI: Comrade, are you Theatre Director Zhao?

ZHAO: Yes, that's right. And you're ....

LI: My name is Zhang Xiaoli.

ZHAO: *(surprised)* Eh? You?

LI: Yes. Did Department Head Ma phone you about me?

ZHAO: Yes, yes. Oh dear—why didn't you tell me before who you are. It's a misunderstanding! A misunderstanding! You shouldn't have disturbed Department Head Ma about such a little thing like this! In the future, whenever you need any tickets, just get in touch with me directly.

LI: I really am a terrible nuisance. A terrible nuisance.

ZHAO: Not at all. Department Head Ma introduced you ... this is the least I can do ... your father is Department Head Ma's ....

LI: My father and Department Head Ma are old comrades-in-arms.

ZHAO: Oh, oh! Please go ahead. After you. After you. *(THEATRE DIRECTOR ZHAO ushers LI inside the theatre. From then on, LI XIAOZHANG becomes ZHANG XIAOLI.)*

BYSTANDER B: Hey! How come that fellow can get in?

ZHAO: His father is a high level cadre. Is yours?

(CURTAIN)

ACT II

The same evening, after the performance.

The VIP room of the theatre. A door at either side; one leading to the stage, the other backstage. Armchairs line the walls. Photographs of a performance of "The Inspector General" hang on one wall, and a poster advertising the same play hangs on the another wall.

As the curtain rises, enthusiastic applause from the audience, and the shuffling of feet as they leave the theatre can be heard.

THEATRE DIRECTOR ZHAO leads ZHANG XIAO-LI into the VIP room through the door leading from the stage.

ZHAO: *(warmly)* Sit down, relax. Just sit any-where. This theatre is not very comfortable—nothing like those in Peking, I suppose.
    (A THEATRE ATTENDANT *brings in two cups of tea, gives them to* ZHAO *and* ZHANG, *and leaves.)*
ZHAO: Well, give me your valuable opinions!
ZHANG: *(sincerely)* It was very good. In fact, I've never seen such a good play.
ZHAO: Do you have any valuable suggestions?
ZHANG: Really, it's really very good. Er . . . I must go now . . . .
ZHAO: Why don't you stay a while longer?
ZHANG: I really must go.
ZHAO: No, don't go yet. I told Division Head Qian and Section Head Sun that you were here. They want to meet you.
ZHANG: *(surprised)* They want to meet me?
ZHAO: They're just chatting with some of the actors backstage, but they'll be here in a moment.
ZHANG: No no no—er—leading comrades are so busy, I don't want to bother them.
    *(*ZHANG *gets up and is about to go, but* ZHAO, *full of enthusiasm, stops him.)*
    (The THEATRE ATTENDANT *brings in some refreshments, then leaves.)*
ZHAO: Just a while longer. Here, have some supper. *(She puts a cake in front of* ZHANG.*)* Wouldn't you like something to eat? Here, try this. *(*ZHANG *has no choice but to sit down and eat the cake, but he appears uneasy.)*
ZHAO: How's the weather in Peking?
ZHANG: Not bad. It's snowing.

ZHAO: Snowing? In such hot weather?
ZHANG: No . . . er . . . I mean, it snows in winter. Like everywhere else in China. It snows in winter.
ZHAO: Yes, that's right. Why have you come down from Peking this time? Do you have a special assignment?
ZHANG: No. I try to avoid special assignments. They're a nuisance.
ZHAO: Did you come to see some friends?
ZHANG: Yes, that's right. I came to see some friends.
ZHAO: Did you have anything else in mind?
ZHANG: *(cautiously)* No, nothing else in mind. The only reason I came to see you today was that I wanted to see this play, that's all.
ZHAO: What I meant was—do you have anything in particular to do—apart from seeing your friends, that is.
ZHANG: No. Just stroll around. See a few plays.
ZHAO: A few plays? Well, I've got plenty of tickets—*(takes out some tickets)*—here are some tickets for some "restricted movies"—American, Japanese, French . . . here, take all of them.
ZHANG: *(delighted)* Great. How much?
ZHAO: But you've come so far—from Peking—how could I charge you for them?
ZHANG: No, no—I couldn't.
ZHAO: The least I can do is to invite you to see a few movies.
ZHANG: *(taking the tickets)* I really couldn't take them . . . oh, I nearly forgot . . . . *(He takes the bottle of* maotai *out of his satchel)* I don't really have anything suitable to give you, but . . . please accept this, Auntie Zhao.
ZHAO: *Maotai*?
ZHANG: It's nothing much.
ZHAO: But I don't drink.
ZHANG: Well, keep it—you can use it as a gift. Please take it—when I want to see a play again, I won't feel bad about coming to you for tickets!
ZHAO: *(taking the wine)* Now you're making me embarrassed! You must have bought this wine in a guesthouse, I suppose.
ZHANG: No, you can't even get it in the guest-houses. This is special quality. For export.

ZHAO: Oh? So it's even classier than ordinary *maotai*?

ZHANG: Well ... you could say the taste is a bit different.

ZHAO: Does your father often drink this special quality *maotai*?

ZHANG: Oh yes. Often. At least thirty bottles a month.

ZHAO: Oh! And your father is ....

ZHANG: You mean, my father's ....

ZHAO: Is it confidential information?

ZHANG: No. Not to you.

ZHAO: Well—who is he?

ZHANG: Guess. My surname's Zhang.

ZHAO: Is your father Zhang Jingfu?[1]

(ZHANG *smiles mysteriously, and shakes his head.*)

ZHAO: Zhang Qilong?[2]

(ZHANG *shakes his head.*)

ZHAO: Zhang Dingcheng?[3]

(ZHANG *shakes his head.*)

ZHAO: Then he must be ... Zhang Tingfa?[4]

(ZHANG *continues shaking his head.*)

ZHAO: Aaah ... Zhang Wentian?[5] No, that can't be right. He's dead ... oh yes! It must be Deputy Chief of Staff Zhang Caiqian!

(ZHANG *continues to shakes his head.*)

ZHAO: Then he must be ... er ....

ZHANG: Keep guessing. He's not Zhang Chunqiao.[6]

ZHAO: Of course not, of course not. He's ... well —which one of our leading cadres is he?

ZHANG: He's just an ordinary cadre.

ZHAO: Impossible. He can't be. He must be a high level one. *(Suddenly gets excited)* Oooh— it must be ....

ZHANG: Who?

[1]The Communist Party First Secretary of Anhui Province.

[2]A member of the Standing Committee of the National People's Congress.

[3]A member of the Standing Committee of the National People's Congress.

[4]Commander of the Army.

[5]Secretary of the Communist Party during the Long March.

[6]One of the "Gang of Four".

ZHAO: It's ... *(whispers in* ZHANG*'s ear)* .... Is that right?

ZHANG: What do you think?

ZHAO: It must be. I'm sure it is.

ZHANG: *(laughing)* Well, if you say so ....

ZHAO: *(surprised, gleeful)* Ah! So it's really him. Good Heavens! Such an important father! You're really lucky.

ZHANG: The sad thing is that not everyone can have such an important father.

ZHAO: Seeing your father is a former superior of Department Head Ma, he must know Secretary Wu, too.

ZHANG: Secretary Wu?

ZHAO: Don't you know him? Municipal Committee Secretary Wu.

ZHANG: Oh—Municipal Committee Secretary Wu? I've heard my father speak of him.

ZHAO: Secretary Wu's wife, Division Head Qian told me that, in the summer of 1953, when Secretary Wu went to Peking to attend a meeting, he went to your home to see your father. You were probably still a baby-in-arms then! On that occasion Secretary Wu presented your father with a rare and unusual cactus. Your father noticed that Secretary Wu was a heavy smoker, so he presented him with two cartons of exclusive cigarettes ... Division Head Qian said that Secretary Wu hasn't seen your father for more than twenty years. I'd better go and find her. When I tell her who you are, she's sure to be thrilled. Just wait a minute.

(ZHAO *goes off through the door leading backstage.*)

(ZHANG *gazes in the direction* ZHAO *has just left, shaking his head. Then he takes a packet of cigarettes from the table, takes out one and puts it in his jacket pocket, and is about to sneak off. He quietly opens the door leading towards the stage, and is about to go. However, he takes one look outside, and quickly retreats into the room.*)

(DIVISION HEAD QIAN *and* SECTION HEAD SUN *arrive.*)

(ZHANG XIAOLI, *full of confidence and charm, walks over to welcome them.*)

ZHANG: Auntie Qian!

QIAN: *(surprised)* Who ... ?

ZHANG: Department Head Ma arranged for me to come here tonight to see the play.

QIAN: Oh yes—I've heard about you ... where's Theatre Director Zhao?

ZHANG: She went out to look for you.

QIAN: Sit down. Relax.

ZHANG: How is Uncle Wu?

QIAN: Not bad.

ZHANG: Does he still smoke as much as he used to?

QIAN: *(curiously)* You little devil! How did you know about that?

ZHANG: My father told me. He's given up smoking, now. He said Uncle Wu should cut down a bit, too.

QIAN: *(confused)* Your father? Oh ... is your father well?

ZHANG: Yes. But he's so busy, he doesn't have time for gardening nowadays. But he still likes that cactus Uncle Wu gave him in 1953, when he went to Peking to attend a meeting.

QIAN: *(delighted)* Oh! So you're ... —oh—why didn't you tell me? No wonder you even know about Secretary Wu's smoking habits!

(SECTION HEAD SUN turns towards QIAN, enquiringly. QIAN whispers in SUN's ear.)

SUN: *(greatly surprised)* Oh! *(SUN hurriedly sits down, at one side.)*

QIAN: Well, that's marvellous. Come on now, come over here. *(She pulls ZHANG towards her, and sits him down at her side.)* How many children are there in your family now? Are you the oldest?

ZHANG: When Uncle Wu went to Peking in 1953, I was still a baby-in-arms.

QIAN: So you must be ... the fifth child ....

ZHANG: Yes, that's right. I'm the fifth in the family.

QIAN: You little devil! What's your name?

ZHANG: You can call me Little Zhang, if you like. *(ZHAO comes hurrying through the door leading from the backstage.)*

ZHAO: Ah, Sister Qian! Ah ... you know each other already!

QIAN: Of course we do! Secretary Wu knew his father more than twenty years ago—Secretary Wu even carried him in his arms. Sister Zhao, do you know who his father is?

ZHAO: Oh yes. I know. I guessed.

QIAN: You needed to guess? One look and you can tell! Just look how much he resembles his father!

SUN: My word! A striking resemblance! The spitting image!

QIAN: Sister Zhao, he can stay with Secretary Wu and me, as our guest. Be sure to invite him to see some plays!

ZHANG: Auntie Qian, you must have a lot to do. I'd better be off now.

QIAN: There's no hurry.

ZHANG: But I have to fly back to Peking tomorrow.

QIAN: Why don't you stay a little longer?

ZHAO: You've got tickets for some "restricted movies" next week!

ZHANG: I'll catch a plane back, just to see them. Auntie Qian, I'll come and see you next time, too.

QIAN: Don't go yet. Stay a little longer. *(She draws ZHANG closer to her, and sits him down.)* We haven't had a chance to have a chat yet. Why did you come down from Peking this time?

ZHANG: I came to see a friend.

QIAN: A girlfriend?

ZHANG: No—a young man.

ZHAO: Oh, you're fibbing!

ZHANG: I never lie.

QIAN: Where is your friend?

ZHANG: At the East Sea State Farm.

QIAN: Oh. Hasn't he been transferred back yet?

ZHANG: His father's just an ordinary worker—he hasn't got the right connections—I'm really very worried about him.

ZHAO: Why don't you get your father to use his connections?

ZHANG: But my father doesn't know the Farm Director.

ZHAO: *(suddenly remembering)* Section Head Sun —aren't you an old comrade-in-arms of Old Zheng, the Farm Director of the East Sea State Farm?

SUN: Mmm. Yes. That's right.

ZHAO: Well then, Little Zhang. You can ask Section Head Sun to call on Farm Director Zheng, asking him to pay particular attention to this matter.

SUN: *(embarrassed)* Er ....

(ZHAO makes a sign to ZHANG XIAOLI, suggesting he say something to DIVISION HEAD QIAN.)

ZHANG: Auntie Qian, do you think we could

bother Uncle Sun with this matter?

QIAN: Come on, Old Sun. Why don't you just pop over there?

SUN: *(quickly)* Oh, very well then. I'll try. Mmm . . . what's his name?

ZHANG: His name is Li Xiaozhang. He's in the May Seventh Brigade.

SUN: *(writing in his notebook)* All right.

ZHANG: *(surprised and extremely happy, but not changing his expression)* That's great. If Uncle Sun can help Li Xiaozhang get transferred off the farm—I won't go back to Peking for the time being.

QIAN: That's good. Stay here a while longer. Enjoy yourself for a few more days.

ZHANG: Uncle Sun, when do you think I can hear from you—about this matter?

SUN: Em . . . . Come to my place in a week.

ZHANG: All right. I'll call on you in a week's time then.

QIAN: Well, that's that. Where are you staying now, Little Zhang?

ZHANG: *(off the top of his head)* The South Lake Guesthouse.

QIAN: Your room number?

ZHANG: Room 102.

QIAN: Seeing you're not going back to Peking yet, you'd better come and stay with us.

ZHANG: No no no . . . the guesthouse is just fine.

QIAN: My home is not bad, either!

ZHANG: But I'll have to check out . . . it's a lot of bother . . . forget it . . . .

QIAN: It's no bother to check out. *(Lifts the receiver)* I'll speak to them.

ZHANG: *(hurriedly taking the receiver)* No, I'll do it. You just sit down. Don't you bother about this.

QIAN: Do you know their number?

ZHANG: Yes. (ZHANG *dials a number at random.)* *(A telephone appears at the side of the stage. A middle aged man answers.)*

ZHANG: Hello? Is that the South Lake Guesthouse?

MAN: What? South Lake Guesthouse? No! This is the Funeral Parlour!

ZHANG: *(nodding his head to* QIAN, *indicating that he has been connected)* My name is Zhang. Room 102.

MAN: You've dialled the wrong number. This is the Funeral Parlour.

ZHANG: Oh, Comrade Ba Le ... No, nothing wrong ... just that I won't be spending tonight in my room, that's all.

MAN: *(talking to himself)* Eh? Since when have I been called Comrade Ba Le? *(Into the telephone)* My name's Ding!

ZHANG: My things? Oh, never mind. I'll pick them up in a few days.

MAN: *(exasperated)* Are you crazy? Is this some sort of joke? It's getting on for midnight. Come on now, what are you after?

ZHANG: My father? Oh, no letters? No telegrams? Nothing at all?

MAN: *(shouting)* You must be off your rocker! *(Slams the phone down, and leaves.)*

ZHANG: You're too kind! Thank you, thank you very much. *(He hangs up.)* The service there is really excellent.

ZHAO: Of course—so it should be, it's one of the top guesthouses!

QIAN: *(rising to her feet)* Come along then, Little Zhang.

ZHANG: Coming. Uncle Sun, I'll get some news from you in a week, I hope.

SUN: All right. All right.

(ZHANG gleefully pounds SUN on the shoulder. Suddenly he remembers who he is supposed to be, and quickly pulls back his hand, smiling sheepishly.)

(CURTAIN)

ACT III

One week afterwards.

Morning.

SECTION HEAD SUN's lounge-room. There is a door on either side, one leading to the bedroom, the other to the kitchen. In the middle there is a third door, leading to a veranda and the courtyard. In the room there is a colour television set, a console radio set, a sofa, a rattan reclining chair, a low table and a telephone.

The curtain rises. ZHOU MINGHUA is barefoot, her trousers rolled up, kneeling on the floor, scrubbing it. She has obviously been working for a long time, and is covered in sweat. Suddenly she feels nauseous and is about to vomit, but, with a great effort, she restrains herself. She rests for a few moments, then continues scrubbing the floor. SECTION HEAD SUN comes in from the veranda and walks into the lounge room.

SUN: *(dissatisfied)* Oh, really! This is a waxed floor. How can you scrub it with water?

(ZHOU MINGHUA is surprised. She is at a loss.)

SUN: There are guests coming for dinner today—just look at what you've done. Oh well. All right. You may as well stop now.

(ZHOU MINGHUA picks up the bucket and the mop, and walks through the door to the kitchen. JUANJUAN comes in through the other door, carrying a book.)

JUANJUAN: Hello, Daddy! You're back!

SUN: Have you just got up?

JUANJUAN: I woke up at nine, but stayed in bed. I was reading a novel.

SUN: You really know how to enjoy life! Just because your mother's not at home, you even employed a servant!

JUANJUAN: I didn't.

SUN: Well, who was that scrubbing the floor just now?

JUANJUAN: Oh—she's a friend of mine—from school.

SUN: From school?

JUANJUAN: She's very capable. Rough work, delicate work—she's good at everything. Just look *(pointing at her skirt)* she made me this skirt yesterday. She said she's going to knit me a sweater, too.

SUN: Eh? How is it that I haven't seen her here before?

JUANJUAN: She's come here because she's after a favour—from you.

SUN: *(annoyed)* I'm already too busy!
(ZHOU MINGHUA enters, carrying a big basket of clothes.)

JUANJUAN: Minghua, come over here. Let me introduce you. This is my father.

ZHOU: Hello, Uncle Sun.

JUANJUAN: Her name is Zhou Minghua. She was transferred back from the countryside last year, and now she works at a cotton mill.

SUN: Oh . . . I thought you'd come to . . . . *(He points at the clothes-basket* ZHOU MINGHUA *is carrying.)* Put it down! Let Juanjuan do the washing!

JUANJUAN: Really. How can I wash so much? I told you to buy a washing machine, but you still haven't bought me one. You'd better send them to the laundry!

ZHOU: *(worried that she might miss the chance to wash the clothes)*—No no no! I'll wash them . . . . *(ZHOU is about to leave, carrying the clothes basket.)*

JUANJUAN: Just a minute, Minghua. Daddy!

SUN: What do you want?

JUANJUAN: Minghua has a boyfriend—he's still in the countryside. They've known each other for years, and they'd like to get married, but her father won't agree to it. He insists that her boyfriend must get transferred back from the countryside before he'll agree. I feel so sorry for her. Do try to think of a way to help her!

SUN: She's your friend. You go and talk to her father—a bit of "ideological persuasion", eh! Tell her father that his attitude is incorrect, that in our country there's no distinction between high and low occupations—all work,

whether on the farm or in a factory, is the same—all work "serves the people" and all workers have a bright future.

JUANJUAN: You make it seem so simple—you go and tell him! As if anybody is willing to listen to that sort of stuff nowadays!

SUN: Well, they can wait a couple of years before getting married. Her boyfriend will be transferred back sooner or later, I suppose.

ZHOU: Uncle Sun—we can't wait . . . .

SUN: You're still young—you should concentrate on your work and your studies.

JUANJUAN: Daddy, don't be like that! You know the Director of the East Sea State Farm, Farm Director Zheng, don't you? Just a few words will do—just ring him up, even!

SUN: How can you ask your father to do such a thing? I'm a government official—how could I do anything so unprincipled?

ZHOU: Juanjuan, I think we'd better forget it. We shouldn't give Uncle Sun so much trouble.

JUANJUAN: He's just putting on an act. All right then *(she takes the clothes basket off* ZHOU MINGHUA *and thrusts it in* SUN's *hands)*—you go and wash these clothes, then! She's been helping us so much for the past few days, but it's all been for nothing!

SUN: You, you . . . . Come on, now. We'll talk about it another time *(He takes* JUANJUAN *to one side.)* I have some guests coming from Peking. Pekingese like to eat *mantou*—go and buy some for me, will you?

JUANJUAN: It's too far! I'm not going.

SUN: Use the car.

JUANJUAN: I want to read.

ZHOU: Juanjuan—what's the matter?

JUANJUAN: He wants me to go and buy some *mantou*.

ZHOU: Uncle Sun, you don't need to buy them. I know how to make them.

SUN: Oh? Good. Off you go to the kitchen then. But be sure to have them ready by midday.

ZHOU: I will.

JUANJUAN: Minghua, you're marvellous.
(ZHOU MINGHUA leaves, by the door leading to the kitchen.)

JUANJUAN: Daddy, you're rotten. People help you so much, but you're not willing to help them.

SUN: Juanjuan—when you're talking in front of people outside our own family you should watch what you say.

JUANJUAN: Everything I said is true.

SUN: But you have to consider the circumstances.

JUANJUAN: So when you're telling the truth you have to "consider the circumstances", do you? What about when you're telling lies?

SUN: Who's been telling lies?

JUANJUAN: You. I hear you telling lies all day.

SUN: You . . . ! You're getting worse and worse. Wait till your mother gets back. I'll get her to take you in hand!

JUANJUAN: *I'm* not afraid of Mummy. You're the one who's afraid of her!

SUN: You, you . . . what can I do with you? Nothing at all. (SUN *shakes his head, resignedly, and leaves by the door to the bedroom.*)

(JUANJUAN *sits on the sofa, and starts to read her book.*)

JUANJUAN: Minghua . . . what are you doing?

(ZHOU MINGHUA'*s voice from offstage: Kneading the* dough.)

JUANJUAN: Come and sit with me.

(ZHOU *comes in, carrying a basin of flour.*)

JUANJUAN: Mummy's not home—I have to rely on you for everything.

ZHOU: It doesn't matter. If you and your father are able to get my boyfriend back from the countryside, I'll do anything for you!

JUANJUAN: Don't worry. My father's just putting on a righteous front. At the moment he's busy making some arrangements for me. When that's fixed, I'll talk to him again.

ZHOU: Arrangements for you? But you were transferred back long ago.

JUANJUAN: My husband's still in the North-East. A few days ago my mother went up there, carrying a letter Daddy got some VIP to write for him. She's going to see my husband's boss, so as to get my husband transferred back there.

ZHOU: What are his chances?

JUANJUAN: Daddy will be able to fix it.

ZHOU: I really envy you.

JUANJUAN: Your boyfriend will be transferred back, too. Minghua—I haven't met your boyfriend yet. Is he handsome?

ZHOU: (*shyly*) Just ordinary.

JUANJUAN: Do you love him very much?

ZHOU: I used to . . . .

JUANJUAN: Used to?

ZHOU: When he first arrived at the farm he was marvellous—idealistic, intelligent, able to turn his mind to anything—he was good at acting, too. But afterwards life on the farm got worse and worse, and the ones with connections managed to get transferred out. According to the official policy, he should have been transferred back the year before last, but his place was taken by other people, and he became very despondent. He took up smoking and drinking, and he's been getting . . . .

JUANJUAN: So you don't love him any more?

ZHOU: It's not that. I think he'll get better.

(THEATRE DIRECTOR ZHAO *enters, from the veranda.*)

ZHAO: Juanjuan!

JUANJUAN: Auntie Zhao!

(ZHOU MINGHUA *leaves.*)

ZHAO: Look. I've bought you some tickets.

JUANJUAN: Oh—that's great!

ZHAO: (*holding out the tickets*) These are all for foreign movies. Restricted circulation. For reference purposes.

JUANJUAN: (*taking the tickets*) Do you have any more?

ZHAO: You're really greedy! There are three hundred people in our Company, and we only get ten tickets for each movie. Everybody scrambles for them as soon as they arrive and there are always awful fights—but I've given you two tickets for each film—aren't you satisfied?

JUANJUAN: Oh yes. Thank you, Auntie Zhao.

ZHAO: Where's your father?

JUANJUAN: Inside. (*calls out*) Daddy! Auntie Zhao's here! (JUANJUAN *leaves.*)

(SECTION HEAD SUN *enters, from the bedroom.*)

SUN: (*coolly*) Oh? What are you doing here today?

ZHAO: Didn't you say you'd have news for that Little Zhang from Peking within a week?

SUN: (*unhappily*) So you're involved in this, too?

ZHAO: Just making a little extra effort. Everyone knows what a concerned person I am. (*She takes the bottle of* maotai *out of her satchel*) I managed to get this for you.

SUN: (*surprised and gleeful, but suddenly looks serious*) What's this for?

ZHAO: I don't drink, and there's no point leaving it at home. I know you like *maotai* so I've brought it for you.

SUN: I don't like people to be . . . like that . . . .

ZHAO: You're right. If it were any other sort of wine, I wouldn't have brought it. But this isn't just ordinary *maotai*. It's specially made for export—I think it has some sort of tonic in it.

SUN: Oh? Specially made? It's not ordinary *maotai*?

ZHAO: Of course not. It wasn't easy to get hold of.

SUN: Well . . . all right, just put it down there. But I insist, I must pay for it.

ZHAO: If you offer me money, I'll take it back!

SUN: *(laughing)* You! Very well then, we'll talk about it later. *(SUN puts the maotai in a cupboard.)*

ZHAO: Now—what about Little Zhang?

SUN: We'll talk about it when he arrives.

ZHAO: *(enquiringly)* Has Juanjuan's husband been transferred back from the North-East yet?

SUN: Don't listen to Juanjuan's prattle. I don't do that kind of thing.

　　(Silence)

ZHAO: Section Head Sun—about my accommodation . . . .

SUN: Haven't I told you already? There's nothing I can do about it.

ZHAO: But you're the Section Head!

SUN: Your flat is perfectly satisfactory—why do you need a bigger one? You're a party member and a government official. What about "hard work and plain living", eh?

ZHAO: But some people who joined the revolution when I did already have more than seventy square metres living space!

SUN: There will always be differences . . . .

ZHAO: Section Head Sun!

SUN: You'd be better off talking to the Propaganda Department of the Municipal Committee!

ZHAO: *(takes out a report)* I've written a report on the matter. Would you mind passing it on to Department Head Ma?

SUN: Department Head Ma's gone overseas.

ZHAO: Well, give it to his secretary.

SUN: That's no good. If I pass it on, that implies that I approve. I think we should let this matter rest for a while.

ZHAO: What about Little Zhang's problem? Aren't you dealing with that?

SUN: That was given me directly by the wife of

the Secretary of the Municipal Committee herself. If my superiors gave me the nod about
your problem, I could fix that, too.

ZHAO: Section Head Sun.

> *(The phone rings.* SUN *is about to answer it
> when* JUANJUAN *runs in from the door on
> the right.)*

JUANJUAN: Daddy, I'll get it. *(Lifts the phone)*
Yes, yes—that's right. *(Excitedly, to* SUN*)*
Daddy, it's a long distance call from Mummy,
in the North-East!

SUN: Don't make such a racket! *(To* ZHAO*)* Come
on, come along and sit down inside . . .

ZHAO: All right then. *(She stands up slowly, then
suddenly deliberately twists her ankle)* Ouch!
(She nimbly falls back onto the sofa again)
Oooh!

SUN: What's up?

ZHAO: I've twisted my ankle.

SUN: How opportune.

JUANJUAN: Is it serious?

ZHAO: I'll have to massage it. *(*ZHAO *massages her
ankle.)*

> *(*SUN *is extremely agitated.)*

JUANJUAN: *(into the phone)* Mummy? It's me,
Juanjuan! . . . . What? . . . . The letter Daddy
got that VIP to write was very useful? . . . .
Marvellous . . . . Great! They've agreed to transfer him back? *(Excitedly, to* SUN*)* Daddy! Did
you hear? Did you hear?

ZHAO: Section Head Sun, Juanjuan's asking you
whether you heard or not?

SUN: Hang up! Hang up!

JUANJUAN: *(into the telephone)* Oh . . . good.
(Hangs up, to SUN*)* Mummy said that they've
agreed to let him go, but you must get the
transfer arranged here, and send the forms to
them immediately.

SUN: I'm not responsible for your affairs. None
of you! It's none of my business!

JUANJUAN: None of your business? Ha! *(*JUAN-
JUAN *leaves through the door on the right.)*

> *(*SUN *is very angry. He is about to leave
> through the door on the left. The sound of
> a car horn outside is heard.)*

SUN: *(turns to* THEATRE DIRECTOR ZHAO, *in an
urgent tone)* Do you have anything else?

ZHAO: *(pretending to be in pain)* Oooh! My poor
ankle.

> *(*SUN *leaves via the door to the veranda.)*

> *(In a few moments,* SUN *and* ZHANG XIAOLI
> *enter, together.* ZHANG *is carrying a platter
> of fruit.)*

ZHANG: Uncle Sun, Auntie Qian asked me to give
you this platter of fruit.

SUN: Oh! When you go back, please thank Division
Head Qian for me.

ZHANG: It's only a small gift. No need to say
thank you.

ZHAO: Hello, Little Zhang!

ZHANG: Auntie Zhao! Nice to see you again!

ZHAO: Come and sit down.

> *(*ZHANG XIAOLI *sits on the sofa.)*

SUN: *(offering* ZHANG *a cigarette)* Would you like
a cigarette?

ZHANG: No, thanks all the same. *(Takes out an
exclusive brand)* Try one of these! *(*ZHANG
hands the cigarettes to SECTION HEAD SUN *and*
THEATRE DIRECTOR ZHAO.*)*

ZHAO: Did you come by car?

ZHANG: Yeah. Secretary Wu's car.

ZHAO: Oh? Secretary Wu's car?

ZHANG: Uncle Wu's gone to Huang Shan[7] to
attend a meeting. He left the day I shifted in.
Auntie Qian's letting me use his car.

SUN: So you haven't met Secretary Wu yet?

ZHANG: He doesn't even know I'm here.

ZHAO: Auntie Qian is very good to you.

ZHANG: She has no children, so she's treating me
like her own son. Uncle Sun, Auntie Qian asked
me to ask you if you've fixed up that matter
yet?

SUN: *(embarrassed)* It's not so easy.

ZHANG: *(attentively)* Why's that?

SUN: I went to see Farm Director Zheng yesterday.
He said that the whole business of transferrals
back from the countryside and people jumping
the queue has been in a terrible mess recently,
so much so that it's come under criticism from
the Municipal Committee. At the moment
they're taking disciplinary measures and re-
organizing the system, and all transferrals have
been temporarily halted.

ZHAO: What a lot of bureaucratic humbug!

ZHANG: Didn't you tell him that Li Xiaozhang is
a special case, and that his case had been given
to you personally by the wife of the Secretary
of the Municipal Committee?

---

[7] A famous mountain resort.

SUN: I told him, but it did no good. Farm Director Zheng said that it was Secretary Wu himself who issued the order to "close the door". If we want to open the door again—either the front door or the back door—we'll need a note, personally signed by Secretary Wu.

ZHANG: Is it absolutely necessary to get a note signed by Secretary Wu?

SUN: Well, as they say, "an oral order offers no proof" and he's worried that if there's an investigation afterwards, he'll be in trouble.

ZHANG: Do you mean to say that the word of the wife of the Secretary of the Municipal Committee counts for nought? Hmmmph! All right, I'll go and tell Auntie Qian . . . .

SUN: Little Zhang, just wait a minute . . . .

ZHANG: I've already waited a week!

SUN: Without that note . . . no one will take the responsibility!

ZHAO: I've heard Sister Qian say that Secretary Wu is a man of very high principles. Perhaps he won't be prepared to sign such a note.

SUN: I'm afraid that's right.

ZHANG: Auntie Zhao—what can we do?
  (Silence)

ZHAO: *(pensively)* I think we'll just have to get your father involved.

ZHANG: What's that?

ZHAO: You could tell Secretary Wu that Li Xiaozhang has a "special relationship" with your father.

ZHANG: What sort of special relationship?

ZHAO: *(suddenly inspired)* He saved your father's life!

ZHANG: He saved my father's life?

ZHAO: Yes! *(Thinking out loud, getting more and more excited)* Tell him that when the Cultural Revolution started, Li Xiaozhang went to Peking to "exchange revolutionary experiences" with other Red Guards . . . um . . . and that he just happened to see your father being beaten, and that he saved his life, and hid him, and . . . um . . . hid him for several months. When your father's name was cleared, and he was reinstated, he still remembered this, and is very grateful to him, so that's why he's sent you specially to ask Secretary Wu to help Li Xiaozhang get transferred off the farm. As soon as Secretary Wu hears you've been sent by your father, and that Li Xiaozhang once protected him, he might very well sign that paper. *(Pleased with herself)* What about that?

ZHANG: *(nodding his head)* Uncle Sun, what do you think?

SUN: Well, it will do no harm to try. No harm at all.

ZHANG: All right then. Auntie Zhao, thank you for thinking up such a good story. I'm sure Secretary Wu will sign.

SUN: If he does, the rest will be easy to arrange.
  (A restaurant attendant comes in, carrying a multi-tiered food container.)

SUN: Just put it over there!
  (The attendant sets the food out on the table, and leaves.)

SUN: We have no adequate way of entertaining you, Little Zhang, but we'd like you to have a simple meal with us here. I'll see if the *mantou* are ready yet. Please sit down, everyone. *(SUN leaves via the door on the right.)*

ZHAO: It's a pity my flat is so small—otherwise I'd invite you home for a meal, too.

ZHANG: How big is your flat?

ZHAO: Oh, don't talk about it—it's so small— three people living in just over fifty square metres. I've written a report on it, applying to exchange it for a larger one, but I'm afraid our leading comrades are so busy, they have had no time to deal with it . . . Little Zhang . . . I wonder if you could help me to get my request directly to Department Head Ma . . . or, better still, give it directly to Secretary Wu . . . Yes? Just mention my housing problem to him, in passing—just a word from Secretary Wu will solve everything.

ZHANG: All right. No problem. Leave it to me.

ZHAO: *(handing over the report to ZHANG)* Thank you so much.

ZHANG: It's I who should thank you.
  (SECTION HEAD SUN comes in, from the door on the right.)

SUN: The *mantou* will be ready soon. Come and sit down.

ZHAO: Section Head Sun, I'll have to leave now.

ZHANG: Are you leaving now?

ZHAO: My ankle's better now, so there's no reason for me to stay.

SUN: Well, don't let me detain you.

ZHAO: Goodbye. See you later. *(ZHAO leaves through the door leading to the veranda.)*

SUN: Little Zhang, did Theatre Director Zhao ask you to do something for her?

ZHANG: Oh, only a minor matter. To hand over a report. About her accommodation.

SUN: Little Zhang, you belong to a family of high officials—you should pay attention to the impression you make on people. You really oughtn't agree to help people who come to you directly, asking you to fix things for them, instead of going through the correct channels.

ZHANG: It doesn't matter. I always help whenever I can.

SUN: *(surprised and gleeful)* Oh? Really?

ZHANG: Really. Uncle Sun, if I can help you in any way, just say the word.

SUN: Er.... *(He is about to say something, but stops)* No no no—it's so embarrassing to trouble you.

ZHANG: Come on now, it's not as if we were strangers—what are you afraid of?

SUN: Er.... I have a son-in-law—in the North-East. His unit there has already agreed to let him come back, but we have to arrange the transfer from here....

ZHANG: Ah. Yes. All right, all right. Just write a report about it, and I'll say a few words to Secretary Wu—no problem....

SUN: Oh, good. I'll write it immediately.
(SECTION HEAD SUN excitedly leaves from the door on the left.)
(ZHANG XIAOLI walks around admiring the furniture and fittings in SECTION HEAD SUN's apartment.)
(ZHOU MINGHUA brings in the mantou and puts them on the table. She is about to leave when she notices ZHANG XIAOLI. She stops, trying to make out who he is. At last she realizes it is LI XIAOZHANG.)

ZHOU: Li Xiaozhang!
(ZHANG XIAOLI jumps with surprise.)

ZHOU: Li Xiaozhang!
(ZHANG XIAOLI slowly turns his head.)

ZHOU: Li Xiaozhang—it *is* you!

ZHANG: *(extremely surprised)* Minghua! *(He runs over to her.)* What are you doing here?

ZHOU: It's all for you.

ZHANG: For me?

ZHOU: I used to go to school with Section Head Sun's daughter.

ZHANG: *(realizing what she means)* Oh.... *(He looks ZHOU MINGHUA up and down; he is obviously moved. Full of gratitude, he takes MINGHUA by the hand.)* Minghua, you....
(ZHANG takes out his handkerchief, and lovingly wipes away the sweat on her forehead.)

ZHOU: And what are *you* doing here?

ZHANG: Don't ask me that now. I'll tell you later.
(JUANJUAN comes in through the door on the left.)

JUANJUAN: Minghua!
(ZHANG XIAOLI and ZHOU MINGHUA hurriedly separate.)

ZHANG: *(goes over to greet JUANJUAN)* You must be Juanjuan!

JUANJUAN: Yes, I am. Hello! Er—Minghua—do you know him?

ZHOU: He's my boyfriend....

ZHANG: *(hurriedly interrupts her again)* Her boyfriend's friend—Li Xiaozhang's friend.

JUANJUAN: What? Do you know Li Xiaozhang?

ZHOU: He's....

ZHANG: Li Xiaozhang is a "rusticated intellectual youth" assigned to the East Sea State Farm; he's the same age as I am, and looks a bit like me. I've known him for a long time. I've come down from Peking, to try to get him transferred off the farm, back to the city.

JUANJUAN: Oh? Great! Minghua, his father is a high-level cadre—he's got more ways and means than my father has!

ZHOU: His father is a high-level cadre?

JUANJUAN: You didn't know? I just heard my father say so.

ZHOU: Eh?

ZHANG: I suppose you didn't realize . . . .

ZHOU: You . . . !

ZHANG: I'm doing this for Li Xiaozhang and you!

JUANJUAN: That's great. I'll go and tell my father that the matter's fixed! *(JUANJUAN runs off through the left door.)*

ZHOU: *(angrily)* Li Xiaozhang! How can you deceive people like this?

ZHANG: Minghua, they're also deceiving people. Don't be so naive.

ZHOU: But it's not right!

ZHANG: Don't you want me to find a way of getting transferred off the farm?

ZHOU: It's still not right to go about things this way.

ZHANG: Well, what way is there then? You want me to marry you as soon as possible, don't you? Didn't you say you can't wait?

ZHOU: *(calming down, to herself)* That's right. We can't wait much longer . . . .

(SECTION HEAD SUN and JUANJUAN enter

through the left hand door.)

JUANJUAN: My father's finished it. You're really great—able to solve two problems at once. No wonder my father's invited you to a meal!

SUN: Come on, come on, all sit down.

(SUN, JUANJUAN and ZHANG XIAOLI sit down. ZHOU MINGHUA is about to leave through the door on the right.)

ZHANG: Zhou Minghua!

(ZHOU stops.)

JUANJUAN: That's right, Minghua is here too— why don't you join us . . . ?

SUN: Juanjuan!

ZHANG: Uncle Sun—she's Li Xiaozhang's girl-friend—and she's a friend of mine, too.

SUN: Oh! Well, in that case, let's all sit down, then, together . . . .

ZHANG: Uncle Sun, move the table over here. Juanjuan, you sit here. Uncle Sun, you sit here. *(Goes over to ZHOU MINGHUA, and leads her over.)* Minghua, you sit here.

(ZHOU MINGHUA sits at the table, her body slanted to one side, not daring to move.)

ZHANG: *(passing a mantou to ZHOU MINGHUA)* Eat them while they're hot!

(ZHOU MINGHUA lifts her head, and stares in amazement at ZHANG XIAOLI.)

(CURTAIN)

ACT IV

A week later, in the morning.

The home of the Secretary of the Municipal Committee, SECRETARY WU.

What does a Municipal Secretary's home look like? Unfortunately, the authors of this play, and the vast majority of the audience watching it, have never been to one, so there's no way of knowing.

If the homes of Municipal Committee Secretaries were not so heavily protected, such absolutely forbidden places, such deep inner sanctums (as they always have been), but instead were places where Comrade Municipal Party Secretaries could be visited by anybody, where ordinary folk could be invited for a meal . . . then the authors would not have to make such outrageous guesses as to what the inside of a Municipal Committee's Secretary's home looks like.

As the curtain rises, ZHANG XIAOLI is sitting in the lounge room, reading a book.

DIVISION HEAD QIAN arrives.

QIAN: Little Zhang! You're up already!

ZHANG: Hello, Auntie Qian. Is Uncle Wu up yet?

QIAN: Not yet. The meeting at Huang Shan lasted two weeks—he's dead tired. He only got back last night, so I'm letting him sleep in a little this morning.

ZHANG: Have you mentioned Li Xiaozhang to him yet?

QIAN: Yes.

ZHANG: What did he say?

QIAN: He said that the decision to suspend the transfers back from the countryside for the time being, and to clean up the business of people coming back out of turn, was a decision of the whole Municipal Committee—he can't disregard it.

ZHANG: Oh? Did you tell him that Li Xiaozhang protected my father—that he has a special relationship with my father?

QIAN: I told him. I told him that Li Xiaozhang had saved your father's life—even that he himself had been wounded while protecting your father. I made the story more detailed than the version I heard—even more realistic! *(Laughing)* I even had myself believing it!

ZHANG: What did Uncle Wu say?

QIAN: He said that even though Li Xiaozhang has

a special relationship with your father, one can't use one's personal feeling to sabotage Party policy.

ZHANG: It's not that serious!

QIAN: The old man's just like that—"scrupulous and methodical"—always quoting some policy or other. He's the same with me. On his trip to Huang Shan this year, I asked him to bring me back a monkey—a Golden Hair Monkey—but he absolutely refused. Another thing—the Central Committee's going to send a large delegation overseas soon—I asked him to get me included in the quota—a couple of places would be better—so that we could both go on an overseas tour, but he wouldn't agree to that! I'm afraid he really does suffer from "ultra-leftist thinking"—he really hasn't liberated his thoughts at all!

ZHANG: So it seems there's no hope at all for Li Xiaozhang.

QIAN: If only you had come a month or two earlier—before the Municipal Committee made its decision—it would have been easy to fix.

ZHANG: But how was I to know that? Sometimes they tighten up, sometimes they relax, sometimes they allow some liberalization, and then they draw the reins in again . . . . I've already written to Li Xiaozhang, and gave him a guarantee his problem would be solved. But now I'll have to . . . . *(He suddenly starts sobbing.)*

QIAN: You poor devil—don't worry, don't worry! I'll think of something.

ZHANG: It doesn't matter—but when my father finds out that this matter was not resolved, I'm afraid he might have something to say . . . .

QIAN: Don't tell your father yet. All they've done is to stop transfers for the time being. Wait until this phase is over, and I'll make sure that Li Xiaozhang is the first to be transferred back.
      (SECRETARY WU enters, from an inside room.)

WU: What's up?

QIAN: Just look! You won't agree to sign that note, and the poor devil's started crying!

ZHANG: *(wiping his tears with a handkerchief)* Uncle Wu!!

WU: It's hard for you to understand, isn't it? This

matter's not easy to handle—it would make a bad impression—it would be no good for that "intellectual youth" of yours, or for your father, or for you.

QIAN: Aren't you worried his father might have something to say, if you carry on like this?

WU: We're having difficulties here. I might ring him up this evening, and explain the situation to him.

ZHANG: *(surprised)* You want to telephone my father?

WU: What do you think? I haven't seen him for more than twenty years—just a quick phone call to pass on my best wishes. *(Paying closer attention to* ZHANG's *expression)* Don't you think that's a good idea?

ZHANG: *(quickly regaining his cool)* Of course it is. Then he won't blame me for this, and think I'm not able to fix things. All right, Uncle Wu, let's do it that way. Well, you must be busy . . . . *(ZHANG is about to leave.)*

WU: Where are you going?

ZHANG: I've been going to the movies every night for the past few nights, and I'm feeling tired. I think I'll take a nap.

WU: Stay a while, come on now. Sit down. Would you like a cigarette? *(Gives him a cigarette)* Here you are.

ZHANG: Thanks. I'll help myself.

WU: You were born and brought up in Peking, I suppose?

ZHANG: Yeah.

WU: No wonder your Mandarin is so good. Where did your father come from?

ZHANG: My father?

WU: Mmm.

QIAN: You silly old fool—his father's from Sichuan—who doesn't know that?

WU: Just making conversation . . . .

ZHANG: Auntie Qian's right. Dad's from Sichuan.

WU: And he joined the revolution in 1934, it must have been . . . .

QIAN: How could it have been in 1934?

WU: *(interrupting* QIAN*)* You know everything, don't you!!

ZHANG: Uncle Wu, your memory's let you down. It wasn't 1934, it was 1924. He joined the Party in June, 1925 and went to Jinggangshan[8]

[8]The main Communist base area.

in October, 1927. In 1928 he was promoted to platoon leader, in 1929 he became a regimental commander, he was wounded in 1930, in 1931 he . . . .

QIAN: Oh, damn. Why does the old fool want to know all this? *(She hands the book* ZHANG *has just been reading to* SECRETARY WU*)* This is his father's memoirs—it's all in here, in detail.

ZHANG: Uncle Wu—was there anything else?

WU: No, no . . . nothing else. Just chatting. I'll phone your father, and explain about that matter. You go and rest.

ZHANG: All right. *(ZHANG leaves.)*

QIAN: Are you really going to ring him up?

WU: Just to find out what's really going on. You didn't look carefully at this whole business at all, but you put my car at his disposal . . . how will it look if there's something wrong?

QIAN: What's so special about your car? He rides around in a *Hongqi*[9] in Peking. Oh . . . you're suspicious of him, are you? No wonder you asked those questions.

WU: But you kept interrupting, and stopped me from pursuing my questions.

QIAN: I tell you, he's for real. If he weren't, why would have Department Head Ma have introduced him to Theatre Director Zhao? If he were an impostor, how could he have known that you visited his home in 1953, and that you gave his father a cactus?

WU: It doesn't hurt to investigate things. Avoids making mistakes.

QIAN: There's no mistake! He must be real—who would have the gall to shift in here with us if he weren't real? In my opinion, you'd better just fix that matter for him and be done with it.

WU: We'll discuss signing that note afterwards.

QIAN: I've had enough! You're just looking for an excuse. You just don't want to help him at all. When I ask you to fix something for me you're just the same—why didn't you bring me back a Golden Hair Monkey!

WU: I'm a Municipal Committee Secretary—how can I get on a plane carrying a monkey? It'd look ridiculous.

QIAN: Well, what about getting me a place on that overseas delegation?

[9]A luxury limousine.

WU: There are no places left.

QIAN: Can't you get in touch with the Central Committee, and wangle a couple of extra places?

WU: You think that's easy?

QIAN: You never care about me. Some people get a lot of extra tickets. How come you can't even wangle one or two?

WU: You're the Head of the Political Division of the Organization Department of the Municipal Committee. Why do you want to go overseas?

QIAN: To make a study tour of inspection so as to make greater contributions to the Four Modernizations!

WU: You want to go to a capitalist country to study Party political and ideological work? Ridiculous!

QIAN: It's you who's ridiculous. A lot of people— some of them have only been cadres since 1938 —have taken their wives on overseas trips! And you? Have you ever taken me? Eh? What about the ten years of the Cultural Revolution? Haven't we been through enough trouble—we were treated like criminals—almost killed! Now that the Gang of Four has been overthrown, you and I should go on an overseas trip to recuperate—what's wrong with enjoying ourselves? *(QIAN sits to one side, angry.)*

WU: *(comforting her)* All right, all right. We'll talk about it later.

QIAN: Later? When? When you retire? When they hold your memorial ceremony?

WU: Very well. I'll reconsider the matter . . . if I can wangle it, I'll let you go. Come on now, what's wrong with that? Oh dear! What can I do with you? *(SECRETARY WU leaves.)*

(At the same time, ZHANG XIAOLI *rushes onto the stage on his bike, and stops in front of the curtain. A telephone appears at the side of the stage. He lifts up the receiver, dials a number, and the telephone in* SECRETARY WU*'s lounge room rings.* DIVISION HEAD QIAN *answers.)*

QIAN: Hello . . . Who?

ZHANG: Is that the residence of Secretary Wu?

QIAN: Yes, it is.

ZHANG: This is the Garrison Command Headquarters. There's a long distance telephone call from Peking for you. Please stand by. *(He imitates a Sichuanese accent)* Hello! Who's that?

QIAN: I'm Secretary Wu's wife. Who's speaking, please?

ZHANG: I'm Zhang Xiaoli's father.

QIAN: *(surprised and happy)* Ooooo! Venerable Comrade Zhang!

ZHANG: Your name must be Qian.

QIAN: Yes yes yes yes!

ZHANG: We've never met . . . should I call you "Old Qian" or just "Little Qian"?

QIAN: Oh—Little Qian—Little Qian, of course!

ZHANG: Well, Little Qian, my lad, Xiaoli, wrote me that he's living in your house . . . that's such a bother . . . you are both so busy with your work, and he's given you so much extra trouble . . . you shouldn't let him stay there—you ought to throw him out!

QIAN: No, no—we're really happy to have him here—I invited him here—don't worry about it!

ZHANG: He's just a kid—there's a lot he doesn't understand. Very wild, too—discipline him if needs be—you'll have to be strict with him!

QIAN: No, no—he's very good—Secretary Wu and I both like him. Er—Venerable Comrade Zhang—how's your work been recently? Very busy, I suppose?

ZHANG: Yes, very busy. I'm responsible for organizing a large overseas delegation.

QIAN: *(very happy)* Oh? Venerable Comrade Zhang—are there a lot of people in this large delegation?

ZHANG: Of course—it's a *large* delegation.

QIAN: Have the members of the delegation already been decided?

ZHANG: Not completely—are you interested?

QIAN: Of course. I'm interested in going overseas —er—for study purposes, of course. Secretary Wu's also interested.

ZHANG: In that case I'll include your names.

QIAN: Marvellous!

ZHANG: Er—is Old Wu home?

QIAN: Yes, he is. Just wait a minute. *(Towards the inside room)* Old Wu! *(SECRETARY WU enters.)*

QIAN: *(excitedly)* It's Venerable Comrade Zhang —for you!

WU: *(quizzically)* Oh? *(He lifts the phone)* Is that Venerable Comrade Zhang?

ZHANG: Yes, yes—is that Old Wu?

WU: Yes, yes.

ZHANG: Hello!

WU: Hello!

ZHANG: I've just been telling Little Qian that the Central Committee has decided to include the two of you on an overseas delegation.

WU: *(surprised)* Oh? *(Looks at* QIAN*)* Did you ...?

QIAN: It's been decided by the Central Committee!

ZHANG: What do you think about that?

WU: I'm afraid I might not be able to spare the time to get away!

QIAN: *(snatching the phone from him)* No—no—he'll be able to get away—he'll manage!

ZHANG: You can give the responsibility of running the Municipal Committee to someone else.

WU: I can't just do that!

QIAN: *(directly into the receiver)* Of course he can. Quite easily done!

> *(*SECRETARY WU *and* QIAN *argue, through hand gestures.)*

ZHANG: This is an organizational decision—you'll just have to put up with it!

QIAN: *(directly into the receiver)* Yes, of course— we don't mind suffering!

ZHANG: In that case it's decided. Old Wu, how's your health nowadays?

WU: Not bad, Venerable Comrade Zhang. How's yours?

ZHANG: My leg's still playing up.

WU: Oh? Why is that?

ZHANG: When I was being beaten up by the Red Guards, somebody threw me off a platform, and I hurt my leg. Luckily there was a young fellow there who protected me; otherwise my leg would have been finished for good!

QIAN: *(into the phone)* Was that young man's name Li Xiaozhang?

ZHANG: That's right, that's him. I like him very much—like my own son . . . . I've heard he's still in the countryside and hasn't been transferred back yet . . . .

WU: Mmm . . . .

> *(*QIAN *is making desperate hand gestures to* WU, *exhorting him to offer to help.)*

WU: Don't worry about it—we should be able to solve that problem.

ZHANG: Good. Now I can put my mind at ease. How's production down in your area nowadays?

WU: Much better this year than last. Now we're

acting according to the Party's "Eight-Character" policy.[10]

ZHANG: And how about the discussion on "Practice is the Only Criterion of Truth"?[11]

WU: We're catching up. It's not going too badly at all.

ZHANG: Good, good. Well, good luck in your work —I'll visit you when I get a chance.

WU: Good. We'll look forward to your visit!

ZHANG: I might be with you very soon, in fact!

WU: We would like that very much.

ZHANG: Goodbye for now.

WU: Goodbye, goodbye.

> *(As soon as* ZHANG XIAOLI *hangs up, he cycles off the stage. The phone at the side of the stage also disappears.)*

QIAN: Isn't that marvellous! I didn't realise Venerable Comrade Zhang cared so much about us!

WU: I suppose you're satisfied now?

QIAN: Hmmph. No thanks to you! Good old Venerable Comrade Zhang! And you were just wondering if his son is real or not!

WU: I was worried about being taken for a ride.

QIAN: I'm sure there's no mistake. I'm very good at telling a person's character. If he's not real . . . well, I think he's even realler than real! He can't be an impostor. You'd better get Li Xiaozhang transferred back quickly. Venerable Comrade Zhang fought for decades in campaigns all over the country . . . it's such a small favour. You'd better agree to do it.

WU: All right, all right. I'll sign that note.

QIAN: Now you're doing the right thing! Write it immediately.

> *(*SECTION HEAD SUN *enters.)*

SUN: Hello, Division Head Qian!

QIAN: Ah, Section Head Sun. Secretary Wu's agreed to help us with that matter. Look—he's writing a note right now.

SUN: Great! *(He takes the bottle of* maotai *out of his satchel.)* Division Head Qian, I've heard that Secretary Wu has a taste for *maotai*. Here's a bottle—here—you have it . . . .

QIAN: But he's got plenty! You keep it for yourself!

---

[10]Tuanjie, zhengdun, gaige, tigao: unite, rectify, re-form, raise standards—a common slogan in 1978.

[11]A slogan launched by Deng Xiaoping in 1978.

SUN: Perhaps you don't have this sort of *maotai*—it's not ordinary *maotai*. It's specially made for export—it has different ingredients.

QIAN: How did you get it?

SUN: The XXX Foreign Trading Company.

QIAN: I'll put it there, then. Please sit down. I'll go and get Little Zhang. *(QIAN puts the maotai in a cupboard, and leaves.)*

(SECRETARY WU finishes writing the note, and stands up.)

SUN: Hello, Secretary Wu.

WU: Section Head Sun—you can make the necessary arrangements about Li Xiaozhang now.

SUN: *(taking the note)* Ah, that's good.

(QIAN enters.)

QIAN: That young fellow really sleeps like a top. I kept calling him for such a long time before he woke up. I told him his father telephoned us—such a grin he had on his face—he's really still a kid!

(ZHANG XIAOLI runs onto the stage, buttoning up his coat as he does so.)

ZHANG: Uncle Wu—did my father ring you?

WU: Mmmm. Well, I've written that note, and I've given it to Section Head Sun.

ZHANG: Great!

QIAN: Section Head Sun—deal with that as a matter of priority, won't you?

SUN: Of course. I'll go to the State Farm now. Little Zhang—would you like to go with me, to see Li Xiaozhang?

ZHANG: Eh? Me? Oh no . . . I'll see him tomorrow.

SUN: Well, I'm off.

ZHANG: *(walking in front of him)* Uncle Sun—I've been an awful nuisance.

SUN: No problem. Nothing at all. *(In a low voice)* How are you managing with that problem of mine?

ZHANG: It takes time. Secretary Wu only came back yesterday.

SUN: All right then. Well, I'm off now. *(SECTION HEAD SUN leaves.)*

ZHANG: Uncle Wu, I'd like to borrow your car for a while.

WU: Do you want to go out?

ZHANG: Just on a private matter.

WU: Very well. Get Auntie Qian to have a word with the driver.

ZHANG: Thanks.

WU: The little devil! *(SECRETARY WU leaves.)*

(ZHANG XIAOLI jumps for joy.)

QIAN: The little devil—just look how happy he is!

ZHANG: Auntie Qian, as soon as Li Xiaozhang's problem is solved, I'll have to go back to Peking.

QIAN: Can't you stay a few days longer?

ZHANG: I've been away a long time already.

QIAN: You must be homesick, poor boy. All right—but next time you must stay with us again—just make yourself at home.

ZHANG: It's much better here than it is at home!

QIAN: You little devil! When you go back to Peking, I'd like to give your father a present—Secretary Wu brought it back from Huang Shan, specially for you . . . . *(She takes the bottle of maotai out of the cupboard.)* It's a special kind . . . .

(ZHANG XIAOLI accepts the bottle.)

ZHANG: Thanks a lot! *(He laughs heartily.)*

(CURTAIN)

ACT V

Immediately following the previous act. Afternoon.

The Office of the Director of the East Sea State Farm. It is very disorderly. All sorts of office equipment are mixed up with everyday kitchen utensils, none in their proper place. An old silk banner is hanging, close to the floor, on a tattered wall. An old broom is tied to a string leading to the light switch. Instructions issued from an office such as this would obviously not be very effective—perhaps they die young, after just having left the door. The most symbolic thing is the clusters of weeds running riot in one corner of the room—from this the audience can get some idea of what the general appearance of the fields must be like.

As the curtain rises, FARM DIRECTOR ZHENG enters, carrying a herbicide spraying container on his back. He lackadaisically sits down at the office

desk, and has a few mouthfuls of wine.
YOUNG MAN A runs onto the stage.

YOUNG MAN A: Farm Director Zheng!

ZHENG: Whad'ya want?

YOUNG MAN A: *(takes out a telegram; with a mournful expression on his face)* My grandmother's suddenly been taken ill. My family's sent me a telegram, wanting me to hurry back!

ZHENG: What's wrong with her?

YOUNG MAN A: Cancer!

ZHENG: Don't try to scare people, do you mind? If you want some leave, just apply for it—why do you want to wish cancer on your grandmother?

YOUNG MAN A: She's really got cancer!

ZHENG: You're not a doctor. If you go back, will it cure her cancer? If it does, and I ever get cancer, I won't need to go to hospital—I'll just get you to call me every day, and my cancer will disappear.

YOUNG MAN A: *(imploringly)* Farm Director Zheng!

ZHENG: All right, all right. Have you spoken to your company commander?

YOUNG MAN A: The company commander's father is sick—he went home two days ago.

ZHENG: What about the deputy company commander?

YOUNG MAN A: The deputy company commander's mother's sick—he left yesterday afternoon.

ZHENG: How come they're all sick? It must be some sort of contagious disease. Oh well . . . how many days leave do you want?

YOUNG MAN A: That depends on how long it takes my grandmother to get well again.

ZHENG: When the relatives of people like you get sick, they never get well quickly. It takes them at least a fortnight, sometimes half a year. How many days do you want?

YOUNG MAN A: How about a month for a start?

ZHENG: Very well. Leave the telegram there.

YOUNG MAN A: Farm Director Zheng—you're really great!

(YOUNG MAN A leaves happily. YOUNG MAN B comes running in.)

YOUNG MAN B: Farm Director Zheng!

ZHENG: Is your father ill?

YOUNG MAN B: No.

ZHENG: Then it must be your mother.

YOUNG MAN B: No, it's my sister—she's getting married. Oh—*(taking out a letter)* I just got a letter.

ZHENG: And you want leave to go home.

YOUNG MAN B: Yeah.

ZHENG: I suppose if you don't go back your sister won't marry her boyfriend, eh?

YOUNG MAN B: No, it's not that—I just want to go to their wedding, that's all.

ZHENG: Have you spoken to your company commander?

YOUNG MAN B: The company commander's brother is getting married—he's left to attend the wedding.

ZHENG: What about the deputy company commander?

YOUNG MAN B: His sister got married not long ago—he's not back yet.

ZHENG: Oh well. The contagious diseases are over. Now it's time for collective marriages. How many days do you want?

YOUNG MAN B: Not many. A week.

ZHENG: All right. Leave the letter there.

YOUNG MAN B: Great! I'll bring you back a piece of wedding cake!

(Without lifting his head, ZHENG waves the young man out. YOUNG MAN B leaves.)
(ZHENG sighs, deeply, and starts to hum a song from the Korean War. The sound of a car horn is heard. ZHENG leans through the window to take a look. The sound of brakes. In a few moments SECTION HEAD SUN enters.)

ZHENG: I've been expecting you for quite a few days—I knew you'd come!

SUN: Eh? . . . Have you been drinking?

ZHENG: Would you like a mouthful?

SUN: Drinking during office hours! Really! If you're not worried about the impression you make, I am!

ZHENG: More hypocrisy! What office hours? There's no office to have hours in! Just look through the window at the fields. Who's at work? Who's doing anything? Come on, have one!

SUN: *(taking a drink and talking at the same time)* You shouldn't stay here drinking. You should go around the work teams doing ideological work—"getting close to the masses", eh?

ZHENG: What masses? They've all run off into the cities. Some have jumped the queue, some have wangled transfers, and some have left through the "back door".

SUN: Why are you complaining? It's your management which is at fault.

ZHENG: My management at fault? You come here and manage the place, then! I'll kowtow to you, and beat my head on the ground so hard you'll be able to hear it!

SUN: All right, all right. *(Takes out the note from* SECRETARY WU, *and hands it over to* ZHENG.*)* Look at this.

ZHENG: *(takes it, very surprised)* Oh? The Secretary of the Municipal Committee has really written a note?

SUN: Before coming here, I went to the Labour Office. As soon as they saw this note, I was able to wangle a transfer. You'd better transfer Li Xiaozhang's registration at once. Secretary Wu says the quicker the better.

ZHENG: Can't be done. You're one step behind.

SUN: What?

ZHENG: The State Farm Party Committee has decided that, in view of the fact that the whole policy of transferrals is under investigation, we should "restrict the backdoor battlefront" as much as possible. So it has been decided that, for the second half of this year, a quota of no more than twenty will be allowed to leave through the back door.

SUN: The case that Secretary Wu has asked you to handle can hardly be considered "leaving through the back door"!

ZHENG: Oh, come now, Old Sun—don't feel bad about it. *(He fingers* SECRETARY WU*'s note.)* This is one-hundred-per-cent backdoorism!

SUN: Are you daring to insinuate that the Secretary of the Municipal Committee dabbles in backdoorism?

ZHENG: Not only the Secretary of the Municipal Committee . . . even Ministers of the State Council and members of the Central Committee —they all do it!

SUN: You're drunk! This isn't backdoorism!

ZHENG: It is backdoorism!

SUN: It's not!

ZHENG: It is!

SUN: It's definitely not. It's frontdoorism! *(Realizing he's made a slip of the tongue)* Oh

no, it's not—no—that's wrong, that's wrong. I must be drunk, too. All right then. What do you think we should do about this matter?

ZHENG: He'll have to ease someone else out of the quota.

SUN: How can you call this "easing someone out of the quota"? It's "paying attention to that which is important". Get out the quota name list, and let me have a look at it.

ZHENG: *(handing over a list of names to* SUN*)* There are twenty names here. Which one do you think we can ease out?

SUN: *(pointing at the list)* What about this one?

ZHENG: No chance. He's the nephew of the Chief of Staff of the Local Command Garrison.

SUN: Oh. *(Pointing at the list)* What about this one?

ZHENG: The niece of the sister of the Vice-Minister of Health!

SUN: Good Lord! *(Points at the list)* This one?

ZHENG: The grandson of the brother-in-law of the cousin of the Vice-Premier!

SUN: Bigger and bigger! I suppose this one's got relatives who are high-level cadres, too.

ZHENG: No—they're not high officials.

SUN: Oh? Well, that's good then.

ZHENG: But there's no chance there, either. She's the girlfriend of the State Farm Party Committee's Secretary's son!

SUN: Damn. Isn't there someone just related to an ordinary official?

ZHENG: *(pointing at the list)* This one. His father is the Eighth Deputy Section Head of the Housing Bureau.

SUN: Only a Deputy Section Head! And number eight, at that! Fine—he can wait until next year. Give his place to Li Xiaozhang. All right?

ZHENG: All right. Of course an Eighth Deputy Section Head has to cede to a Municipal Committee Secretary. The higher up an official is, the greater his power—power, power, power—you can do anything if you have power—that's the truth of the matter—and practice is its criterion!

SUN: Well, that's how we'll do it, then.

ZHENG: *(opens a drawer and takes out some papers)* This is Li Xiaozhang's file—the amount of oil and grain he's entitled to, his residence transfer permit . . . here—you take the lot.

SUN: Oh? You've already completed all the formalities for him to leave the farm?

ZHENG: A case handed me by my superiors . . . that young man obviously has the right connections . . . of course I smelt it coming, so I made some preparations.

SUN: You've been having me on!

ZHENG: Not at all. I was only waiting for the note from the Municipal Committee Secretary.

SUN: *(taking up the file)* Are you going to notify Li Xiaozhang right away? Then he can leave the farm as soon as possible.

ZHENG: Of course. I'll phone now. *(Takes up the phone)* May Seventh Company, please . . . . Is that the May Seventh Company? Is that Company Commander Chen? . . . Farm Director Zheng here . . . . Is Li Xiaozhang in your Company at the moment? Oh? He's just come back this afternoon? No, don't criticize him—he's about to leave—transferred out—back to the city—yes, that's right. What? You won't agree to it? Good! Still a bit of the old rebellious spirit left, eh? You want to know if it's all in accordance with the prescribed rules and regulations? Or if it's a case of backdoorism?

Wait a minute *(He gives the phone to* SECTION HEAD SUN*)* Here—you answer him!

SUN: *(taking the phone—slightly drunk)* Hello—you want to know who I am? You'll jump when I tell you. I'm the Municipal Committee Secretary . . . .

ZHENG: *(surprised)* You're the Municipal Committee Secretary?

SUN: . . . Secretary's special envoy!

ZHENG: Oh! You really did make me jump.

SUN: Oh! You're asking if all this is in accordance with the prescribed rules and regulations? I can tell you quite categorically, that it certainly doesn't . . . .

ZHENG: Eh?

SUN: . . . deviate at all from the prescribed rules and regulations.

ZHENG: Good grief!

SUN: Officials ought to have special privileges . . . "backdoorism" is completely legal . . . .

ZHENG: What?

SUN: . . . that's what the Gang of Four said.

ZHENG: Come on now, that's enough. Just leave this to me. *(Takes the phone off him)* Hello—Old Chen? The Secretary of the Municipal Committee has written me a note, specifically requesting that Li Xiaozhang be transferred out. Immediately. Yes yes yes. Eh? You refuse to go along with this? I'm afraid you won't be able to resist the pressure . . . you'd better get Li Xiaozhang himself to come to the State Farm Office. Yes. Get him to come here immediately. *(He hangs up.)* Do you want to wait, and leave with him?

SUN: No—he'll still have to do his packing, and I can't wait that long. I'd better leave first—I might look as if I'm a bit drunk—no! I'm not drunk, I'm not drunk! Goodbye!

ZHENG: All right. I won't see you off.

(SUN leaves. After a few moments, the sound of a car door is heard. FARM DIRECTOR ZHENG *looks through the window watching* SECTION HEAD SUN *leave. He shakes his head, and continues drinking. Suddenly, he picks up a piece of paper from his desk, and starts writing furiously.)*

*(*LI XIAOZHANG, *having returned to his real identity from* ZHANG XIAOLI, *looks around cautiously inside and outside the office. He then steps in. His manner of speech and his*

actions are the same as before he assumed his new role.)

LI: *(cheekily)* Li Xiaozhang, valiantly battling May Seventh warrior in the glorious May Seventh Company on the East Sea State Farm reporting for duty, sah!

ZHENG: So you're Li Xiaozhang.

LI: The real thing. One metre 76 high, 66 kilos in weight, 26 years old, and in sixty-six days . . . .

ZHENG: Well?

LI: I will have been valiantly battling in the East Sea State Farm for eight years. Let's have a drink to celebrate it!

ZHENG: Don't be so cheeky. You might laugh a lot, but you're depressed as anything inside.

LI: Wow! Farm Director Zheng really has insight!

ZHENG: Has the Company Commander told you you're being transferred out?

LI: I heard something about it.

ZHENG: All the formalities have been completed. Your file and identity papers have all been taken away by Section Head Sun. You can leave our farm now.

LI: Thank heavens for that!

ZHENG: Should I offer you my congratulations, or my apologies?

LI: Your apologies?

ZHENG: This farm hasn't been managed well . . . we've wasted a lot of land, and . . . we've wasted your youth. So . . . so . . . everybody wants to leave . . . every time someone leaves, I feel . . . just so . . . so sad, as if I owe them something. But then—what could I have done about it? Even the Municipal Committee Secretary abuses his power and demands special privileges . . . he dabbles in backdoorism and doesn't care about running the State Farm well—he doesn't care . . . how can we "work flat out for the revolution"—there's no point . . . Not only you young people want to get off the Farm through the back door, even the State Farm's leading officials want to leave the same way . . . .

LI: *(not unsympathetically)* What about you?

ZHENG: I'm so depressed. *(He points at the wine)* I rely on this to drown my sorrows . . . the farm should be managed, but . . . not this way. If it goes on this way, I don't . . . I don't want to stay here any longer. The longer I stay here the less I can stand it . . . .

LI: *(surprised)* You want to leave too?

ZHENG: *(sadly)* I've written a report, requesting a transfer. You know some high official's son, don't you—his name is Zhang Xiaoli. Couldn't you ask him . . . to help me . . . to have a word to the Municipal Committee Secretary . . . to get me transferred out, too?

LI: *(stunned)* How . . . how could I do that!?
    (YOUNG MAN A enters.)

ZHENG: Why can't you? *(He takes SECRETARY WU's note)* Just ask him. He wrote you a note, authorizing you to leave . . . why can't he write me a note, authorizing me to leave too? *(He takes the report he has just written, requesting a transfer)* This is my request for a transfer— I've got two reasons—one is that my grand- mother has cancer, and the other is that my sister is getting married!

    (ZHENG hands the transfer request to LI XIAOZHANG, but LI is stunned, and doesn't move. Suddenly, ZHENG withdraws his hand, and sorrowfully shakes his head. He waves LI away.)
    (LI leaves.)
    (ZHENG slowly, but firmly, starts to tear the transfer request into small pieces.)

ZHENG: *(loudly)* Oh! My farm! *(He holds his head in his hands and sobs.)*

    (YOUNG MAN A stands behind ZHENG, and tears his own leave application form into small pieces.)
    (CURTAIN)

ACT VI

A few days afterwards. Afternoon.

SECRETARY WU's home. The setting is as in Act IV. The stage is empty when the curtain rises. After a few moments ZHANG XIAOLI's voice can be heard offstage, saying "Now just turn your attention this way, please". ZHANG XIAOLI leads ZHOU MINGHUA onto the stage.

ZHANG: *(standing at the side of the door, politely)* Please come in! *(ZHOU MINGHUA stares at the furnishings, stunned.)*

ZHANG: *(like a tourist guide)* Kindly observe— this is the guest room of a Municipal Com- mittee Secretary's home—it's like this both upstairs and downstairs—electric lights and telephones, steel windows and built-in cup- boards, carpets and sofas, television, radio and tape-recorders—air-conditioning too. *(He points towards a room at one side.)* The bed- room's inside. Please come in.

ZHOU: *(standing at the door, and looking at ZHANG)* What?

ZHANG: Would you normally be allowed to come in? Please do!

ZHOU: No, no, no!

ZHANG: *(opening a cupboard)* Would you like a glass of orangeade? *(Pours a glass for ZHOU)* Here we are!

ZHOU: How can you just take other people's things like that—when they're not even at home?!

ZHANG: It doesn't matter. It's my special privilege. Come on now.

ZHOU: No! I've never taken anything off somebody without their knowing about it.

ZHANG: Oh, I take a lot. The more I take, the happier they are.

ZHOU: Is this the way you've been living for the last ten days or so?

ZHANG: Yes. Do you envy me?

ZHOU: No.

ZHANG: Minghua . . . all the time I've been enjoying this I've been thinking of you—as if I could see you again in Section Head Sun's house, barefoot, covered in sweat, washing clothes, polishing the floor . . . .

ZHOU: Did you ask me to come over here today to see how rich you are nowadays?

ZHANG: I wanted to show you what sort of changes can happen to a man's life if he pretends he has an important father. There's something else I want to show you.

ZHOU: What?

ZHANG: Guess.

ZHOU: You're up to so many tricks . . . I can't guess.

ZHANG: *(takes out his work transfer permit)* Just look at this.

ZHOU: *(takes it and looks at it, wildly happy)* What? You've got it? Wow!

ZHANG: Yes, I've got it. Section Head Sun has arranged all the formalities. Tomorrow I can report for work at the most up-to-date factory in the whole city!

ZHOU: I . . . I must be dreaming . . . .

ZHANG: No. The dream is over.

ZHOU: Wonderful!

ZHANG: *(imitating ZHOU)* Wonderful! Didn't you scold me for pretending to be the son of a high official?

ZHOU: It's still not right. Not proper.

ZHANG: But if I hadn't done it *(waving the transfer permit)*—could we have ever got this? And how about the year before last, when I should have been transferred back, but my place in the queue was taken by some high official's son—was that "proper"?

ZHOU: It's still . . . .

ZHANG: Minghua—I'm not a crook. I haven't stolen anything, or robbed anybody, I haven't killed anyone or set fire to anything, I didn't conspire with the Gang of Four to usurp Party and State power, I didn't try to start the Third World War. I just played a little trick on some officials, that's all.

ZHOU: I've been worried sick about you every day.

ZHANG: I've been pretty scared myself, too. Anyway, from tomorrow on, the scheming and cunning Zhang Xiaoli will be changed back into honest, law-abiding Li Xiaozhang, and I won't have to run this sort of risk again. This is the first and last time.

ZHOU: Really?

ZHANG: Of course. Aren't you unhappy with me the way I am? *(Serious, in a way he has not been before)* I'm that way because I felt empty inside, my life was meaningless . . . I had no future . . . I'd written myself off, hated myself —and I could only take it out on other people . . . but from tomorrow on—I can guarantee you'll be one hundred percent satisfied!

ZHOU: Good—well—I—er—I'd like to tell you some good news . . . .

ZHANG: You poor devil—how could you have any good news?

ZHOU: Haven't you noticed?

ZHANG: Noticed what?

ZHOU: *(shyly)* I'm already . . . .

ZHANG: Already what?

ZHOU: Oh, really! You . . . . *(She whispers in his ear.)*

ZHANG: *(surprised and happy)* Eh? Really? Minghua, Minghua! *(He takes MINGHUA in his arms and caresses her.)* Thank you . . . thank you . . . . Why didn't you tell me earlier?

ZHOU: Didn't I tell you we wouldn't be able to wait much longer?

ZHANG: Oh!

ZHOU: When do you think we'll be able to . . . .

ZHANG: Ummm. I'll register tomorrow . . . perhaps next month . . . .

ZHOU: No, no . . . we can't put it off till then!

ZHANG: Well—what do you think?

ZHOU: Let's get married tomorrow!

ZHANG: *(excited)* All right then, tomorrow. Minghua, from tomorrow on—I'll be someone you can really like . . . .

ZHOU: *(seriously)* I hope so much that you will. You are not satisfied with yourself the way you are—and, to tell you the truth, I'm not happy with the way I am at the moment, either. I wasn't happy with your recent activities, but I've forgiven you—perhaps that's because I'm selfish, too—I'm only concerned about getting married to you, and about our child. So instead of saying I've forgiven you, I should say I've forgiven myself.

ZHANG: Why are you telling me all this?

ZHOU: Perhaps to rekindle our lost ideals, our lost enthusiasm. We should be grateful for this chance. In the future we should work hard, and act like decent citizens. Promise me that from tomorrow on you won't smoke anymore!

ZHANG: *(sincerely)* I promise.

ZHOU: And you won't drink anymore?

ZHANG: I won't.

ZHOU: And you won't deceive people anymore, either!

ZHANG: That's for sure.

ZHOU: For ourselves, and for the sake of our child . . . .

ZHANG: Don't worry. I'll be a good father.

ZHOU: I believe you.

ZHANG: *(holding* MINGHUA's *hand, emotionally)* Minghua!

ZHOU: We'd better leave here soon.

ZHANG: I can't. My performance is not over yet. The last act is tonight.

ZHOU: What's happening?

ZHANG: I told them that first thing tomorrow morning I'd be flying back to Peking and Division Head Qian is insisting on taking me to a play tonight. I'll have to wait until tomorrow before I can say goodbye to this place, and to that impostor, Zhang Xiaoli.

ZHOU: I'd better leave first.

ZHANG: Stay a while longer.

ZHOU: I have to go and tell my father about you being transferred off the farm—and I'll have to make some arrangements about tomorrow.

ZHANG: Will the old fool—er—I mean, my future father-in-law—still be against it?

ZHOU: No. I'm sure he won't.

ZHANG: If your father agrees, you must come and tell me.

ZHOU: How can I tell you? There are too many people here.

ZHANG: If your father agrees just wear your most beautiful dress—and you won't need to say a word—I'll know . . . .

ZHOU: All right.

*(*ZHOU MINGHUA *leaves.* ZHANG *follows her lovingly with his eyes.* DIVISION HEAD QIAN *enters, excited.)*

QIAN: I've got some good news for you!

ZHANG: More good news? What is it?

QIAN: Someone's come to see you.

ZHANG: Who is it?

QIAN: Guess.

ZHANG: Do I know whoever it is?

QIAN: Of course you do.

ZHANG: Auntie Zhao?

QIAN: Wrong.

ZHANG: Section Head Sun?

QIAN: Wrong.

ZHANG: I don't know anybody else here—except Li Xiaozhang, that is. Oh . . . is it Department Head Ma?

QIAN: I'll tell you . . . it's your father.

ZHANG: *(shocked)* My father? What father?

QIAN: What? How many fathers do you have?

ZHANG: No . . . what I meant was—whose father?

QIAN: *Your* father, of course! He's just come from Peking.

*(*ZHANG's *whole body feels weak. He collapses into the sofa.)*

QIAN: What's up with you?

ZHANG: Oh . . . I'm just so happy . . . so happy . . . .

QIAN: You scared me.

ZHANG: Where is he now?

QIAN: He'll be here any moment.

*(*VENERABLE COMRADE ZHANG *arrives, and takes one look at* ZHANG XIAOLI. ZHANG XIAOLI *slowly rises from the sofa. He and* VENERABLE COMRADE ZHANG *stand at opposite ends of the lounge room, staring at each other, without saying a word.* VENERABLE COMRADE ZHANG *inspects* ZHANG XIAOLI *in silence—*ZHANG XIAOLI *looks as if he is expecting a storm to break at any moment.)*

QIAN: *(twittering)* Venerable Comrade Zhang— please sit down—do sit down—oh—why don't you sit down? And you, Little Zhang— why are you looking at your father as if he were a tiger? *(She looks at* VENERABLE COMRADE ZHANG, *and at* ZHANG XIAOLI *again, but they are still staring at each other, silently.)* It's really strange to see the two of you there, father and son . . . when you meet you just stand there, without uttering a word. Oh! I know what it is! Just like in a play: "a reunion after a long separation"—you're both so choked with emotion you can't even talk!

VENERABLE COMRADE ZHANG: I certainly can talk. I have something I want to say. To him.

QIAN: *(continuing to twitter)* Oh, you don't want to talk in front of me, is that it? Of course, of course. I should let the two of you have a good little tête-à-tête. Little Zhang, you stay here with your father—but you will still have to come with me to see the play tonight. I'll be off now. You two have a nice little chat! *(QIAN leaves.)*

VENERABLE COMRADE ZHANG: Don't just stand there. Sit down.

> *(ZHANG XIAOLI sits down, as does VENE-RABLE COMRADE ZHANG.)*
> *(Silence)*

VENERABLE COMRADE ZHANG: Is your name Zhang?

ZHANG: No—it's Li.

VENERABLE COMRADE ZHANG: This is really a case of "Zhang's hat on Li's head"! What is your full name?

ZHANG: Li Xiaozhang.

VENERABLE COMRADE ZHANG: So—you're back to being yourself again. How old are you?

ZHANG: Twenty-six.

VENERABLE COMRADE ZHANG: Are you assigned to the East Sea State Farm?

ZHANG: *(nods his head, surprised)* Yes.

VENERABLE COMRADE ZHANG: Why did you pretend to be my son?

ZHANG: I was miserable. I wanted to be transferred out.

VENERABLE COMRADE ZHANG: You didn't commit any criminal acts?

ZHANG: I could have. But I didn't.

VENERABLE COMRADE ZHANG: Did you manage to get yourself transferred out?

ZHANG: *(glaring at VENERABLE COMRADE ZHANG)* It's all been destroyed by you. You've destroyed my hopes, you've destroyed my happiness—the happiness of three people.

VENERABLE COMRADE ZHANG: Three people?

ZHANG: I was planning to get married to my girlfriend tomorrow.

VENERABLE COMRADE ZHANG: And the third?

ZHANG: Our unborn child.

VENERABLE COMRADE ZHANG: Why did the two of you conceive a child before you were married?

ZHANG: Partly out of love. Partly because we were bored.

VENERABLE COMRADE ZHANG: Why didn't you get married, then?

ZHANG: If you get married you've got no hope of getting off the farm.

> *(Silence)*

VENERABLE COMRADE ZHANG: Why did you impersonate my son? Why did you deceive so many people?

ZHANG: *(excitedly)* Surely I'm not the only one guilty of deception. On the contrary, this hoax is a communal effort. Aren't the very people I am deceiving, deceiving others in their turn? Not only did they provide me with the means and opportunity to perpetrate this hoax— some of them even showed me how to set about deceiving others. I can't deny that I used your position and status to achieve my own personal aims, but didn't they try to make use of my assumed position and status to achieve their much greater personal aims?

VENERABLE COMRADE ZHANG: They? Who are *they*?

ZHANG: *(taking out a pile of reports, letters and papers.)* Look at these. This is from Theatre Director Zhao—she wants to get a bigger flat; this is from Section Head Sun—he wants to get his son-in-law transferred back from the North-East; this is a personal request to you, written last night by Division Head Qian, trying to get herself and Secretary Wu on an overseas delegation. Almost all of them had requests to make of me, but to whom can I address my requests? They all crawl to me, wanting me to solve their problems—but who's going to solve my problem?

> *(VENERABLE COMRADE ZHANG leafs through the letters, papers and reports. He frowns and he walks up and down the room, in deep thought. He seems to forget that ZHANG XIAOLI is there.)*

VENERABLE COMRADE ZHANG: *(in a low voice, but forcefully)* They're all corrupt! Were you going to help them?

ZHANG: They're insatiable. I kept these things just in case I ever needed evidence to prove that they're not as pure as they make out!

VENERABLE COMRADE ZHANG: Did you want to

use that evidence to bring a lawsuit against them?

ZHANG: No. To stop them bringing a lawsuit against me!

VENERABLE COMRADE ZHANG: You thought of everything.

ZHANG: I have no power or influence—this was the only way I had of protecting myself.

VENERABLE COMRADE ZHANG: But do you realize what you're guilty of? Fraud! That's illegal!

ZHANG: Because I impersonated your son.

VENERABLE COMRADE ZHANG: It is fraud to impersonate anybody's son!

ZHANG: But why did I impersonate *your* son? Because when I did, they became so flattering, so toadying—they made everything so easy for me—so easy to do all sorts of things I'd never even dreamt of doing before. If I were to impersonate an ordinary worker's son or a peasant's son, would they have swarmed around me like that? Would all those doors have opened so easily for me? Of course not. Why? Isn't it because you—or people of your status—have special privileges which give you unimpeded access to everything—which give you unrestricted power? If you didn't have such special privileges, neither I, nor anyone else, would want to impersonate your son!

VENERABLE COMRADE ZHANG: Surely that's no justification for you to commit fraud. Because special privileges exist, you want to abuse them —because other people practise deceit, you want to deceive people too? That's a swindler's logic—it's not what decent young men ought to think. It's true that our present cadre system affords a few people unreasonable privileges— but not all officials abuse their special privileges!

ZHANG: So you're the Grand Lord of Incorruptibility, are you?

(ZHANG XIAOLI guffaws sarcastically. VENERABLE COMRADE ZHANG glares at him with such an authoritative air that ZHANG XIAOLI gradually stops his sniggering.)

VENERABLE COMRADE ZHANG: You may have impersonated my son, but you don't understand me at all. You lack a basic understanding of our Party, of our cadre system. I'd like you to give those notes and reports to me.

ZHANG: Why should I give them to you?

VENERABLE COMRADE ZHANG: It's my responsibility to deal with such matters.

(ZHANG XIAOLI hands him the papers.)

ZHANG: All right then. Are you going to arrest me?

VENERABLE COMRADE ZHANG: The departments concerned will deal with you in the appropriate manner.

ZHANG: I see. I know what to expect then.

(SECTION HEAD SUN enters.)

SUN: Come along. Little Zhang. Come and see the play. I've come to pick you up.

ZHANG: *(to* VENERABLE COMRADE ZHANG*)* You see how friendly they are—they've even specially sent a car to pick me up.

VENERABLE COMRADE ZHANG: Who's he?

ZHANG: Section Head Sun—Head of the Cultural Section.

SUN: Er . . . Little Zhang, who is . . . .

ZHANG: My father!

SUN: *(surprised)* Oh! Venerable Comrade Zhang!

ZHANG: *(to* VENERABLE COMRADE ZHANG *)* Can I go and see the play?

SUN: Venerable Comrade Zhang—it's the last performance tonight—let him go, eh?

VENERABLE COMRADE ZHANG: *(to* ZHANG XIAOLI*)* You're responsible for your own behaviour!

(SECRETARY WU and DIVISION HEAD QIAN *enter.)*

QIAN: Venerable Comrade Zhang! This is Comrade Wu.

WU: How are you, Venerable Comrade Zhang.

ZHANG: I'm well. And you, Old Wu?

WU: Have a seat. I didn't expect you so soon.

QIAN: Old Sun, I suppose you've come to take Little Zhang to the play?

SUN: That's right. It's time now. We should be off.

QIAN: Good, let's go, and let them have a chat. Come along Little Zhang!

(DIVISION HEAD QIAN leads ZHANG XIAOLI off, followed by SUN.)

WU: Venerable Comrade Zhang, I suppose you've come about . . . .

VENERABLE COMRADE ZHANG: I've been sent by the Committee for the Investigation of Party Discipline!

WU: Oh?

VENERABLE COMRADE ZHANG: *(taking out a*

letter) This is a letter to the Committee for the Investigation of Party Discipline, sent by the Director of the East Sea State Farm. He's sent a note, signed by you.

WU: Er . . . don't you know about this?

VENERABLE COMRADE ZHANG: *(taking it)* Don't I know about what? You've been had! Swindled!

WU: What? Oh . . . *(suddenly understanding)* Zhang Xiaoli . . . .

VENERABLE COMRADE ZHANG: Zhang Xiaoli isn't my son.

WU: But he's been using your name . . . .

VENERABLE COMRADE ZHANG: Even if I'd asked you personally, you should have refused. *(Takes out the letters and reports written by* DIVISION HEAD QIAN *and the others.)* Look at these! Even worse!

WU: Theatre Director Zhao, Section Head Sun— even my wife!?

VENERABLE COMRADE ZHANG: *(angrily)* It's really sad. Our Party wasn't like this before—it had glorious revolutionary traditions! Don't you remember, Old Wu, during the war, how your children were lost? We gave up everything, in those days—for the revolution. When we took the cities we were still wearing straw sandals, sleeping by the roadside, going through thick and thin with the ordinary people. But what's happened to all those revolutionary traditions nowadays? Of course we can blame the Gang of Four—but they fell more than two years ago, and some comrades still haven't realized that things have changed. This is our Party's tragedy! Old Wu, we've been in the Party for decades—surely this must make us stop and think.

WU: You're right. I'm going to write a self-criticism for my role in the whole business to the Central Committee. And a bit of "ideological re-education" within the ranks of the Party for the other comrades, eh?

VENERABLE COMRADE ZHANG: Yes, they need some "ideological re-education". But those comrades have been involved in a criminal act. The Ministry of Justice might want to prosecute Li Xiaozhang, and the comrades involved might have to appear in court.

WU: I'm not worried about that. But it concerns me that, seeing the prestige of the Party is particularly low at the moment, if this case comes to court, it might . . . .

VENERABLE COMRADE ZHANG: That's the rub. But it can't be covered up. The masses will find out about it sooner or later, and, if they can't tell you what they think to your face, they'll talk behind your back. This sort of thing has been going on for a long time now, and the Party's prestige is getting lower and lower. We can only make our Party open and above board if we allow it to be subject to criticism—only if we openly expose the abuse of privilege and the corruption of some Party Members can the Party overcome its defects—only then does it have any hope!

(ZHOU MINGHUA runs on, wearing an extremely beautiful dress.)

VENERABLE COMRADE ZHANG: We should try Li Xiaozhang in open court. This will give our cadres a lesson, and will also educate our young people—it will save them, get them on our side —and this will avoid a second or third Li Xiaozhang appearing under the name of Zhang Xiaoli.

(ZHOU MINGHUA is shocked. She loses colour.)

WU: All right. I'll ring the Public Security Bureau. *(SECRETARY WU goes over to the phone, and is about to dial.)*

ZHOU: *(crying out)* No! Don't!

(ZHOU screams and faints. SECRETARY WU and VENERABLE COMRADE ZHANG run over to her.)

(CURTAIN)

EPILOGUE

Unfortunately, we can't remember who it was that said "the stage is a forum". In any case, at the moment our stage is a courtroom, and our respected, loyal audience have become spectators at an open trial. We hope that, after they have witnessed the whole proceedings, they will be able to come to their own conclusions about the correctness of the Court's decision.

The JUDGE and the two ASSESSORS are on the podium. LI XIAOZHANG is in the dock. Two bailiffs are sitting behind him. SECRETARY WU, DIVISION HEAD QIAN, SECTION HEAD SUN, THEATRE DIRECTOR ZHAO and STATE FARM DIRECTOR ZHENG are on the witness stand. VENERABLE COMRADE ZHANG is sitting at the desk of the defence attorney. The prosecutor sits at this desk. As the curtain rises, the prosecutor is reading the indictment.

PROSECUTOR: ... and the investigation shows that the case is absolutely watertight. So we have decided to prosecute in Court. That is all.

JUDGE: We have just heard the prosecution read the indictment, and explain the circumstances of this case. Li Xiaozhang—do you admit that the case as presented by the prosecution is true?

LI: *(standing up)* Completely true.

JUDGE: Do you believe what you did constitutes a crime?

LI: I'm not familiar with the law—but I do admit I made a mistake.

QIAN: What?! A mistake? As simple as that?

ZHAO: What was your mistake? Tell us!

JUDGE: Silence!

LI: My mistake is that I was not real. If I were really Venerable Comrade Zhang's son—or the son of some other high official—then everything I did would have been completely legal.

ZHAO: What's that supposed to mean?

QIAN: What impertinence!

SUN: He must be dealt with severely!

JUDGE: Witnesses may not speak without permission of the Court!

LI: I would like to express my thanks to the witnesses in this case. The fact that I was able to do all I did, and that I almost succeeded in getting off the farm, all began with Theatre Director Zhao giving me a start, Section Head Sun giving me a way, Secretary Wu and Division Head Qian giving me a note and Farm Director Zheng giving me a transfer. *(He bows deeply to the witnesses.)* Thank you very much for all your good intentions, thank you for making

things easy for me, thank you for all your kind assistance!

> *(THEATRE DIRECTOR ZHAO is choking with anger, DIVISION HEAD QIAN is fuming, silently, SECTION HEAD SUN just stares vacantly, his mouth open.)*

ZHAO: Comrade Judge, please permit me to say a few words.

JUDGE: Go ahead.

ZHAO: What the accused just said is irrelevant to the case. Please direct him to remain silent!

FARM DIRECTOR ZHENG: No! Comrade Judge, please permit me to speak.

JUDGE: Go ahead.

FARM DIRECTOR ZHENG: I think what the accused just said is completely relevant: it's the truth.

JUDGE: What do the other witnesses think?

WU: *(rising)* I agree with Farm Director Zheng. We should let the accused tell the whole story. That will be—er—helpful.

JUDGE: What else do you have to say, accused?

LI: I would like to ask why Zhou Minghua is not in court.

> *(The JUDGE and the two ASSESSORS converse in a whisper.)*

ASSESSOR: Zhou Minghua has been taken ill. She's in hospital. She can't attend the court.

LI: What's wrong with her?

ASSESSOR: She's undergoing emergency treatment.

LI: *(stunned)* What?

JUDGE: Do you have any other questions?

LI: *(weakly)* No. None. *(LI XIAOZHANG holds his head in his hands and sobs.)*

JUDGE: Now the defence attorney will conduct the defence.

VENERABLE COMRADE ZHANG: *(standing)* I didn't expect the accused to ask me to be his defence attorney. But, seeing I had a clear understanding of the circumstances of the case, I had several conversations with the accused and decided to accept. In the first place, I believe that what he did does constitute the crime of fraud, and that the judicial organs should prosecute him. Otherwise we will not be able to maintain social order, and save young people from straying from the straight and narrow. But two questions presented themselves to me, and I would like Comrade Judge and Comrade Assessors to consider them in their deliberations. First, apart from subjective factors concerning this young man's attitudes and character already existent when he embarked upon this erroneous and dangerous course, I think there are also deeper social and historical factors involved. In my opinion, during the decade of the Cultural Revolution and rule by Lin Biao and the Gang of Four, the policy of sending young people "down into the villages and up into the mountains" was distorted, and this poisoned the minds of many young people. This is a major factor in understanding Li Xiaozhang's behaviour. From this standpoint the accused, Li Xiaozhang, is also a victim. This being the case, should we not deal with the accused leniently? Please consider this. Secondly, the reason the accused could proceed so smoothly in his deceit and his swindling was not due to any particularly brilliant methods he may have employed, but due to the fact that our society still tolerates special privileges and unreasonable ways of getting things done— these can provide any swindler with a fertile ground to perpetrate his fraud. For example, some of the Party members and high officials who were taken in by Li Xiaozhang actually helped him in his crime. Those comrades acted the way they did because, on the one hand, they were influenced by certain feudal ways of behaviour, and, on the other, because they wanted to satisfy their own selfish desires. Consequently, they were not only victims of this fraud—they were accomplices. They should accept that responsibility. When the Court is deciding the punishment for this crime, it should also take that into account.

ZHAO: What? We're accomplices?

SUN: Why should we accept any responsibility for it?

QIAN: Venerable Comrade Zhang! Really, that's too much! I can't understand—I can't agree with you! We're all victims of the Gang of Four!

VENERABLE COMRADE ZHANG: Are you the only victims of the Gang of Four? Our Party, our Country, our People—have suffered much more than you have. Why are you all so concerned with your own interests, and not the interests of the Party—of the Country, of our

People? Just reflect for a moment: while we were being persecuted by the Gang of Four, and longing for liberation from them, what was in our thoughts? Weren't we all looking forward to getting back to work, so as to dedicate our efforts to the revolution? At that time, the masses gave us unlimited sympathy and support. They hoped that we would be able to save the country, and bring happiness to the people. But now—you've forgotten all about that! You let the masses worry about the future of the country, you let them work for the common good—while you worry about getting better accommodation and looking after your own private interests. You let other people's children settle in the countryside, while you dream up thousands of plots and schemes to get your own children back into the cities. You expect the ordinary people to "work hard and live plainly", while you yourselves long for an even more luxurious life. If we don't go through thick and thin with the ordinary people, how can we expect them to be "of one heart and one mind" with us? What really concerns me is that many of our officials—even those who survived the Gang of Four—will fall victim to their own corruption. So, Comrades—watch out! Otherwise some of you who are in the witness stand in this court may well end up in the dock of the Party's Discipline Committee!

(CURTAIN)

沙葉新：馬克思秘史

The Secret History of Marx: Prelude

By Sha Yexin

Translated by Geremie Barmé

On the stage is the solitary form of Marx's grave.

The base of the grave is rectangular with a raised platform of grey granite on which is set a square, marble plaque recording the birth and death dates of Marx. On the gravestone the following words are carved, "Workers of the world, Unite!" Below this are the words, "Philosophers have used different means to explain the world, but the thing is to change it." Below the tombstone stands a bronze bust of Marx[1] around which a number of wreaths and baskets of flowers have been placed.

The curtain rises revealing Marx on the platform of his own grave, sitting in a posture reminiscent of Rodin's 'The Thinker'.

MARX: *(looking around)* Why so many flowers? Oh, I see, it's been a hundred years! *(addressing the audience in a familiar tone)* Did you put them here? Thank you. Unfortunately, I didn't know any of you when I was alive; and, of course, you've never seen me. Even though many of my believers have said they are 'going to see Marx' just before they die, I haven't met any of them. If I had, I certainly would have expressed my gratitude. *(feeling his pockets for cigarettes)* I would be even more grateful if, in the future, you put some boxes of cigars on my grave. After all, I am a materialist, so you should present me with material things.

[1]The bust is actually on top of the tombstone, not at its base.

(The PLAYWRIGHT enters holding two sprigs of plum blossom.)

PLAYWRIGHT: Comrade Marx, I have some cigarettes.

MARX: *(delighted)* Ooh? Excellent. You're a materialist, I see.

(The PLAYWRIGHT hands MARX a cigarette and lights it for him)

MARX: *(drawing deeply)* Thank you.

PLAYWRIGHT: *(presenting the flowers)* These are for you.

MARX: Plum blossom! That's Chinese; are you Chinese?

PLAYWRIGHT: That's right.

MARX: China's a mysterious land. I wrote a lot of articles about the Opium Wars and the Taiping Rebellion back then. I've always thought a lot of the Chinese.

PLAYWRIGHT: Comrade Marx, would it be all right if we had a talk?

MARX: Certainly.

PLAYWRIGHT: You see, I'm a playwright.

MARX: Really, like Shakespeare. I adore Shakespeare; he's eclipsed all other writers in my mind. I'm honoured to have an opportunity to talk with one of Shakespeare's colleagues.

PLAYWRIGHT: What I'd like to talk about with you is your life, work and struggle.

MARX: Ah, an interview for professional purposes.

PLAYWRIGHT: I'm thinking of writing a play about you.

MARX: About me?

PLAYWRIGHT: You're the mentor of the proletarian revolution, the author of the bible of the workers—*Das Kapital*—and a great man.

MARX: No, you are greater than me. After all, I only wrote *Das Kapital*, you want to write *Marx*!

PLAYWRIGHT: You mean to say that I'm taking on more than I can cope with.

MARX: Not at all. I see you don't understand my joke. What I mean is that it will be harder for you to write *Marx* than it was for me to write *Das Kapital*.

PLAYWRIGHT: But why?

MARX: Engels said here at my grave: 'Marx is the most despised and vilified man of our age. All governments, be they autocracies or republics, expelled him; capitalists, whether conservative or absolute democrats, vied with each other to libel and denigrate him.' They decried me as a pitiless God of Thunder, a spirit over Europe, a devil who was scheming to annihilate everything held sacred by man.

PLAYWRIGHT: But you never wanted your enemies to praise you.

MARX: Certainly not. But then even some of my friends thought me to be proud, violent, eccentric, morbid and completely without compassion.

PLAYWRIGHT: Didn't that hurt you?

MARX: As my compatriot and the father of German literature Lessing said, 'I do not crave the approbation of others; yet, though the cold indifference with which I am regarded by those worldly men who find in me no worth whatsoever causes me no terrible grief, it does fill me with feelings of lassitude and dejection.' But, then again, I was more detached than Lessing ever was. I didn't give a thought to the apathy and calumny of my contemporaries, for what I wanted was the recognition of future generations.

PLAYWRIGHT: Well, you have achieved that. If that were not the case then there would not be so many flowers here on your grave. Your portrait hangs in countries throughout the world, your works are published in dozens of languages, and the proletarian political party that you and Engels founded has developed into communist parties with millions of members on all of the continents of the world. The prestige you have today is unparalleled.

MARX: If that is so then it is going to be even more difficult for you to write about me.

PLAYWRIGHT: And why do you say that?

MARX: People in my day slandered me, giving me no 'face' at all; while the people of today have showered me with overwhelming praise, so much so that my face has been buried in cosmetics. But that isn't the real me. I want to make a point of reminding those who praise me: you must depict historical figures in all honesty and entirely in accordance with historical reality. You must beware not to fall into the trap of bourgeois historians and make idols out of your heroes—all done up in platform-sole shoes and with haloes around their heads. Actually, I'm a normal person, just like anybody else.

PLAYWRIGHT: Don't worry, I'm no bourgeois historian; I'm a Marxist.

MARX: Oh, are you? *(taking a gold-rimmed monocle out of his pocket, puts it to his eye and studies the* PLAYWRIGHT *from head to toe)* A Marxist, eh? I'm not a Marxist.

PLAYWRIGHT: *(Shocked)* What? Oh, oh, I see; that's because there are so many false Marxists: the May student movement in Paris in 1968; the recent activities of the Red Brigade in Italy; and even the various religious groups that claim to be your followers. So . . . .

MARX: So it is no surprise that Hegel said only one of his students understood him, and even his understanding wasn't completely accurate. Do you have a proper understanding of me?

PLAYWRIGHT: I'll do my utmost to have one.

MARX: Don't you perhaps think that the philosophy and political ideas I expressed a century ago are stale and out-of-date? Or that they are incapable of explaining the new phenomena that have appeared in socialist and capitalist society?

PLAYWRIGHT: In my opinion, your basic principles still hold true.

MARX: That means you still believe in me?

PLAYWRIGHT: Yes, I do.

MARX: Thank you! Well, then, what were you thinking of writing about me?

PLAYWRIGHT: Your wife Jenny once said that she could write a secret history about the writing of *Das Kapital* . . . .

MARX: So that's it—you want to write a secret history? Jenny also said that such a history would reveal all of the anxieties, worries and fretting . . . it's quite a tragedy.

PLAYWRIGHT: You're not against tragedies, are you?

MARX: No. After all, Aristotle said tragedy can purify the soul.

PLAYWRIGHT: Then please tell me your secret history.

MARX: Let me first say that this so-called secret history is nothing more than the record of the trivia of everyday existence and family life; a collection of minor episodes dispersed through the major struggle.

PLAYWRIGHT: But that's exactly what I want to find out about. Because in your involvement in social, economic and political activities you were Marx the Revolutionary; but Marx the Man disappears entirely, or at least becomes very blurred, in the shadow of those all-important and epoch-making activities. It may well be that in your secret history, amidst the everyday trivia, the episodic and private detail, you will reveal your personality to me, and that your character, inner world and feelings will become clearer to all of us; enabling us to get closer to you.

MARX: I can only hope that will be the case. Would you happen to have another cigarette?

PLAYWRIGHT: Yes, yes.

MARX: *(taking the cigarette)* Let's begin with something that happened in 1894.
   (The PLAYWRIGHT *takes out a tape-recorder)*

MARX: What's that?

PLAYWRIGHT: It's called a tape-recorder.

MARX: A tape-recorder?

PLAYWRIGHT: Yes, it can record everything you say.

MARX: *(fiddling with the machine with great interest)* Things certainly have changed; you can even record my voice. Do you want me to sit closer?

PLAYWRIGHT: No, that's just fine where you are. Please go on.

MARX: *(staring at the recorder)* One day in May 1849, the European revolution was coming to an end, and Engels and I were living in Cologne, editing the *Neue Rheinische Zeitung* . . . .[2]

---

[2]For the full text of this play, see *October* 十月, No. 3, 1983, pp. 4-37.

A Touch of the Absurd
—introducing Gao Xingjian, and his play *The Bus-stop*

By Geremie Barmé

IN JUNE 1983 the controversial playwright Gao Xingjian staged his second play, *The Bus-stop* (*Chezhan* 車站), in the small theatre-in-the-round studio of the Capital Theatre in Peking. Gao's earlier production *Alarm Signal* (*Juedui xinhao* 絕對信號), a deft psychological study of an unemployed youth torn between love and revenge on an uncaring society, had been staged in the same theatre in late 1982 to marvellous effect and widespread public acclaim. Both stylistically and thematically *The Bus-stop* goes further than *Alarm Signal* in breaking away from the staid fifty year-old conventions of the Chinese theatre. It is also the first play to introduce elements of the Theatre of the Absurd to a Chinese audience.[1]

The Bus-stop, not surprisingly, is a play all about waiting. A number of people more or less representing a cross-section of Chinese urban society gather at a bus-stop on the outskirts of a large city on a Saturday afternoon expecting to catch a ride into town. There is an avuncular old man who is looking forward to a crucial game of chess at the cultural palace; a garrulous young ruffian bent on spending his wages on the strange new food that he has heard so much about—yoghurt; a studious bespectacled young man preparing for his university entrance exams by mumbling English sentences such as, 'Open your books! Open your pigs! . . . ' like grace-bestowing mantras; a mother with a job in the local township off to spend the weekend with her husband and child who live in the city; a girl approaching the age of spinsterhood going to meet a prospective husband; an earthy carpenter with a jovial manner and a job in the city, off to teach his trade to a group of young apprentices; and, Director Ma, the porcine but jocular head of a general supplies store off to town to be fêted by some of his cronies. A mysterious and silent stranger stands with the group waiting for the bus. Although none of the others knows what he is doing there, the audience recognizes him as the weary wayfarer of Lu Xun's one-scene play *The Passer-By*, used by playwright Gao as a prelude to *The Bus-stop*. *The Passer-By* is one of the works in Lu Xun's sombre and brooding

---

[1] For a full Chinese text of *Alarm Signal* by Gao Xingjian and Liu Huiyuan, see *Works and Criticism* 作品與爭鳴, No. 3, 1983, pp. 17-36; the text of *The Bus-stop* can be found in *October* 十月, No. 3, 1983, pp. 119-38.

collection of prose-poetry, *Wild Grass*. Written in 1925, it is a heavily symbolic work about a lone traveller who stops to ask for a drink of water from an old man and a young girl who live in a hovel on the wayside. The old man, drained of all energy and hope, offers no solace or guidance to the traveller, while the young girl scampers to get him a drink and cloth to bandage his feet. Not detained by the old man's advice to give up his trek, and beckoned onwards by a voice, the Passer-By trudges on. Gao gives a very orthodox interpretation of this play as an allegory of the journey and struggle of the Chinese people for a more hopeful albeit uncertain future. Thus, nearly sixty years later, the Passer-By appears alongside the other passengers waiting at a bus-stop. A number of buses, represented by sound recordings and lighting effects, flash past heedless of the motley band of travellers who are busy arguing with each other and jostling for a place in line. The silent stranger, still consumed by his ancient *Wanderlust*, picks up his sack and continues his journey on foot.

Buses continue to roll past as the group push and shove so as to be first to get on. When none of the buses stop, they get into an orderly line in the belief that this will bring the next bus to a halt. Again a bus passes without stopping. The dialogue is fast moving and highly colloquial, combining the tempo of cross-talk 相聲 with the sardonic humour of Beijing dialect. Gao and the talented director of the production, Lin Zhaohua, are careful to avoid the leaden pedagogy and unconvincing characterization of other recent drama. The play continues in a light, semi-farcical naturalistic mood until the last bus whooshes past the small group. The bad-tempered recriminations and selfish jostling gradually give way to panic and fear that they will never get into town. Will a bus ever stop for them? Is it really a bus-stop they're waiting at? The sharp-tongued yobbo cries that he would have been able to *crawl* into the city by now if he hadn't stayed hanging around for the bus. Each character is caught in the dilemma of whether to go back or walk on into town. Nobody moves. The group is frozen by what appears to be a mass paralysis of will. A vision of the stranger entices some of them to action, and jarring music strikes up. The young student declares that five, no six, seven, eight . . . months have passed. In a dizzying play of disco lights accompanied by the ponderous ticking of a clock the years fly by, eight, nine, ten. Things fall apart, but the show goes on.

'Plus ça change, plus c'est la même chose.' The band of travellers is as bewildered by the flight of time as is the unsuspecting audience; yet still they do nothing. Time, just like all those buses earlier, speeds by as they squabble, sigh over lost opportunities and dream about a future that in a flash has turned into an unredeemable past. Catapulted far into the future, they lose themselves for a while in talk of change, growth, decay and death, yet always come back to the central question of whether they should walk into the city. They still keep pulling in different directions. 'Life must have a meaning!' cries the earnest, now somewhat pedantic, young student: they should walk into town together. It starts to rain. Following a few frenzied moments during which each person tries to keep dry regardless of the others, they huddle together under a large sheet of plastic. As the rain comes to a stop they split into groups discussing their predicament with each other and then directly with the audience. They talk over each other; it is the first time polyphonic dialogue and direct address have been used on the Chinese stage, so the actors are a little hesitant to really let go, still more concerned with verbal clarity than dramatic effect. This, along with the experimental use of a theatre-in-the-round stage, is all part of Gao and Lin's attempts to break down the 'glass wall' that still separates audiences from the stage in a country where Brecht and Artaud have never been given a hearing.

No bus will stop for them. There is no easy way out, no instant salvation. A casual Saturday afternoon outing has turned into a topsy-turvy nightmare. The fractionated interests and efforts of the passengers are gradually over-shadowed by the common realization of a need for resolution and action. The young student is the first to decide to walk, the others still talk on. 'I really don't understand . . . perhaps . . . they're waiting   time is not a bus-stop . . . life isn't a bus stop . . . . Yet they don't really want to go . . . . Let's move, we've said everything that can be said . . . come on!'[2] They take up his call 'Let's go', echoing it in an impotent refrain. Eventually, as they make to go the podgy Director Ma calls out for everyone to wait a moment: he bends down to tie up his shoe-lace. The lights go out.

Perhaps all this smacks a little too obviously of Samuel Beckett's *Waiting for Godot*? In fact, Gao Xingjian is frank about his debt to Beckett, Artaud and a host of writers and theorists of the Theatre of the Absurd. Beckett said in his monumental play, 'Nothing happens, nobody comes, nobody goes, it's awful'.[3] If *The Bus-stop* is nothing more than a Chinese version of *Waiting for Godot*, then Gao has got it all wrong: nothing happens and nobody comes, but the irrepressible passer-by from the 1920s appears, waits momentarily with the others and then forges on regardless; the other passengers, forced to look beyond their petty differences and individual concerns, frustrated by their own inaction and weighed on by the relentless passing of time, become wayfarers in turn, united in the hope of getting to the city by their own efforts. Ma stops to tie up his shoelace and the play ends; maybe they will all be reduced to meaningless back-biting again; they might simply just keep on talking about walking into town; or, perhaps they will finally make a start. A group of prisoners who saw *Waiting for Godot* in San Quentin took to the play immediately; they had no trouble understanding Vladimir and Estragon's dilemma, 'Godot is society . . . . He's the outside'. The prisoners knew 'what is meant by waiting . . . . They knew if Godot finally came, he would only be a disappointment'.[4] Gao Xingjian's passengers are waiting too; the bus comes but never stops, though that is more their fault than anything else. They are left waiting, certainly, but they have an aspired direction; their dilemma is far from being either existential or absurd. It is rather one of strategy and means—when and how they should move on. There is never any real doubt that they can and must go towards the city. Gao's work does not aim at forcing the audience to confront the half-realized fears and anxieties of the human mind. Rather his positivistic view of contemporary Chinese society has a definite moral undertone: unite and work together, but be careful not to neglect the importance and value of the individual. Gao might be inspired

[2]See *October*, p. 138.

[3]*Waiting for Godot*, Faber & Faber, London 1959, p. 41.

[4]See *The Theatre of the Absurd*, Martin Esslin, Penguin Books, 1968, p. 20.

by Beckett and Ionesco, but he is keeping his themes well within the didactic tradition of Ibsen and Stanislavsky.

Gao Xingjian is well-suited to be the first writer to introduce erstwhile European *avant-garde* culture to a receptive young Chinese audience. Now in his early forties, Gao studied French as a university student, and was given work as a translator on the French-language edition of *China Reconstructs* after graduation. While at university he read widely in French as well as making a systematic study of classical Chinese literature; a familiarity with the literature of both Europe and China, though expected among writers of the 1930s, is all but unheard of among his contemporaries. Five years in a cadre school during the Cultural Revolution brought him into direct contact with the crude realities of life in the Chinese countryside, while at the same time providing him with ample opportunity to read and write. Following a short period back at the Foreign Languages Press, Gao was transferred to work as a translator in the Chinese Writers' Association, continuing to write in his spare time. Caught up in the post-Cultural Revolution writing boom, he published his first novella in early 1978. Three years later he was given another transfer, this time to the People's Art Troupe 人民藝術劇院, China's foremost performing arts company, as a writer, not a translator. He has written eleven plays to date, the first of these to be performed being *Alarm Signal*, which though controversial at the time has cleared the way for more 'abstract' and daring works to be staged, such as *The Bus-stop*. *Alarm Signal* enjoyed a solid run of one hundred performances in Beijing, an impressive record for an art form badly hit by the recent upsurge in television entertainment and a revived film culture. Restaged by companies throughout the country, the play, which relies heavily on the use of unconventional sound and lighting effects—unconventional for Chinese audiences, heavily overused in the West—has given some Chinese writers and directors a glimpse at a range of new potentials for the theatre as a medium for artistic expression and human communication. Though some critics bewailed the nearly heretical break the People's Art Troupe had made with its solid socialist-realist traditions in performing *Alarm Signal*, more kindly disposed commentators hailed it as a 'new signal for experimentation and reform in Chinese drama'.[5]

In both *Alarm Signal* and *The Bus-stop* the influence of the formidable French dramatist, God-madman, Antonin Artaud is evident. Gao Xingjian is open about his interest in Artaud's view of 'theatre as the double of life' and desire for a drama in which each performance is 'une sorte d'événement' (a kind of happening) which can shake the audience and have a cathartic effect on them. Gao's use of the theatre-in-the-round, various stage effects, polyphonic dialogue, and so on, are all part of post-War western theatre conventions that Chinese audiences are just beginning to learn about. Yet it has only been five years between the publication of Harold Pinter's *The Birthday Party* in Chinese, introduced in a lengthy article about the Theatre of the Absurd by the literary historian Zhu Hong in 1978,[6] and the performance of China's first attempt at a Theatre of the Absurd drama, *The Bus-stop*.

---

[5] "A Signal Worthy of Our Attention—Introducing the play *Alarm Signal* performed by the People's Art Troupe" 一個引人注目的信號——介紹北京人藝演出的《絕對信號》, by Tang Sixia and Luo Jun.

[6] See *World Literature* 世界文學, No. 2, 1978, pp. 213-310.

As is usual in such cases of adaptation and experimentation, purists of either western or Chinese drama are likely to take umbrage at Gao Xingjian and Lin Zhaohua's hard-won achievement. I personally see these plays as a striking departure from outdated theatrical convention, stereotyped characterization and acting, as well as unimaginative and unpopular playwriting. Gao's plays have positively enriched the range of expression open to artists involved in all forms of the performing arts in China, and have encouraged people to look into their own cultural heritage and literature to see what positive contributions it can make to the contemporary arts scene.

The *avant-garde* might just be coming into its own in mainland China after a hiatus of nearly fifty years,[7] but elsewhere it is all somewhat *passé*. It is more than likely that the present interest in 'modernism' among the educated urban élite will come under increasing attack by those in favour of 'national forms', as it did in Taiwan in the late 60s and the 70s. In fact, just such a 'popular reaction' is presently being orchestrated by the authorities in the form of a debate about 'national forms' in the arts. Gao Xingjian is an adept at the juggling of mainland cultural jargon, and so far he has been careful to emphasize the 'traditional' and 'Chinese' aspects of his experimentation in the theatre and writing. Taiwanese writers managed to weather that period of 'native soil' reaction—during which a large body of well-written 'native soil literature' was produced—along with its slight touches of xenophobia, to create what appears to be a unique and modern Chinese culture. It is doubtful that 'modernism' will have a similar fate in the mainland. That 'modernism' has been able to develop in mainland China over the last few years at all is astounding; that it will flourish and result in a revolution in content and not just a faddish experimentation with artistic forms is unlikely. I personally think that the movement, though interesting and much needed, is doomed, as it is hard to imagine that the authorities would ever allow the arts to outstrip official policy, much less venture into areas where Communist orthodoxy is loth to go, and where the *avant-garde* will perforce lead it.

On a more optimistic note, towards the end of the year Gao Xingjian's third play is due to be performed in Peking. This time he will be concentrating his efforts more on a melding of Western stage craft with traditional Chinese theatre in what he calls 'modern opera-drama sketches' 現代折子戲. With his background in Western literature and culture as well as a thorough grounding in Chinese theatre and writing, Gao is the first member of the middle-aged generation of Chinese writers to be capable of such experimentation. As such, his work is naturally given more attention than it would otherwise deserve, but until more writers like him come along everything he does will be eagerly awaited by audiences in China and those interested in the Chinese cultural scene overseas.[8]

---

[7]As early as the 20s even relatively obscure young writers like Li Jinfa and Feng Zikai used journals such as *Literature Weekly* 文學週報 to introduce the Western *avant-garde*. Li continued to write his little-understood poetry (see "Modernism in Modern Chinese Literature", 浪漫之餘 by Leo Lee, Taiwan 1981, pp. 39-74), while Feng wrote and lectured about Dadaism, the Constructionists and abstract art (see 西洋美術史, by Feng Zikai, Kaiming Shudian, Shanghai 1928, pp. 233-46).

[8]Editor's note: The Spiritual Pollution compaign intervened at the end of 1983, and Gao's plans had to be shelved.

PHOTOGRAPHS of the original Peking stage production of *The Bus-stop*, courtesy Wolfgang Kubin.

高行健：車站

The Bus-stop

By Gao Xingjian
Translated by Geremie Barmé

THE FOLLOWING EXCERPT is translated from the Chinese text of The Bus-stop *as publish-ed in the bimonthly literature journal,* Shiyue *(October), 1983 No. 3, pp. 119-38. This translation starts from the third line on page 129 and finishes with the third last line on page 133 of the published text. The original play would have taken over four and a half hours to be performed on stage; the present version of the work lasts for just over an hour. The text of the play may well have been further altered following the first performances of* The Bus-stop *in June, 1983. The descriptions of the characters have been added by the translator, who saw the play at a preview in Peking.*

Characters (in order of appearance)

SILENT MAN:	A middle-aged man carrying a bag. He impatiently waits for the bus and, as if responding to some inaudible call, starts out for the city by himself without a word to any of the others. His silhouetted form reappears from time to time along with the music of his 'signature tune'.
DIRECTOR MA:	An ageing and porcine cadre, approximately fifty years old. He is a petty dealer and seeming expert in *guanxixue* (the 'science of connections and backdoorism' as presently practised on all levels of Chinese society) who is going to town for a banquet which, he claims, he doesn't care if he misses.
GLASSES:	A studious young man of thirty years who breaks off conversations to swot English. He generally affects the attitude of a somewhat idealistic young intellectual.
OLD MAN:	A man in his late sixties who is going to the Cultural Palace in the city to have the chess game of his life.
MOTHER:	Forty years old; very obviously on the threshold of a mid-life crisis.
GIRL:	An ungainly woman in her late-twenties, paranoid about becoming a spinster and tormented by bouts of melancholia and hysteria as a result. She's off into town to meet a last-hope blind date.
LOUT:	A brash and inconsiderate young man of about nineteen. He has his heart set on testing the latest 'city-side' taste sensation — yoghurt.
CARPENTER:	About forty-five. A dull-witted, 'salt of the earth' type with a heavy (Shandong) accent.

(Up to this point the action of the play has largely consisted of the characters getting angry with the LOUT *for jumping the queue, squabbling between themselves and making various ineffectual attempts to get onto one of the buses that occasionally speed by. One by one they have revealed their reasons for going into the city. Meanwhile,* GLASSES *has noticed to his astonishment that time is slipping by at an alarming rate—one year has passed since they started waiting at the bus-stop. The* SILENT MAN *has also disappeared; presumed to be walking into town.)*

DIRECTOR MA: Wait here if you want to, I'm going back. Any of you going to come with me?

(Silence. The lights dim and the sound of a bus can be heard in the distance. The signature tune of the SILENT MAN *becomes audible again, soft yet distinct. The searching beat of the music becomes clearer.)*

GLASSES: Listen, can you hear it? It's . . . .
(The music fades.)

GLASSES: Why couldn't you hear it? That fellow must have got into the city ages ago. We can't wait any longer; it's useless to keep on waiting. This is meaningless torture.

OLD MAN: You're absolutely right. I've been waiting my whole life. Waiting just like this, always waiting. Now I'm an old man.

MOTHER: *(at the same time as the* GIRL*)* If I'd known there was going to be so much bother, I wouldn't have brought such a large bag with me. It would be such a waste to throw these dates and sesame seeds away.

GIRL: *(at the same time as the* MOTHER*)* I'm exhausted, and I probably look a wreck. I know I'd feel much better if I could just have a short nap.

LOUT: Cut the crap. We could have all crawled into town by now if you lot hadn't just hung around here yapping.

CARPENTER: Why didn't you make a start then?

LOUT: If you go first, we'll all crawl after you.

CARPENTER: I'm no damned maggot that crawls around in a cesspool. I use my hands for my work.

GLASSES: *(facing the audience)* Hey, still waiting for the bus, are you? That's strange, no reply.

(Louder) Anybody over there waiting for a bus?

GIRL: It's pitch black. I can't see a thing; it's night. Now there really won't be any buses.

CARPENTER: We'll wait till dawn. The bus-stop's not going to disappear. They can't fool me.

DIRECTOR MA: And if the bus still doesn't come? I suppose, like a right ass, you're going to wait here for it for the rest of your life.

CARPENTER: I've got my trade—they need people like me in the city. What would anyone want you for?

DIRECTOR MA: *(feeling slighted)* I'm invited for a meal, but I don't care if I never make it.

CARPENTER: Why don't you get off back home then?

DIRECTOR MA: I've been thinking about it for a while now. *(Troubled)* I'll have to go all the way back through the open countryside; no houses or villages for miles. What if a dog leaps out at me from the darkness—Hey, which one of you wants to go back with me?

OLD MAN: I've been thinking of going back, too. But it seems to be the less inviting alternative: walking along that path in the dead of night.

LOUT: I'm gonna have a taste of yoghurt if it's the last thing I do. I'll have five jars of it in one go.[1] *(To* GLASSES*)* Don't waste your time on them. Let's just the two of us get going.

GLASSES: What if the bus comes after we leave? *(Faces the audience and continues as if thinking out loud.)* And if it comes but fails to stop again? Looking at the problem rationally, I know I should start walking; it's just that I'm not one hundred percent sure. What's stopping me is the nagging suspicion that it'll come. I must make a plan! *Desk, dog, pig, book,*[2]

[1] In China yoghurt is presently packaged in small jars not unlike old-fashioned honey pots, which are sealed with a thin paper cover. Generally sold chilled as a beverage in the warmer months, it is commonly 'drunk' through a straw, though spoons are occasionally provided at road-side stalls for those who prefer to eat it. Yoghurt has only become fashionable, indeed only deemed edible at all, in the last few years.

[2,3] GLASSES, being a pseudo-intellectual, prefers English red herrings. The words and sentences in italics here were in English in the original text. GLASSES mumbles mysterious English incantations throughout the play.

should I stay or go? It's the enigma of our existence. Perhaps Fate has decreed that we must wait here forever, till we all grow old and die. But why do people accept the capricious rulings of Fate? Then again, what exactly is Fate? *(Addressing the* GIRL*)* Do you believe in Fate?

GIRL: *(softly)* Yes.

GLASSES: You can think of life as a coin. *(Takes a coin out of his pocket.)* Do you believe in this? *(He flicks the coin in the air and catches it.)* Heads or tails? *Pig, book, desk, dog,* that's decided it! *Are you teachers? No. Are you pig?* No, I'm none of those, *I am I.*[3] I am who I am. You don't believe in yourself, but you do believe in this? *(Self-mockingly he flicks the coin again and catches it.)*

GIRL: What do you think we should do? I don't even have the strength to make a decision.

GLASSES: Let's gamble with Fate: heads we wait, tails we go. It all depends on the coin—*(He flicks the coin into the air. It falls to the ground and* GLASSES *covers it over with the palm of his hand.)* Do we stay or do we go? Stay or go? Let's see what Fate has decreed.

GIRL: *(hurriedly pressing her hand over his)* I'm scared. *(Realizing that she's touching his hand she recoils suddenly.)*

GLASSES: What, scared of your own fate?

GIRL: I don't know; I don't know anything any more.

LOUT: Those two really take the cake. Oi, are you two going or aren't you?

CARPENTER: Haven't you gone on enough already? Whoever is going to walk, get moving and be done with it. Look, here's the bus-stop and there are people waiting at it. How come there's no bus? How can they expect to stay in business if they don't pick up any passengers?
(Silence. The sound of an approaching bus and the tune of the SILENT MAN *can be heard, and gradually become more distinct.)*

DIRECTOR MA: *(waving his hands as if to disperse the disturbing sounds)* Hey, any of you going to walk?
(The sounds stop. The OLD MAN, *who has been leaning against the bus-stop napping, lets out a snort.)*

OLD MAN: *(without opening his eyes)* Is a bus coming?

(No one replies.)

LOUT: It's like we're all glued to this bus-stop. What a bummer! *(Takes a* wok *and then flops down on the ground despondently.)*
(The others variously crouch or sit on the ground. A bus can be heard approaching. All listen intently, but no one makes a move. The sound gets louder as the lights in the theatre become brighter.)

LOUT: *(still lolling on the ground)* A bus, wow.

MOTHER: It's about time. Come on, old man, wake up—it's dawn and a bus is coming.

OLD MAN: Uh, a bus? *(Getting up hurriedly)* You're right.

GIRL: It won't drive by and leave us standing here again, will it?

GLASSES: If it looks like it's not going to stop we'll block the road.

GIRL: I just know it isn't going to stop.

OLD MAN: They wouldn't dare; it's their job.

MOTHER: Yes, but what if it really doesn't stop?

LOUT: *(jumping to his feet)* Hey, carpenter, do you have any nails in your bag?

CARPENTER: Why?

LOUT: If he doesn't stop, we can blow his tyres; then no one'll be going into the city.

GIRL: You can't—it's against the law to disrupt transportation services.

GLASSES: I still say we should block its path. All right everyone, line up along the road.

CARPENTER: Right you are.

LOUT: *(picking up a stick)* Hurry up, it's coming.
(Everyone stands up at the sound of the approaching bus.)

GIRL: *(shouting)* S—t—o—p!

MOTHER: We've been waiting a whole year.

OLD MAN: Hey you—stop! Stop I say.

DIRECTOR MA: Ahoooy . . . .
(They all push to the front of the stage and make to block the road. A horn sounds.)

GLASSES: *(directing everyone)* One, two . . . .

ALL TOGETHER: Stop! . . . Stop!

GLASSES: It's been a whole year!

ALL TOGETHER: *(waving and shouting)* We can't wait any longer! Stop, stop. S—t—o—p . . . .
(The sound of a horn blaring wildly.)

LOUT: *(running forward with his stick upraised)* I'll show you.

GLASSES: *(holding him back)* You'll be run over.

GIRL: *(closing her eyes in horror)* Dear . . . .

CARPENTER: *(rushing forward he pulls the* LOUT *to a halt)* Do ya' wanna' get yourself killed?

LOUT: *(breaking free and running after the bus, he throws the stick after it)* Damned well hope ya' flip into a river and the fish suck ya' brains.
(The sound of the horn fades into the distance.)

CARPENTER: *(at a loss)* It was full of foreigners.

MOTHER: It was a bus-load of tourists.

GLASSES: Thinks he's some big deal, that driver does. Just because he's driving a bus full of foreigners.

OLD MAN: *(grumbling)* Wasn't even full.

CARPENTER: *(baffled and hurt)* We're waiting here at the bus-stop just like we should. We'll buy tickets; what's wrong with our money?

DIRECTOR MA: Do you have foreign currency?[4] You need foreign money to get onto that bus.

OLD MAN: *(stamping his feet in frustration)* But this isn't a foreign country.

GIRL: I knew it—I said they wouldn't stop for us.
(At this moment a number of vehicles flash past them. They are represented by different colours and sounds, and are moving in opposite directions.)

DIRECTOR MA: This is just too much. They're playing games with us. If no one's going to stop, we might as well not wait here any more. But let me tell you something: if the Bus Company isn't given a shake up, there's no way the transportation situation will improve. What you all have to do is to write an official complaint. I'll take it to the Transportation Department personally. *(Pointing at* GLASSES.*)* You can write it.

GLASSES: All right, but what should I say?

DIRECTOR MA: What? Oh, well, you say, . . . see, well . . . . What type of intellectual are you supposed to be? Why, you don't even know how to write a letter of complaint.

GLASSES: What good would it do anyhow? Won't we still be left standing here?

DIRECTOR MA: You can keep on waiting here if you want, I'm not in any particular hurry. I

---

[4]Or in full, Foreign Currency Exchange Certificates *(waihuiquan)*, known to foreigners as 'funny money'. This is a clone currency of China's *Renminbi*, except for the fifty *yuan* note, and is supposedly restricted for use by people who are not citizens of the People's Republic.

didn't want to have that meal in town in the first place; and what should I care about any of you? Go on and wait if you want. See if I care.
(They all remain silent. The signature tune of the SILENT MAN *starts up and becomes a quick and taunting melody in triple time.)*

GLASSES: *(looks at his watch. Shocked)* I don't believe it.
(The GIRL *goes over to look at his watch. They count the numbers indicated on the face of the watch in time with the music.)*

GLASSES: *(continuously pressing the indicator button on his digital watch)* Five, six, seven, eight, nine, ten, eleven, twelve, thirteen months . . . .

GIRL: . . . one month, two months, three months, four months . . . .

GLASSES: . . . five months, six months, seven months, eight months . . . .

GIRL: . . . one year and eight months altogether.

GLASSES: Another year has just gone by.

GIRL: That makes it two years and eight months.

GLASSES: Two years and eight months, . . . no, it's three years and eight months. No, I'm wrong— five years and six months . . . . Seven, eight, nine, ten months.
(They all look at each other in amazement.)

LOUT: This is crazy.

GLASSES: I can assure you that I'm quite sane.

LOUT: Wasn't talkin' about you. I said my watch's had a nervous breakdown.

GLASSES: Mechanical devices don't have nerves. A watch is a mechanism that measures time and it isn't influenced by the psychological states of its owner.

GIRL: Please don't, I beg of you.

GLASSES: Don't try to stop me. None of this is up to me. There's no way you can hold back the passage of time. Come on everyone and have a look at this watch.
(All crowd around GLASSES *and peer at his watch.)*

GLASSES: Six years, seven years, eight years, nine years. See, ten whole years have passed just while we were talking.

CARPENTER: Are you sure you haven't got it wrong? *(Grabs his wrist, shakes it, holds it to his ear and listens, then looks at the face of the watch.)*

LOUT: *(coming forward he grabs the button on*

the watch.) See—no numbers now, just a blank dial. *(Raising* GLASSES' *arm for all to see.)* One touch of that knob and it's all over. *(Smugly)* Nearly got taken in that time.

GLASSES: *(gravely)* How can you be so stupid? Just because you've swtiched off my watch, it doesn't mean that Time itself has stopped. The existence of Time is an objective reality; it can be proven by mathematical formulae—T= $\sqrt{a}+\beta \times \Sigma^2$, or something.... It's all in Einstein's Theory of Relativity.

GIRL: *(hysterical)* I can't take it any more.

OLD MAN: This is a disgrace; *(coughs)* making passengers stand around waiting till their hair turns grey.... *(Suddenly becoming quite decrepit.)* Preposterous, absolutely preposterous.

CARPENTER: *(pained)* The Bus Company must be trying to get even with us for something. But we haven't done anything to them, have we?

MOTHER: *(overcome with exhaustion)* What's going to happen to my darling Peipei and her father now? They don't even have a decent change of clothes... and him without a clue about sewing.

(The LOUT *walks to one side and kicks stones along the ground, then sitting down despondently he spreads his legs out and stares straight ahead in a daze.)*

GIRL: *(numbly)* I want to cry.

MOTHER: Yes, dear, have a good cry. It's nothing to be ashamed of.

GIRL: But I can't....

MOTHER: It's not our fault that we were born women. We're doomed to wait, it's simply our lot in life. It starts when we wait for the right man to come along, and then we wait until we get married. Then we wait for a child, after which we wait till the child grows up. By then we've already grown old, and....

GIRL: I'm old already.... *(Leaning on the* MOTHER's *shoulder.)*

MOTHER: Go on and cry if you want; you'll feel much better if you do. If he was here and held me in his arms, I'd just cry and cry... I can't tell you why I feel like this, it's hard to explain.

DIRECTOR MA: *(turns to the* OLD MAN *balefully)* I'm telling you it's not worth it, old man. Why not grow old in the peace and calm of your own home. All this playing of the lute, chess, calligraphy and painting[5] is for whiling away the hours at home. Why do you have to go into the city to find yourself a partner anyway? Is it worth throwing your last years away here on the road?

OLD MAN: What would you know about it? All you can think about is your infernal wheeling and dealing. The whole point of chess is the feeling of exhilaration you get from it; it's all a matter of the spirit of the thing. The spirit of the thing, that's what life's all about.

(The LOUT, *looking extremely bored, swaggers up behind* GLASSES *and gives him a hard slap on the shoulder which snaps him out of his silent reverie.)*

GLASSES: *(angrily)* You don't understand what pain is—that's why you're so indifferent. We've been cast aside by life, forgotten. The world is fleeting by in front of you and you don't even see it. You might be happy to muddle along like this, but I'm not.

CARPENTER: *(sadly)* I can't go back. I'm a carpenter, I make hardwood furniture. I'm not going into the city just to make money, I've got a service to provide. Back home I get by pretty well—with my tools I can knock a bed together, make a dining-room table or a cabinet. We get by all right we do, my family and me. I can't let the craft that's been handed down to me by my ancestors die out like this. You might be a big-wig Director, but there's no way you can understand how I feel.

GLASSES: *(pushing the* LOUT *aside)* Leave me alone. *(In a sudden fury)* I need some quiet. Can't you understand? I need to be left alone.

(The LOUT *moves away obediently, makes to whistle but then takes his fingers out of his mouth.)*

GIRL: *(facing the audience and thinking out loud)* I've had many dreams in the past, some of them very beautiful....

MOTHER: *(facing the audience and saying to herself)* Sometimes I wanted to dream.

(The following speeches are spoken simultaneously and weave together as the characters address the audience, ignoring each other.)

GIRL: I've dreamt that the moon can laugh out loud....

[5] *Qin, qi, shu, hua,* the elegant pastimes of the 'retired scholar' in classical times.

MOTHER: But then I'd always collapse on the bed dead tired. I could never got enough sleep . . . .

GIRL: I dreamt he was holding my hand and speaking in my ear softly. I really wanted to stay close to him . . . .

MOTHER: From the moment I opened my eyes Peipei would be standing there in front of me with a toe sticking out of one of her socks . . . .

GIRL: I don't have any dreams left now . . . .

MOTHER: The hem on the sleeve of her father's sweater would have come undone, too . . . .

GIRL: No black bear would ever jump out at me now . . . .

MOTHER: Peipei wants a little battery-drive car . . . .

GIRL: And no one chases after me ferociously . . . .

MOTHER: Twenty cents for a kilo of tomatoes . . . .

GIRL: I won't be having any more dreams now.

MOTHER: That's how mothers are. *(Turning her head in the* GIRL*'s direction)* I wasn't a bit like you when I was your age.
(The following is a dialogue between the GIRL *and the* MOTHER.*)*

GIRL: You can't imagine how much I've changed —I've become so petty. I can't stand to see prettily dressed girls. I know it's not right for me to feel the way I do, but whenever I see city girls all done up and wearing those high-heel shoes, it makes me feel as though they've walked all over me and are flaunting themselves in front of me just to rub it in. But I know I shouldn't have these feelings.

MOTHER: I understand. I don't blame you . . . .

GIRL: You'd never believe how jealous I feel; I hate them all.

MOTHER: Come now, don't be so silly. You shouldn't be so hard on yourself.

GIRL: I've always wanted to wear one of those floral dresses. You know, the type that's all just one piece, with a little zip at the waist. But I don't even dare make one,—in the city it's different, everyone walks around in public in dresses like that. How could I ever wear something like that here?

MOTHER: *(caressing the* GIRL*'s hair)* Let me give you some advice: whatever you want to do don't wait until you're my age to do it. You're still young, there's sure to be boys who'd be interested in you. You'll fall in love, then

you'll bear his child and he'll care for you for the rest of your life.

GIRL: Go on, don't stop. Have you really found some grey hairs?

MOTHER: *(inspecting her hair)* No, no. Really, I haven't.

GIRL: Don't lie to me.

MOTHER: Well, yes; but there's only one or two strands.

GIRL: Pull them out.

MOTHER: But you can't tell, honestly. If I pull them out you'll only get more.

GIRL: Please, I beg of you.
(The MOTHER *pulls out a strand of grey hair. Suddenly hugging the girl to her she starts to cry.)*

GIRL: What's wrong?

MOTHER: I've got so much grey hair—my hair's almost white.

GIRL: No it isn't. *(Hugging her they cry in each other's arms.)*

LOUT: *(sitting on the ground. He slaps a banknote down, takes some playing cards out of his pocket and throws them on the ground as well)* Okay, I'll take on any of ya' for a fiver. All or nothing.
(The OLD MAN *feels his pocket fretfully.)*

LOUT: Don't worry, I made it all doing odd jobs. If luck's with ya' you can make yourself a little ready cash, no sweat. I don't care—there's no way I'm going to hang around here any longer.
(DIRECTOR MA and the OLD MAN move closer.)

LOUT: All right, which one of you's puttin' up the stake? Three dollars in one hand, four in the other—I've only been able to harvest a 'crop' of five bucks—just enough for a return fare to town and a drink of yoghurt. It's all here.

DIRECTOR MA: How's a young fellow like yourself managed to fall into such bad ways?

LOUT: Aw, give over. Keep your speeches for your own kids. How about you old man, feelin' lucky? Come on, you can put money on two of the cards. It's only a fiver. If you pick the right card it proves luck's on your side; if you lose, well, a few dollars isn't anything to a man of your age and stature. If you wanna bet for a round of drinks, don't worry—I'm buying.
(The CARPENTER *walks over to join them.)*

LOUT: Gate to Heaven, Gate to Earth, Green

Dragon, White Tiger.[6] Come on, which'll it be?
   (The CARPENTER *cuffs him.)*
LOUT: If I can't go into the city and have my
   yoghurt, what else is there for me to do?
   (Bursts into tears.) Let the bloody city dudes
   prance along their damned roads then . . . .
OLD MAN: Come on m'lad, pick 'em up.
   (The LOUT *rubs his eyes with the back of his
   dirty hand, blows his nose and picks up the
   money and cards. Lowering his head he continues to whimper. Silence. Gradually, the
   sound of traffic intermingled with the tune
   of the* SILENT MAN *becomes audible in the
   distance, rising and falling in pitch. The
   tempo of the music speeds up and it turns
   into a lively melody.)*
GLASSES: There's not going to be any bus. *(With
   finality)* Let's start walking, like that man.
   While we've been wasting all this time at this
   bus-stop, he's had time enough to get into the
   city and really do something. There's nothing
   worth waiting for here.
OLD MAN: You're absolutely right. *(To the* GIRL*)*
   Don't cry any more. If you'd gone along with
   that man you'd have been married long ago,
   and your child would be walking by now. Instead we've all stayed here waiting, getting
   more and more bent with age. *(With difficulty)*
   Come on . . . . *(Staggers forward.)*
   (The GIRL *hurries over to support him.)*
OLD MAN: I'm only worried that I won't be able
   to make it. *(To the* MOTHER.*)* Are you coming
   with us?
GIRL: Do you still want to go into the city?
MOTHER: *(smoothing down the* GIRL*'s hair with
   her hands)* How unfair. You can't tell me no
   one wants a nice girl like you. I'll introduce you
   to someone. *(Picks up her travelling-bag.)* I only
   wish I hadn't brought such a heavy bag.
GIRL: Here, let me take it.
DIRECTOR MA: You've been buying up for your
   organization?
OLD MAN: Are you coming or not?
DIRECTOR MA: *(thoughtfully)* If comfort's what
   you're after, it's nice and quiet in a country
   town. Even if you can put up with everything

   6 *Tianmen, dimen, qinglong* and *baihu* are names used
to indicate the position of the cards in relation to the
'bank'. In other contexts these terms may have an as-
trological, military or indeed sexual significance.

else, let me tell you old man, the roads in the
   city—what with those confusing red and green
   traffic lights—before you know what's happened you'll have got yourself run over.
CARPENTER: I'm going.
LOUT: *(having regained his composure)* Do you
   expect us to carry you in a litter or something?
DIRECTOR MA: What are you making such a fuss
   about, eh? I've got high blood pressure and
   hardening of the arteries. *(Angrily)* I don't have
   to take this. *(Moves to exit; looks back.)* I
   forgot to take my medicine: it's a compound
   of wolfberry and formalin sedative with special
   nutritive additives.
   (All watch him exit.)
OLD MAN: Has he gone back?
MOTHER: *(muttering)* He's gone back.
GIRL: *(feebly)* Don't go.
LOUT: Let 'im go. Come on.
CARPENTER: *(to* GLASSES*)* Are you coming?
GLASSES: I'm just taking one last look to see if a
   bus is coming. *(He takes off his glasses, polishes
   them and puts them back on.)*
   *(They all split up and pace up and down the
   stage, some of them obviously wanting to
   make a start, others remaining motionless;
   they collide.)*
OLD MAN: Get out of my way!
LOUT: Go on then!
MOTHER: What chaos.
GLASSES: Ah, life . . . .
GIRL: Do you call this living?
GLASSES: Sure it is. Despite everything we're still
   alive.
GIRL: We might as well be dead.
GLASSES: Why don't you end it all, then?
GIRL: Because it seems like such a waste to come
   into this world and then get nothing out of life.
GLASSES: There should be some meaning to life.
GIRL: To live on like this, not really alive and not
   dead either—it's so boring!
   *(All walk on the spot and then turn around
   in circles as if possessed.)*
CARPENTER: Let's go.
GIRL: No—
GLASSES: No?
LOUT: Come on.
MOTHER: Yes, coming.
OLD MAN: Let's go—
   (Silence. The sound of falling rain.)

Author's Suggestions for the Performance of The Bus-stop:

Note: Following the resounding success of Gao's first play, *Alarm Signal*, in October 1982, drama troupes throughout the country performed it, often ignoring or completely unaware of the tremendous attention the writer and director had given to stage effects, lighting and characterization in the original performance. Gao Xingjian appended a list of *Playwright's Suggestions* to the published text of *The Bus-stop*, clearly in the hope of avoiding similar 'misinterpretations' of this play. These 'suggestions' are of interest not only in that they give us something of an insight into the author's artistic perceptions, but that they also show just how far the average 'drama worker' is from an immediate understanding of Gao's style of theatre.   *G.B.*

1. In creating this play I have experimented with the use of the 'multiple soliloquy'. At times there are two or three, or even as many as seven, characters speaking at once. Due to the technical limitations of the printed text, it has not been possible to indicate the use of this device here effectively. But then, drama is primarily for presentation on the stage.
2. Just as one does not demand that every instrument in an orchestra be played at the same pitch, so the multiple voice-over soliloquies need not be delivered at the same volume. The main [vocal] theme should be complimented by different harmonies and accompaniment, but not overwhelmed by them . . . .
3. As drama, like music, is an art governed by time, I believe that the various forms of music can be applied to it. In this play I have used both the *sonata* and *rondo* forms to replace the conventional Ibsenesque dramatic structure . . . .
4. Sound [effects], including music itself, should not be purely expository. In the play sound effects and dramatic situations work as a combined whole, sound often being added as counterpoint, and the contrast between combinations of harmony and disharmony is used to give the music an independent role, allowing it to carry on a dialogue with both the characters and the audience. If when presenting this play conditions permit the composition of music for the whole work, the music for the SILENT MAN should act as a *leitmotif* attenuated by musical variations.
5. In traditional Chinese Opera drama and poetic force have always been closely allied. This play is an attempt to meld modern drama and contemporary poetry. I hope that the actors who perform this play will pay particular attention to expressing the poetic qualities of the work.
6. In this play artistic abstraction, or what can be termed an 'essential likeness' (神似), is of more importance that mere realistic detail. Precedents for such an approach can be found in traditional opera, especially in the vivid and subtle performance of Mei Lanfang in *The Consort Gets Tipsy* (貴妃醉酒) and Zhou Xinfang in *Xu Ce Rushes to the City* (徐策跑城). Care must be taken to create characters similar to those in contemporary society, and exaggeration is to be avoided.
7. This play aims at combining dramatic action and inaction. When emphasis is to be given to action then attention should be paid to the clarity of physical movement, while at those times when inactivity is indicated physical stasis should be stressed while language takes over from the action.
8. The *parole* of the characters is at times clear and direct, while at other times it is vague and purposely inept, or uttered merely for the sake of speech, just as the very act of waiting for the bus comes to preclude the reasons and meaning for doing so. This use of dialogue can express the comic aspect of the characters . . . .
9. This play is best suited to performance in theatre-in-the-round, assembly halls and open air theatres. If it is performed on a conventional stage, the performing area should ideally be extended in length and the action concentrated on the front end of the stage.

The above suggestions are for your reference only.

何聞：話劇「車站」觀後

Postscript: On Seeing the Play *The Bus-stop*
He Wen's Critique in *Literary Gazette*

Translated by Chan Sin-wai

THE SCRIPT OF the play *The Bus-stop* was published in the journal *Shiyue* (October) in May, 1983. Beginning in June that year, several experimental performances were staged by the Peking People's Art Troupe. Watching the live performance is a more vivid experience than reading the script.

1

... THE IMPRESSION one gets from the play is this: a particular bus route and the Bus Company which operates it were originally set up to serve the public, but have now come to disregard the needs of the public and are instead a cause for public indignation. The passengers are ordinary members of society, each with his own quite reasonable and ordinary wishes to fulfil ('being fêted by cronies' is hardly reasonable, but has become deplorably customary). But these very ordinary wishes are frustrated by the extreme irresponsibility of the Bus Company. The bus-stop sign is so worn and faded as to be illegible and the would-be passengers have to wait interminably for the bus to come. It is such a long distance from the suburbs into town and all their hopes are pinned on the bus. But they have been made fools of.

... Is this play, which conveys so strongly the would-be passengers' anger, pain, pessimism, humiliation, and despair at their failure to get onto their bus, simply criticizing the problems existing in one particular transport department in real life? Of course it is doing more than that. *The Bus-stop*, while depicting the despair of the would-be passengers, also relates, through the mouths of its main characters, all kinds of malpractice, various unhealthy tendencies existing in our society: traffic disorder, bad service, shortage of supply of certain goods, the science of "connections", "backdoorism", lack of civilized manners, job-transfer through powerful connections in town, poor rural education, and so on and so forth. Watching this performance, we are made to feel that our lives are in total disarray, and that there is hardly any hope or future.

There are, to be sure, many serious malpractices and great difficulties in our present life. And we are now waging an arduous struggle to overcome them, a struggle in which we have achieved considerable, if gradual, progress. Despite the difficulties, our future is full of hope, China is sure to be revitalized, and the socialist cause is certain of an even greater victory. Creative writers and artists should truthfully reflect this struggle and the course of its development. Naturally, art should expose the dark side of life, but this exposure should do more than merely arouse attention; it should also enhance the confidence to find a remedy. *The Bus-stop* has failed to produce this effect; it has actually encouraged the loss of confidence.

The author once made the remark that this play, "attaches great importance to artistic abstraction, or what may be termed an 'essential likeness'." He also said that the play has a "certain symbolic meaning". The question is: what does it symbolize? It is possible that the play contains abstruse doctrines such as "freedom of choice", deriving from existentialism, but the direct impression it creates is this—the Bus Company and the fate of those waiting would-be passengers symbolize the general condition of our present lives.

Perhaps some may say: Surely we are allowed to expose the dark side of life. But the problem with *The Bus-stop* is not that it exposes the dark side of life; it is the way it exposes, and the things it "symbolizes", that constitute a distortion of our real life. There is a line in the play which summarizes this: "Everyone sees it, but there is no solution." If "there is no solution", how can there be any hope at all?

2

SOME SAY that *The Bus-stop* aims at attacking some kind of "national characteristic" of the present time—the vacillation, waiting, frustration, discontent, and inertia. These failings can hardly be called a "national characteristic." But even if they are simply the individual weaknesses of a certain number of people, they still ought to be criticized. However, what the play shows is in fact something quite different. The fault, in this whole bus-waiting incident, lies entirely with the Bus Company: to go into town from the suburbs, the public is dependent on the bus service. It is only too understandable that they should go on waiting and waiting for the bus to come. They truly deserve our sympathy. Is there anything that we can find fault with in it? What the play mocks and criticizes is not the vacillation and waiting, but the way in which this group of people, while waiting for the bus, continue to cherish illusions about a Bus Company which totally ignores them and fools them again and again. The dilemma the play presents us with is: these people rest their hopes on something which is patently corrupt and unreliable, and the lessons derived from reality will not awaken them, so much so that it is only after they fail to make out whether the bus-stop sign is still in use, that they start to walk hesitantly. How pitiful, lamentable, and laughable are their illusions about life!

So what is the way out? In contrast to those pitiful, lamentable, and laughable common people, the play features a Silent Man who slips away from the group and walks into town while the others begin their long hopeless wait for the bus. Although his appearance on the stage is brief and quite wordless, the Silent Man has a special signature tune of his own, a prominent *leitmotif* which runs throughout the play. (After the Silent Man leaves, his signature tune can be heard several times, and the author compares the tune to "exploration", "satire", "the voice of the universe", and "a march".) This is clearly the real message of the play.

But is this Silent Man really so superior to the rest of the group; is he really an ideal figure for us to emulate? The programme-notes for *The Bus-stop* say: "The Silent Man symbolizes the call of the times; the future belongs to those who talk no nonsense, waste no time, and have a genuine sense of initiative." In real life, there are indeed many such enterprising individuals. They have their revolutionary ideals and their world outlook, and, working together with the masses, are boldly innovative, persistent in struggle, and diligent in enterprise. They are part of the masses, and at the same time life's pioneers. How can there be the slightest similarity between the symbolic figure in *The Bus-stop* and those new socialist men whose initiative responds to the call of the times? The Silent Man is no more than a "Superman", a narcissistic figure setting himself apart from the masses. He is the kind of person who claims to be "sober while all men are drunk". Disillusioned and deprived of hope, he disdains the fantasies and expectations that people have towards life and goes his own way. The pitiful and sad experiences of the other would-be passengers only serve to prove him right. Such is the ideal personified by this figure in the play. But is this the correct attitude towards reality and towards the masses? People cannot help asking why the ideal figure in the author's mind does not care about the suffering of the people, does not join with the masses to change the present situation, but instead adopts an indifferent attitude towards those around him and simply stalks away? This attitude towards life and way of behaviour, which we should strongly oppose, is whole-heartedly endorsed in the play. What hope does the play offer to the passengers or the audience?

3

WHEN *THE BUS-STOP* was performed, *The Passer-By*, a one-scene dramatic prose-poem from Lu Xun's collection *Wild Grass*, was staged as a prelude. Furthermore, the actor playing the role of the Passer-By also played the role of the Silent Man in *The Bus-stop*. Why should it have been so arranged? Let us put aside the appropriateness of presenting Lu Xun's prose-poem *The Passer-By* on the stage at all; even with regard to the philosophical content of these two works, it is impossible to see how they can be related. However, the performers proclaim in their programme-notes that *The Bus-stop* "is the descendant of the theatrical technique created by Lu Xun half a century ago; it is an attempt to take Lu Xun's technique a step further by introducing some new ideas . . . . " This gives the impression that *The Bus-stop*'s reflection of life is also inherited from Lu Xun.

The Passer-By was written in March 1925. In it, Lu Xun created the figure of a revolutionary Passer-By who severs all ties with the dark old society; fearless, and regardless of personal gain or loss, he moves resolutely forward. The Passer-By also feels lonely, bewildered and weary, but he believes neither the old man nor the young girl. He faces reality soberly, accepts no charity, and trudges doggedly on. *The Passer-By* and other works in *Wild Grass* truthfully reflect the process of transformation that Lu Xun underwent at this time, from a Darwinist to a fighter for communism. What we see in *The Passer-By* is the scientific attitude of Lu Xun, his strict ideological self-examination, and his thoroughgoing revolutionary spirit as a fearless fighter for anti-imperialism and anti-feudalism.

The age of *The Passer-By*, needless to say, is gone. Our social ideals and spiritual condition have far transcended the historical and philosophical limitations of *The Passer-By*. Even when judging the two works on their own merits, we can barely mention the Silent Man of *The Bus-stop* and the Passer-By of *The Passer-By* in the same breath. How can we put a lonely, arrogant individualist who sets himself above the masses on a par with an indomitable revolutionary? To stage two plays of contradictory philosophical composition at the same time, and to describe *The Bus-stop* as a theatrical descendant of *The Passer-By* is to say the least rash, and at worst a deliberative confusion.

The Bus-stop does not continue the tradition of *The Passer-By*. It is a product of the blind worship and mechanical copying of the social viewpoints and creative theories of modernist drama in the West. The author of *The Bus-stop* has written a book entitled *A Preliminary Discussion of Contemporary Narrative Techniques* (hereafter abbreviated as *Preliminary Discussion*). In this small book, which contains many philosophical and theoretical contradictions and distortions, the author twice approvingly mentions Samuel Beckett's *Waiting for Godot*. In his other writings and speeches, he also repeatedly discusses this work. The two-act play *Waiting for Godot*, written by the Irish playwright Beckett in 1952, is one of the representative works of the Theatre of the Absurd in the West. The play is about two wretched-looking tramps who wait aimlessly for Godot on a deserted country road. The play does not tell us who Godot is, and why he should be waited for. Even when the play ends, Godot has not come. Like other playwrights of the Theatre of the Absurd, Beckett considers the objective world absurd, cruel, and unthinkable, and that is why the words and deeds of the characters in the play *Waiting for Godot* are also unthinkable. Some critics in the West consider that this play "exposes the dilemma of humanity in an absurd universe." This work mirrors to some extent the life and the human spiritual condition of a capitalist society, and can be of some help in understanding the absurdities of capitalist society; but the world outlook, the philosophical and social stance of the playwright are "idealistic" and nihilistic. We support the discriminating use of the best modern literature from the West. It has already been shown that when this is done properly, it helps our own creative writers. But we must certainly not lavish uncritical praise on the social attitudes and creative concepts of the Theatre of the Absurd. Let us see how the author of *The Bus-stop* evaluated *Waiting for Godot* in his *Preliminary Study*:

> After World War II, (Samuel) Beckett, the representative figure of the *avant-garde*, wrote a modern tragedy *Waiting for Godot* that shocked the Western world . . . . Beckett's message is very clear: The Godot who never appears, however long the characters in the play wait for him, is the future that men wait for, pray to as if it were a deity. They hope to free themselves from poverty and suffering, and therefore wait endlessly for Godot; but he never appears.
>
> Godot represents Beckett's observation of modern society, or to put it another way, it is the artistic condensation of his world outlook.

His audience and his readers can freely draw their own conclusions from this abstract figure . . . . Here we have to admit that in artistic presentation, the playwright's technique is outstanding. We may call the method employed by Beckett to portray the figure of Godot a method of artistic abstraction.

The dialogue in Beckett's *Waiting for Godot* is written in a deadpan style, something like fragments of conversation in real life. Taken as a whole, the play is both utterly absurd and, on closer reflection, surprisingly profound.

Since the contents of the play are so "surprisingly profound," we can read between the lines that the author has an enormous veneration for Beckett. It is therefore not too difficult to understand why there is so much resemblance between *Waiting for Godot* as Gao sees it, and his own creation, *The Bus-stop*. The two plays are both about "waiting": waiting for Godot, waiting for the bus. And they both deal with "the futility of waiting": waiting in capitalist society, where the future offers no solution to those wishing to free themselves from poverty and hardship; and waiting in socialist society.

The Passer-By as depicted by Lu Xun is a fighter who abhors the old society, who never looks back, but keeps forging ahead to look to the future. The Silent Man in *The Bus-stop*, on the other hand, is a lonely individualist who goes his own way. Since the social connotation of these two figures is so strikingly different, how can it be said that *The Bus-stop* is the theatrical descendant of Lu Xun? Is it not more appropriate to say that it has been influenced by the social viewpoints and artistic outlook of such "idealistic" and nihilistic works as *Waiting for Godot*?

4

THE APPEARANCE of *The Bus-stop* is not fortuitous: it reflects the influence in literature and art of a certain erroneous trend in social thought.

The policies laid down by the Third Plenum of the Central Committee at the Eleventh National Party Congress have since led our country onto a prosperous broad road to build a modernized socialist society. In the last five years, we have achieved great success. There are still many problems and difficulties to be over-come, and we are now trying to do this and have achieved significant results. This is the present situation. Most of the people follow the Party line closely, and move forward with full confidence. However, as a consequence of the ten years of turbulence and of the corrosive effect of foreign bourgeois ideology, the thoughts of a certain number of people have for a long time been confused and unstable. Their individualism, liberalism, and anarchism have gradually developed into a kind of negative, pessimistic, and indifferent outlook with which they judge our reality, and have reached the point where they even express doubts and adopt a negative attitude towards the leadership of the Communist Party and the future of socialism.

A certain trend of thought in artistic and literary creation is often the mani-festation of a certain trend of social thinking. Our writers and artists should, through their creative artistic activities and through their true reflection of life, enlighten the benighted, and, with a clear-cut standard of love and hatred, exert a transforming influence on the people to heighten their awareness, and encourage them to have the will to fight for the great cause of socialist construction. Many of our works have given play to the progressive function of socialist art and literature. However, after a certain period, amidst an unprecedented literary and artistic blooming, some deviant works which distort history, twist the facts, spread all kinds of negative, pessimistic, corrupt, and vulgar ideas, and propagate all manner of bourgeois, idealistic, egoistic world views, creating harmful effects on readers and theatre-going public, have appeared. In literary and artistic theories, some comrades enthusiastically advocate Western modernist art and literature, trying to develop our country's art and literature along the lines of the Western modernists. Under the pretext of "discriminative borrowing", "blazing new trails", and "achieving eminence", they blindly laud the modernist school in the West to the skies, and plan to "transplant" indiscriminately the entire world outlook and artistic philosophy of the modernist school to China, and use it to serve as the guiding ideology for our creative writers and artists. *The Bus-stop* is surely a case in point.

March 1984

ILLUSTRATION from *Shiyue*

NOTES ON CONTRIBUTORS

GEREMIE BARMÉ (白杰明) was born in Sydney in 1954. He graduated from the Australian National University, and then studied in China from 1974 to 1977. His recent translations include Yang Jiang's *A Cadre School Life: Six Chapters* and Ba Jin's *Random Thoughts*. He has also published a volume of essays in Chinese.

CHAN SIN-WAI (陳善偉) received his Ph.D. from the University of London in 1977. His major publications include two books on T'an Ssu-t'ung published by The Chinese University Press: *T'an Ssu-t'ung: An Annotated Bibliography* (1980) and *An Exposition of Benevolence: The Jen-hsüeh of T'an Ssu-t'ung* (1984). His forthcoming work is *Buddhism in Late Ch'ing Political Thought* by the same publisher.

DOMINIC CHEUNG (張錯) is Associate Professor of Chinese and Comparative Literature at the University of Southern California. He graduated from National Chengchi University, Taiwan, and received his Ph.D. in Comparative Literature from the University of Washington at Seattle. His published works include a critical biography of Feng Zhi in English, Chinese translations of W.C. Williams and Harry Martinson, and many volumes of poetry in Chinese.

LING CHUNG (鍾玲) first appeared in *Renditions* in the Inaugural Issue with her poem 'The Fall of Moon Lady', from the book *Woman Poets of China*, which she translated with Kenneth Rexroth. She and Rexroth have also translated the complete poems of Li Qingzhao. She received her Ph.D. from the University of Wisconsin, and is at present teaching translation and Chinese literature at the University of Hong Kong. She has published several volumes of poetry and prose in Chinese.

SUSETTE COOKE (孔蘇珊) obtained her B.A. in Asian Studies from the Australian National University and the University of Sydney. Following two years as an exchange student in the Chinese Department of Peking University, 1978-1980, she is currently working on her M.A. in modern Chinese literature at Sydney University.

SEÁN GOLDEN (高而登) was born in London in 1948 of Irish parents who emigrated to the U.S.A. He graduated from Holy Cross College, and took an M.A. and Ph.D. from the University of Connecticut, specializing in modernism and the works of James Joyce. He taught Irish and Modern literature at the University of Notre Dame before going to China in 1981 and teaching there for almost three years. Edited *Soft Day: A Miscellany of Contemporary Irish Writing* with Peter Fallon in 1980.

DAVID S.G. GOODMAN (戈大衛) was educated at the Universities of Manchester, Peking and London. He has been in the Department of Politics, University of Newcastle upon Tyne, since 1974. His most recent publication is *Groups and Politics in the People's Republic of China*, and he is currently working on a project concerned with provincial leadership in China.

HUANG GUOBIN (黃國彬) was born in Hong Kong in 1946, and read English and Translation at the University of Hong Kong, where he is currently a Lecturer in Translation. His publications include six books of poems, all in Chinese.

ALISA JOYCE (趙愛素) studied Chinese at Middlebury College in the U.S.A. and at The Chinese University of Hong Kong. She currently teaches English at Peking Normal University.

DANIEL KANE (康大年) studied Chinese at the University of Melbourne and the Australian National University. From 1976 to 1981 he was employed at the Australian Embassy in Peking. He is interested in the interaction between literature and politics in China, but his current research interests are in the field of Chinese historical linguistics and dialectology.

GINGER LI (李潔珍) obtained her B.A. in English Studies from The Chinese University of Hong Kong in 1981 and is now writing a dissertation on the realism of 16th-century Chinese short stories for the M.Phil. degree in East-West Comparative Literature.

TAO TAO LIU (劉陶陶), M.A., D.Phil., teaches Chinese Language and Literature at the Oriental Institute, Oxford University. Her main interest is in poetry, especially the *shi* from the Han to the Tang, and also *baihua* verse.

RACHEL MAY (梅瑞琦) studied English literature and trained as a teacher in England. From 1980 to 1982 she taught English in China, and is now living in Hong Kong and working on her first collection of short stories.

BONNIE S. McDOUGALL (杜博妮) has taught modern Chinese literature and language at the University of Sydney and Harvard University, and spent three years as editor/translator for the Foreign Languages Press in Peking. Her recent publications include *Mao Zedong's "Talks at the Yan'an Conference on Literature and Art"* and *Popular Chinese Literature and Performing Arts*, which she has edited for California U.P. She is at present editing a collection of stories by Zhao Zhenkai (Bei Dao), including 'Waves' and 'Moon on the Manuscript'.

LUCIEN MILLER (米樂山) is Associate Professor of Comparative Literature at the University of Massachusetts, Amherst. He is author of *Masks of Fiction in Dream of the Red Chamber* and of many scholarly articles in the field of Comparative Literature. He has translated a collection of the stories of Chen Yingzhen, including 'A Race of Generals' and 'Poor Poor Dumb Mouths'.

JOHN MINFORD (閔福德) has translated the last forty chapters of *The Story of the Stone* for Penguin Classics, and is currently Executive Editor of *Renditions*.

MOK WING-YIN (莫詠賢) last appeared in Vol. 15 of *Renditions*. She received her B.A., M.A. and Ph.D. from the University of Hong Kong, specializing in the study of Tang poetry. She is now a Lecturer in the Department of Chinese Language and Literature of The Chinese University of Hong Kong.

NG MAU-SANG (吳茂生) received his B.A. and M.Phil. from the University of Hong Kong. From 1975 to 1978 he was a Commonwealth Scholar at New College, Oxford, where he was tutored by Prof. John Bayley in Russian and Comparative Literature. After getting his D. Phil., he taught for two years at the National University of Singapore, and since 1981 has been Lecturer in Chinese literature and Translation at The Chinese University of Hong Kong. His articles on modern Chinese literature have appeared in journals in Peking, Hong Kong and the U.S.A.

SU KUICHUN (蘇奎春) graduated from the Tianjin Foreign Languages Institute in 1980 and taught English at the Tianjin Foreign Languages School for two years. She now resides in San Francisco and is studying at City College there.

CECILIA TSIM (詹左玉艮) was born in Hong Kong and graduated in English and Comparative Literature from the University of Hong Kong. She did postgraduate studies in Victorian literature at the University of Manchester. While working in London, she spent some time doing research into the May Fourth Movement and modern Chinese writers (1919-1949). She also translated King Hu's *Lao She and His Times*.

DAVID WAKEFIELD (魏達維) received his M.A. in History from San Francisco State University in 1980. He lived in China from 1980 to 1982, and now teaches ESL and History at City College of San Francisco.

XIANG LIPING (相麗萍) studied English at Nanjing University, and is currently completing an M.Phil. in Comparative Literature at The Chinese University of Hong Kong.

YANG QINGHUA (楊淸華) was born in 1922 and graduated from the Catholic University of Peking. He is one of the oldest interpreters and translators of the English Language in the People's Republic of China. He went to Yan'an in the early 40s and subsequently held various posts in the diplomatic service. He then taught English for thirty years, and is now Associate Professor of English at the Tianjin Foreign Languages Institute.

YIP WAI-LIM (葉維廉) is Professor of Comparative Literature at the University of California at San Diego. He is author of *Ezra Pound's Cathay* and of many other books in both English and Chinese.

DIANA YU (余丹) was born in China and educated in Hong Kong. She graduated from the University of Hong Kong. In 1973 she joined The Chinese University's Translation Centre, and served *Renditions* first as its Assistant Editor and then as its Managing Editor. From 1976 to 1982 she taught translation and Chinese literature in the Department of Chinese of the University of Hong Kong. She is currently Senior Lecturer in Translation at the Hong Kong Polytechnic.

ZHU ZHIYU (朱志瑜) studied English at the Tianjin Foreign Languages Institute, and is currently completing an M.Phil. in Comparative Literature at The Chinese University of Hong Kong.